THE OXFORD BOOK OF

ENGLISH MYSTICAL VERSE

ED. BY
D.H.S. NICHOLSON
AND A.H.E. LEE

the apocryphile press
BERKELEY, CA
www.apocryphile.org

apocryphile press
BERKELEY, CA

Apocryphile Press
1700 Shattuck Ave #81
Berkeley, CA 94709
www.apocryphile.org

First published by Oxford University Press, 1917.
Apocryphile Press Edition, 2012.

ISBN 978-1-937002-31-2

Contents

Verse

Author **Page**

Contents

Contents

Contents

Contents

Contents

Contents

CONTENTS

Contents

Contents

Contents

CONTENTS

CONTENTS

Contents

Contents

Contents

Contents

Contents

Contents

Introduction

IN the early days of English mysticism the first translation of Dionysius' *Mystical Theology* was so readily welcomed that it is said, in a quaintly expressive phrase, to have 'run across England like deere'. Since that time the fortunes of mysticism in these islands have been various, but, despite all the chances of repute and disrepute which it has undergone, there has been a continual undercurrent of thought by which it has been not only tolerated but welcomed. There have been, of course, heights of enthusiasm as well as profound depths of apathy in regard to it, but even if the limitations of the greatest enthusiasm have always been evident, so also has been the continuing readiness of some portion of the religious consciousness of the people to respond to what has been most vital in it. It is, in fact, the hypothesis of mysticism that it is not utterly without its witness in any age, even though the voice of that witness be lost in the turmoil of surrounding things.

And now it appears–it has in fact been appearing for some years–that the fortunes of mysticism are mending. It has emerged from the morass of apathy which characterized the eighteenth and the greater part of the nineteenth century; it is reawakening to the value of its own peculiar treasure of thought and word: on all sides there are signs that it is on the verge of entering into a kingdom of such breadth and fertility as it has perhaps never known. It is as though the world were undergoing a spiritual revitalization, spurring it on to experience–even through destruction and death–a further measure of reality and truth.

At such a time it is of interest to look back over the past and discover something of what has been already accomplished in the way of poetic expression of mystical themes and feelings. The most essential part of mysticism cannot, of course, ever pass into expression, inasmuch as it consists in an experience which is in the most literal sense ineffable. The secret of the inmost sanctuary is not in danger of profanation, since none but those who penetrate into that sanctuary can understand it, and those even who penetrate find, on passing out again, that their lips are sealed by the sheer insufficiency of language as a medium for conveying the sense of their supreme adventure. The speech of every day has no terms for what they have seen and known, and least of all can they hope for adequate expression through the phrases and apparatus of logical reasoning. In despair of moulding the stubborn stuff of prose into a form that will even approximate to their need, many of them turn, therefore, to poetry as the medium which will convey least inadequately some hint of their experience. By the rhythm and the glamour of their verse, by its peculiar quality of suggesting infinitely more than it ever says directly, by its very elasticity, they struggle to give what hints they may of the reality that is eternally underlying all things. And it is precisely through that rhythm and that glamour and the high enchantment of their writing that some rays gleam from the light which is supernal.

The ways in which mystical experience will translate itself into such measure of expression as is possible must evidently vary, both in kind and degree, with the experience itself. In sending out this anthology we have no desire to venture on a definition of what actually constitutes mysticism and what does not, since such an attempt would be clearly outside our province. Our conception of mysticism must be found in the poetry we have gathered together. But it may serve as a ground for comprehension to say that in making our selection we have been governed by a desire to include only such poems and extracts from poems as contain intimations of a consciousness wider and deeper than the normal. This is the connecting link between them–the thread, as it were, on which the individual pieces are strung. It is less a question of a common subject than of a common standpoint and in some sense a common atmosphere, and our attempt has been to steer a middle course between the twin dangers of an uninspired piety on the one hand and mere intellectual speculation on the other. The claim to inclusion has in no case been that any particular poet is of sufficient importance to demand representation as such, but that a poet of no matter what general rank has written one or more poems which testify to the greater things and at the same time reach a certain level of expression. For similar reasons we have not included the work of any poet when there seemed no better reason for so doing than that he was representative of some particular period or style.

It should be remembered, further, that this anthology makes no claim to be representative even of any poet whose work is included, since the great mass of writing by which he or she is commonly known may fall without our limits, and some little known poem or poems may have seemed to answer our requirements. The difficulty of selection has of course been greatest in the cases, like that of Thomas Traherne, where nearly all the poems are definitely mystical, and it is evident that, here and elsewhere, we have been compelled to choose from among many possible pieces. We cannot, therefore, pretend to have made an exhaustive collection of the mystical poetry of the English language or of any poet, but hope rather that our selections may be found to be adequately representative both of the one and the other.

Beyond this question of the immediate ground for choice, it may be well to mention the limits we have set ourselves in other directions. We have felt it desirable to admit any poetry written in English, from whatever country the poet may have hailed, as well as any native poetry written in Great Britain and Ireland in some other tongue than English, and subsequently translated. Thus translations from any European language have been excluded, often with very great regret, but translations from the Gaelic have been gladly admitted. In point of time we have set ourselves no limits, but have rather sought to show that the torch of the Inner Light has been handed down from age to age until the present day, when, as we believe, the world is near to a spiritual vitalization hitherto unimagined.

We offer our sincere thanks to the following authors for permission to include their own poems:

Mr. Lascelles Abercrombie, Mrs. de Bary (Anna Bunston), Mr. Clifford Bax, the Dean of Norwich (Dr. H. C. Beeching), Mr. A. C. Benson, Mr. F. W. Bourdillon, Mr. F. G. Bowles, Miss A. M. Buckton (for two poems from *Songs of Joy*), Mr. Bliss Carman, Mr. Edward Carpenter, Miss Amy Clarke, Mr. Aleister Crowley, Dr. W. J. Dawson, Mrs. Margaret Deland, Mr. E. J. Ellis, Mr. Darrell Figgis, Mr. H. E. Goad, Mr. Edmund Gosse, Father John Gray, Miss Emily Hickey, Mrs. K. Tynan Hinkson, Mr. E. G. A. Holmes, Mr. Paul Hookham, Miss G. M. Hort, Mr. Laurence Housman, Mrs. H. E. Hamilton King, Mr. John Masefield, Mr. Eugene

Mason, Mrs. Stuart Moore (Miss Evelyn Underhill), Mr. Henry Newbolt (for his own poem from *Poems New and Old*, published by Mr. John Murray, and for Miss Mary Coleridge's work from *Poems*, published by Mr. Elkin Mathews), Mr. Alfred Noyes, Mr. John Oxenham, Mr. James Rhoades, Sir Rennell Rodd, Mr. G. W. Russell ('A. E.'), Mr. G. Santayana, Mr. R. A. E. Shepherd, Mr. Arthur Symons, Mr. Herbert Trench, Mr. Samuel Waddington, Mr. A. E. Waite, the Rev. F. W. Orde Ward, and Mr. W. L. Wilmhurst (for his own poems and, as editor of *The Seeker*, for confirming Mr. Goad's permission).

We are further indebted for a similar courtesy to many publishers and private owners of copyrights, of whom the full list follows:

The editor of the *Academy* for confirming the permission given by Miss Hort; Messrs. George Allen & Unwin for two poems from *The Mockers* by Miss Barlow, and for the text of Richard Rolle's poem from Dr. Horstmann's edition of his works; Messrs. Angus & Robertson of Sydney for a poem from *At Dawn and Dusk* by Mr. V. J. Daley; Messrs. Appleton & Co. for three of the poems by Walt Whitman; Mr. Edward Arnold for confirming the permission given by Sir Rennell Rodd; Messrs. G. Bell & Sons for Coventry Patmore; Mr. Mackenzie Bell for A. C. Swinburne; Mr. B. H. Blackwell for the work of the Rev. A. S. Cripps, Mr. W. R. Childe, and Mr. J. S. Muirhead; Messrs. Blackwood & Sons for confirming the permission given by Mr. Noyes for poems from his *Collected Works*; Mr. Robert Bridges for Father Gerard Hopkins; Mr. A. H. Bullen for Mr. Horace Holley; Messrs. Burns & Oates for Mgr. R. H. Benson, Mr. J. C. Earle, Hon. Mrs. Lindsay, Mrs. Meynell, Father J. B. Tabb, and Francis Thompson; the late Lady Victoria Buxton for the Hon. Roden Noel; Messrs. Chatto & Windus for George MacDonald and for confirming Miss Jay's permission for Robert Buchanan's work; Mr. W. H. Chesson for Mrs. Chesson; the Clarendon Press for its texts of Donne, Herrick, and Vaughan; Messrs. Constable & Co. for George Meredith (by permission of Constable & Co., Ltd., London, and Charles Scribner's Sons, New York), for confirming Mr. E. G. A. Holmes's permission and for Mr. Harold Monro; Mrs. P. L. Deacon for A. W. E. O'Shaughnessy; Messrs. J. M. Dent & Sons for Mr. G. K. Chesterton; Mr. Stephen de Vere for Aubrey de Vere; Messrs. P. J. & A. E. Dobell for Thomas Traherne (printed here from Mr. Bertram Dobell's modernized text); Mrs. Dowden for Edward Dowden (including the poem 'Love's Lord' from *A Woman's Reliquary*); the Very Reverend Mother Provincial O. S. D. for Augusta Theodosia Drane; Messrs. Duffield & Co. for Mrs. Elsa Barker; the Early English Text Society for the text of *Quia Amore Langueo*; Mr. H. J. Glaisher as literary executor for Mr. G. Barlow: Canon Greenwell for Miss Dora Greenwell; Messrs. Heinemann for 'The Soul's Prayer' and 'In Salutation to the Eternal Peace', from *The Bird of Time* by Sarojini Nayadu, London, Heinemann, and for 'To a Buddha seated on a Lotus' from *The Golden Threshold* by Sarojini Nayadu, London, Heinemann; Mrs. Henley for W. E. Henley; the Houghton Mifflin Company for poems by Mr. H. B. Carpenter, Mr. C. P. Cranch, and Miss E. M. Thomas; Miss Harriett Jay for Robert Buchanan; Messrs. Kegan Paul & Co. for Archbishop Alexander, Sir Edwin Arnold, P. J. Bailey, and A. Gurney, as well as for confirming the permission given by Mrs. Hamilton King; Mr. John Lane for Richard le Gallienne and for 'The Immortal Hour' from *Poems* by Mrs. R. A. Taylor and for confirming permissions given by Mr. Lascelles Abercrombie, Mr. A. C. Benson, and Mr. James Rhoades; Messrs. Longmans, Green & Co.

for poems by F. W. H. Myers and Miss E. Gore Booth; Messrs. Lothrop, Lee & Shepard Co. for D. A. Wasson; Messrs. Macmillan & Co. for T. E. Brown, Mrs. D. M. Craik (Miss Mulock), Christina Rossetti, Lord Tennyson, and Mrs. Fraser-Tytler, and for confirming the permission given by Mr. G. W. Russell; Mr. Elkin Mathews for Miss May Probyn, Mrs. R. A. Taylor, and the Rev. A. S. Cripps ('The Death of St. Francis'); Messrs. Maunsel & Co. for Mr. J. H. Cousins, Miss S. L. Mitchell, J. M. Plunkett, and Mr. James Stephens; Messrs. Methuen & Co. for Oscar Wilde; Lady Miller for Sir Alfred Lyall; Mr. Arthur Morris for Sir Lewis Morris; Mr. Eveleigh Nash for Michael Field; Messrs. James Nisbet & Co., Ltd., for Frances Ridley Havergal; the Rev. Conrad Noel for concurring in permission for the Hon. Roden Noel; The Page Company for confirming Mr. Bliss Carman's permission; Mr. Herbert Paul for D. M. Dolben; Messrs. Putnam's Sons for 'Sibylline' from Madison Cawein's *Intimations of the Beautiful*, and for Mr. C. A. Walworth; Messrs. Routledge for P. J. Bailey and for confirming the permission given by Lady Miller; Mr. Duncan C. Scott for Archibald Lampman; Mrs. Elizabeth Sharp for William Sharp (Fiona Macleod); Mr. Clement Shorter for Mrs. D. S. Shorter; Messrs. Small, Maynard & Co. for two poems from *The Poet, the Fool and the Faeries* by Madison Cawein; Messrs. Smith, Elder & Co. for J. A. Symonds; the editor of the *Spectator* for confirming Mr. F. W. Bourdillon's permission; Mr. Fisher Unwin for poems from Mr. W. B. Yeats's *Poems* and *The Secret Rose*, and from the *Collected Poems* of Mrs. Duclaux, and for Mr. C. Weekes; Mr. A. S. Walker for J. S. Blackie; and Mr. J. M. Watkins for Miss C. M. Verschoyle.

This completes the record of our indebtedness. We would simply add an expression of our regret that it has been impossible to obtain permission to include any of

Sidney Lanier's writing, owing to copyright restrictions. But if we cannot reprint 'A Ballad of Trees and the Master', which is the chief object of our regret, we can at least point to it as deserving inclusion in any such anthology as the present, and we can further draw attention to such other poems as 'The Marshes of Glynn' and 'A Florida Sunday'. We would gladly have included all these and even more, but we must now content ourselves with this mention of them. It is with equal regret that we offer a mere extract from George Meredith's 'Outer and Inner', but in his case the rules now laid down for quotation from his poems make it impossible to do him justice.

There are a very few poems the copyright-holders of which we have been unable to discover or to trace in spite of repeated efforts. To these unknown owners of treasure we would offer our acknowledgements and our apologies, as to those, if any, whose claims we have unknowingly overlooked.

D. H. S. Nicholson.
A. H. E. Lee.

ANONYMOUS

Date unknown

Amergin

I AM the wind which breathes upon the sea,
I am the wave of the ocean,
I am the murmur of the billows,
I am the ox of the seven combats,
I am the vulture upon the rocks,
I am a beam of the sun,
I am the fairest of plants,
I am a wild boar in valour.
I am a salmon in the water,
I am a lake in the plain,
I am a word of science,
I am the point of the lance in battle,
I am the God who creates in the head the fire.
Who is it who throws light into the meeting on the
mountain?
Who announces the ages of the moon?
Who teaches the place where couches the sun?

RICHARD ROLLE OF HAMPOLE

1290?-1349

Love is Life

I

LUF es lyf þat lastes ay, þar it in Criste es feste,
For wele ne wa it chaunge may, als wryten has men
wyseste.
Þe nyght it tournes in til þe day, þi trauel in tyll reste;
If þou wil luf þus as I say, þou may be wyth þe beste.

þar] when feste] fastened trauel] toil

MYST. B

II

Lufe es thoght, wyth grete desyre, of a fayre louyng;
Lufe I lyken til a fyre þat sloken may na thyng;
Lufe vs clenses of oure syn, lufe vs bote sall bryng;
Lufe þe keynges hert may wyn, lufe of ioy may syng.

III

Þe settel of lufe es lyft hee, for in til heuen it ranne;
Me thynk in erth it es sle, þat makes men pale and wanne.
Þe bede of blysse it gase ful nee, I tel þe as I kanne,
Þof vs thynk þe way be dregh: luf copuls god & manne.

IV

Lufe es hatter þen þe cole, lufe may nane be-swyke;
Þe flawme of lufe wha myght it thole, if it war ay I-lyke?
Luf vs comfortes, & mase in qwart, & lyftes tyl heuen-ryke;
Luf rauysches Cryste in tylowr hert, I wate na lust it lyke.

V

Lere to luf, if þou wyl lyfe when þou sall hethen fare.
All þi thoght til hym þou gyf, þat may þe kepe fra kare;
Loke þi hert fra hym noght twyn, if þou in wandreth ware,
Sa þou may hym welde & wyn and luf hym euer-mare.

VI

Ihesu þat me lyfe hase lent, In til þi lufe me bryng,
Take til þe al myne entent, þat þow be my ȝhernyng.
Wa fra me away war went & comne war my couytyng,
If þat my sawle had herd & hent þe sang of þi louyng.

louyng] object of love, beloved sloken] quench bote] remedy settel] seat lyft] lifted hee] high sle] deceitful? bede] bed? nee] nigh Þof] Though dregh] long hatter] hotter be-swyke] deceive thole] bear I-lyke] the same mase in qwart] makes healthy heuen-ryke] heaven's kingdom lust]desire Lere] Learn hethen] hence twyn] separate in wandreth ware] shouldst be in trouble welde] possess lent] given ȝhernyng] desire hent] grasped, apprehended

VII

Þi lufe es ay lastand, fra þat we may it fele:
Þare-in make me byrnand, þat na thyng gar it kele.
My thoght take in to þi hand, & stabyl it ylk a dele,
Þat I be noght heldand to luf þis worldes wele.

VIII

If I lufe any erthly thyng þat payes to my wyll,
& settes my ioy & my lykyng when it may com̄ me tyll,
I mai drede of partyng, þat wyll be hate and yll:
For al my welth es bot wepyng, when pyne mi saule sal spyll.

IX

Þe ioy þat men hase sene, es lyckend tyl þe haye,
Þat now es fayre & grene, and now wytes awaye.
Swylk es þis worlde, I wene, & bees till domes-daye,
All in trauel & tene, fle þat na man it maye.

X

If þou luf in all þi thoght, and hate þe fylth of syn,
And gyf hym þi sawle þat it boght, þat he þe dwell with-in:
Als Crist þi sawle hase soght & þer-of walde noght blyn,
Sa þou sal to blys be broght, & heuen won with-in.

XI

Þe kynd of luf es þis, þar it es trayst and trew:
To stand styll in stabylnes, & chaunge it for na new.
Þe lyfe þat lufe myght fynd or euer in hert it knew,
Fra kare it tornes þat kyend, & lendes in myrth & glew.

fra þat] from the time that gar it kele] may cause it to cool ylk a dele] every whit, completely [lit. every one part] heldand] inclined payes to] pleases hate] grievous pyne] pain spyll] destroy haye] grass ready for mowing wytes] passes Swylk] such tene] affliction þat...it] which blyn] cease won] dwell kynd] nature, quality þar] when trayst] faithful Þe lyfe] The man, the soul kyend] nature, quality lendes] places glew] joy

XII

For now lufe þow, I rede, Cryste, as I þe tell:
And with aungels take þi stede–þat ioy loke þou noght sell!
In erth þow hate, I rede, all þat þi lufe may fell:
For luf es stalworth as þe dede, luf es hard as hell.

XIII

Luf es a lyght byrthen, lufe gladdes ȝong and alde,
Lufe es with-owten pyne, als lofers hase me talde;
Lufe es a gastly wynne, þat makes men bygge & balde,
Of lufe sal he na thyng tyne þat hit in hert will halde.

XIV

Lufe es þe swettest thyng þat man in erth hase tane,
Lufe es goddes derlyng, lufe byndes blode & bane.
In lufe be owre lykyng, Ine wate na better wane,
For me & my lufyng lufe makes bath be ane.

XV

Bot fleschly lufe sal fare as dose þe flowre in may,
And lastand be na mare þan ane houre of a day,
And sythen syghe ful sare þar lust, þar pride, þar play,
When pai er casten in kare, til pyne þat lastes ay.

XVI

When þair bodys lyse in syn, þair sawls mai qwake & drede:
For vp sal ryse al men, and answer for þair dede;
If þai be fonden in syn, als now þair lyfe þai lede,
Þai sall sytt hel within, & myrknes hafe to mede.

For now] Therefore rede] advise stede] place fell] abate þe dede] death gastly] spiritual wynne] wine bygge] strong tyne] lose wane] dwelling sythen] afterwards syghe] lament myrknes] darkness

XVII

Riche men þair handes sal wryng, & wicked werkes sal by
In flawme of fyre bath knyght & keyng, with sorow schamfully.
If þou wil lufe, þan may þou syng til Cryst in melody,
Þe lufe of hym ouercoms al thyng, þarto þou traiste trewly.

XVIII

[I] sygh & sob, bath day & nyght, for ane sa fayre of hew.
Þar es na thyng my hert mai light, bot lufe, þat es ay new.
Wha sa had hym in his syght, or in his hert hym knew,
His mournyng turned til ioy ful bryght, his sang in til glew.

XIX

In myrth he lyfes, nyght & day, þat lufes þat swete chylde:
It es Ihesu, forsoth I say, of all mekest & mylde.
Wreth fra hym walde al a-way, þof he wer neuer sa wylde;
He þat in hert lufed hym, þat day fra euel he wil hym schylde.

XX

Of Ihesu mast lyst me speke, þat al my bale may bete.
Me thynk my hert may al to-breke, when I thynk on pat swete.
In lufe lacyd he hase my thoght, þat I sal neuer forgete:
Ful dere me thynk he hase me boght, with blodi hende & fete.

XXI

For luf my hert es bowne to brest, when I þat faire behalde.
Lufe es fair þare it es fest, þat neuer will be calde.
Lufe vs reues þe nyght rest, in grace it makes vs balde;
Of al warkes luf es þe best, als haly men me talde.

by] pay dearly for hew] form, aspect turned] would turn Wreth] Anger þof] though bale] woe bete] amend lacyd] caught hende] hands bowne to brest] ready to burst reues] bereaves

XXII

Na wonder gyf I syghand be & siþen in sorow be sette:
Ihesu was nayled apon þe tre, & al blody for-bette;
To þynk on hym es grete pyte, how tenderly he grette–
Þis hase he sufferde, man, for þe, if þat þou syn wyll lette.

XXIII

Þare es na tonge in erth may tell of lufe þe swetnesse;
Þat stedfastly in lufe kan dwell, his ioy es endlesse.
God schylde þat he sulde til hell þat lufes & langand es,
Or euer his enmys sulde hym qwell, or make his luf be
lesse!

XXIV

Ihesu es lufe þat lastes ay: til hym es owre langyng;
Ihesu þe nyght turnes to þe day, þe dawyng in til spryng.
Ihesu, þynk on vs, now & ay: for þe we halde oure keyng;
Ihesu, gyf vs grace, as þou wel may, to luf þe with-owten
endyng.

ANONYMOUS

?15th century

Quia Amore Langueo

IN the vaile of restles mynd
I sowght in mownteyn & in mede,
trustyng a treulofe for to fynd:
vpon an hyll than toke I hede;
a voise I herd (and nere I yede)
in gret dolour complaynyng tho,
'see, dere soule, my sydes blede
Quia amore langueo.'

for-bette] scourged — grette] wept — lette] leave
sulde] should [go] — qwell] destroy, slay — dawyng] dawn
spryng] day-spring — nere] nearer — yede] went

Vpon thys mownt I fand a tree;
 vndir thys tree a man sittyng;
from hede to fote wowndyd was he,
 hys hert blode I saw bledyng;
 A semely man to be a kyng,
 A graciose face to loke vnto.
 I askyd hym how he had paynyng,
 he said, '*Quia amore langueo.*'

I am treulove that fals was neuer;
 my sistur, mannys soule, I loued hyr thus;
By-cause I wold on no wyse disseuere,
 I left my kyngdome gloriouse;
 I purueyd hyr a place full preciouse;
 she flytt, I folowyd, I luffed her soo
 that I suffred thes paynès piteuouse
 Quia amore langueo.

My faire love and my spousë bryght,
 I saued hyr fro betyng, and she hath me bett;
I clothed hyr in grace and heuenly lyght,
 this blody surcote she hath on me sett;
 for langyng love I will not lett;
 swetë strokys be thes, loo;
 I haf loued euer als I hett,
 Quia amore langueo.

I crownyd hyr with blysse and she me with thorne,
 I led hyr to chambre and she me to dye;
I browght hyr to worship and she me to skorne,
 I dyd hyr reuerence and she me velanye.
 To love that loueth is no maistrye,
 hyr hate made neuer my love hyr foo,
 ask than no moo questions whye,
 but *Quia amore langueo.*

hett] promised

Loke vnto myn handys, man!
thes gloues were geuen me whan I hyr sowght;
they be nat white, but rede and wan,
embrodred with blode my spouse them bowght;
they wyll not of, I lefe them nowght,
I wowe hyr with them where euer she goo;
thes handes full frendly for hyr fowght,
Quia amore langueo.

Maruell not, man, thof I sitt styll,
my love hath shod me wondyr strayte;
she boklyd my fete as was hyr wyll
with sharp nailes, well thow maist waite!
in my love was neuer dissaite,
for all my membres I haf opynd hyr to;
my body I made hyr hertys baite,
Quia amore langueo.

In my syde I haf made hyr nest,
loke, in me how wyde a wound is here!
this is hyr chambre, here shall she rest,
that she and I may slepe in fere.
here may she wasshe, if any filth were;
here is socour for all hyr woo;
cum if she will, she shall haf chere,
Quia amore langueo.

I will abide till she be redy,
I will to hyr send or she sey nay;
If she be rechelesse I will be gredi,
If she be dawngerouse I will hyr pray.
If she do wepe, than byd I nay;
myn armes ben spred to clypp hyr to;
crye onys, 'I cum!' now, soule, assaye!
Quia amore langueo.

waite] take heed baite] enticement, nourishment in fere] together dawngerouse] difficult of approach, haughty

I sitt on an hille for to se farre,
I loke to the vayle, my spouse I see;
now rynneth she awayward, now cummyth she narre,
yet fro myn eye syght she may nat be;
sum waite ther pray, to make hyr flee,
I rynne tofore to chastise hyr foo;
recouer, my soule, agayne to me,
Quia amore langueo.

My swete spouse, will we goo play?
apples ben rype in my gardine;
I shall clothe the in new array,
thy mete shall be mylk, honye, & wyne,
now, dere soule, latt us go dyne,
thy sustenance is in my skrypp, loo!
tary not now, fayre spousë myne,
Quia amore langueo.

Yf thow be fowle, I shall make thee clene,
if thow be seke, I shall the hele;
yf thow owght morne, I shall be-mene;
spouse, why will thow nowght with me dele?
thow fowndyst neuer love so lele;
what wilt thow, sowle, that I shall do?
I may of vnkyndnes the appele,
Quia amore langueo.

What shall I do now with my spouse?
abyde I will hyre iantilnesse;
wold she loke onys owt of hyr howse
of flesshely affeccions and vnclennesse;
hyr bed is made, hyr bolstar is in blysse,
hyr chambre is chosen, suche ar no moo;
loke owt at the wyndows of kyndnesse,
Quia amore langueo.

farre] farther narre] nearer

Long and love thow neuer so hygh,
  yit is my love more than thyñ may be;
thow gladdyst, thow wepist, I sitt the bygh,
  yit myght thow, spouse, loke onys at me!
  spouse, shuld I alway fede the
    with childys mete? nay, love, nat so!
  I pray the, love, with aduersite,
    Quia amore langueo.

My spouse is in chambre, hald ȝoure pease!
  make no noyse, but lat hyr slepe;
my babe shall sofre noo disease,
  I may not here my dere childe wepe,
  for with my pappe I shall hyr kepe;
    no wondyr thowgh I tend hyr to,
  thys hoole in my side had neuer ben so depe,
    but *Quia amore langueo.*

Wax not wery, myñ owne dere wyfe!
  what mede is aye to lyffe in comfort?
for in tribulacion, I ryñ more ryfe
  ofter tymes than in disport;
  In welth, in woo, euer I support;
    than, dere soule, go neuer me fro!
  thy mede is markyd, whan thow art mort,
    in blysse; *Quia amore langueo.*

11

ROBERT SOUTHWELL

?1561-1595

I dye alive

O LIFE! what letts thee from a quicke decease?
O death! what drawes thee from a present praye?
My feast is done, my soule would be at ease,
My grace is saide; O death! come take awaye.

I live, but such a life as ever dyes;
I dye, but such a death as never endes;
My death to end my dying life denyes,
And life my living death no whitt amends.

Thus still I dye, yet still I do revive;
My living death by dying life is fedd;
Grace more then nature kepes my hart alive,
Whose idle hopes and vayne desires are deade.

Not where I breath, but where I love, I live;
Not where I love, but where I am, I die;
The life I wish, must future glory give,
The deaths I feele in present daungers lye.

Of the Blessed Sacrament of the Aulter

THE angells' eyes, whome veyles cannot deceive,
Might best disclose that best they do descerne;
Men must with sounde and silent faith receive
More then they can by sence or reason lerne;
God's poure our proofes, His workes our witt exceede,
The doer's might is reason of His deede.

A body is endew'd with ghostly rightes;
And Nature's worke from Nature's law is free;
In heavenly sunne lye hidd eternall lightes,
Lightes cleere and neere, yet them no eye can see;
Dedd formes a never-dyinge life do shroude;
A boundlesse sea lyes in a little cloude.

The God of hoastes in slender hoste doth dwell,
Yea, God and man with all to ether dewe,
That God that rules the heavens and rifled hell,
That man whose death did us to life renewe:
That God and man that is the angells' blisse,
In forme of bredd and wyne our nurture is.

Whole may His body be in smallest breadd,
Whole in the whole, yea whole in every crumme;
With which be one or be tenn thowsand fedd,
All to ech one, to all but one doth cumme;
And though ech one as much as all receive,
Not one too much, nor all too little have.

One soule in man is all in everye part;
One face at once in many mirrhors shynes;
One fearefull noyse doth make a thowsand start;
One eye at once of countlesse thinges defynes;
If proofes of one in many, Nature frame,
God may in straunger sort performe the same.

God present is at once in everye place,
Yett God in every place is ever one;
So may there be by giftes of ghostly grace,
One man in many roomes, yett filling none;
Sith angells may effects of bodyes shewe,
God angells' giftes on bodyes may bestowe.

HENRY CONSTABLE

?1562-?1613

To the Blessed Sacrament

WHEN thee (O holy sacrificed Lambe)
In severed sygnes I whyte and liquide see,
As on thy body slayne I thynke on thee,
Which pale by sheddyng of thy bloode became.

And when agayne I doe behold the same
Vayled in whyte to be receav'd of mee,
Thou seemest in thy syndon wrapt to bee
Lyke to a corse, whose monument I am.

Buryed in me, vnto my sowle appeare,
Pryson'd in earth, and bannisht from thy syght,
Lyke our forefathers who in lymbo were,
Cleere thou my thoughtes, as thou did'st gyve them light,
And as thou others freed from purgyng fyre
Quenche in my hart the flames of badd desyre.

JOSHUA SYLVESTER

1563-1618

The Father

ALPHA and Omega, God alone:
Eloi, My God, the Holy-One;
Whose Power is Omnipotence:
Whose Wisedome is Omni-science:
Whose Beeing is All Soveraigne Blisse:
Whose Worke Perfection's Fulnesse is;
Under All things, not under-cast;
Over All things, not over-plac't;

Within All things, not there included;
Without All things, not thence excluded:
   Above All, over All things raigning;
Beneath All, All things aye sustayning:
Without All, All conteyning sole:
Within All, filling-full the Whole:
   Within All, no where comprehended;
Without All, no where more extended;
Under, by nothing over-topped:
Over, by nothing under-propped:

Unmov'd, Thou mov'st the World about;
Unplac't, Within it, or Without:
Unchanged, time-lesse, Time Thou changest:
Th' unstable, Thou, still stable, rangest;
No outward Force, nor inward Fate,
Can Thy drad Essence alterate:

To-day, To-morrow, yester-day,
With Thee are One, and instant aye;
Aye undivided, ended never:
To-day, with Thee, indures for-ever.

Thou, Father, mad'st this mighty Ball;
Of nothing thou created'st All,
After th' *Idea* of thy Minde,
Conferring Forme to every kinde.

Thou wert, Thou art, Thou wilt be ever:
And Thine *Elect*, rejectest never.

15

JOHN DONNE

1573-1631

Sonnet

BATTER my heart, three person'd God; for, you
As yet but knocke, breathe, shine, and seeke to mend;
That I may rise, and stand, o'erthrow mee, 'and bend
Your force, to breake, blowe, burn and make me new.
I, like an usurpt towne, to'another due,
Labour to'admit you, but Oh, to no end,
Reason your viceroy in mee, mee should defend,
But is captiv'd, and proves weake or untrue.
Yet dearely' I love you, 'and would be loved faine,
But am betroth'd unto your enemie:
Divorce mee,'untie, or breake that knot againe,
Take mee to you, imprison mee, for I
Except you'enthrall mee, never shall be free,
Nor ever chast, except you ravish mee.

From 'The Crosse'

WHO can blot out the Crosse, which th'instrument
Of God, dew'd on mee in the Sacrament?
Who can deny mee power, and liberty
To stretch mine armes, and mine owne Crosse to be?
Swimme, and at every stroake, thou art thy Crosse;
The Mast and yard make one, where seas do tosse;
Looke downe, thou spiest out Crosses in small things;
Looke up, thou seest birds rais'd on crossed wings;
All the Globes frame, and spheares, is nothing else
But the Meridians crossing Parallels.
Material Crosses then, good physicke bee,
But yet spirituall have chiefe dignity.
These for extracted chimique medicine serve,
And cure much better, and as well preserve;

Then are you your own physicke, or need none,
When Still'd, or purg'd by tribulation.
For when that Crosse ungrudg'd, unto you stickes,
Then are you to your selfe, a Crucifixe.
As perchance, Carvers do not faces make,
But that away, which hid them there, do take;
Let Crosses, soe, take what hid Christ in thee,
And be his image, or not his, but hee.

Resurrection, imperfect

SLEEP sleep old Sun, thou canst not have repast
As yet, the wound thou took'st on friday last;
Sleepe then, and rest; The world may beare thy stay,
A better Sun rose before thee to day,
Who, not content to'enlighten all that dwell
On the earths face, as thou, enlightned hell,
And made the darke fires languish in that vale,
As, at thy presence here, our fires grow pale.
Whose body having walk'd on earth, and now
Hasting to Heaven, would, that he might allow
Himselfe unto all stations, and fill all,
For these three daies become a minerall;
Hee was all gold when he lay downe, but rose
All tincture, and doth not alone dispose
Leaden and iron wills to good, but is
Of power to make even sinfull flesh like his.
Had one of those, whose credulous pietie
Thought, that a Soule one might discerne and see
Goe from a body, 'at this sepulcher been,
And, issuing from the sheet, this body seen,
He would have justly thought this body a soule,
If not of any man, yet of the whole.

Desunt cœtera

Goodfriday, 1613. Riding Westward

LET mans Soule be a Spheare, and then, in this,
The intelligence that moves, devotion is,
And as the other Spheares, by being growne
Subject to forraigne motions, lose their owne,
And being by others hurried every day,
Scarce in a yeare their naturall forme obey:
Pleasure or businesse, so, our Soules admit
For their first mover, and are whirld by it.
Hence is't, that I am carryed towards the West
This day, when my Soules forme bends toward the East.
There I should see a Sunne, by rising set,
And by that setting endlesse day beget;
But that Christ on this Crosse, did rise and fall,
Sinne had eternally benighted all.
Yet dare I'almost be glad, I do not see
That spectacle of too much weight for mee.
Who sees Gods face, that is selfe life, must dye;
What a death were it then to see God dye?
It made his owne Lieutenant Nature shrinke,
It made his footstoole crack, and the Sunne winke.
Could I behold those hands which span the Poles,
And turne all spheares at once, peirc'd with those holes?
Could I behold that endlesse height which is
Zenith to us, and our Antipodes,
Humbled below us? or that blood which is
The seat of all our Soules, if not of his,
Made durt of dust, or that flesh which was worne
By God, for his apparell, rag'd, and torne?
If on these things I durst not looke, durst I
Upon his miserable mother cast mine eye,
Who was Gods partner here, and furnish'd thus
Halfe of that Sacrifice, which ransom'd us?

Though these things, as I ride, be from mine eye,
They'are present yet unto my memory,
For that looks towards them; and thou look'st towards
mee,
O Saviour, as thou hang'st upon the tree;
I turne my back to thee, but to receive
Corrections, till thy mercies bid thee leave.
O thinke mee worth thine anger, punish mee,
Burne off my rusts, and my deformity,
Restore thine Image, so much, by thy grace,
That thou may'st know mee, and I'll turne my face.

A Hymne to Christ, at the Authors last going into Germany

IN what torne ship soever I embarke,
That ship shall be my embleme of thy Arke;
What sea soever swallow mee, that flood
Shall be to mee an embleme of thy blood;
Though thou with clouds of anger do disguise
Thy face; yet through that maske I know those eyes,
Which, though they turne away sometimes,
They never will despise.

I sacrifice this Iland unto thee,
And all whom I lov'd there, and who lov'd mee;
When I have put our seas twixt them and mee,
Put thou thy sea betwixt my sinnes and thee.
As the trees sap doth seeke the root below
In winter, in my winter now I goe,
Where none but thee, th'Eternall root
Of true Love I may know.

Nor thou nor thy religion dost controule,
The amorousnesse of an harmonious Soule,
But thou would'st have that love thy selfe: As thou
Art jealous, Lord, so I am jealous now,
That lov'st not, till from loving more, thou free
My soule: Who ever gives, takes libertie:
O, if thou car'st not whom I love
Alas, thou lov'st not mee.

Seale then this bill of my Divorce to All,
On whom those fainter beames of love did fall;
Marry those loves, which in youth scattered bee
On Fame, Wit, Hopes (false mistresses) to thee.
Churches are best for Prayer, that have least light:
To see God only, I goe out of sight:
And to scape stormy dayes, I chuse
An Everlasting night.

PHINEAS FLETCHER

1580-1650

The Divine Lover

I

ME Lord? can'st thou mispend
One word, misplace one look on me?
Call'st me thy Love, thy Friend?
Can this poor soul the object be
Of these love-glances, those life-kindling eyes?
What? I the Centre of thy arms embraces?
Of all thy labour I the prize?
Love never mocks, Truth never lies.
O how I quake: Hope fear, fear hope displaces:
I would, but cannot hope: such wondrous love amazes.

II

See, I am black as night,
See I am darkness: dark as hell.
Lord thou more fair than light;
Heav'ns Sun thy Shadow; can Sunns dwell
With Shades? 'twixt light, and darkness what commerce?
True: thou art darkness, I thy Light: my ray
Thy mists, and hellish foggs shall pierce.
With me, black soul, with me converse.
I make the foul *December* flowry *May*,
Turn thou thy night to me: I'le turn thy night to day.

III

See Lord, see I am dead:
Tomb'd in my self: my self my grave
A drudge: so born, so bred:
My self even to my self a slave.
Thou Freedome, Life: can Life, and Liberty,
Love bondage, death? Thy Freedom I: I tyed
To loose thy bonds: be bound to me:
My Yoke shall ease, my bonds shall free.
Dead soul, thy Spring of life, my dying side:
There dye with me to live: to live in thee I dyed.

ROBERT HERRICK

1591-1674

Eternitie

O YEARES! and Age! Farewell;
Behold I go,
Where I do know
Infinitie to dwell.

And these mine eyes shall see
All times, how they
Are lost i' th' Sea
Of vast Eternitie.

Where never Moone shall sway
The Starres; but she,
And Night, shall be
Drown'd in one endlesse Day.

FRANCIS QUARLES

1592-1644

Christ and Our Selves

I WISH a greater knowledge, then t'attaine
The knowledge of *my selfe:* A greater Gaine
Then to augment *my selfe*; A greater Treasure
Then to enjoy *my selfe*: A greater Pleasure
Then to content *my selfe*; How slight, and vaine
Is all selfe-Knowledge, Pleasure, Treasure, Gaine;
Vnlesse my better knowledge could retrive
My Christ; unles my better Gaine could thrive
In Christ; unles my better Wealth grow rich
In Christ; unles my better Pleasure pitch
On Christ; Or else my Knowledge will proclaime
To my owne heart how ignorant I am:
Or else my Gaine, so ill improv'd, will shame
My Trade, and shew how much declin'd I am;
Or else my Treasure will but blurre my name
With *Bankrupt*, and divulge how poore I am;
Or else my Pleasures, that so much *inflame*
My Thoughts, will blabb how full of sores I am:
Lord, keepe me from *my Selfe*; 'Tis best for me,
Never to owne my *Selfe*, if not in *Thee*.

My beloved is mine, and I am his;
He feedeth among the lilies

EV'N like two little bank-dividing brooks,
That wash the pebbles with their wanton streams,
And having rang'd and search'd a thousand nooks,
Meet both at length in silver-breasted Thames,
Where in a greater current they conjoin:
So I my best-beloved's am; so he is mine.

Ev'n so we met; and after long pursuit,
Ev'n so we joyn'd; we both became entire;
No need for either to renew a suit,
For I was flax and he was flames of fire:
Our firm-united souls did more than twine;
So I my best-beloved's am; so he is mine.

If all those glitt'ring Monarchs that command
The servile quarters of this earthly ball,
Should tender, in exchange, their shares of land,
I would not change my fortunes for them all:
Their wealth is but a counter to my coin:
The world's but theirs; but my beloved's mine.

Nay, more; If the fair Thespian Ladies all
Should heap together their diviner treasure:
That treasure should be deem'd a price too small
To buy a minute's lease of half my pleasure;
'Tis not the sacred wealth of all the nine
Can buy my heart from him, or his, from being mine.

Nor Time, nor Place, nor Chance, nor Death can bow
My least desires unto the least remove;
He's firmly mine by oath; I his by vow;
He's mine by faith; and I am his by love;
He's mine by water; I am his by wine,
Thus I my best-beloved's am; thus he is mine.

He is my Altar; I, his Holy Place;
I am his guest; and he, my living food;
I'm his by penitence; he mine by grace;
I'm his by purchase; he is mine, by blood;
He's my supporting elm; and I his vine;
Thus I my best beloved's am; thus he is mine.

He gives me wealth; I give him all my vows:
I give him songs; he gives me length of dayes;
With wreaths of grace he crowns my conqu'ring brows,
And I his temples with a crown of Praise,
Which he accepts as an everlasting signe,
That I my best-beloved's am; that he is mine.

GEORGE HERBERT

1593-1632

Easter Song

I GOT me flowers to straw Thy way,
I got me boughs off many a tree;
But Thou wast up by break of day,
And brought'st Thy sweets along with Thee.

The sunne arising in the East,
Though he give light, and th'East perfume,
If they should offer to contest
With Thy arising, they presume.

Can there be any day but this,
Though many sunnes to shine endeavour?
We count three hundred, but we misse:
There is but one, and that one ever.

Affliction

MY heart did heave, and there came forth 'O God!'
By that I knew that Thou wast in the grief,
To guide and govern it to my relief,
Making a scepter of the rod:
Hadst thou not had Thy part,
Sure the unruly sigh had broke my heart.

But since Thy breath gave me both life and shape,
Thou know'st my tallies; and when there's assign'd
So much breath to a sigh, what's then behinde?
Or if some yeares with it escape,
The sigh then onely is
A gale to bring me sooner to my blisse.

Thy life on earth was grief, and Thou art still
Constant unto it, making it to be
A point of honour now to grieve in me,
And in Thy members suffer ill.
They who lament one crosse,
Thou dying dayly, praise Thee to Thy losse.

Man

MY God, I heard this day
That none doth build a stately habitation
But he that means to dwell therein.
What house more stately hath there been,
Or can be, then is Man? to whose creation
All things are in decay.

For Man is ev'ry thing,
And more: he is a tree, yet bears no fruit;
A beast, yet is, or should be, more:
Reason and speech we onely bring;
Parrats may thank us, if they are not mute,
They go upon the score.

Man is all symmetrie,
Full of proportions, one limbe to another,
And all to all the world besides;
Each part may call the farthest brother,
For head with foot hath private amitie,
And both with moons and tides.

Nothing hath got so farre
But Man hath caught and kept it as his prey;
His eyes dismount the highest starre;
He is in little all the sphere;
Herbs gladly cure our flesh, because that they
Find their acquaintance there.

For us the windes do blow,
The earth doth rest, heav'n move, and fountains flow;
Nothing we see but means our good,
As our delight or as our treasure;
The whole is either our cupboard of food
Or cabinet of pleasure.

The starres have us to bed,
Night draws the curtain, which the sunne withdraws;
Musick and light attend our head,
All things unto our flesh are kinde
In their descent and being; to our minde
In their ascent and cause.

Each thing is full of dutie:
Waters united are our navigation;
Distinguished, our habitation;
Below, our drink; above, our meat;
Both are our cleanlinesse. Hath one such beautie?
Then how are all things neat!

More servants wait on Man
Than he'l take notice of: in ev'ry path
He treads down that which doth befriend him
When sicknesse makes him pale and wan.
Oh mightie love! Man is one world, and hath
Another to attend him.

Since then, my God, Thou hast
So brave a palace built, O dwell in it,
That it may dwell with Thee at last!
Till then afford us so much wit,
That, as the world serves us, we may serve Thee,
And both Thy servants be.

Dialogue

Man

SWEETEST Saviour, if my soul
Were but worth the having,
Ouickly should I then controll
Any thought of waving.
But when all my cares and pains
Cannot give the name of gains
To Thy wretch so full of stains,
What delight or hope remains?

Saviour

What, childe, is the ballance thine,
    Thine the poise and measure?
If I say, 'Thou shalt be Mine,'
    Finger not My treasure.
What the gains in having thee
Do amount to, onely He
Who for man was sold can see;
That transferr'd th' accounts to Me.

Man

But as I can see no merit
    Leading to this favour,
So the way to fit me for it
    Is beyond my savour.
As the reason, then, is Thine,
So the way is none of mine:
I disclaim the whole designe;
Sinne disclaims and I resigne.

Saviour

That is all:–if that I could
    Get without repining;
And My clay, My creature, would
    Follow my resigning;
That as I did freely part
With my glorie and desert,
Left all joyes to feel all smart––

Man

Ah, no more: Thou break'st my heart.

Clasping of Hands

LORD, Thou art mine, and I am Thine,
If mine I am; and Thine much more
Then I or ought or can be mine.
Yet to be Thine doth me restore,
So that again I now am mine,
And with advantage mine the more,
Since this being mine brings with it Thine,
And thou with me dost Thee restore:
If I without Thee would be mine,
I neither should be mine nor Thine.

Lord, I am Thine, and Thou art mine;
So mine Thou art, that something more
I may presume Thee mine then Thine,
For Thou didst suffer to restore
Not Thee, but me, and to be mine:
And with advantage mine the more,
Since Thou in death wast none of Thine,
Yet then as mine didst me restore:
O, be mine still; still make me Thine;
Or rather make no Thine and Mine.

The Pulley

WHEN God at first made man,
Having a glasse of blessings standing by,
Let us,' said He, 'poure on him all we can;
Let the world's riches, which dispersed lie,
Contract into a span.'

So strength first made a way;
Then beautie flow'd, then wisdome, honour, pleasure;
When almost all was out, God made a stay,
Perceiving that, alone of all His treasure,
Rest in the bottome lay.

'For if I should,' said He,
'Bestow this jewell also on My creature,
He would adore My gifts in stead of Me,
And rest in Nature, not the God of Nature:
So both should losers be.

'Yet let him keep the rest,
But keep them with repining restlesnesse;
Let him be rich and wearie, that at least,
If goodnesse leade him not, yet wearinesse
May tosse him to My breast.'

The Elixer

TEACH me, my God and King,
In all things Thee to see,
And what I do in any thing
To do it as for Thee.

Not rudely, as a beast,
To runne into an action;
But still to make Thee prepossest,
And give it his perfection.

A man that looks on glasse,
On it may stay his eye;
Or if he pleaseth, through it passe,
And then the heav'n espie.

All may of Thee partake:
Nothing can be so mean
Which with his tincture, 'for Thy sake,'
Will not grow bright and clean.

A servant with this clause
Makes drudgerie divine;
Who sweeps a room as for Thy laws
Makes that and th' action fine.

This is the famous stone
That turneth all to gold;
For that which God doth touch and own
Cannot for lesse be told.

The Collar

I STRUCK the board, and cry'd, 'No more;
I will abroad.'
What, shall I ever sigh and pine?
My lines and life are free; free as the rode,
Loose as the winde, as large as store.
Shall I be still in suit?
Have I no harvest but a thorn
To let me bloud, and not restore
What I have lost with cordiall fruit?
Sure there was wine
Before my sighs did drie it; there was corn
Before my tears did drown it.
Is the yeare onely lost to me?
Have I no bayes to crown it,
No flowers, no garlands gay? all blasted,
All wasted?
Not so, my heart; but there is fruit,
And thou hast hands.
Recover all thy sigh-blown age
On double pleasures; leave thy cold dispute
Of what is fit and not; forsake thy cage,
Thy rope of sands,

Which pettie thoughts have made; and made to thee
Good cable, to enforce and draw,
And be thy law,
While thou didst wink and wouldst not see.
Away! take heed;
I will abroad.
Call in thy death's-head there, tie up thy fears;
He that forbears
To suit and serve his need
Deserves his load.
But as I rav'd and grew more fierce and wilde
At every word,
Me thought I heard one calling, 'Childe';
And I reply'd, 'My Lord.'

CHRISTOPHER HARVEY

1597-1663

The Nativity

UNFOLD thy face, unmaske thy ray,
Shine forth, bright Sunne, double the day.
Let no malignant misty fume,
Nor foggy vapour, once presume
To interpose thy perfect sight
This day, which makes us love thy light
For ever better, that we could
That blessèd object once behold,
Which is both the circumference,
And center of all excellence:
Or rather neither, but a treasure
Unconfinèd without measure,
Whose center and circumference,
Including all preheminence,

Excluding nothing but defect,
And infinite in each respect,
Is equally both here and there,
And now and then and every where,
And alwaies, one, himselfe, the same.
A beeing farre above a name.
Draw neer then, and freely poure
Forth all thy light into that houre,
Which was crownèd with his birth,
And made heaven envy earth.
Let not his birth-day clouded be,
By whom thou shinest, and we see.

RICHARD CRASHAW

?1613-1649

'I am not worthy that thou should'st come under my roofe.'

THY God was making hast into thy roofe,
Thy humble faith, and feare, keepes him aloofe:
Hee'l be thy guest, because he may not be,
Hee'l come–into thy house? no, into thee.

The Recommendation

THESE Houres, and that which hovers o're my End,
Into thy hands, and hart, lord, I commend.

Take Both to Thine Account, that I and mine
In that Hour, and in these, may be all thine.

That as I dedicate my devoutest Breath
To make a kind of Life for my lord's Death,

So from his living, and life-giving Death,
My dying Life may draw a new, and never fleeting Breath.

To the Name above every Name, the Name of Jesus

A HYMN

I SING the Name which None can say
But touch't with An interiour Ray:
The Name of our New Peace; our Good:
Our Blisse: and Supernaturall Blood:
The Name of All our Lives and Loves.
Hearken, And Help, ye holy Doves!
The high-born Brood of Day; you bright
Candidates of blissefull Light,
The Heirs Elect of Love; whose Names belong
Unto The everlasting life of Song;
All ye wise Soules, who in the wealthy Brest
Of This unbounded Name build your warm Nest.
Awake, My glory. Soul, (if such thou be,
And That fair Word at all referr to Thee)
Awake and sing
And be All Wing;
Bring hither thy whole Self; and let me see
What of thy Parent Heavn yet speakes in thee,
O thou art Poore
Of noble Powres, I see,
And full of nothing else but empty Me,
Narrow, and low, and infinitely lesse
Then this Great mornings mighty Busynes.
One little World or two
(Alas) will never doe.
We must have store.
Goe, Soul, out of thy Self, and seek for More.
Goe and request
Great Nature for the Key of her huge Chest

Of Heavns, the self involving Sett of Sphears
(Which dull mortality more Feeles then heares)
Then rouse the nest
Of nimble Art, and traverse round
The Aiery Shop of soul-appeasing Sound:
And beat a summons in the Same
All-soveraign Name
To warn each severall kind
And shape of sweetnes, Be they such
As sigh with supple wind
Or answer Artfull Touch,
That they convene and come away
To wait at the love-crowned Doores of
This Illustrious Day.
Shall we dare This, my Soul? we'l doe't and bring
No Other note for't, but the Name we sing.
Wake Lute and Harp
And every sweet-lipp't Thing
That talkes with tunefull string;
Start into life, And leap with me
Into a hasty Fitt-tun'd Harmony.
Nor must you think it much
T'obey my bolder touch;
I have Authority in Love's name to take you
And to the worke of Love this morning wake you;
Wake; In the Name
Of Him who never sleeps, All Things that Are,
Or, what's the same,
Are Musicall;
Answer my Call
And come along;
Help me to meditate mine Immortall Song.
Come, ye soft ministers of sweet sad mirth,
Bring All your houshold stuffe of Heavn on earth;

O you, my Soul's most certain Wings,
Complaining Pipes, and prattling Strings,
Bring All the store
Of Sweets you have; And murmur that you have no
more.
Come, nére to part,
Nature and Art!
Come; and come strong,
To the conspiracy of our Spatious song.
Bring All the Powres of Praise
Your Provinces of well-united Worlds can raise;
Bring All your Lutes and Harps of Heavn and Earth;
What ére cooperates to The common mirthe
Vessells of vocall Ioyes,
Or You, more noble Architects of Intellectuall Noise,
Cymballs of Heav'n, or Humane sphears,
Solliciters of Soules or Eares;
And when you'are come, with All
That you can bring or we can call;
O may you fix
For ever here, and mix
Your selves into the long
And everlasting series of a deathlesse Song;
Mix All your many Worlds, Above,
And loose them into One of Love.
Chear thee my Heart!
For Thou too hast thy Part
And Place in the Great Throng
Of This unbounded All-imbracing Song.
Powres of my Soul, be Proud!
And speake lowd
To All the dear-bought Nations This Redeeming Name,
And in the wealth of one Rich Word proclaim
New Similes to Nature.

May it be no wrong
Blest Heavns, to you, and your Superiour song,
That we, dark Sons of Dust and Sorrow,
A while Dare borrow
The Name of Your Dilights and our Desires,
And fitt it to so farr inferior Lyres.
Our Murmurs have their Musick too,
Ye mighty Orbes, as well as you,
Nor yeilds the noblest Nest
Of warbling Seraphim to the eares of Love,
A choicer Lesson then the joyfull Brest
Of a poor panting Turtle-Dove.
And we, low Wormes have leave to doe
The Same bright Busynes (ye Third Heavens) with you.
Gentle Spirits, doe not complain.
We will have care
To keep it fair,
And send it back to you again.
Come, lovely Name! Appeare from forth the Bright
Regions of peacefull Light,
Look from thine own Illustrious Home,
Fair King of Names, and come.
Leave All thy native Glories in their Georgeous Nest,
And give thy Self a while The gracious Guest
Of humble Soules, that seek to find
The hidden Sweets
Which man's heart meets
When Thou art Master of the Mind.
Come, lovely Name; life of our hope!
Lo we hold our Hearts wide ope!
Unlock thy Cabinet of Day
Dearest Sweet, and come away.
Lo how the thirsty Lands
Gasp for thy Golden Showres! with longstretch't Hands.

Lo how the laboring Earth
That hopes to be
All Heaven by Thee,
Leapes at thy Birth.
The' attending World, to wait thy Rise,
First turn'd to eyes;
And then, not knowing what to doe;
Turn'd Them to Teares, and spent Them too.
Come Royall Name, and pay the expence
Of All this Pretious Patience.
O come away
And kill the Death of This Delay.
O see, so many Worlds of barren yeares
Melted and measur'd out in Seas of Teares.
O see, The Weary liddes of wakefull Hope
(Love's Eastern windowes) All wide ope
With Curtains drawn,
To catch The Day-break of Thy Dawn.
O dawn, at last, long look't for Day!
Take thine own wings, and come away.
Lo, where Aloft it comes! It comes, Among
The Conduct of Adoring Spirits, that throng
Like diligent Bees, And swarm about it.
O they are wise;
And know what Sweetes are suck't from out it.
It is the Hive,
By which they thrive,
Where All their Hoard of Honey lyes.
Lo where it comes, upon The snowy Dove's
Soft Back; And brings a Bosom big with Loves.
Welcome to our dark world, Thou
Womb of Day!
Unfold thy fair Conceptions; And display
The Birth of our Bright Ioyes.

O thou compacted
Body of Blessings: spirit of Soules extracted!
O dissipate thy spicy Powres
(Clowd of condensed sweets) and break upon us
In balmy showrs;
O fill our senses, And take from us
All force of so Prophane a Fallacy
To think ought sweet but that which smells of Thee.
Fair, flowry Name; In none but Thee
And Thy Nectareall Fragrancy,
Hourly there meetes
An universall Synod of All sweets;
By whom it is defined Thus
That no Perfume
For ever shall presume
To passe for Odoriferous,
But such alone whose sacred Pedigree
Can prove it Self some kin (sweet name) to Thee.
Sweet Name, in Thy each Syllable
A Thousand Blest Arabias dwell;
A Thousand Hills of Frankincense;
Mountains of myrrh, and Beds of species,
And ten Thousand Paradises,
The soul that tasts thee takes from thence.
How many unknown Worlds there are
Of Comforts, which Thou hast in keeping!
How many Thousand Mercyes there
In Pitty's soft lap ly a sleeping!
Happy he who has the art
To awake them,
And to take them
Home, and lodge them in his Heart.
O that it were as it was wont to be!
When thy old Freinds of Fire, All full of Thee,

Fought against Frowns with smiles; gave Glorious chase
To Persecutions; And against the Face
Of Death and feircest Dangers, durst with Brave
And sober pace march on to meet A Grave.
On their Bold Brests about the world they bore thee
And to the Teeth of Hell stood up to teach thee,
In Center of their inmost Soules they wore thee,
Where Rackes and Torments striv'd, in vain, to reach thee.
        Little, alas, thought They
Who tore the Fair Brests of thy Freinds,
        Their Fury but made way
For Thee; And serv'd them in Thy glorious ends.
What did Their weapons but with wider pores
Inlarge thy flaming-brested Lovers
        More freely to transpire
        That impatient Fire
The Heart that hides Thee hardly covers.
What did their Weapons but sett wide the Doores
For Thee: Fair, purple Doores, of love's devising;
The Ruby windowes which inrich't the East
Of Thy so oft repeated Rising.
Each wound of Theirs was Thy new Morning;
And reinthron'd thee in thy Rosy Nest,
With blush of thine own Blood thy day adorning,
It was the witt of love óreflowd the Bounds
Of Wrath, and made thee way through All Those wounds.
Wellcome dear, All-Adored Name!
        For sure there is no Knee
        That knowes not Thee.
Or if there be such sonns of shame,
        Alas what will they doe
        When stubborn Rocks shall bow
And Hills hang down their Heavn-saluting Heads
        To seek for humble Beds

Of Dust, where in the Bashfull shades of night
Next to their own low Nothing they may ly,
And couch before the dazeling light of thy dread majesty.
They that by Love's mild Dictate now
Will not adore thee,
Shall Then with Just Confusion, bow
And break before thee.

A Hymn to the Name and Honor of the Admirable Sainte Teresa

Fovndresse of the Reformation of the Discalced Carmelites, both men and Women; a Woman for Angelicall heigth of speculation, for Masculine courage of performance, more then a woman. Who yet a child, out ran maturity, and durst plott a Martyrdome.

LOVE, thou art Absolute sole lord
Of Life and Death. To prove the word,
Wee'l now appeal to none of all
Those thy old Souldiers, Great and tall,
Ripe Men of Martyrdom, that could reach down
With strong armes, their triumphant crown;
Such as could with lusty breath
Speak lowd into the face of death
Their Great Lord's glorious name, to none
Of those whose spatious Bosomes spread a throne
For Love at larg to fill, spare blood and sweat;
And see him take a private seat,
Making his mansion in the mild
And milky soul of a soft child.
Scarse has she learn't to lisp the name
Of Martyr; yet she thinks it shame
Life should so long play with that breath
Which spent can buy so brave a death.

She never undertook to know
What death with love should have to doe;
Nor has she e're yet understood
Why to show love, she should shed blood
Yet though she cannot tell you why,
She can Love, and she can Dy.
    Scarse has she Blood enough to make
A guilty sword blush for her sake;
Yet has she'a Heart dares hope to prove
How much lesse strong is Death then Love.
    Be love but there; let poor six yeares
Be pos'd with the maturest Feares
Man trembles at, you straight shall find
Love knowes no nonage, nor the Mind.
'Tis Love, not Yeares or Limbs that can
Make the Martyr, or the man.
    Love touch't her Heart, and lo it beates
High, and burnes with such brave heates;
Such thirsts to dy, as dares drink up,
A thousand cold deaths in one cup.
Good reason. For she breathes All fire.
Her weake brest heaves with strong desire
Of what she may with fruitles wishes
Seek for amongst her Mother's kisses.
    Since 'tis not to be had at home
She'l travail to à Martyrdom.
No home for hers confesses she
But where she may à Martyr be.
    Sh'el to the Moores; And trade with them,
For this unvalued Diadem.
She'l offer them her dearest Breath,
With Christ's Name in't, in change for death.
Sh'el bargain with them; and will give
Them God; teach them how to live

In him: or, if they this deny,
For him she'l teach them how to Dy.
So shall she leave amongst them sown
Her Lord's Blood; or at lest her own.
Farewel then, all the world! Adieu.
Teresa is no more for you.
Farewell, all pleasures, sports, and ioyes,
(Never till now esteemed toyes)
Farewell what ever deare may be,
Mother's armes or Father's knee.
Farewell house, and farewell home!
She's for the Moores, and Martyrdom.
Sweet, not so fast ! lo thy fair Spouse
Whom thou seekst with so swift vowes,
Calls thee back, and bidds thee come
T'embrace a milder Martyrdom.
Blest powres forbid, Thy tender life
Should bleed upon a barborous knife;
Or some base hand have power to race
Thy Brest's chast cabinet, and uncase
A soul kept there so sweet, ô no;
Wise heavn will never have it so.
Thou art love's victime; and must dy
A death more mysticall and high.
Into love's armes thou shalt let fall
A still-surviving funerall.
His is the Dart must make the Death
Whose stroke shall tast thy hallow'd breath;
A Dart thrice dip't in that rich flame
Which writes thy spouse's radiant Name
Upon the roof of Heav'n; where ay
It shines, and with a soveraign ray
Beates bright upon the burning faces
Of soules which in that name's sweet graces

Find everlasting smiles. So rare,
So spirituall, pure, and fair
Must be th' immortall instrument
Upon whose choice point shall be sent
A life so lov'd; And that there be
Fitt executioners for Thee,
The fair'st and first-born sons of fire
Blest Seraphim, shall leave their quire
And turn love's souldiers, upon Thee
To exercise their archerie.
O how oft shalt thou complain
Of a sweet and subtle Pain.
Of intolerable Ioyes;
Of a Death, in which who dyes
Loves his death, and dyes again.
And would for ever so be slain.
And lives, and dyes; and knowes not why
To live, But that he thus may never leave to Dy.
How kindly will thy gentle Heart
Kisse the sweetly-killing Dart!
And close in his embraces keep
Those delicious Wounds, that weep
Balsom to heal themselves with. Thus
When These thy Deaths, so numerous,
Shall all at last dy into one,
And melt thy Soul's sweet mansion;
Like a soft lump of incense, hasted
By too hott a fire, and wasted
Into perfuming clouds, so fast
Shalt thou exhale to Heavn at last
In a resolving Sigh, and then
O what? Ask not the Tongues of men.
Angells cannot tell, suffice,
Thy selfe shall feel thine own full ioyes

And hold them fast for ever there
So soon as you first appear,
The Moon of maiden starrs, thy white
Mistresse, attended by such bright
Soules as thy shining self, shall come
And in her first rankes make thee room;
Where 'mongst her snowy family
Immortall wellcomes wait for thee.
O what delight, when reveal'd Life shall stand
And teach thy lipps heav'n with his hand;
On which thou now maist to thy wishes
Heap up thy consecrated kisses.
What ioyes shall seize thy soul, when she
Bending her blessed eyes on thee
(Those second Smiles of Heav'n) shall dart
Her mild rayes through thy melting heart!
Angels, thy old freinds, there shall greet thee
Glad at their own home now to meet thee.
All thy good Workes which went before
And waited for thee, at the door,
Shall own thee there; and all in one
Weave a constellation
Of Crowns, with which the King thy spouse
Shall build up thy triumphant browes.
All thy old woes shall now smile on thee
And thy paines sitt bright upon thee,
All thy Suffrings be divine.
Teares shall take comfort, and turn gemms
And Wrongs repent to Diademms.
Ev'n thy Death shall live; and new
Dresse the soul that erst they slew.
Thy wounds shall blush to such bright scarres
As keep account of the Lamb's warres.
Those rare Workes where thou shalt leave writt

Love's noble history, with witt
Taught thee by none but him, while here
They feed our soules, shall cloth Thine there.
Each heavnly word by whose hid flame
Our hard Hearts shall strike fire, the same
Shall flourish on thy browes, and be
Both fire to us and flame to thee;
Whose light shall live bright in thy Face
By glory, in our hearts by grace.
    Thou shalt look round about, and see
Thousands of crown'd Soules throng to be
Themselves thy crown. Sons of thy vowes
The virgin-births with which thy soveraign spouse
Made fruitfull thy fair soul, goe now
And with them all about thee bow
To Him, put on (hee'l say) put on
(My rosy love) That thy rich zone
Sparkling with the sacred flames
Of thousand soules, whose happy names
Heav'n keep upon thy score. (Thy bright
Life brought them first to kisse the light
That kindled them to starrs.) and so
Thou with the Lamb, thy lord, shalt goe;
And whereso'ere he setts his white
Stepps, walk with Him those wayes of light
Which who in death would live to see,
Must learn in life to dy like thee.

The Flaming Heart

Vpon the book and Picture of the seraphicall saint Teresa,
(as she is usually expressed with a Seraphim biside her)

WELL meaning readers! you that come as freinds
And catch the pretious name this peice pretends;
Make not too much hast to' admire
That fair-cheek't fallacy of fire.
That is a Seraphim, they say
And this the great Teresia.
Readers, be rul'd by me; and make
Here a well-plac't and wise mistake.
You must transpose the picture quite,
And spell it wrong to read it right;
Read Him for her, and her for him;
And call the Saint the Seraphim.
Painter, what didst thou understand
To put her dart into his hand!
See, even the yeares and size of him
Showes this the mother Seraphim.
This is the mistresse flame; and duteous he
Her happy fire-works, here, comes down to see.
O most poor-spirited of men!
Had thy cold Pencil kist her Pen
Thou couldst not so unkindly err
To show us This faint shade for Her.
Why man, this speakes pure mortall frame;
And mockes with female Frost love's manly flame.
One would suspect thou meant'st to print
Some weak, inferiour, woman saint.
But had thy pale-fac't purple took
Fire from the burning cheeks of that bright Booke
Thou wouldst on her have heap't up all
That could be found Seraphicall;

What e're this youth of fire weares fair,
Rosy fingers, radiant hair,
Glowing cheek, and glistering wings,
All those fair and flagrant things,
But before all, that fiery Dart
Had fill'd the Hand of this great Heart.
Doe then as equall right requires,
Since His the blushes be, and her's the fires,
Resume and rectify thy rude design;
Undresse thy Seraphim into Mine.
Redeem this injury of thy art;
Give Him the vail, give her the dart.
Give Him the vail; that he may cover
The Red cheeks of a rivall'd lover.
Asham'd that our world, now, can show
Nests of new Seraphims here below.
Give her the Dart for it is she
(Fair youth) shootes both thy shaft and Thee
Say, all ye wise and well-peirc't hearts
That live and dy amidst her darts,
What is't your tastfull spirits doe prove
In that rare life of Her, and love?
Say and bear wittnes. Sends she not
A Seraphim at every shott?
What magazins of immortall Armes there shine!
Heavn's great artillery in each love-spun line.
Give then the dart to her who gives the flame;
Give him the veil, who gives the shame.
But if it be the frequent fate
Of worst faults to be fortunate;
If all's præscription; and proud wrong
Hearkens not to an humble song;
For all the gallantry of him,
Give me the suffring Seraphim.

His be the bravery of all those Bright things.
The glowing cheekes, the glistering wings;
The Rosy hand, the radiant Dart;
Leave Her alone The Flaming Heart.
    Leave her that; and thou shalt leave her
Not one loose shaft but love's whole quiver.
For in love's feild was never found
A nobler weapon then a Wound.
Love's passives are his activ'st part.
The wounded is the wounding heart.
O Heart! the æquall poise of love's both parts
Bigge alike with wound and darts.
Live in these conquering leaves; live all the same;
And walk through all tongues one triumphant Flame.
Live here, great Heart; and love and dy and kill;
And bleed and wound; and yeild and conquer still.
Let this immortall life wherere it comes
Walk in a crowd of loves and Martyrdomes.
Let mystick Deaths wait on't; and wise soules be
The love-slain wittnesses of this life of thee.
O sweet incendiary! shew here thy art,
Upon this carcasse of a hard, cold, hart,
Let all thy scatter'd shafts of light, that play
Among the leaves of thy larg Books of day,
Combin'd against this Brest at once break in
And take away from me my self and sin,
This gratious Robbery shall thy bounty be;
And my best fortunes such fair spoiles of me.
O thou undanted daughter of desires!
By all thy dowr of Lights and Fires;
By all the eagle in thee, all the dove;
By all thy lives and deaths of love;
By thy larg draughts of intellectuall day,
And by thy thirsts of love more large then they;

By all thy brim-fill'd Bowles of feirce desire
By thy last Morning's draught of liquid fire;
By the full kingdome of that finall kisse
That seiz'd thy parting Soul, and seal'd thee his;
By all the heav'ns thou hast in him
(Fair sister of the Seraphim!)
By all of Him we have in Thee;
Leave nothing of my Self in me.
Let me so read thy life, that I
Unto all life of mine may dy.

A Song

LORD, when the sense of thy sweet grace
Sends up my soul to seek thy face.
Thy blessed eyes breed such desire,
I dy in love's delicious Fire.
  O love, I am thy Sacrifice.
Be still triumphant, blessed eyes.
Still shine on me, fair suns! that I
Still may behold, though still I dy.

  Though still I dy, I live again;
Still longing so to be still slain,
So gainfull is such losse of breath.
I dy even in desire of death.
  Still live in me this loving strife
Of living Death and dying Life.
For while thou sweetly slayest me
Dead to my selfe, I live in Thee.

Prayer

An Ode which was præfixed to a little Prayer-book given to a young Gentle-woman

LO here a little volume, but great Book
A nest of new-born sweets;
Whose native fires disdaining
To ly thus folded, and complaining
Of these ignoble sheets,
Affect more comly bands
(Fair one) from the kind hands
And confidently look
To find the rest
Of a rich binding in your Brest.
It is, in one choise handfull, heavenn; and all
Heavn's Royall host; incamp't thus small
To prove that true schooles use to tell,
Ten thousand Angels in one point can dwell.
It is love's great artillery
Which here contracts itself, and comes to ly
Close couch't in their white bosom: and from thence
As from a snowy fortresse of defence,
Against their ghostly foes to take their part,
And fortify the hold of their chast heart.
It is an armory of light
Let constant use but keep it bright,
You'l find it yeilds
To holy hands and humble hearts
More swords and sheilds
Then sin hath snares, or Hell hath darts.

Only be sure
The hands be pure
That hold these weapons; and the eyes
Those of turtles, chast and true;
Wakefull and wise;
Here is a freind shall fight for you,
Hold but this book before their heart;
Let prayer alone to play his part,
But ô the heart
That studyes this high Art
Must be a sure house-keeper;
And yet no sleeper.
Dear soul, be strong.
Mercy will come e're long
And bring his bosom fraught with blessings,
Flowers of never fading graces
To make immortall dressings
For worthy soules, whose wise embraces
Store up themselves for Him, who is alone
The Spouse of Virgins and the Virgin's son.
But if the noble Bridegroom, when he come
Shall find the loytering Heart from home;
Leaving her chast aboad
To gadde abroad
Among the gay mates of the god of flyes;
To take her pleasure and to play
And keep the devill's holyday;
To dance th' sunshine of some smiling
But beguiling
Spheares of sweet and sugred Lyes,
Some slippery Pair
Of false, perhaps as fair,
Flattering but forswearing eyes;

Doubtlesse some other heart
        Will gett the start
Mean while, and stepping in before
Will take possession of that sacred store
Of hidden sweets and holy ioyes.
Words which are not heard with Eares
(Those tumultuous shops of noise)
Effectuall wispers, whose still voice
The soul it selfe more feeles then heares;
Amorous languishments; luminous trances;
Sights which are not seen with eyes;
Spirituall and soul-peircing glances
Whose pure and subtil lightning flyes
Home to the heart, and setts the house on fire
And melts it down in sweet desire
        Yet does not stay
To ask the windows leave to passe that way;
Delicious Deaths; soft exalations
Of soul; dear and divine annihilations;
        A thousand unknown rites
Of ioyes and rarefy'd delights;
A hundred thousand goods, glories, and graces,
        And many a mystick thing
        Which the divine embraces
Of the deare spouse of spirits with them will bring
        For which it is no shame
That dull mortality must not know a name.
        Of all this store
Of blessings and ten thousand more
        (If when he come
        He find the Heart from home)
        Doubtlesse he will unload
        Himself some other where,
        And poure abroad

His pretious sweets
On the fair soul whom first he meets.
O fair, ô fortunate! O riche, ô dear!
O happy and thrice happy she
Selected dove
Who ere she be,
Whose early love
With winged vowes
Makes hast to meet her morning spouse
And close with his immortall kisses.
Happy indeed, who never misses
To improve that pretious hour,
And every day
Seize her sweet prey
All fresh and fragrant as he rises
Dropping with a baulmy Showr
A delicious dew of spices;
O let the blissfull heart hold fast
Her heavnly arm-full, she shall tast
At once ten thousand paradises;
She shall have power
To rifle and deflour
The rich and roseall spring of those rare sweets
Which with a swelling bosome there she meets
Boundles and infinite
Bottomles treasures
Of pure inebriating pleasures
Happy proof! she shal discover
What ioy, what blisse,
How many Heav'ns at once it is
To have her God become her Lover.

ANDREW MARVELL

1621-1678

On a Drop of Dew

SEE how the orient dew
Shed from the bosom of the Morn
Into the blowing roses,
Yet careless of its mansion new,
For the clear region where 'twas born,
Round in its self incloses:
And in its little globe's extent
Frames, as it can, its native element.
How it the purple flow'r does slight,
Scarce touching where it lyes,
But gazing back upon the skies,
Shines with a mournful light,
Like its own tear,
Because so long divided from the sphear.
Restless it roules, and unsecure,
Trembling, lest it grow impure;
Till the warm sun pitty its pain
And to the skies exhale it back again.
So the soul, that drop, that ray,
Of the clear fountain of eternal day,
(Could it within the humane flow'r be seen)
Rememb'ring still its former height,
Shuns the sweat leaves and blossoms green,
And, recollecting its own light,
Does in its pure and circling thoughts express
The greater heaven in an heaven less.
In how coy a figure wound,
Every way it turns away;
(So the world-excluding round)
Yet receiving in the day.

Dark beneath, but bright above,
Here disdaining, there in love.
How loose and easie hence to go;
How girt and ready to ascend;
Moving but on a point below,
It all about does upwards bend.
Such did the manna's sacred dew destil,
White and intire, though congeal'd and chill;
Congeal'd on Earth; but does, dissolving, run
Into the glories of th' almighty sun.

The Coronet

WHEN for the thorns with which I long, too long,
With many a piercing wound,
My Saviour's head have crown'd,
I seek with garlands to redress that wrong;
Through every garden, every mead,
I gather flow'rs (my fruits are only flow'rs),
Dismantling all the fragrant towers
That once adorn'd my shepherdesse's head:
And now, when I have summ'd up all my store,
Thinking (so I my self deceive)
So rich a chaplet thence to weave
As never yet the King of Glory wore,
Alas! I find the Serpent old,
That, twining in his speckled breast
About the flowers disguis'd, does fold,
With wreaths of fame and interest.
Ah, foolish man, that would'st debase with them
And mortal glory, Heaven's diadem!
But Thou who only could'st the Serpent tame,
Either his slipp'ry knots at once untie.

And disintangle all his winding snare;
Or shatter too with him my curious frame,
And let these wither–so that he may die–
Though set with skill, and chosen out with care;
That they, while Thou on both their spoils dost tread,
May crown Thy feet, that could not crown Thy head.

HENRY VAUGHAN

1621-1695

The Search

LEAVE, leave, thy gadding thoughts;
Who Pores
and spies
Still out of Doores,
descries
Within them nought.

The skinne, and shell of things
Though faire,
are not
Thy wish, nor pray'r,
but got
By meer Despair
of wings.

To rack old Elements,
or Dust
and say
Sure here he must
needs stay,
Is not the way,
nor just.
Search well another world; who studies this,
Travels in Clouds, seeks *Manna,* where none is.

The Retreate

HAPPY those early dayes! when I
Shin'd in my Angell-infancy.
Before I understood this place
Appointed for my second race,
Or taught my soul to fancy ought
But a white, Celestiall thought;
When yet I had not walkt above
A mile, or two, from my first love,
And looking back (at that short space,)
Could see a glimpse of his bright-face;
When on some *gilded Cloud*, or *flowre*
My gazing soul would dwell an houre,
And in those weaker glories spy
Some shadows of eternity;
Before I taught my tongue to wound
My Conscience with a sinfull sound,
Or had the black art to dispence
A sev'rall sinne to ev'ry sence,
But felt through all this fleshly dresse
Bright *shootes* of everlastingnesse.
O how I long to travell back
And tread again that ancient track!
That I might once more reach that plaine,
Where first I left my glorious traine,
From whence th' Inlightned spirit sees
That shady City of Palme trees;
But (ah!) my soul with too much stay
Is drunk, and staggers in the way.
Some men a forward motion love,
But I by backward steps would move,
And when this dust falls to the urn
In that state I came return.

The Morning Watch

O JOYES! Infinite sweetnes! with what flowres,
And shoots of glory, my soul breakes, and buds!
All the long houres
Of night, and Rest,
Through the still shrouds
Of sleep, and Clouds,
This Dew fell on my Breast;
O how it *Blouds*,
And *Spirits* all my Earth! heark! In what Rings,
And *Hymning Circulations* the quick world
Awakes, and sings;
The rising winds,
And falling springs,
Birds, beasts, all things
Adore him in their kinds.
Thus all is hurl'd
In sacred *Hymnes*, and *Order*, The great *Chime*
And *Symphony* of nature. Prayer is
The world in tune,
A spirit-voyce,
And vocall joyes
Whose *Eccho is* heav'ns blisse.
O let me climbe
When I lye down! The Pious soul by night
Is like a clouded starre, whose beames though sed
To shed their light
Under some Cloud
Yet are above,
And shine, and move
Beyond that mistie shrowd.
So in my Bed
That Curtain'd grave, though sleep, like ashes, hide
My lamp, and life, both shall in thee abide.

Rules and Lessons

WHEN first thy Eies unveil, give thy Soul leave
To do the like; our Bodies but forerun
The spirits duty; True hearts spread, and heave
Unto their God, as flow'rs do to the Sun.
Give him thy first thoughts then; so shalt thou keep
Him company all day, and in him sleep. . . .

Walk with thy fellow-creatures: note the *hush*
And *whispers* amongst them. There's not a *Spring*,
Or *Leafe* but hath his *Morning-hymn*; Each *Bush*
And *Oak* doth know *I AM*; canst thou not sing?
O leave thy Cares, and follies! go this way
And thou art sure to prosper all the day. . . .

Spend not an hour so, as to weep another,
For tears are not thine own; If thou giv'st words
Dash not thy *friend*, nor *Heav'n*; O smother
A vip'rous thought; some *Syllables* are *Swords*.
Unbitted tongues are in their penance double,
They shame their *owners*, and the *hearers* trouble. . . .

When Seasons change, then lay before thine Eys
His wondrous *Method*; mark the various *Scenes*
In heav'n; *Hail, Thunder, Rain-bows, Snow*, and *Ice*,
Calmes, Tempests, Light, and *darknes* by his means;
Thou canst not misse his Praise; Each *tree, herb, flowre*
Are shadows of his *wisedome*, and his Pow'r.

The World

I SAW Eternity the other night
Like a great *Ring* of pure and endless light,
All calm, as it was bright,

And round beneath it, Time in hours, days, years
        Driv'n by the spheres
Like a vast shadow mov'd, In which the world
    And all her train were hurl'd;
The doting Lover in his queintest strain
        Did their Complain,
Neer him, his Lute, his fancy, and his flights,
        Wits sour delights,
With gloves, and knots the silly snares of pleasure
        Yet his dear Treasure
All scatter'd lay, while he his eys did pour
        Upon a flowr.

The darksome States-man hung with weights and woe
Like a thick midnight-fog mov'd there so slow
    He did nor stay, nor go;
Condemning thoughts (like sad Ecclipses) scowl
        Upon his soul,
And Clouds of crying witnesses without
    Pursued him with one shout.
Yet dig'd the Mole, and lest his ways be found
        Workt under ground,
Where he did Clutch his prey, but one did see
        That policie,
Churches and altars fed him, Perjuries
        Were gnats and flies,
It rain'd about him bloud and tears, but he
        Drank them as free.

The fearfull miser on a heap of rust
Sate pining all his life there, did scarce trust
    His own hands with the dust,
Yet would not place one peece above, but lives
        In feare of theeves.

Thousands there were as frantick as himself
And hug'd each one his pelf,
The down-right Epicure plac'd heav'n in sense
And scornd pretence
While others slipt into a wide Excesse
Said little lesse;
The weaker sort slight, triviall wares Inslave
Who think them brave,
And poor, despised truth sate Counting by
Their victory.

Yet some, who all this while did weep and sing,
And sing, and weep, soar'd up into the *Ring*,
But most would use no wing.
O fools (said I,) thus to prefer dark night
Before true light,
To live in grots, and caves, and hate the day
Because it shews the way,
The way which from this dead and dark abode
Leads up to God,
A way where you might tread the Sun, and be
More bright than he.
But as I did their madnes so discusse
One whisper'd thus,
This Ring the Bride-groome did for none provide
But for his bride.

The Knot

BRIGHT Queen of Heaven! Gods Virgin Spouse
The glad worlds blessed maid!
Whose beauty tyed life to thy house,
And brought us saving ayd.

Thou art the true Loves-knot; by thee
  God is made our Allie,
And mans inferior Essence he
  With his did dignifie.

For Coalescent by that Band
  We are his body grown,
Nourished with favors from his hand
  Whom for our head we own.

And such a Knot, what arm dares loose,
  What life, what death can sever?
Which us in him, and him in us
  United keeps for ever.

The Dwelling-place

WHAT happy, secret fountain,
  Fair shade, or mountain,
Whose undiscover'd virgin glory
Boasts it this day, though not in story,
Was then thy dwelling? did some cloud
Fix'd to a Tent, descend and shrowd
My distrest Lord? or did a star,
Becken'd by thee, though high and far,
In sparkling smiles haste gladly down
To lodge light, and increase her own?
My dear, dear God! I do not know
What lodgd thee then, nor where, nor how;
But I am sure, thou dost now come
Oft to a narrow, homely room,
Where thou too hast but the least part,
My God, I mean *my sinful heart.*

Quickness

FALSE life! a foil and no more, when
Wilt thou be gone?
Thou foul deception of all men
That would not have the true come on.

Thou art a Moon-like toil; a blinde
Self-posing state;
A dark contest of waves and winde;
A meer tempestuous debate.

Life is a fix'd, discerning light,
A knowing Joy;
No chance, or fit: but ever bright,
And calm and full, yet doth not cloy.

'Tis such a blissful thing, that still
Doth vivifie,
And shine and smile, and hath the skill
To please without Eternity.

Thou art a toylsom Mole, or less
A moving mist
But life is, what none can express,
A quickness, which my God hath kist.

THOMAS TRAHERNE

?1636-1674

Wonder

HOW like an Angel came I down!
How bright are all things here!
When first among His works I did appear
O how their glory me did crown!

The world resembled His Eternity,
In which my soul did walk;
And every thing that I did see
Did with me talk.

The skies in their magnificence,
The lively, lovely air,
Oh how divine, how soft, how sweet, how fair!
The stars did entertain my sense,
And all the works of God, so bright and pure,
So rich and great did seem,
As if they ever must endure
In my esteem.

A native health and innocence
Within my bones did grow,
And while my God did all his Glories show,
I felt a vigour in my sense
That was all Spirit. I within did flow
With seas of life, like wine;
I nothing in the world did know
But 'twas divine.

Harsh ragged objects were concealed,
Oppressions, tears and cries,
Sins, griefs, complaints, dissensions, weeping eyes
Were hid, and only things revealed
Which heavenly Spirits and the Angels prize.
The state of Innocence
And bliss, not trades and poverties,
Did fill my sense.

The streets were paved with golden stones,
The boys and girls were mine,
Oh how did all their lovely faces shine!
The sons of men were holy ones,

In joy and beauty they appeared to me,
And every thing which here I found,
While like an Angel I did see,
Adorned the ground.

Rich diamond and pearl and gold
In every place was seen;
Rare splendours, yellow, blue, red, white and green,
Mine eyes did everywhere behold.
Great wonders clothed with glory did appear,
Amazement was my bliss,
That and my wealth was everywhere;
No joy to this!

Cursed and devised proprieties,
With envy, avarice
And fraud, those fiends that spoil even Paradise,
Flew from the splendour of mine eyes,
And so did hedges, ditches, limits, bounds,
I dreamed not aught of those,
But wandered over all men's grounds,
And found repose.

Proprieties themselves were mine,
And hedges ornaments;
Walls, boxes, coffers, and their rich contents
Did not divide my joys, but all combine.
Clothes, ribbons, jewels, laces, I esteemed
My joys by others worn:
For me they all to wear them seemed
When I was born.

The Vision

FLIGHT is but the preparative. The sight
Is deep and infinite,
Ah me! 'tis all the glory, love, light, space,
Joy, beauty and variety
That doth adorn the Godhead's dwelling-place;
'Tis all that eye can see.
Even trades themselves seen in celestial light,
And cares and sins and woes are bright.

Order the beauty even of beauty is,
It is the rule of bliss,
The very life and form and cause of pleasure;
Which if we do not understand,
Ten thousand heaps of vain confused treasure
Will but oppress the land.
In blessedness itself we that shall miss,
Being blind, which is the cause of bliss.

First then behold the world as thine, and well
Note that where thou dost dwell.
See all the beauty of the spacious case,
Lift up thy pleas'd and ravisht eyes,
Admire the glory of the Heavenly place
And all its blessings prize.
That sight well seen thy spirit shall prepare,
The first makes all the other rare.

Men's woes shall be but foils unto thy bliss,
Thou once enjoying this:
Trades shall adorn and beautify the earth,
Their ignorance shall make thee bright;

Were not their griefs Democritus his mirth?
Their faults shall keep thee right:
All shall be thine, because they all conspire
To feed and make thy glory higher.

To see a glorious fountain and an end,
To see all creatures tend
To thy advancement, and so sweetly close
In thy repose: to see them shine
In use, in worth, in service, and even foes
Among the rest made thine:
To see all these unite at once in thee
Is to behold felicity.

To see the fountain is a blessed thing,
It is to see the King
Of Glory face to face: but yet the end,
The glorious, wondrous end is more;
And yet the fountain there we comprehend,
The spring we there adore:
For in the end the fountain best is shown,
As by effects the cause is known.

From one, to one, in one to see all things,
To see the King of Kings
But once in two; to see His endless treasures
Made all mine own, myself the end
Of all his labours! 'Tis the life of pleasures!
To see myself His friend!
Who all things finds conjoined in Him alone,
Sees and enjoys the Holy One.

The Rapture

SWEET Infancy!
O fire of heaven! O sacred Light
How fair and bright,
How great am I,
Whom all the world doth magnify!

O Heavenly Joy!
O great and sacred blessedness
Which I possess!
So great a joy
Who did into my arms convey?

From God above
Being sent, the Heavens me enflame:
To praise his Name
The stars do move!
The burning sun doth shew His love.

O how divine
Am I! To all this sacred wealth,
This life and health,
Who raised? Who mine
Did make the same? What hand divine?

Dumbness

SURE Man was born to meditate on things,
And to contemplate the eternal springs
Of God and Nature, glory, bliss, and pleasure;
That life and love might be his Heavenly treasure;
And therefore speechless made at first, that He
Might in himself profoundly busied be:

And not vent out, before he hath ta'en in
Those antidotes that guard his soul from sin.
　Wise Nature made him deaf, too, that He might
Not be disturbed, while he doth take delight
In inward things, nor be depraved with tongues,
Nor injured by the errors and the wrongs
That mortal words convey. For sin and death
Are most infused by accursed breath,
That flowing from corrupted entrails, bear
Those hidden plagues which souls may justly fear.
　This, my dear friends, this was my blessed case;
For nothing spoke to me but the fair face
Of Heaven and Earth, before myself could speak,
I then my Bliss did, when my silence, break.
My non-intelligence of human words
Ten thousand pleasures unto me affords;
For while I knew not what they to me said,
Before their souls were into mine conveyed,
Before that living vehicle of wind
Could breathe into me their infected mind,
Before my thoughts were leavened with theirs, before
There any mixture was; the Holy Door,
Or gate of souls was close, and mine being one
Within itself to me alone was known.
Then did I dwell within a world of light,
Distinct and separate from all men's sight,
Where I did feel strange thoughts, and such things see
That were, or seemed, only revealed to me,
There I saw all the world enjoyed by one;
There I was in the world myself alone;
No business serious seemed but one; no work
But one was found; and that did in me lurk.
　D'ye ask me what? It was with clearer eyes
To see all creatures full of Deities;

Especially one's self: And to admire
The satisfaction of all true desire:
'Twas to be pleased with all that God hath done;
'Twas to enjoy even all beneath the sun:
'Twas with a steady and immediate sense
To feel and measure all the excellence
Of things; 'twas to inherit endless treasure,
And to be filled with everlasting pleasure:
To reign in silence, and to sing alone,
To see, love, covet, have, enjoy and praise, in one:
To prize and to be ravished; to be true,
Sincere and single in a blessed view
Of all His gifts. Thus was I pent within
A fort, impregnable to any sin:
Until the avenues being open laid
Whole legions entered, and the forts betrayed:
Before which time a pulpit in my mind,
A temple and a teacher I did find,
With a large text to comment on. No ear
But eyes themselves were all the hearers there,
And every stone, and every star a tongue,
And every gale of wind a curious song.
The Heavens were an oracle, and spake
Divinity: the Earth did undertake
The office of a priest; and I being dumb
(Nothing besides was dumb), all things did come
With voices and instructions; but when I
Had gained a tongue, their power began to die.
Mine ears let other noises in, not theirs,
A noise disturbing all my songs and prayers.
My foes pulled down the temple to the ground;
They my adoring soul did deeply wound
And casting that into a swoon, destroyed
The Oracle, and all I there enjoyed:

And having once inspired me with a sense
Of foreign vanities, they march out thence
In troops that cover and despoil my coasts,
Being the invisible, most hurtful hosts.
   Yet the first words mine infancy did hear,
The things which in my dumbness did appear,
Preventing all the rest, got such a root
Within my heart, and stick so close unto 't,
It may be trampled on, but still will grow
And nutriment to soil itself will owe.
The first Impressions are Immortal all,
And let mine enemies hoop, cry, roar, or call,
Yet these will whisper if I will but hear,
And penetrate the heart, if not the ear.

My Spirit

MY naked simple Life was I;
      That Act so strongly shin'd
   Upon the earth, the sea, the sky,
   It was the substance of my mind;
      The sense itself was I.
I felt no dross nor matter in my soul,
No brims nor borders, such as in a bowl
We see. My essence was capacity,
      That felt all things;
      The thought that springs
Therefrom's itself. It hath no other wings
   To spread abroad, nor eyes to see,
      Nor hands distinct to feel,
         Nor knees to kneel;
But being simple like the Deity
   In its own centre is a sphere
   Not shut up here, but everywhere.

It acts not from a centre to
Its object as remote,
But present is when it doth view,
Being with the Being it doth note
Whatever it doth do.
It doth not by another engine work,
But by itself; which in the act doth lurk.
Its essence is transformed into a true
And perfect act.
And so exact
Hath God appeared in this mysterious fact,
That 'tis all eye, all act, all sight,
And what it please can be,
Not only see,
Or do; for 'tis more voluble than light,
Which can put on ten thousand forms,
Being cloth'd with what itself adorns.

This made me present evermore
With whatsoe'er I saw.
An object, if it were before
My eye, was by Dame Nature's law,
Within my soul. Her store
Was all at once within me; all Her treasures
Were my immediate and internal pleasures,
Substantial joys, which did inform my mind.
With all she wrought
My soul was fraught,
And every object in my heart a thought
Begot, or was; I could not tell,
Whether the things did there
Themselves appear,
Which in my Spirit truly seem'd to dwell;
Or whether my conforming mind
Were not even all that therein shin'd.

But yet of this I was most sure,
That at the utmost length,
(So worthy was it to endure)
My soul could best express its strength.
It was so quick and pure,
That all my mind was wholly everywhere,
Whate'er it saw, 'twas ever wholly there;
The sun ten thousand legions off, was nigh:
The utmost star,
Though seen from far,
Was present in the apple of my eye.
There was my sight, my life, my sense,
My substance, and my mind;
My spirit shin'd
Even there, not by a transient influence:
The act was immanent, yet there:
The thing remote, yet felt even here.
O Joy! O wonder and delight!
O sacred mystery!
My Soul a Spirit infinite!
An image of the Deity!
A pure substantial light!
That Being greatest which doth nothing seem!
Why, 'twas my all, I nothing did esteem
But that alone. A strange mysterious sphere!
A deep abyss
That sees and is
The only proper place of Heavenly Bliss.
To its Creator 'tis so near
In love and excellence,
In life and sense,
In greatness, worth, and nature; and so dear,
In it, without hyperbole,
The Son and friend of God we see.

A strange extended orb of Joy,
Proceeding from within,
Which did on every side, convey
Itself, and being nigh of kin
To God did every way
Dilate itself even in an instant, and
Like an indivisible centre stand,
At once surrounding all eternity.
'Twas not a sphere,
Yet did appear,
One infinite. 'Twas somewhat every where,
And though it had a power to see
Far more, yet still it shin'd
And was a mind
Exerted, for it saw Infinity.
'Twas not a sphere, but 'twas a might
Invisible, and yet gave light.

O wondrous Self! O sphere of light,
O sphere of joy most fair
O act, O power infinite;
O subtile and unbounded air!
O living orb of sight!
Thou which within me art, yet me! Thou eye,
And temple of His whole infinity!
O what a world art Thou! A world within!
All things appear,
All objects are
Alive in Thee! Supersubstantial, rare,
Above themselves, and nigh of kin
To those pure things we find
In His great mind
Who made the world! Tho' now eclipsed by sin
There they are useful and divine,
Exalted there they ought to shine.

Amendment

THAT all things should be mine,
This makes His bounty most divine.
But that they all more rich should be,
And far more brightly shine,
As used by me;
It ravishes my soul to see the end,
To which this work so wonderful doth tend.

That we should make the skies
More glorious far before Thine eyes
Than Thou didst make them, and even Thee
Far more Thy works to prize,
As used they be
That as they're made, is a stupendous work,
Wherein Thy wisdom mightily doth lurk.

Thy greatness, and Thy love,
Thy power, in this, my joy doth move;
Thy goodness, and felicity
In this exprest above
All praise I see:
While Thy great Godhead over all doth reign,
And such an end in such a sort attain.

What bound may we assign,
O God, to any work of Thine!
Their endlessness discovers Thee
In all to be divine;
A Deity,
That will for evermore exceed the end
Of all that creature's wit can comprehend.

Am I a glorious spring
Of joys and riches to my King?
Are men made Gods? And may they see
So wonderful a thing
As God in me?
And is my soul a mirror that must shine
Even like the sun and be far more divine?

Thy Soul, O God, doth prize
The seas, the earth, our souls, the skies;
As we return the same to Thee
They more delight Thine eyes,
And sweeter be
As unto Thee we offer up the same,
Than as to us from Thee at first they came.

O how doth Sacred Love
His gifts refine, exalt, improve!
Our love to creatures makes them be
In Thine esteem above
Themselves to Thee!
O here His goodness evermore admire!
He made our souls to make His creatures higher.

The Anticipation

MY contemplation dazzles in the End
Of all I comprehend,
And soars above all heights,
Diving into the depths of all delights.
Can He become the End,
To whom all creatures tend,
Who is the Father of all Infinites?
Then may He benefit receive from things,
And be not Parent only of all springs.

The End doth want the means, and is the cause,
    Whose sake, by Nature's laws,
    Is that for which they are.
Such sands, such dangerous rocks we must beware:
    From all Eternity
    A perfect Deity
Most great and blessed He doth still appear;
His essence perfect was in all its features,
He ever blessed in His joys and creatures.

From everlasting He those joys did need,
    And all those joys proceed
    From Him eternally.
From everlasting His felicity
    Complete and perfect was,
    Whose bosom is the glass,
Wherein we all things everlasting see.
His name is Now, His Nature is For-ever:
None can His creatures from their Maker sever.

The End in Him from everlasting is
    The fountain of all bliss:
    From everlasting it
Efficient was, and influence did emit,
    That caused all. Before
    The world, we do adore
This glorious End. Because all benefit
From it proceeds: both are the very same,
The End and Fountain differ but in Name.

That so the End should be the very Spring
    Of every glorious thing;
    And that which seemeth last,
The fountain and the cause; attained so fast

That it was first; and mov'd
The Efficient, who so lov'd
All worlds and made them for the sake of this;
It shews the End complete before, and is
A perfect token of His perfect bliss.

The End complete, the means must needs be so,
By which we plainly know,
From all Eternity
The means whereby God is, must perfect be.
God is Himself the means
Whereby He doth exist:
And as the Sun by shining's cloth'd with beams,
So from Himself to all His glory streams,
Who is a Sun, yet what Himself doth list.

His endless wants and His enjoyments be
From all Eternity
Immutable in Him:
They are His joys before the Cherubim.
His wants appreciate all,
And being infinite,
Permit no being to be mean or small
That He enjoys, or is before His sight.
His satisfactions do His wants delight.

Wants are the fountains of Felicity;
No joy could ever be
Were there no want. No bliss,
No sweetness perfect, were it not for this.
Want is the greatest pleasure
Because it makes all treasure.
O what a wonderful profound abyss
Is God! In whom eternal wants and treasures
Are more delightful since they both are pleasures.

He infinitely wanteth all His joys;
(No want the soul e'er cloys.)
And all those wanted pleasures
He infinitely hath. What endless measures,
What heights and depths may we
In His felicity
Conceive! Whose very wants are endless pleasures.
His life in wants and joys is infinite,
And both are felt as His Supreme Delight.

He's not like us; possession doth not cloy,
Nor sense of want destroy;
Both always are together;
No force can either from the other sever.
Yet there's a space between
That's endless. Both are seen
Distinctly still, and both are seen for ever.
As soon as e'er He wanteth all His bliss,
His bliss, tho' everlasting, in Him is.

His Essence is all Act: He did that He
All Act might always be.
His nature burns like fire;
His goodness infinitely does desire
To be by all possesst;
His love makes others blest.
It is the glory of His high estate,
And that which I for evermore admire,
He is an Act that doth communicate.

From all to all Eternity He is
That Act: an Act of bliss:
Wherein all bliss to all
That will receive the same, or on Him call,

Is freely given: from whence
'Tis easy even to sense
To apprehend that all receivers are
In Him, all gifts, all joys, all eyes, even all
At once, that ever will or shall appear.

He is the means of them, they not of Him.
The Holy Cherubim,
Souls, Angels from Him came
Who is a glorious bright and living Flame,
That on all things doth shine,
And makes their face divine.
And Holy, Holy, Holy is His Name:
He is the means both of Himself and all,
Whom we the Fountain, Means, and End do call.

Love

O NECTAR! O delicious stream!
O ravishing and only pleasure! Where
Shall such another theme
Inspire my tongue with joys or please mine ear!
Abridgement of delights!
And Queen of sights!
O mine of rarities! O Kingdom wide!
O more! O cause of all! O glorious Bride!
O God! O Bride of God! O King!
O soul and crown of everything!

Did not I covet to behold
Some endless monarch, that did always live
In palaces of gold,
Willing all kingdoms, realms, and crowns to give
Unto my soul! Whose love
A spring might prove

Of endless glories, honours, friendships, pleasures,
Joys, praises, beauties and celestial treasures!
Lo, now I see there's such a King,
The fountain-head of everything!

Did my ambition ever dream
Of such a Lord, of such a love! Did I
Expect so sweet a stream
As this at any time! Could any eye
Believe it? Why all power
Is used here;
Joys down from Heaven on my head do shower,
And Jove beyond the fiction doth appear
Once more in golden rain to come
To Danae's pleasing fruitful womb.

His Ganymede! His life! His joy!
Or He comes down to me, or takes me up
That I might be His boy,
And fill, and taste, and give, and drink the cup.
But those (tho' great) are all
Too short and small,
Too weak and feeble pictures to express
The true mysterious depths of Blessedness.
I am His image, and His friend,
His son, bride, glory, temple, end.

An Hymn upon St. Bartholomew's Day

WHAT powerful Spirit lives within!
What active Angel doth inhabit here!
What heavenly light inspires my skin,
Which doth so like a Deity appear!

A living Temple of all ages, I
Within me see
A Temple of Eternity!
All Kingdoms I descry
In me.

An inward Omnipresence here
Mysteriously like His within me stands,
Whose knowledge is a Sacred Sphere
That in itself at once includes all lands.
There is some Angel that within me can
Both talk and move,
And walk and fly and see and love,
A man on earth, a man
Above.

Dull walls of clay my Spirit leaves,
And in a foreign Kingdom doth appear,
This great Apostle it receives,
Admires His works and sees them, standing here.
Within myself from East to West I move
As if I were
At once a Cherubim and Sphere,
Or was at once above
And here.

The Soul's a messenger whereby
Within our inward Temple we may be
Even like the very Deity
In all the parts of His Eternity.
O live within and leave unwieldy dross!
Flesh is but clay!
O fly my soul and haste away
To Jesus' Throne or Cross
Obey!

83

ISAAC WATTS

1674-1748

The Incomprehensible

FAR in the Heavens my God retires:
My God, the mark of my desires,
And hides his lovely face;
When he descends within my view,
He charms my reason to pursue,
But leaves it tir'd and fainting in th' unequal chase.

Or if I reach unusual height
Till near his presence brought,
There floods of glory check my flight,
Cramp the bold pinions of my wit,
And all untune my thought;
Plunged in a sea of light I roll,
Where wisdom, justice, mercy, shines;
Infinite rays in crossing lines
Beat thick confusion on my sight, and overwhelm my
soul. . . .

Great God! behold my reason lies
Adoring: yet my love would rise
On pinions not her own:
Faith shall direct her humble flight,
Through all the trackless seas of light,
To Thee, th' Eternal Fair, the infinite Unknown.

ALEXANDER POPE

1688-1744

From 'An Essay on Man'

ALL are but parts of one stupendous whole,
Whose body Nature is, and God the soul;
That, changed through all, and yet in all the same,
Great in the earth, as in th' ethereal frame,
Warms in the sun, refreshes in the breeze,
Glows in the stars, and blossoms in the trees,
Lives through all life, extends through all extent,
Spreads undivided, operates unspent:
Breathes in our soul, informs our mortal part;
As full, as perfect, in a hair as heart;
As full, as perfect, in vile man that mourns
As the rapt Seraphim, that sings and burns:
To him no high, no low, no great, no small–
He fills, he bounds, connects, and equals all. . . .
All nature is but art, unknown to thee:
All chance, direction, which thou canst not see:
All discord, harmony not understood;
All partial evil, universal good.

JOHN BYROM

1691-1763

A Poetical Version of a Letter from Jacob Behmen

TIS Man's own Nature, which in its own Life,
Or Centre, stands in Enmity and Strife,
And anxious, selfish, doing what it lists,
(Without God's Love) that tempts him, and resists;
The Devil also shoots his fiery Dart,
From Grace and Love to turn away the Heart.

This is the greatest Trial; 'tis the Fight
Which Christ, with His internal Love and Light,
Maintains within Man's Nature, to dispel
God's Anger, Satan, Sin, and Death, and Hell;
The human Self, or Serpent, to devour,
And raise an Angel from it by His Pow'r.

Now if God's Love in Christ did not subdue
In some Degree this Selfishness in you,
You would have no such Combat to endure;
The Serpent, then, triumphantly secure,
Would unoppos'd exert its native Right,
And no such Conflict in your Soul excite.

For all the huge Temptation and Distress
Rises in Nature, tho' God seeks to bless;
The Serpent feeling its tormenting State,
(Which of itself is a mere anxious Hate,)
When God's amazing Love comes in, to fill
And change the selfish to a God-like Will.

Here Christ, the Serpent-bruiser, stands in Man,
Storming the Devil's hellish, self-built Plan;
And hence the Strife within the human Soul,–
Satan's to kill, and Christ's to make it whole;
As by Experience, in so great Degree,
God in his Goodness causes you to see. . . .

The next Temptation, which befalls of Course
From Satan and from Nature's selfish Force,
Is, when the Soul has tasted of the Love
And been illuminated from above;
Still in its Self-hood it would seek to shine,
And as its own possess the Light Divine.

That is, the soulish Nature,–take it right,
As much a Serpent, if without God's Light,
As Lucifer,–this Nature still would claim
For own Propriety the Heav'nly Flame,
And elevate its Fire to a Degree
Above the Light's Good Pow'r, which cannot be.

This domineering Self, this Nature-Fire,
Must be transmuted to a Love-Desire.
Now, when this Change is to be undergone,
It looks for some own Pow'r, and, finding none,
Begins to doubt of Grace, unwilling quite
To yield up its self-willing Nature's Right.

It never quakes for Fear, and will not die
In Light Divine, tho' to be blest thereby:
The Light of Grace it thinks to be Deceit,
Because it worketh gently without Heat;
Mov'd too by outward Reason, which is blind,
And of itself sees nothing of this Kind.

Who knows, it thinketh, whether it be true
That God is in thee, and enlightens too?
Is it not Fancy? For thou dost not see
Like other People, who as well as thee
Hope for Salvation by the Grace of God,
Without such Fear and Trembling at his Rod. . . .

The own Self-will must die away, and shine,
Rising thro' Death, in Saving Will Divine;
And from the Opposition which it tries
Against God's Will such great Temptations rise;
The Devil too is loth to lose his Prey,
And see his Fort cast down, if it obey.

For, if the Life of Christ within arise,
Self-Lust and false Imagination dies,–
Wholly, it cannot in this present Life,
But by the Flesh maintains the daily Strife,–
Dies, and yet lives; as they alone can tell
In whom Christ fights against the Pow'rs of Hell.

The third Temptation is in Mind and Will,
And Flesh and Blood, if Satan enter still;
Where the false Centres lie in Man, the Springs
Of Pride and Lust, and Love of earthly Things,
And all the Curses wish'd by other Men,
Which are occasion'd by this Devil's Den.

These in the Astral Spirit make a Fort,
Which all the Sins concentre to support;
And human Will, esteeming for its Joy
What Christ, to save it, combats to destroy,
Will not resign the Pride-erected Tow'r,
Now live obedient to the Saviour's Pow'r. . . .

Let go all earthly Will, and be resign'd
Wholly to Him with all your Heart and Mind!
Be Joy or Sorrow, Comfort or Distress,
Receiv'd alike, for He alike can bless,
To gain the Victory of Christian Faith
Over the World and all Satanic Wrath!

WILLIAM COWPER

1731-1800

From 'The Task'

THE Lord of all, himself through all diffus'd,
Sustains, and is the life of all that lives.
Nature is but a name for an effect,
Whose cause is God. He feeds the secret fire

By which the mighty process is maintain'd,
Who sleeps not, is not weary; in whose sight
Slow circling ages are as transient days;
Whose work is without labour; whose designs
No flaw deforms, no difficulty thwarts;
And whose beneficence no charge exhausts.
Him blind antiquity profan'd, not serv'd,
With self-taught rites, and under various names,
Female and male, Pomona, Pales, Pan,
And Flora, and Vertumnus; peopling earth
With tutelary goddesses and gods
That were not; and commending, as they would,
To each some province, garden, field, or grove.
But all are under one. One spirit–His
Who wore the platted thorns with bleeding brows–
Rules universal nature. Not a flow'r
But shows some touch, in freckle, streak, or stain,
Of his unrivall'd pencil. He inspires
Their balmy odours, and imparts their hues,
And bathes their eyes with nectar, and includes,
In grains as countless as the sea-side sands,
The forms with which he sprinkles all the earth.
Happy who walks with him! whom what he finds
Of flavour or of scent in fruit or flow'r,
Or what he views of beautiful or grand
In nature, from the broad majestic oak
To the green blade that twinkles in the sun,
Prompts with remembrance of a present God!

89

WILLIAM BLAKE

1757-1827

The Divine Image

TO Mercy, Pity, Peace, and Love
All pray in their distress;
And to these virtues of delight
Return their thankfulness.

For Mercy, Pity, Peace, and Love
Is God, our Father dear,
And Mercy, Pity, Peace, and Love
Is man, His child and care.

For Mercy has a human heart,
Pity a human face,
And Love, the human form divine,
And Peace, the human dress.

Then every man, of every clime,
That prays in his distress,
Prays to the human form divine,
Love, Mercy, Pity, Peace.

And all must love the human form,
In heathen, Turk, or Jew;
Where Mercy, Love, and Pity dwell
There God is dwelling too.

Night

THE sun descending in the west,
The evening star does shine;
The birds are silent in their nest,
And I must seek for mine.
The moon, like a flower,
In heaven's high bower,
With silent delight
Sits and smiles on the night.

Farewell, green fields and happy groves,
Where flocks have took delight.
Where lambs have nibbled, silent moves
The feet of angels bright;
Unseen they pour blessing,
And joy without ceasing,
On each bud and blossom,
And each sleeping bosom.

They look in every thoughtless nest,
Where birds are cover'd warm;
They visit caves of every beast,
To keep them all from harm.
If they see any weeping
That should have been sleeping,
They pour sleep on their head,
And sit down by their bed.

When wolves and tigers howl for prey,
They pitying stand and weep;
Seeking to drive their thirst away,
And keep them from the sheep.

But if they rush dreadful,
The angels, most heedful,
Receive each mild spirit,
New worlds to inherit.

And there the lion's ruddy eyes
Shall flow with tears of gold,
And pitying the tender cries,
And walking round the fold,
Saying: 'Wrath, by His meekness,
And, by His health, sickness
Is driven away
From our immortal day.

'And now beside thee, bleating lamb,
I can lie down and sleep;
Or think on Him who bore thy name,
Graze after thee and weep.
For, wash'd in life's river,
My bright mane for ever
Shall shine like the gold
As I guard o'er the fold.'

Broken Love

MY Spectre around me night and day
Like a wild beast guards my way;
My Emanation far within
Weeps incessantly for my sin.

'A fathomless and boundless deep,
There we wander, there we weep;
On the hungry craving wind
My Spectre follows thee behind.

'He scents thy footsteps in the snow
Wheresoever thou dost go,
Thro' the wintry hail and rain.
When wilt thou return again?

'Dost thou not in pride and scorn
Fill with tempests all my morn,
And with jealousies and fears
Fill my pleasant nights with tears?

'Seven of my sweet loves thy knife
Has bereavèd of their life.
Their marble tombs I built with tears,
And with cold and shuddering fears.

'Seven more loves weep night and day
Round the tombs where my loves lay,
And seven more loves attend each night
Around my couch with torches bright.

'And seven more loves in my bed
Crown with wine my mournful head,
Pitying and forgiving all
Thy transgressions great and small.

'When wilt thou return and view
My loves, and them to life renew?
When wilt thou return and live?
When wilt thou pity as I forgive?'

'O'er my sins thou sit and moan:
Hast thou no sins of thy own?
O'er my sins thou sit and weep,
And lull thy own sins fast asleep.

'What transgressions I commit
Are for thy transgressions fit.
They thy harlots, thou their slave;
And my bed becomes their grave.

'Never, never, I return:
Still for victory I burn.
Living, thee alone I'll have;
And when dead I'll be thy grave.

'Thro' the Heaven and Earth and Hell
Thou shalt never, never quell:
I will fly and thou pursue:
Night and morn the flight renew.'

'Poor, pale, pitiable form
That I follow in a storm;
Iron tears and groans of lead
Bind around my aching head.

'Till I turn from Female love
And root up the Infernal Grove,
I shall never worthy be
To step into Eternity.

'And, to end thy cruel mocks,
Annihilate thee on the rocks,
And another form create
To be subservient to my fate.

'Let us agree to give up love,
And root up the Infernal Grove;
Then shall we return and see
The worlds of happy Eternity.

'And throughout all Eternity
I forgive you, you forgive me.
As our dear Redeemer said:
"This the Wine, and this the Bread." '

The Everlasting Gospel

THE Vision of Christ that thou dost see
Is my vision's greatest enemy.
Thine has a great hook nose like thine;
Mine has a snub nose like to mine.
Thine is the Friend of all Mankind;
Mine speaks in parables to the blind.
Thine loves the same world that mine hates;
Thy heaven doors are my hell gates.
Socrates taught what Meletus
Loath'd as a nation's bitterest curse,
And Caiaphas was in his own mind
A benefactor to mankind.
Both read the Bible day and night,
But thou read'st black where I read white.

Was Jesus gentle, or did He
Give any marks of gentility?
When twelve years old He ran away,
And left His parents in dismay.
When after three days' sorrow found,
Loud as Sinai's trumpet-sound:
'No earthly parents I confess–
My Heavenly Father's business!
Ye understand not what I say,
And, angry, force Me to obey.
Obedience is a duty then,
And favour gains with God and men.'

John from the wilderness loud cried;
Satan gloried in his pride.
'Come,' said Satan, 'come away,
I'll soon see if you'll obey!
John for disobedience bled,
But you can turn the stones to bread.
God's high king and God's high priest
Shall plant their glories in your breast,
If Caiaphas you will obey,
If Herod you with bloody prey
Feed with the sacrifice, and be
Obedient, fall down, worship me.'
Thunders and lightnings broke around,
And Jesus' voice in thunders' sound:
'Thus I seize the spiritual prey.
Ye smiters with disease, make way.
I come your King and God to seize,
Is God a smiter with disease?'
The God of this world rag'd in vain:
He bound old Satan in His chain,
And, bursting forth, His furious ire
Became a chariot of fire.
Throughout the land He took His course,
And trac'd diseases to their source.
He curs'd the Scribe and Pharisee,
Trampling down hypocrisy.
Where'er His chariot took its way,
There Gates of Death let in the Day,
Broke down from every chain and bar;
And Satan in His spiritual war
Dragg'd at His chariot-wheels: loud howl'd
The God of this world: louder roll'd
The chariot-wheels, and louder still
His voice was heard from Zion's Hill,

And in His hand the scourge shone bright;
He scourg'd the merchant Canaanite
From out the Temple of His Mind,
And in his body tight does bind
Satan and all his hellish crew;
And thus with wrath He did subdue
The serpent bulk of Nature's dross,
Till He had nail'd it to the Cross.
He took on sin in the Virgin's womb
And put it off on the Cross and tomb
To be worshipp'd by the Church of Rome.

Was Jesus humble? Or did He
Give any proofs of humility?
Boast of high things with humble tone,
And give with charity a stone?
When but a child He ran away,
And left His parents in dismay.
When they had wander'd three days long
These were the words upon His tongue:
'No earthly parents I confess:
I am doing My Father's business.'
When the rich learnèd Pharisee
Came to consult Him secretly,
Upon his heart with iron pen
He wrote 'Ye must be born again.'
He was too proud to take a bribe;
He spoke with authority, not like a Scribe.
He says with most consummate art
'Follow Me, I am meek and lowly of heart,
As that is the only way to escape
The miser's net and the glutton's trap.'
What can be done with such desperate fools
Who follow after the heathen schools?

I was standing by when Jesus died;
What I call'd humility, they call'd pride.
He who loves his enemies betrays his friends.
This surely is not what Jesus intends;
But the sneaking pride of heroic schools,
And the Scribes' and Pharisees' virtuous rules;
For He acts with honest, triumphant pride,
And this is the cause that Jesus died.
He did not die with Christian ease,
Asking pardon of His enemies:
If He had, Caiaphas would forgive;
Sneaking submission can always live.
He had only to say that God was the Devil,
And the Devil was God, like a Christian civil;
Mild Christian regrets to the Devil confess
For affronting him thrice in the wilderness;
He had soon been bloody Caesar's elf,
And at last he would have been Caesar himself,
Like Dr. Priestly and Bacon and Newton–
Poor spiritual knowledge is not worth a button!
For thus the Gospel Sir Isaac confutes:
'God can only be known by His attributes;
And as for the indwelling of the Holy Ghost,
Or of Christ and His Father, it's all a boast
And pride, and vanity of the imagination,
That disdains to follow this world's fashion.'
To teach doubt and experiment
Certainly was not what Christ meant.
What was He doing all that time,
From twelve years old to manly prime?
Was He then idle, or the less
About His Father's business?
Or was His wisdom held in scorn
Before His wrath began to burn

In miracles throughout the land,
That quite unnerv'd the Seraph band?
If He had been Antichrist, Creeping Jesus,
He'd have done anything to please us;
Gone sneaking into synagogues,
And not us'd the Elders and Priests like dogs;
But humble as a lamb or ass
Obey'd Himself to Caiaphas.
God wants not man to humble himself:
That is the trick of the Ancient Elf.
This is the race that Jesus ran:
Humble to God, haughty to man,
Cursing the Rulers before the people
Even to the Temple's highest steeple,
And when He humbled Himself to God
Then descended the cruel rod.
'If Thou Humblest Thyself, Thou humblest Me.
Thou also dwell'st in Eternity.
Thou art a Man: God is no more:
Thy own Humanity learn to adore,
For that is My spirit of life.
Awake, arise to spiritual strife,
And Thy revenge abroad display
In terrors at the last Judgement Day.
God's mercy and long suffering
Is but the sinner to judgement to bring.
Thou on the Cross for them shalt pray–
And take revenge at the Last Day.'
Jesus replied, and thunders hurl'd:
'I never will pray for the world.
Once I did so when I pray'd in the Garden;
I wish'd to take with Me a bodily pardon.'
Can that which was of woman born,
In the absence of the morn,

When the Soul fell into sleep,
And Archangels round it weep,
Shooting out against the light
Fibres of a deadly night,
Reasoning upon its own dark fiction,
In doubt which is self-contradiction?
Humility is only doubt,
And does the sun and moon blot out,
Rooting over with thorns and stems
The buried soul and all its gems.
This life's five windows of the soul
Distorts the Heavens from pole to pole,
And leads you to believe a lie
When you see with, not thro', the eye
That was born in a night, to perish in a night,
When the soul slept in the beams of light.

Did Jesus teach doubt? or did He
Give any lessons of philosophy,
Charge Visionaries with deceiving,
Or call men wise for not believing? . . .

Was Jesus born of a Virgin pure
With narrow soul and looks demure?
If He intended to take on sin
The Mother should an harlot been,
Just such a one as Magdalen,
With seven devils in her pen.
Or were Jew virgins still more curs'd,
And more sucking devils nurs'd?
Or what was it which He took on
That He might bring salvation?
A body subject to be tempted,
From neither pain nor grief exempted;
Or such a body as might not feel
The passions that with sinners deal?

Yes, but they say He never fell.
Ask Caiaphas; for he can tell.–
'He mock'd the Sabbath, and He mock'd
The Sabbath's God, and He unlock'd
The evil spirits from their shrines,
And turn'd fishermen to divines;
O'erturn'd the tent of secret sins,
And its golden cords and pins,
In the bloody shrine of war
Pour'd around from star to star,–
Halls of justice, hating vice,
Where the Devil combs his lice.
He turn'd the devils into swine
That He might tempt the Jews to dine;
Since which, a pig has got a look
That for a Jew may be mistook.
"Obey your parents."–What says He?
"Woman, what have I to do with thee?
No earthly parents I confess:
I am doing my Father's business."
He scorn'd Earth's parents, scorn'd Earth's God,
And mock'd the one and the other's rod;
His seventy Disciples sent
Against Religion and Government–
They by the sword of Justice fell,
And Him their cruel murderer tell.
He left His father's trade to roam,
A wand'ring vagrant without home;
And thus He others' labour stole,
The He might live above control.
The publicans and harlots He
Selected for His company,
And from the adulteress turn'd away
God's righteous law, that lost its prey.'

Was Jesus chaste? Or did He
Give any lessons of chastity?
The Morning blushèd fiery red:
Mary was found in adulterous bed;
Earth groan'd beneath, and Heaven above
Trembled at discovery of Love.
Jesus was sitting in Moses' chair.
They brought the trembling woman there.
Moses commands she be ston'd to death.
What was the sound of Jesus' breath?
He laid His hand on Moses' law;
The ancient Heavens, in silent awe,
Writ with curses from pole to pole,
All away began to roll.
The Earth trembling and naked lay
In secret bed of mortal clay;
On Sinai felt the Hand Divine
Pulling back the bloody shrine;
And she heard the breath of God,
As she heard by Eden's flood:
'Good and Evil are no more!
Sinai's trumpets cease to roar!
Cease, finger of God, to write!
The Heavens are not clean in Thy sight.
Thou art good, and Thou alone;
Nor may the sinner cast one stone.
To be good only, is to be
A God or else a Pharisee.
Thou Angel of the Presence Divine,
That didst create this Body of Mine,
Wherefore hast thou writ these laws
And created Hell's dark jaws?
My Presence I will take from thee:
A cold leper thou shalt be.

Tho' thou wast so pure and bright
That Heaven was impure in thy sight,
Tho' thy oath turn'd Heaven pale,
Tho' thy covenant built Hell's jail,
Tho' thou didst all to chaos roll
With the Serpent for its soul,
Still the breath Divine does move,
And the breath Divine is Love.
Mary, fear not! Let me see
The seven devils that torment thee.
Hide not from My sight thy sin,
That forgiveness thou may'st win.
Has no man condemnèd thee?'
'No man, Lord.' 'Then what is he
Who shall accuse thee? Come ye forth,
Fallen fiends of heavenly birth,
That have forgot your ancient love,
And driven away my trembling Dove.
You shall bow before her feet;
You shall lick the dust for meat;
And tho' you cannot love, but hate,
Shall be beggars at Love's gate.
What was thy love? Let Me see it;
Was it love or dark deceit?'
'Love too long from me has fled;
'Twas dark deceit, to earn my bread;
'Twas covet, or 'twas custom, or
Some trifle not worth caring for;
That they may call a shame and sin
Love's temple that God dwelleth in,
And hide in secret hidden shrine
The naked Human Form Divine,
And render that a lawless thing
On which the Soul expands its wing.

But this, O Lord, this was my sin,
When first I let these devils in,
In dark pretence to chastity
Blaspheming Love, blaspheming Thee,
Thence rose secret adulteries,
And thence did covet also rise.
My sin Thou hast forgiven me;
Canst Thou forgive my blasphemy?
Canst Thou return to this dark hell,
And in my burning bosom dwell?
And canst Thou die that I may live?
And canst Thou pity and forgive?'
Then roll'd the shadowy Man away
From the limbs of Jesus, to make them His prey,
An ever devouring appetite,
Glittering with festering venoms bright;
Crying 'Crucify this cause of distress,
Who don't keep the secrets of holiness!
The mental powers by diseases we bind;
But He heals the deaf, the dumb, and the blind.
Whom God has afflicted for secret ends,
He comforts and heals and calls them friends.'
But, when Jesus was crucified,
Then was perfected His galling pride.
In three nights He devour'd His prey,
And still He devours the body of clay;
For dust and clay is the Serpent's meat,
Which never was made for Man to eat.

Seeing this False Christ, in fury and passion
I made my voice heard all over the nation.
What are those...

I am sure this Jesus will not do,
Either for Englishman or Jew.

The Crystal Cabinet

THE Maiden caught me in the wild,
Where I was dancing merrily;
She put me into her Cabinet,
And lock'd me up with a golden key.

This Cabinet is form'd of gold
And pearl and crystal shining bright,
And within it opens into a world
And a little lovely moony night.

Another England there I saw,
Another London with its Tower,
Another Thames and other hills,
And another pleasant Surrey bower,

Another Maiden like herself,
Translucent, lovely, shining clear,
Threefold each in the other clos'd–
O, what a pleasant trembling fear!

O, what a smile! a threefold smile
Fill'd me, that like a flame I burn'd;
I bent to kiss the lovely Maid,
And found a threefold kiss return'd.

I strove to seize the inmost form
With ardour fierce and hands of flame,
But burst the Crystal Cabinet,
And like a weeping Babe became–

A weeping Babe upon the wild,
And weeping Woman pale reclin'd,
And in the outward air again
I fill'd with woes the passing wind.

Auguries of Innocence

TO see a World in a grain of sand,
And a Heaven in a wild flower,
Hold Infinity in the palm of your hand,
And Eternity in an hour. . . .

The bat that flits at close of eve
Has left the brain that won't believe.
The owl that calls upon the night
Speaks the unbeliever's fright. . . .

Joy and woe are woven fine,
A clothing for the soul divine;
Under every grief and pine
Runs a joy with silken twine. . . .

Every tear from every eye
Becomes a babe in Eternity. . . .

The bleat, the bark, bellow, and roar
Are waves that beat on Heaven's shore. . . .

He who doubts from what he sees
Will ne'er believe, do what you please.
If the Sun and Moon should doubt,
They'd immediately go out. . . .

God appears, and God is Light,
To those poor souls who dwell in Night;
But does a Human Form display
To those who dwell in realms of Day.

To Thomas Butts

TO my friend Butts I write
My first vision of light,
On the yellow sands sitting.
The sun was emitting
His glorious beams
From Heaven's high streams.
Over sea, over land,
My eyes did expand
Into regions of air,
Away from all care;
Into regions of fire,
Remote from desire;
The light of the morning
Heaven's mountains adorning:
In particles bright,
The jewels of light
Distinct shone and clear.
Amaz'd and in fear
I each particle gazèd,
Astonish'd, amazèd;
For each was a Man
Human-form'd. Swift I ran,
For they beckon'd to me,
Remote by the sea,
Saying: 'Each grain of sand,
Every stone on the land,
Each rock and each hill,
Each fountain and rill,
Each herb and each tree,
Mountain, hill, earth, and sea,
Cloud, meteor, and star,
Are men seen afar.'

I stood in the streams
Of Heaven's bright beams,
And saw Felpham sweet
Beneath my bright feet,
In soft Female charms;
And in her fair arms
My Shadow I knew,
And my wife's Shadow too,
And my sister, and friend.
We like infants descend
In our Shadows on earth,
Like a weak mortal birth.
My eyes, more and more,
Like a sea without shore,
Continue expanding,
The Heavens commanding;
Till the jewels of light,
Heavenly men beaming bright,
Appear'd as One Man,
Who complacent began
My limbs to enfold
In His beams of bright gold;
Like dross purg'd away
All my mire and my clay.
Soft consum'd in delight,
In His bosom sun-bright
I remain'd. Soft He smil'd,
And I heard His voice mild,
Saying: 'This is My fold,
O thou ram horn'd with gold,
Who awakest from sleep
On the sides of the deep.
On the mountains around
The roarings resound

Of the lion and wolf,
The loud sea, and deep gulf.
These are guards of My fold,
O thou ram horn'd with gold!'
And the voice faded mild;
I remain'd as a child;
All I ever had known
Before me bright shone:
I saw you and your wife
By the fountains of life.
Such the vision to me
Appear'd on the sea.

From 'Milton'

AND did those feet in ancient time
  Walk upon England's mountains green?
And was the holy Lamb of God
  On England's pleasant pastures seen?

And did the Countenance Divine
  Shine forth upon our clouded hills?
And was Jerusalem builded here
  Among these dark Satanic Mills?

Bring me my bow of burning gold!
  Bring me my arrows of desire!
Bring me my spear! O clouds, unfold!
  Bring me my chariot of fire!

I will not cease from mental fight,
  Nor shall my sword sleep in my hand,
Till we have built Jerusalem
  In England's green and pleasant land.

From 'Jerusalem'

To the Christians

I GIVE you the end of a golden string;
Only wind it into a ball,
It will lead you in at Heaven's gate,
Built in Jerusalem's wall. . . .

England! awake! awake! awake!
Jerusalem thy sister calls!
Why wilt thou sleep the sleep of death,
And close her from thy ancient walls?

Thy hills and valleys felt her feet
Gently upon their bosoms move:
Thy gates beheld sweet Zion's ways;
Then was a time of joy and love.

And now the time returns again:
Our souls exult, and London's towers
Receive the Lamb of God to dwell
In England's green and pleasant bowers.

WILLIAM WORDSWORTH

1770-1850

From 'The Excursion'

I

SUCH was the Boy–but for the growing Youth
What soul was his, when, from the naked top
Of some bold headland, he beheld the sun
Rise up, and bathe the world in light! He looked–
Ocean and earth, the solid frame of earth
And ocean's liquid mass, in gladness lay

Beneath him:–Far and wide the clouds were touched,
And in their silent faces could he read
Unutterable love. Sound needed none,
Nor any voice of joy; his spirit drank
The spectacle: sensation, soul, and form,
All melted into him; they swallowed up
His animal being; in them did he live,
And by them did he live; they were his life.
In such access of mind, in such high hour
Of visitation from the living God,
Thought was not; in enjoyment it expired.
No thanks he breathed, he proffered no request;
Rapt into still communion that transcends
The imperfect offices of prayer and praise,
His mind was a thanksgiving to the power
That made him; it was blessedness and love!

II

Thou, who didst wrap the cloud
Of infancy around us, that thyself,
Therein, with our simplicity awhile
Might'st hold, on earth, communion undisturbed;
Who from the anarchy of dreaming sleep,
Or from its death-like void, with punctual care,
And touch as gentle as the morning light,
Restor'st us, daily, to the powers of sense
And reason's steadfast rule–thou, thou alone
Art everlasting, and the blessed Spirits,
Which thou includest, as the sea her waves:
For adoration thou endur'st; endure
For consciousness the motions of thy will;
For apprehension those transcendent truths
Of the pure intellect, that stand as laws
(Submission constituting strength and power)

Even to thy Being's infinite majesty!
This universe shall pass away–a work
Glorious! because the shadow of thy might,
A step, or link, for intercourse with thee.
Ah! if the time must come, in which my feet
No more shall stray where meditation leads,
By flowing stream, through wood, or craggy wild,
Loved haunts like these; the unimprisoned Mind
May yet have scope to range among her own,
Her thoughts, her images, her high desires.
If the dear faculty of sight should fail,
Still, it may be allowed me to remember
What visionary powers of eye and soul
In youth were mine; when, stationed on the top
Of some huge hill, expectant, I beheld
The sun rise up, from distant climes returned
Darkness to chase, and sleep; and bring the day
His bounteous gift! or saw him toward the deep
Sink, with a retinue of flaming clouds
Attended; then, my spirit was entranced
With joy exalted to beatitude;
The measure of my soul was filled with bliss,
And holiest love; as earth, sea, air, with light,
With pomp, with glory, with magnificence!

III

I have seen
A curious child, who dwelt upon a tract
Of inland ground, applying to his ear
The convolutions of a smooth-lipped shell;
To which, in silence hushed, his very soul
Listened intensely; and his countenance soon
Brightened with joy; for from within were heard
Murmurings, whereby the monitor expressed

Mysterious union with its native sea.
Even such a shell the universe itself
Is to the ear of Faith; and there are times,
I doubt not, when to you it doth impart
Authentic tidings of invisible things;
Of ebb and flow, and ever-during power;
And central peace, subsisting at the heart
Of endless agitation.

IV

To every Form of being is assigned
An *active* Principle:–howe'er removed
From sense and observation, it subsists
In all things, in all natures; in the stars
Of azure heaven, the unenduring clouds,
In flower and tree, in every pebbly stone
That paves the brooks, the stationary rocks,
The moving waters, and the invisible air.
Whate'er exists hath properties that spread
Beyond itself, communicating good,
A simple blessing, or with evil mixed;
Spirit that knows no insulated spot,
No chasm, no solitude; from link to link
It circulates, the Soul of all the worlds.
This is the freedom of the universe;
Unfolded still the more, more visible,
The more we know; and yet is reverenced least,
And least respected in the human Mind,
Its most apparent home.

From 'On the Power of Sound'

BY one pervading spirit
Of tones and numbers all things are controlled,
As sages taught, where faith was found to merit
Initiation in that mystery old.
The heavens, whose aspect makes our minds as still
As they themselves appear to be,
Innumerable voices fill
With everlasting harmony;
The towering headlands, crowned with mist,
Their feet among the billows, know
That Ocean is a mighty harmonist;
Thy pinions, universal Air,
Ever waving to and fro,
Are delegates of harmony, and bear
Strains that support the Seasons in their round;
Stern Winter loves a dirge-like sound.

Break forth into thanksgiving,
Ye banded instruments of wind and chords;
Unite, to magnify the Ever-living,
Your inarticulate notes with the voice of words!
Nor hushed be service from the lowing mead,
Nor mute the forest hum of noon;
Thou too be heard, lone eagle! freed
From snowy peak and cloud, attune
Thy hungry barkings to the hymn
Of joy, that from her utmost walls
The six-days' Work by flaming Seraphim
Transmits to Heaven! As Deep to Deep
Shouting through one valley calls,
All worlds, all natures, mood and measure keep
For praise and ceaseless gratulation, poured

Into the ear of God, their Lord!

A Voice to Light gave Being;
To Time, and Man his earth-born chronicler;
A Voice shall finish doubt and dim foreseeing,
And sweep away life's visionary stir;
The trumpet (we, intoxicate with pride,
Arm at its blast for deadly wars)
To archangelic lips applied,
The grave shall open, quench the stars.
O Silence! are Man's noisy years
No more than moments of thy life?
Is Harmony, blest queen of smiles and tears,
With her smooth tones and discords just,
Tempered into rapturous strife,
Thy destined bond-slave? No! though earth be dust
And vanish, though the heavens dissolve, her stay
Is in the WORD, that shall not pass away.

Ode: Intimations of Immortality from Recollections of Early Childhood

THERE was a time when meadow, grove, and stream,
The earth, and every common sight,
To me did seem
Apparelled in celestial light,
The glory and the freshness of a dream.
It is not now as it hath been of yore;–
Turn wheresoe'er I may,
By night or day,
The things which I have seen I now can see no more.

The Rainbow comes and goes,
And lovely is the Rose,
The Moon doth with delight

Look round her when the heavens are bare,
Waters on a starry night
Are beautiful and fair;
The sunshine is a glorious birth;
But yet I know, where'er I go,
That there hath past away a glory from the earth.

Now, while the birds thus sing a joyous song,
And while the young lambs bound
As to the tabor's sound,
To me alone there came a thought of grief:
A timely utterance gave that thought relief,
And I again am strong:
The cataracts blow their trumpets from the steep;
No more shall grief of mine the season wrong;
I hear the Echoes through the mountains throng,
The Winds come to me from the fields of sleep,
And all the earth is gay;
Land and sea
Give themselves up to jollity,
And with the heart of May
Doth every Beast keep holiday;–
Thou Child of Joy,
Shout round me, let me hear thy shouts, thou happy
Shepherd-boy!

Ye blessèd Creatures, I have heard the call
Ye to each other make; I see
The heavens laugh with you in your jubilee;
My heart is at your festival,
My head hath its coronal,
The fulness of your bliss, I feel–I feel it all.
Oh evil day! if I were sullen
While Earth herself is adorning,

This sweet May-morning,
And the Children are culling
On every side,
In a thousand valleys far and wide,
Fresh flowers; while the sun shines warm,
And the Babe leaps up on his Mother's arm:–
I hear, I hear, with joy I hear!
–But there's a Tree, of many, one,
A single Field which I have looked upon,
Both of them speak of something that is gone:
The Pansy at my feet
Doth the same tale repeat:
Whither is fled the visionary gleam?
Where is it now, the glory and the dream?

Our birth is but a sleep and a forgetting:
The Soul that rises with us, our life's Star,
Hath had elsewhere its setting,
And cometh from afar:
Not in entire forgetfulness,
And not in utter nakedness,
But trailing clouds of glory do we come
From God, who is our home:
Heaven lies about us in our infancy!
Shades of the prison-house begin to close
Upon the growing Boy,
But He beholds the light, and whence it flows,
He sees it in his joy;
The Youth, who daily farther from the east
Must travel, still is Nature's Priest,
And by the vision splendid
Is on his way attended;
At length the Man perceives it die away,
And fade into the light of common day.

Earth fills her lap with pleasures of her own;
Yearnings she hath in her own natural kind,
And, even with something of a Mother's mind,
And no unworthy aim,
The homely Nurse doth all she can
To make her Foster-child, her Inmate Man,
Forget the glories he hath known,
And that imperial palace whence he came.

Behold the Child among his new-born blisses,
A six years' Darling of a pigmy size!
See, where 'mid work of his own hand he lies,
Fretted by sallies of his mother's kisses,
With light upon him from his father's eyes!
See, at his feet, some little plan or chart,
Some fragment from his dream of human life,
Shaped by himself with newly-learnèd art;
A wedding or a festival,
A mourning or a funeral;
And this hath now his heart,
And unto this he frames his song:
Then will he fit his tongue
To dialogues of business, love, or strife;
But it will not be long
Ere this be thrown aside,
And with new joy and pride
The little Actor cons another part;
Filling from time to time his 'humorous stage'
With all the Persons, down to palsied Age,
That Life brings with her in her equipage;
As if his whole vocation
Were endless imitation.

Thou, whose exterior semblance doth belie
Thy Soul's immensity;

Thou best Philosopher, who yet dost keep
Thy heritage, thou Eye among the blind,
That, deaf and silent, read'st the eternal deep,
Haunted for ever by the eternal mind,–
        Mighty Prophet! Seer blest!
        On whom those truths do rest,
Which we are toiling all our lives to find,
In darkness lost, the darkness of the grave;
Thou, over whom thy Immortality
Broods like the Day, a Master o'er a Slave,
A Presence which is not to be put by;
Thou little Child, yet glorious in the might
Of heaven-born freedom on thy being's height,
Why with such earnest pains dost thou provoke
The years to bring the inevitable yoke,
Thus blindly with thy blessedness at strife?
Full soon thy Soul shall have her earthly freight,
And custom lie upon thee with a weight,
Heavy as frost, and deep almost as life!

        O joy! that in our embers
        Is something that doth live,
        That nature yet remembers
        What was so fugitive!
The thought of our past years in me doth breed
Perpetual benediction: not indeed
For that which is most worthy to be blest;
Delight and liberty, the simple creed
Of Childhood, whether busy or at rest,
With new-fledged hope still fluttering in his breast:–
        Not for these I raise
        The song of thanks and praise;
    But for those obstinate questionings
    Of sense and outward things,

Fallings from us, vanishings;
Blank misgivings of a Creature
Moving about in worlds not realized,
High instincts before which our mortal Nature
Did tremble like a guilty Thing surprised:
But for those first affections,
Those shadowy recollections,
Which, be they what they may,
Are yet the fountain-light of all our day,
Are yet a master-light of all our seeing;
Uphold us, cherish, and have power to make
Our noisy years seem moments in the being
Of the eternal Silence: truths that wake,
To perish never:
Which neither listlessness, nor mad endeavour,
Nor Man nor Boy,
Nor all that is at enmity with joy,
Can utterly abolish or destroy!
Hence in a season of calm weather
Though inland far we be,
Our Souls have sight of that immortal sea
Which brought us hither,
Can in a moment travel thither,
And see the Children sport upon the shore,
And hear the mighty waters rolling evermore.

Then sing, ye Birds, sing, sing a joyous song!
And let the young Lambs bound
As to the tabor's sound!
We in thought will join your throng,
Ye that pipe and ye that play,
Ye that through your hearts to-day
Feel the gladness of the May!
What though the radiance which was once so bright

Be now for ever taken from my sight,
Though nothing can bring back the hour
Of splendour in the grass, of glory in the flower;
We will grieve not, rather find
Strength in what remains behind;
In the primal sympathy
Which having been must ever be;
In the soothing thoughts that spring
Out of human suffering;
In the faith that looks through death,
In years that bring the philosophic mind.

And O, ye Fountains, Meadows, Hills, and Groves,
Forebode not any severing of our loves!
Yet in my heart of hearts I feel your might;
I only have relinquished one delight
To live beneath your more habitual sway.
I love the Brooks which down their channels fret,
Even more than when I tripped lightly as they;
The innocent brightness of a new-born Day
Is lovely yet;
The Clouds that gather round the setting sun
Do take a sober colouring from an eye
That hath kept watch o'er man's mortality;
Another race hath been, and other palms are won.
Thanks to the human heart by which we live,
Thanks to its tenderness, its joys, and fears,
To me the meanest flower that blows can give
Thoughts that do often lie too deep for tears.

From 'Lines composed a few miles above Tintern Abbey'

FOR I have learned
To look on nature, not as in the hour
Of thoughtless youth; but hearing oftentimes
The still, sad music of humanity,
Nor harsh nor grating, though of ample power
To chasten and subdue. And I have felt
A presence that disturbs me with the joy
Of elevated thoughts; a sense sublime
Of something far more deeply interfused,
Whose dwelling is the light of setting suns,
And the round ocean and the living air,
And the blue sky, and in the mind of man:
A motion and a spirit, that impels
All thinking things, all objects of all thought,
And rolls through all things. Therefore am I still
A lover of the meadows and the woods,
And mountains; and of all that we behold
From this green earth; of all the mighty world
Of eye, and ear,–both what they half create,
And what perceive; well pleased to recognize
In nature and the language of the sense,
The anchor of my purest thoughts, the nurse,
The guide, the guardian of my heart, and soul
Of all my moral being.

From 'The Prelude'

I

THUS while the days flew by, and years passed on,
From Nature and her overflowing soul
I had received so much, that all my thoughts
Were steeped in feeling; I was only then

Contented, when with bliss ineffable
I felt the sentiment of Being spread
O'er all that moves and all that seemeth still;
O'er all that, lost beyond the reach of thought
And human knowledge, to the human eye
Invisible, yet liveth to the heart;
O'er all that leaps and runs, and shouts and sings,
Or beats the gladsome air; o'er all that glides
Beneath the wave, yea, in the wave itself,
And mighty depth of waters. Wonder not
If high the transport, great the joy I felt
Communing in this sort through earth and heaven
With every form of creature, as it looked
Towards the Uncreated with a countenance
Of adoration, with an eye of love.
One song they sang, and it was audible,
Most audible, then, when the fleshly ear,
O'ercome by humblest prelude of that strain,
Forgot her functions, and slept undisturbed.

II

–Of that external scene which round me lay,
Little, in this abstraction, did I see;
Remembered less; but I had inward hopes
And swellings of the spirit, was rapt and soothed,
Conversed with promises, had glimmering views
How life pervades the undecaying mind;
How the immortal soul with God-like power
Informs, creates, and thaws the deepest sleep
That time can lay upon her; how on earth,
Man, if he do but live within the light
Of high endeavours, daily spreads abroad
His being armed with strength that cannot fail.

III

Visionary power
Attends the motions of the viewless winds,
Embodied in the mystery of words:
There, darkness makes abode, and all the host
Of shadowy things work endless changes,–there,
As in a mansion like their proper home,
Even forms and substances are circumfused
By that transparent veil with light divine,
And, through the turnings intricate of verse,
Present themselves as objects recognized,
In flashes, and with glory not their own.

IV

Imagination–here the Power so called
Through sad incompetence of human speech,
That awful Power rose from the mind's abyss
Like an unfathered vapour that enwraps,
At once, some lonely traveller. I was lost;
Halted without an effort to break through;
But to my conscious soul I now can say–
'I recognize thy glory': in such strength
Of usurpation, when the light of sense
Goes out, but with a flash that has revealed
The invisible world, doth greatness make abode,
There harbours; whether we be young or old,
Our destiny, our being's heart and home,
Is with infinitude, and only there;
With hope it is, hope that can never die,
Effort, and expectation, and desire,
And something evermore about to be.
Under such banners militant, the soul
Seeks for no trophies, struggles for no spoils
That may attest her prowess, blest in thoughts

That are their own perfection and reward,
Strong in herself and in beatitude
That hides her, like the mighty flood of Nile
Poured from his fount of Abyssinian clouds
To fertilize the whole Egyptian plain.

V

The brook and road[1]
Were fellow-travellers in this gloomy strait,
And with them did we journey several hours
At a slow pace. The immeasurable height
Of woods decaying, never to be decayed,
The stationary blasts of waterfalls,
And in the narrow rent at every turn
Winds thwarting winds, bewildered and forlorn,
The torrents shooting from the clear blue sky,
The rocks that muttered close upon our ears,
Black drizzling crags that spake by the way-side
As if a voice were in them, the sick sight
And giddy prospect of the raving stream,
The unfettered clouds and region of the Heavens,
Tumult and peace, the darkness and the light–
Were all like workings of one mind, the features
Of the same face, blossoms upon one tree;
Characters of the great Apocalypse,
The types and symbols of Eternity,
Of first, and last, and midst, and without end.

VI

In some green bower
Rest, and be not alone, but have thou there
The One who is thy choice of all the world:
There linger, listening, gazing, with delight

[1]The passage refers to the Simplon Pass.

Impassioned, but delight how pitiable!
Unless this love by a still higher love
Be hallowed, love that breathes not without awe;
Love that adores, but on the knees of prayer,
By heaven inspired; that frees from chains the soul,
Lifted, in union with the purest, best,
Of earth-born passions, on the wings of praise
Bearing a tribute to the Almighty's Throne.

VII

This spiritual Love acts not nor can exist
Without Imagination, which, in truth,
Is but another name for absolute power
And clearest insight, amplitude of mind,
And Reason in her most exalted mood.
This faculty hath been the feeding source
Of our long labour [1]: we have traced the stream
From the blind cavern whence is faintly heard
Its natal murmur; followed it to light
And open day; accompanied its course
Among the ways of Nature, for a time
Lost sight of it bewildered and engulphed;
Then given it greeting as it rose once more
In strength, reflecting from its placid breast
The works of man and face of human life;
And lastly, from its progress have we drawn
Faith in life endless, the sustaining thought
Of human Being, Eternity, and God.

[1]The labour shared between the writer and the reader of the Prelude.

126

SAMUEL TAYLOR COLERIDGE

1772-1834

From 'Religious Musings'

I

THERE is one Mind, one omnipresent Mind,
Omnific. His most holy name is Love.
Truth of subliming import! with the which
Who feeds and saturates his constant soul,
He from his small particular orbit flies
With blest outstarting! From himself he flies,
Stands in the sun, and with no partial gaze
Views all creation; and he loves it all,
And blesses it, and calls it very good!
This is indeed to dwell with the Most High!
Cherubs and rapture-trembling Seraphim
Can press no nearer to the Almighty's throne.
But that we roam unconscious, or with hearts
Unfeeling of our universal Sire,
And that in His vast family no Cain
Injures uninjured (in her best-aimed blow
Victorious Murder a blind Suicide)
Haply for this some younger Angel now
Looks down on Human Nature: and, behold!
A sea of blood bestrewed with wrecks, where mad
Embattling Interests on each other rush
With unhelmed rage!
'Tis the sublime of man,
Our noontide Majesty, to know ourselves
Parts and proportions of one wondrous whole!
This fraternizes man, this constitutes
Our charities and bearings. But 'tis God
Diffused through all, that doth make all one whole;
This the worst superstition, him except
Aught to desire, Supreme Reality!
The plenitude and permanence of bliss!

II

Toy-bewitched,
Made blind by lusts, disherited of soul,
No common centre Man, no common sire
Knoweth! A sordid solitary thing,
Mid countless brethren with a lonely heart
Through courts and cities the smooth savage roams
Feeling himself, his own low self the whole;
When he by sacred sympathy might make
The whole one Self! Self, that no alien knows!
Self, far diffused as Fancy's wing can travel!
Self, spreading still! Oblivious of its own,
Yet all of all possessing! This is Faith!
This is the Messiah's destined victory!

From 'Dejection: an Ode'

MY genial spirits fail;
And what can these[1] avail
To lift the smothering weight from off my breast?
It were a vain endeavour,
Though I should gaze for ever
On that green light that lingers in the west:
I may not hope from outward forms to win
The passion and the life, whose fountains are within.

O Lady! we receive but what we give,
And in our life alone does Nature live:
Ours is her wedding garment, ours her shroud!
And would we aught behold, of higher worth,
Than that inanimate cold world allowed
To the poor loveless ever-anxious crowd,
Ah! from the soul itself must issue forth
A light, a glory, a fair luminous cloud

[1]The clouds, the stars, and the moon, at which the poet was gazing.

Enveloping the earth–
And from the soul itself must there be sent
A sweet and potent voice, of its own birth,
Of all sweet sounds the life and element!

PERCY BYSSHE SHELLEY

1792-1822

Hymn to Intellectual Beauty

I

THE awful shadow of some unseen Power
Floats though unseen among us,–visiting
This various world with as inconstant wing
As summer winds that creep from flower to flower,–
Like moonbeams that behind some piny mountain shower,
It visits with inconstant glance
Each human heart and countenance;
Like hues and harmonies of evening,–
Like clouds in starlight widely spread,–
Like memory of music fled,–
Like aught that for its grace may be
Dear, and yet dearer for its mystery.

II

Spirit of BEAUTY, that dost consecrate
With thine own hues all thou dost shine upon
Of human thought or form,–where art thou gone?
Why dost thou pass away and leave our state,
This dim vast vale of tears, vacant and desolate?
Ask why the sunlight not for ever
Weaves rainbows o'er yon mountain-river,
Why aught should fail and fade that once is shown,
Why fear and dream and death and birth
Cast on the daylight of this earth
Such gloom,–why man has such a scope
For love and hate, despondency and hope?

III

No voice from some sublimer world hath ever
To sage or poet these responses given–
Therefore the names of Demon, Ghost, and Heaven,
Remain the records of their vain endeavour,
Frail spells–whose uttered charm might not avail to sever,
From all we hear and all we see,
Doubt, chance, and mutability.
Thy light alone–like mist o'er mountains driven,
Or music by the night-wind sent
Through strings of some still instrument,
Or moonlight on a midnight stream,
Gives grace and truth to life's unquiet dream.

IV

Love, Hope, and Self-esteem, like clouds depart
And come, for some uncertain moments lent.
Man were immortal, and omnipotent,
Didst thou, unknown and awful as thou art,
Keep with thy glorious train firm state within his heart.
Thou messenger of sympathies,
That wax and wane in lovers' eyes–
Thou–that to human thought art nourishment,
Like darkness to a dying flame!
Depart not as thy shadow came,
Depart not–lest the grave should be,
Like life and fear, a dark reality.

V

While yet a boy I sought for ghosts, and sped
Through many a listening chamber, cave and ruin,
And starlight wood, with fearful steps pursuing
Hopes of high talk with the departed dead.
I called on poisonous names with which our youth is fed;

I was not heard–I saw them not–
When musing deeply on the lot
Of life, at that sweet time when winds are wooing
All vital things that wake to bring
News of birds and blossoming,–
Sudden, thy shadow fell on me;
I shrieked, and clasped my hands in ecstasy!

VI

I vowed that I would dedicate my powers
To thee and thine–have I not kept the vow?
With beating heart and streaming eyes, even now
I call the phantoms of a thousand hours
Each from his voiceless grave: they have in visioned bowers
Of studious zeal or love's delight
Outwatched with me the envious night–
They know that never joy illumed my brow
Unlinked with hope that thou wouldst free
This world from its dark slavery,
That thou–O awful LOVELINESS,
Wouldst give whate'er these words cannot express.

VII

The day becomes more solemn and serene
When noon is past–there is a harmony
In autumn, and a lustre in its sky,
Which through the summer is not heard or seen,
As if it could not be, as if it had not been!
Thus let thy power, which like the truth
Of nature on my passive youth
Descended, to my onward life supply
Its calm–to one who worships thee,
And every form containing thee,
Whom, SPIRIT fair, thy spells did bind
To fear himself, and love all human kind.

From 'Adonais'

HE is made one with Nature: there is heard
His voice in all her music, from the moan
Of thunder, to the song of night's sweet bird;
He is a presence to be felt and known
In darkness and in light, from herb and stone,
Spreading itself where'er that Power may move
Which has withdrawn his being to its own;
Which wields the world with never-wearied love,
Sustains it from beneath, and kindles it above.

He is a portion of the loveliness
Which once he made more lovely: he doth bear
His part, while the one Spirit's plastic stress
Sweeps through the dull dense world, compelling there,
All new successions to the forms they wear;
Torturing th' unwilling dross that checks its flight
To its own likeness, as each mass may bear;
And bursting in its beauty and its might
From trees and beasts and men into the Heaven's light.

The splendours of the firmament of time
May be eclipsed, but are extinguished not;
Like stars to their appointed height they climb
And death is a low mist which cannot blot
The brightness it may veil. When lofty thought
Lifts a young heart above its mortal lair,
And love and life contend in it, for what
Shall be its earthly doom, the dead live there
And move like winds of light on dark and stormy air.

The One remains, the many change and pass;
Heaven's light forever shines, Earth's shadows fly;
Life, like a dome of many-coloured glass,
Stains the white radiance of Eternity,

Until Death tramples it to fragments.–Die,
If thou wouldst be with that which thou dost seek!
Follow where all is fled!–Rome's azure sky,
Flowers, ruins, statues, music, words, are weak
The glory they transfuse with fitting truth to speak.

Why linger, why turn back, why shrink, my Heart?
Thy hopes are gone before: from all things here
They have departed; thou shouldst now depart!
A light is passed from the revolving year,
And man, and woman; and what still is dear
Attracts to crush, repels to make thee wither.
The soft sky smiles,–the low wind whispers near:
'Tis Adonais calls! oh, hasten thither,
No more let Life divide what Death can join together.

That Light whose smile kindles the Universe,
That Beauty in which all things work and move,
That Benediction which the eclipsing Curse
Of birth can quench not, that sustaining Love
Which through the web of being blindly wove
By man and beast and earth and air and sea,
Burns bright or dim, as each are mirrors of
The fire for which all thirst; now beams on me,
Consuming the last clouds of cold mortality.

The breath whose might I have invoked in song
Descends on me; my spirit's bark is driven,
Far from the shore, far from the trembling throng
Whose sails were never to the tempest given;
The massy earth and spherèd skies are riven!
I am borne darkly, fearfully, afar;
Whilst, burning through the inmost veil of Heaven,
The soul of Adonais, like a star,
Beacons from the abode where the Eternal are.

133

JOHN HENRY, CARDINAL NEWMAN

1801- 1890

Melchizedek

Without father, without mother, without descent; having neither beginning of days, nor end of life.

THRICE bless'd are they, who feel their loneliness;
To whom nor voice of friends nor pleasant scene
Brings that on which the sadden'd heart can lean;
Yea, the rich earth, garb'd in her daintiest dress
Of light and joy, doth but the more oppress,
Claiming responsive smiles and rapture high;
Till, sick at heart, beyond the veil they fly,
Seeking His Presence, who alone can bless.
Such, in strange days, the weapons of Heaven's grace;
When, passing o'er the high-born Hebrew line,
He forms the vessel of His vast design;
Fatherless, homeless, reft of age and place,
Sever'd from earth, and careless of its wreck,
Born through long woe His rare Melchizedek.

From 'The Dream of Gerontius'

Choir of Angelicals.

A DOUBLE debt he has to pay–
The forfeit of his sins:
The chill of death is past, and now
The penance-fire begins.

Glory to Him, who evermore
By truth and justice reigns;
Who tears the soul from out its case,
And burns away its stains!

Angel.

They sing of thy approaching agony,
Which thou so eagerly didst question of:
It is the face of the Incarnate God
Shall smite thee with that keen and subtle pain;
And yet the memory which it leaves will be
A sovereign febrifuge to heal the wound;
And yet withal it will the wound provoke,
And aggravate and widen it the more.

Soul.

Thou speakest mysteries: still methinks I know
To disengage the tangle of thy words:
Yet rather would I hear thy angel voice,
Than for myself be thy interpreter.

Angel.

When then–if such thy lot–thou seest thy Judge,
The sight of Him will kindle in thy heart
All tender, gracious, reverential thoughts.
Thou wilt be sick with love, and yearn for Him,
And feel as though thou couldst but pity Him,
That one so sweet should e'er have placed Himself
At disadvantage such, as to be used
So vilely by a being so vile as thee.
There is a pleading in His pensive eyes
Will pierce thee to the quick, and trouble thee.
And thou wilt hate and loathe thyself; for, though
Now sinless, thou wilt feel that thou hast sinn'd,
As never thou didst feel; and wilt desire
To slink away, and hide thee from His sight:
And yet wilt have a longing ay to dwell
Within the beauty of His countenance.

And these two pains, so counter and so keen,–
The longing for Him, when thou seest Him not;
The shame of self at thought of seeing Him,–
Will be thy veriest, sharpest purgatory.

The Pillar of the Cloud

LEAD, Kindly Light, amid the encircling gloom,
Lead Thou me on!
The night is dark, and I am far from home–
Lead Thou me on!
Keep Thou my feet: I do not ask to see
The distant scene,–one step enough for me.

I was not ever thus, nor pray'd that Thou
Shouldst lead me on.
I loved to choose and see my path; but now
Lead Thou me on!
I loved the garish day, and, spite of fears,
Pride ruled my will: remember not past years.

So long Thy power hath blest me, sure it still
Will lead me on,
O'er moor and fen, o'er crag and torrent, till
The night is gone;
And with the morn those angel faces smile
Which I have loved long since, and lost awhile.

136

JAMES CLARENCE MANGAN

1803-1849

S. Patrick's Hymn before Tara

(From the Irish)

CHRIST, as a light,
Illumine and guide me!
Christ, as a shield, o'ershadow and cover me!
Christ be under me! Christ be over me!
Christ be beside me
On left hand and right!
Christ be before me, behind me, about me!
Christ this day be within and without me!

Christ, the lowly and meek,
Christ, the All-powerful, be
In the heart of each to whom I speak,
In the mouth of each who speaks to me!
In all who draw near me,
Or see me or hear me!

At Tara to-day, in this awful hour,
I call on the Holy Trinity!
Glory to Him who reigneth in power,
The God of the Elements, Father, and Son,
And Paraclete Spirit, which Three are the One,
The ever-existing Divinity!

Salvation dwells with the Lord,
With Christ, the Omnipotent Word.
From generation to generation
Grant us, O Lord, Thy grace and salvation!

137

RALPH WALDO EMERSON

1803-1882

The Problem

I LIKE a church; I like a cowl;
I love a prophet of the soul;
And on my heart monastic aisles
Fall like sweet strains, or pensive smiles;
Yet not for all his faith can see
Would I that cowled churchman be.

Why should the vest on him allure,
Which I could not on me endure?

Not from a vain or shallow thought
His awful Jove young Phidias brought;
Never from lips of cunning fell
The thrilling Delphic oracle;
Out from the heart of nature rolled
The burdens of the Bible old;
The litanies of nations came,
Like the volcano's tongue of flame,
Up from the burning core below,–
The canticles of love and woe;
The hand that rounded Peter's dome,
And groined the aisles of Christian Rome,
Wrought in a sad sincerity;
Himself from God he could not free;
He builded better than he knew;–
The conscious stone to beauty grew.

Know'st thou what wove yon woodbird's nest
Of leaves, and feathers from her breast?
Or how the fish outbuilt her shell,
Painting with morn each annual cell?

Or how the sacred pine-tree adds
To her old leaves new myriads?
Such and so grew these holy piles,
Whilst love and terror laid the tiles.
Earth proudly wears the Parthenon,
As the best gem upon her zone;
And Morning opes with haste her lids,
To gaze upon the Pyramids;
O'er England's abbeys bends the sky,
As on its friends, with kindred eye;
For, out of Thought's interior sphere,
These wonders rose to upper air;
And Nature gladly gave them place,
Adopted them into her race,
And granted them an equal date
With Andes and with Ararat.

These temples grew as grows the grass;
Art might obey, but not surpass.
The passive Master lent his hand
To the vast soul that o'er him planned;
And the same power that reared the shrine,
Bestrode the tribes that knelt within.
Ever the fiery Pentecost
Girds with one flame the countless host,
Trances the heart through chanting choirs,
And through the priest the mind inspires.

The word unto the prophet spoken
Was writ on tables yet unbroken;
The word by seers or sibyls told,
In groves of oak, or fanes of gold,
Still floats upon the morning wind,
Still whispers to the willing mind.
One accent of the Holy Ghost
The heedless world hath never lost.

I know what say the fathers wise,–
The Book itself before me lies,
Old *Chrysostom*, best Augustine,
And he who blent both in his line,
The younger *Golden Lips* or mines,
Taylor, the Shakespeare of divines.
His words are music in my ear,
I see his cowled portrait dear;
And yet, for all his faith could see,
I would not the good bishop be.

Ode to Beauty

WHO gave thee, O Beauty,
The keys of this breast,–
Too credulous lover
Of blest and unblest?
Say, when in lapsed ages
Thee knew I of old?
Or what was the service
For which I was sold?
When first my eyes saw thee,
I found me thy thrall,
By magical drawings,
Sweet tyrant of all!
I drank at thy fountain
False waters of thirst;
Thou intimate stranger,
Thou latest and first!
Thy dangerous glances
Make women of men;
New-born, we are melting
Into nature again.

Lavish, lavish promiser,
Nigh persuading gods to err!
Guest of million painted forms,
Which in turn thy glory warms!
The frailest leaf, the mossy bark,
The acorn's cup, the raindrop's arc,
The swinging spider's silver line,
The ruby of the drop of wine,
The shining pebble of the pond,
Thou inscribest with a bond,
In thy momentary play,
Would bankrupt nature to repay.

Ah, what avails it
To hide or to shun
Whom the Infinite One
Hath granted His throne?
The heaven high over
Is the deep's lover;
The sun and sea,
Informed by thee,
Before me run,
And draw me on,
Yet fly me still,
As Fate refuses
To me the heart Fate for me chooses.
Is it that my opulent soul
Was mingled from the generous whole;
Sea-valleys and the deep of skies
Furnished several supplies;
And the sands whereof I'm made
Draw me to them, self-betrayed?
I turn the proud portfolios
Which hold the grand designs

Of Salvator, of Guercino,
And Piranesi's lines.
I hear the lofty paeans
Of the masters of the shell,
Who heard the starry music
And recount the numbers well;
Olympian bards who sung
Divine Ideas below,
Which always find us young,
And always keep us so.
Oft, in streets or humblest places,
I detect far-wandered graces,
Which, from Eden wide astray,
In lonely homes have lost their way.

Thee gliding through the sea of form,
Like the lightning through the storm,
Somewhat not to be possessed,
Somewhat not to be caressed.
No feet so fleet could ever find,
No perfect form could ever bind.
Thou eternal fugitive,
Hovering over all that live,
Quick and skilful to inspire
Sweet, extravagant desire,
Starry space and lily-bell
Filling with thy roseate smell,
Wilt not give the lips to taste
Of the nectar which thou hast.

All that's good and great with thee
Works in close conspiracy;
Thou hast bribed the dark and lonely
To report thy features only,

And the cold and purple morning
Itself with thoughts of thee adorning;
The leafy dell, the city mart,
Equal trophies of thine art;
E'en the flowing azure air
Thou hast touched for my despair;
And, if I languish into dreams,
Again I meet the ardent beams.
Queen of things! I dare not die
In Being's deeps past ear and eye;
Lest there I find the same deceiver,
And be the sport of Fate for ever.
Dread Power, but dear! if God thou be,
Unmake me quite, or give thyself to me!

Brahma

IF the red slayer think he slays,
    Or if the slain think he is slain,
They know not well the subtle ways
    I keep, and pass, and turn again.

Far or forgot to me is near;
    Shadow and sunlight are the same;
The vanished gods to me appear;
    And one to me are shame and fame.

They reckon ill who leave me out;
    When me they fly, I am the wings;
I am the doubter and the doubt,
    And I the hymn the Brahmin sings.

The strong gods pine for my abode,
    And pine in vain the sacred Seven;
But thou, meek lover of the good!
    Find me and turn thy back on heaven.

Worship

THIS is he, who, felled by foes,
Sprung harmless up, refreshed by blows
He to captivity was sold,
But him no prison-bars would hold:
Though they sealed him in a rock,
Mountain chains he can unlock:
Thrown to lions for their meat,
The crouching lion kissed his feet:
Bound to the stake, no flames appalled,
But arched o'er him an honouring vault.
This is he men miscall Fate,
Threading dark ways, arriving late,
But ever coming in time to crown
The truth, and hurl wrong-doers down.
He is the oldest, and best known,
More near than aught thou call'st thy own,
Yet, greeted in another's eyes,
Disconcerts with glad surprise.
This is Jove, who, deaf to prayers,
Floods with blessings unawares.
Draw, if thou canst, the mystic line
Severing rightly his from thine,
Which is human, which divine.

ROBERT STEPHEN HAWKER

1803-1875

Aishah Shechinah

A SHAPE, like folded light, embodied air,
Yet wreathed with flesh, and warm:
All that of heaven is feminine and fair,
Moulded in visible form,

She stood, the Lady Shechinah of earth,
   A chancel for the sky:
Where woke, to breath and beauty, God's own Birth,
   For men to see Him by.

Round her, too pure to mingle with the day,
   Light, that was life, abode;
Folded within her fibres meekly lay
   The link of boundless God.

So linked, so blent, that when, with pulse fulfilled,
   Moved but that Infant Hand,
Far, far away, His conscious Godhead thrilled,
   And stars might understand.

Lo! where they pause, with inter-gathering rest,
   The Threefold, and the One;
And lo, He binds them to her orient breast,
   His manhood girded on.

The zone, where two glad worlds for ever meet,
   Beneath that bosom ran:
Deep in that womb the conquering Paraclete
   Smote Godhead on to man.

Sole scene among the stars, where, yearning, glide
   The Threefold and the One;
Her God upon her lap, the Virgin Bride,
   Her awful Child, her Son!

From 'The Quest of the Sangraal'

THEN came Sir Joseph, hight, of Arimathèe,
Bearing that awful vase, the Sangraal!
The vessel of the Pasch, Shere Thursday night:
The selfsame Cup, wherein the faithful Wine
Heard God, and was obedient unto Blood!
Therewith he knelt, and gathered blessèd drops
From his dear Master's Side that sadly fell,
The ruddy dews from the great Tree of Life:
Sweet Lord! what treasures! like the priceless gems,
Hid in the tawny casket of a king–
A ransom for an army, one by one.
That wealth he cherished long; his very soul
Around his ark; bent, as before a shrine!
He dwelt in orient Syria: God's own land:
The ladder-foot of heaven–where shadowy shapes
In white apparel glided up and down!
His home was like a garner, full of corn
And wine and oil: a granary of God!
Young men, that no one knew, went in and out,
With a far look in their eternal eyes!
All things were strange and rare: the Sangraal
As though it clung to some etherial chain,
Brought down high heaven to earth at Arimathèe.
He lived long centuries! and prophesied.
A girded pilgrim ever and anon:
Cross-staff in hand, and folded at his side,
The mystic marvel of the feast of blood!
Once in old time he stood in this dear land,
Enthralled:–for lo! a sign! his grounded staff
Took root, and branched, and bloomed, like Aaron's rod,
Thence came the shrine, the cell: therefore he dwelt,
The vassal of the vase, at Avalon!

ELIZABETH BARRETT BROWNING

1806-1861

Chorus of Eden Spirits

(Chanting from Paradise, while Adam and Eve fly across the Sword-glare)

HEARKEN, oh hearken! let your souls behind you
Turn, gently moved!
Our voices feel along the Dread to find you,
O lost, beloved!
Through the thick-shielded and strong-marshalled angels,
They press and pierce:
Our requiems follow fast on our evangels,–
Voice throbs in verse.
We are but orphaned spirits left in Eden
A time ago:
God gave us golden cups, and we were bidden
To feed you so.
But now our right hand hath no cup remaining,
No work to do,
The mystic hydromel is spilt, and staining
The whole earth through.
Most ineradicable stains, for showing
(Not interfused!)
That brighter colours were the world's foregoing,
Than shall be used.
Hearken, oh hearken! ye shall hearken surely
For years and years,
The noise beside you, dripping coldly, purely,
Of spirits' tears.
The yearning to a beautiful denied you,
Shall strain your powers.

Ideal sweetnesses shall over-glide you,
 Resumed from ours.
In all your music, our pathetic minor
 Your ears shall cross;
And all good gifts shall mind you of diviner,
 With sense of loss.
We shall be near you in your poet-languors
 And wild extremes,
What time ye vex the desert with vain angers,
 Or mock with dreams.
And when upon you, weary after roaming,
 Death's seal is put,
By the foregone ye shall discern the coming,
 Through eyelids shut.

From 'The Soul's Travelling'

GOD, God!
 With a child's voice I cry,
Weak, sad, confidingly–
 God, God!
Thou knowest, eyelids, raised not always up
Unto Thy love (as none of ours are), droop
 As ours, o'er many a tear!
Thou knowest, though Thy universe is broad,
Two little tears suffice to cover all:
Thou knowest, Thou, who art so prodigal
Of beauty, we are oft but stricken deer
Expiring in the woods–that care for none
Of those delightsome flowers they die upon.

O blissful Mouth which breathed the mournful breath
We name our souls, self-spoilt!–by that strong passion

Which paled Thee once with sighs,–by that strong death
Which made Thee once unbreathing–from the wrack
Themselves have called around them, call them back,
Back to Thee in continuous aspiration!
    For here, O Lord,
For here they travel vainly,–vainly pass
From city-pavement to untrodden sward,
Where the lark finds her deep nest in the grass
Cold with the earth's last dew. Yea, very vain
The greatest speed of all these souls of men
Unless they travel upward to the throne
Where sittest THOU, the satisfying ONE,
With help for sins and holy perfectings
For all requirements–while the archangel, raising
Unto Thy face his full ecstatic gazing,
Forgets the rush and rapture of his wings.

Human Life's Mystery

WE sow the glebe, we reap the corn,
    We build the house where we may rest,
And then, at moments, suddenly,
We look up to the great wide sky,
Inquiring wherefore we were born. . .
    For earnest or for jest?

The senses folding thick and dark
    About the stifled soul within,
We guess diviner things beyond,
And yearn to them with yearning fond;
We strike out blindly to a mark
    Believed in, but not seen.

We vibrate to the pant and thrill
Wherewith Eternity has curled
In serpent-twine about God's seat;
While, freshening upward to His feet,
In gradual growth His full-leaved will
Expands from world to world.

And, in the tumult and excess
Of act and passion under sun,
We sometimes hear–oh, soft and far,
As silver star did touch with star,
The kiss of Peace and Righteousness
Through all things that are done.

God keeps His holy mysteries
Just on the outside of man's dream;
In diapason slow, we think
To hear their pinions rise and sink,
While they float pure beneath His eyes,
Like swans adown a stream.

Abstractions, are they, from the forms
Of His great beauty?–exaltations
From His great glory?–strong previsions
Of what we shall be?–intuitions
Of what we are–in calms and storms,
Beyond our peace and passions?

Things nameless! which, in passing so,
Do stroke us with a subtle grace.
We say, 'Who passes?'–they are dumb.
We cannot see them go or come:
Their touches fall soft, cold, as snow
Upon a blind man's face.

Yet, touching so, they draw above
   Our common thoughts to Heaven's unknown,
Our daily joy and pain advance
To a divine significance,
Our human love–O mortal love,
   That light is not its own!

And sometimes horror chills our blood
   To be so near such mystic Things,
And we wrap round us for defence
Our purple manners, moods of sense–
As angels from the face of God
   Stand hidden in their wings.

And sometimes through life's heavy swound
   We grope for them!–with strangled breath
We stretch our hands abroad and try
To reach them in our agony,–
And widen, so, the broad life-wound
   Which soon is large enough for death.

From 'Aurora Leigh'

TRUTH, so far, in my book;–the truth which draws
Through all things upwards,–that a twofold world
Must go to a perfect cosmos. Natural things
And spiritual,–who separates those two
In art, in morals, or the social drift
Tears up the bond of nature and brings death,
Paints futile pictures, writes unreal verse,
Leads vulgar days, deals ignorantly with men,
Is wrong, in short, at all points. We divide
This apple of life, and cut it through the pips,–
The perfect round which fitted Venus' hand
Has perished as utterly as if we ate
Both halves. Without the spiritual, observe,

The natural's impossible,–no form,
No motion: without sensuous, spiritual
Is inappreciable,–no beauty or power:
And in this twofold sphere the twofold man
(For still the artist is intensely a man)
Holds firmly by the natural, to reach
The spiritual beyond it,–fixes still
The type with mortal vision, to pierce through,
With eyes immortal, to the antetype
Some call the ideal,–better call the real,
And certain to be called so presently
When things shall have their names. Look long enough
On any peasant's face here, coarse and lined,
You'll catch Antinous somewhere in that clay,
As perfect featured as he yearns at Rome
From marble pale with beauty; then persist,
And, if your apprehension's competent,
You'll find some fairer angel at his back,
As much exceeding him as he the boor,
And pushing him with empyreal disdain
For ever out of sight. Aye, Carrington
Is glad of such a creed: an artist must,
Who paints a tree, a leaf, a common stone
With just his hand, and finds it suddenly
A-piece with and conterminous to his soul.
Why else do these things move him, leaf, or stone?
The bird's not moved, that pecks at a spring-shoot;
Nor yet the horse, before a quarry, a-graze:
But man, the twofold creature, apprehends
The twofold manner, in and outwardly,
And nothing in the world comes single to him,
A mere itself,–cup, column, or candlestick,
All patterns of what shall be in the Mount;
The whole temporal show related royally,

And built up to eterne significance
Through the open arms of God. 'There's nothing great
Nor small', has said a poet of our day,
Whose voice will ring beyond the curfew of eve
And not be thrown out by the matin's bell:
And truly, I reiterate, nothing's small!
No lily-muffled hum of a summer-bee,
But finds some coupling with the spinning stars;
No pebble at your foot, but proves a sphere;
No chaffinch, but implies the cherubim;
And (glancing on my own thin, veinèd wrist),
In such a little tremor of the blood
The whole strong clamour of a vehement soul
Doth utter itself distinct. Earth's crammed with heaven,
And every common bush afire with God;
But only he who sees, takes off his shoes,
The rest sit round it and pluck blackberries,
And daub their natural faces unaware
More and more from the first similitude.

RICHARD CHENEVIX TRENCH, ARCHBISHOP OF DUBLIN

1807-1886

'If there had anywhere'

IF there had anywhere appeared in space
    Another place of refuge, where to flee,
Our hearts had taken refuge in that place,
        And not with Thee.

For we against creation's bars had beat
    Like prisoned eagles, through great worlds had sought
Though but a foot of ground to plant our feet,
        Where Thou wert not.

And only when we found in earth and air,
  In heaven or hell, that such might nowhere be–
That we could not flee from Thee anywhere,
      We fled to Thee.

EDGAR ALLAN POE

1809-1849

The Goddess's Song from 'Al Aaraaf'

SPIRIT! that dwellest where,
  In the deep sky,
The terrible and fair,
  In beauty vie!
Beyond the line of blue–
  The boundary of the star
Which turneth at the view
  Of thy barrier and thy bar–
Of the barrier overgone
  By the comets who were cast
From their pride and from their throne
  To be drudges till the last–
To be carriers of fire
  (The red fire of their heart)
With speed that may not tire
  And with pain that shall not part–
Who livest–*that* we know–
  In Eternity–we feel–
But the shadow of whose brow
  What spirit shall reveal?
Though the beings whom thy Nesace,
  Thy messenger hath known,
Have dreamed for thy Infinity
  A model of their own–

Thy will is done, O God!
The star hath ridden high
Through many a tempest, but she rode
Beneath thy burning eye;
And here, in thought, to thee–
In thought that can alone
Ascend thy empire, and so be
A partner of thy throne–
By wingèd Fantasy,
My embassy is given,
Till secrecy shall knowledge be
In the environs of Heaven.

RICHARD MONCKTON MILNES, LORD HOUGHTON

1809-1885

The Sayings of Rabia

I

A PIOUS friend one day of Rabia asked,
How she had learnt the truth of Allah wholly?
By what instructions was her memory tasked–
How was her heart estranged from this world's folly?

She answered–'Thou, who knowest God in parts,
Thy spirit's moods and processes can tell;
I only know that in my heart of hearts
I have despised myself and loved Him well.'

II

Some evil upon Rabia fell,
And one who loved and knew her well
Murmured that God with pain undue
Should strike a child so fond and true:

But she replied–'Believe and trust
That all I suffer is most just;
I had in contemplation striven
To realize the joys of heaven;
I had extended fancy's flights
Through all that region of delights,–
Had counted, till the numbers failed,
The pleasures on the blest entailed,–
Had sounded the ecstatic rest
I should enjoy on Allah's breast;
And for those thoughts I now atone
That were of something of my own,
And were not thoughts of Him alone.'

III

When Rabia unto Mekkeh came,
  She stood awhile apart–alone,
Nor joined the crowd with hearts on flame
  Collected round the sacred stone.

She, like the rest, with toil had crossed
  The waves of water, rock, and sand,
And now, as one long tempest-tossed,
  Beheld the Kaabeh's promised land.

Yet in her eyes no transport glistened;
  She seemed with shame and sorrow bowed;
The shouts of prayer she hardly listened,
  But beat her heart and cried aloud:–

'O heart! weak follower of the weak,
  That thou should'st traverse land and sea,
In this far place that God to seek
  Who long ago had come to thee!'

IV

Round holy Rabia's suffering bed
The wise men gathered, gazing gravely–
'Daughter of God!' the youngest said,
'Endure thy Father's chastening bravely;
They who have steeped their souls in prayer
Can every anguish calmly bear.'

She answered not, and turned aside,
Though not reproachfully nor sadly;
'Daughter of God!' the eldest cried,
'Sustain thy Father's chastening gladly;
They who have learnt to pray aright,
From pain's dark well draw up delight.'

Then she spoke out–'Your words are fair;
But, oh! the truth lies deeper still;
I know not, when absorbed in prayer,
Pleasure or pain, or good or ill;
They who God's face can understand
Feel not the motions of His hand.'

From 'Ghazeles'

ALL things once are things for ever,
Soul, once living, lives for ever;
Blame not what is only once,
When that once endures for ever;
Love, once felt, though soon forgot,
Moulds the heart to good for ever;
Once betrayed from childly faith,
Man is conscious man for ever;
Once the void of life revealed,
It must deepen on for ever,

Unless God fill up the heart
With Himself for once and ever:
Once made God and man at once,
God and man are one for ever.

ALFRED, LORD TENNYSON

1809-1892

St. Agnes' Eve

DEEP on the convent-roof the snows
   Are sparkling to the moon:
My breath to heaven like vapour goes:
   May my soul follow soon!
The shadows of the convent-towers
   Slant down the snowy sward,
Still creeping with the creeping hours
   That lead me to my Lord:
Make Thou my spirit pure and clear
   As are the frosty skies,
Or this first snowdrop of the year
   That in my bosom lies.

As these white robes are soil'd and dark,
   To yonder shining ground;
As this pale taper's earthly spark,
   To yonder argent round;
So shows my soul before the Lamb,
   My spirit before Thee;
So in mine earthly house I am,
   To that I hope to be.
Break up the heavens, O Lord! and far,
   Thro' all yon starlight keen,
Draw me, thy bride, a glittering star,
   In raiment white and clean.

He lifts me to the golden doors;
  The flashes come and go;
All heaven bursts her starry floors,
  And strows her lights below,
And deepens on and up! the gates
  Roll back, and far within
For me the Heavenly Bridegroom waits,
  To make me pure of sin.
The sabbaths of Eternity,
  One sabbath deep and wide–
A light upon the shining sea–
  The Bridegroom with his bride!

Sir Galahad

MY good blade carves the casques of men,
  My tough lance thrusteth sure,
My strength is as the strength of ten,
  Because my heart is pure.
The shattering trumpet shrilleth high,
  The hard brands shiver on the steel,
The splinter'd spear-shafts crack and fly,
  The horse and rider reel:
They reel, they roll in clanging lists,
  And when the tide of combat stands,
Perfume and flowers fall in showers,
  That lightly rain from ladies' hands.

How sweet are looks that ladies bend
  On whom their favours fall!
For them I battle till the end,
  To save from shame and thrall:

But all my heart is drawn above,
    My knees are bow'd in crypt and shrine:
I never felt the kiss of love,
    Nor maiden's hand in mine.
More bounteous aspects on me beam,
    Me mightier transports move and thrill;
So keep I fair thro' faith and prayer
    A virgin heart in work and will.

When down the stormy crescent goes,
    A light before me swims,
Between dark stems the forest glows,
    I hear a noise of hymns:
Then by some secret shrine I ride;
    I hear a voice, but none are there;
The stalls are void, the doors are wide,
    The tapers burning fair.
Fair gleams the snowy altar-cloth,
    The silver vessels sparkle clean,
The shrill bell rings, the censer swings,
    And solemn chaunts resound between.

Sometimes on lonely mountain-meres
    I find a magic bark;
I leap on board: no helmsman steers:
    I float till all is dark.
A gentle sound, an awful light!
    Three angels bear the holy Grail:
With folded feet, in stoles of white.
    On sleeping wings they sail.
Ah, blessed vision! blood of God!
    My spirit beats her mortal bars,
As down dark tides the glory slides,
    And star-like mingles with the stars.

When on my goodly charger borne
    Thro' dreaming towns I go,
The cock crows ere the Christmas morn,
    The streets are dumb with snow.
The tempest crackles on the leads,
    And, ringing, springs from brand and mail;
But o'er the dark a glory spreads,
    And gilds the driving hail.
I leave the plain, I climb the height;
    No branchy thicket shelter yields;
But blessed forms in whistling storms
    Fly o'er waste fens and windy fields.

A maiden knight–to me is given
    Such hope, I know not fear;
I yearn to breathe the airs of heaven
    That often meet me here.
I muse on joy that will not cease,
    Pure spaces clothed in living beams,
Pure lilies of eternal peace,
    Whose odours haunt my dreams;
And, stricken by an angel's hand,
    This mortal armour that I wear,
This weight and size, this heart and eyes,
    Are touch'd, are turn'd to finest air.

The clouds are broken in the sky,
    And thro' the mountain-walls
A rolling organ-harmony
    Swells up, and shakes and falls.
Then move the trees, the copses nod,
    Wings flutter, voices hover clear:
'O just and faithful knight of God!
    Ride on! the prize is near.'

So pass I hostel, hall, and grange;
By bridge and ford, by park and pale,
All-arm'd I ride, whate'er betide,
Until I find the holy Grail.

The Higher Pantheism

THE sun, the moon, the stars, the seas, the hills and the plains–
Are not these, O Soul, the Vision of Him who reigns?

Is not the Vision He? tho' He be not that which He seems?
Dreams are true while they last, and do we not live in dreams?

Earth, these solid stars, this weight of body and limb,
Are they not sign and symbol of thy division from Him?

Dark is the world to thee: thyself art the reason why;
For is He not all but thou, that hast power to feel 'I am I'?

Glory about thee, without thee; and thou fulfillest thy doom,
Making Him broken gleams, and a stifled splendour and gloom.

Speak to Him thou for He hears, and Spirit with Spirit can meet–
Closer is He than breathing, and nearer than hands and feet.

God is law, say the wise; O Soul, and let us rejoice,
For if He thunder by law the thunder is yet His voice.

Law is God, say some: no God at all, says the fool;
For all we have power to see is a straight staff bent in
a pool;

And the ear of man cannot hear, and the eye of man cannot see;
But if we could see and hear, this Vision–were it not He?

'Flower in the crannied wall'

FLOWER in the crannied wall,
I pluck you out of the crannies;–
Hold you here, root and all, in my hand,
Little flower–but if I could understand
What you are, root and all, and all in all,
I should know what God and man is.

From 'In Memoriam'

I

DEAR friend, far off, my lost desire,
So far, so near in woe and weal;
O loved the most, when most I feel
There is a lower and a higher;

Known and unknown; human, divine;
Sweet human hand and lips and eye;
Dear heavenly friend that canst not die,
Mine, mine, for ever, ever mine;

Strange friend, past, present, and to be;
Loved deeplier, darklier understood;
Behold, I dream a dream of good,
And mingle all the world with thee.

II

Thy voice is on the rolling air;
I hear thee where the waters run;
Thou standest in the rising sun,
And in the setting thou art fair.

What art thou then? I cannot guess;
But tho' I seem in star and flower
To feel thee some diffusive power,
I do not therefore love thee less:

My love involves the love before;
My love is vaster passion now;
Tho' mix'd with God and Nature thou,
I seem to love thee more and more.

Far off thou art, but ever nigh;
I have thee still, and I rejoice;
I prosper, circled with thy voice;
I shall not lose thee tho' I die.

III

O living will that shalt endure
When all that seems shall suffer shock,
Rise in the spiritual rock,
Flow thro' our deeds and make them pure,

That we may lift from out of dust
A voice as unto him that hears,
A cry above the conquer'd years
To one that with us works, and trust,

With faith that comes of self-control,
The truths that never can be proved
Until we close with all we loved
And all we flow from, soul in soul.

From 'The Holy Grail'

I

BUT she, the wan sweet maiden, shore away
Clean from her forehead all that wealth of hair
Which made a silken mat-work for her feet;
And out of this she plaited broad and long
A strong sword-belt, and wove with silver thread
And crimson in the belt a strange device,
A crimson grail within a silver beam;
And saw the bright boy-knight, and bound it on him,
Saying, 'My knight, my love, my knight of heaven,
O thou, my love, whose love is one with mine,
I, maiden, round thee, maiden, bind my belt.
Go forth, for thou shalt see what I have seen,
And break thro' all, till one will crown thee king
Far in the spiritual city:' and as she spake
She sent the deathless passion in her eyes
Thro' him, and made him hers, and laid her mind
On him, and he believed in her belief.

Then came a year of miracle: O brother,
In our great hall there stood a vacant chair,
Fashion'd by Merlin ere he past away,
And carven with strange figures; and in and out
The figures, like a serpent, ran a scroll
Of letters in a tongue no man could read.
And Merlin call'd it 'The Siege perilous,'
Perilous for good and ill; 'for there,' he said,
'No man could sit but he should lose himself:'
And once by misadvertence Merlin sat
In his own chair, and so was lost; but he,
Galahad, when he heard of Merlin's doom,
Cried, 'If I lose myself, I save myself!'

II

. . .When the hermit made an end,
In silver armour suddenly Galahad shone
Before us, and against the chapel door
Laid lance, and enter'd, and we knelt in prayer.
And there the hermit slaked my burning thirst,
And at the sacring of the mass I saw
The holy elements alone; but he:
'Saw ye no more? I, Galahad, saw the Grail,
The Holy Grail, descend upon the shrine:
I saw the fiery face as of a child
That smote itself into the bread, and went;
And hither am I come; and never yet
Hath what thy sister taught me first to see,
This Holy Thing, fail'd from my side, nor come
Cover'd, but moving with me night and day,
Fainter by day, but always in the night
Blood-red, and sliding down the blacken'd marsh
Blood-red, and on the naked mountain top
Blood-red, and in the sleeping mere below
Blood-red. And in the strength of this I rode,
Shattering all evil customs everywhere,
And past thro' Pagan realms, and made them mine,
And clash'd with Pagan hordes, and bore them down,
And broke thro' all, and in the strength of this
Come victor. But my time is hard at hand,
And hence I go; and one will crown me king
Far in the spiritual city; and come thou, too,
For thou shalt see the vision when I go.'

While thus he spake, his eye, dwelling on mine,
Drew me, with power upon me, till I grew
One with him, to believe as he believed.
Then, when the day began to wane, we went.

There rose a hill that none but man could climb,
Scarr'd with a hundred wintry watercourses–
Storm at the top, and when we gain'd it, storm
Round us and death; for every moment glanced
His silver arms and gloom'd: so quick and thick
The lightnings here and there to left and right
Struck, till the dry old trunks about us, dead,
Yea, rotten with a hundred years of death,
Sprang into fire: and at the base we found
On either hand, as far as eye could see,
A great black swamp and of an evil smell,
Part black, part whiten'd with the bones of men,
Not to be crost, save that some ancient king
Had built a way, where, link'd with many a bridge,
A thousand piers ran into the great Sea.
And Galahad fled along them bridge by bridge,
And every bridge as quickly as he crost
Sprang into fire and vanish'd, tho' I yearn'd
To follow; and thrice above him all the heavens
Open'd and blazed with thunder such as seem'd
Shoutings of all the sons of God: and first
At once I saw him far on the great Sea,
In silver-shining armour starry-clear;
And o'er his head the Holy Vessel hung
Clothed in white samite or a luminous cloud.
And with exceeding swiftness ran the boat,
If boat it were–I saw not whence it came.
And when the heavens open'd and blazed again
Roaring, I saw him like a silver star–
And had he set the sail, or had the boat
Become a living creature clad with wings?
And o'er his head the Holy Vessel hung
Redder than any rose, a joy to me,
For now I knew the veil had been withdrawn.

Then in a moment when they blazed again
Opening, I saw the least of little stars
Down on the waste, and straight beyond the star
I saw the spiritual city and all her spires
And gateways in a glory like one pearl–
No larger, tho' the goal of all the saints–
Strike from the sea; and from the star there shot
A rose-red sparkle to the city, and there
Dwelt, and I knew it was the Holy Grail,
Which never eyes on earth again shall see.

The Human Cry

HALLOWED be Thy name–Halleluiah!–
Infinite Ideality!
  Immeasurable Reality!
  Infinite Personality!
Hallowed be Thy name–Halleluiah!

We feel we are nothing–for all is Thou and in Thee;
We feel we are something–*that* also has come from Thee;
We know we are nothing–but Thou wilt help us to be.
Hallowed be Thy name–Halleluiah!

From 'The Ancient Sage'

IF thou would'st hear the Nameless, and wilt dive
Into the Temple-cave of thine own self,
There, brooding by the central altar, thou
May'st haply learn the Nameless hath a voice,
By which thou wilt abide, if thou be wise,
As if thou knewest, tho' thou canst not know;
For Knowledge is the swallow on the lake
That sees and stirs the surface-shadow there

But never yet hath dipt into the abysm,
The Abysm of all Abysms, beneath, within
The blue of sky and sea, the green of earth,
And in the million-millionth of a grain
Which cleft and cleft again for evermore,
And ever vanishing, never vanishes,
To me, my son, more mystic than myself,
Or even than the Nameless is to me.
   And when thou sendest thy free soul thro' heaven,
Nor understandest bound nor boundlessness,
Thou seest the Nameless of the hundred names.
   And if the Nameless should withdraw from all
Thy frailty counts most real, all thy world
Might vanish like thy shadow in the dark.

'And since–from when this earth began–
   The Nameless never came
Among us, never spake with man,
   And never named the Name'–

Thou canst not prove the Nameless, O my son,
Nor canst thou prove the world thou movest in
Thou canst not prove that thou art body alone,
Nor canst thou prove that thou art spirit alone,
Nor canst thou prove that thou art both in one:
Thou canst not prove thou art immortal, no
Nor yet that thou art mortal–nay my son,
Thou canst not prove that I, who speak with thee,
Am not thyself in converse with thyself,
For nothing worthy proving can be proven,
Nor yet disproven: wherefore thou be wise,
Cleave ever to the sunnier side of doubt,
And cling to Faith beyond the forms of Faith
She reels not in the storm of warring words,

She brightens at the clash of 'Yes' and 'No',
She sees the Best that glimmers thro' the Worst,
She feels the Sun is hid but for a night,
She spies the summer thro' the winter bud,
She tastes the fruit before the blossom falls,
She hears the lark within the songless egg,
She finds the fountain where they wail'd 'Mirage'!

JOHN STUART BLACKIE

1809-1895

All things are full of God

ALL things are full of God. Thus spoke
   Wise Thales in the days
When subtle Greece to thought awoke
   And soared in lofty ways.
And now what wisdom have we more?
   No sage divining-rod
Hath taught than this a deeper lore,
   ALL THINGS ARE FULL OF GOD.

The Light that gloweth in the sky
   And shimmers in the sea,
That quivers in the painted fly
   And gems the pictured lea,
The million hues of Heaven above
   And Earth below are one,
And every lightful eye doth love
   The primal light, the Sun.

Even so, all vital virtue flows
   From life's first fountain, God;
And he who feels, and he who knows,
   Doth feel and know from God.

As fishes swim in briny sea,
    As fowl do float in air,
From Thy embrace we cannot flee;
    We breathe, and Thou art there.

Go, take thy glass, astronomer,
    And all the girth survey
Of sphere harmonious linked to sphere,
    In endless bright array.
All that far-reaching Science there
    Can measure with her rod,
All powers, all laws, are but the fair
    Embodied thoughts of God.

Trimurti

TRIMURTI, Trimurti,
        Despise not the name;
Think and know
    Before thou blame!

Look upon the face of Nature
    In the flush of June;
BRAHMA is the great Creator,
    Life is Brahma's boon.
Dost thou hear the zephyr blowing?
    That is Brahma's breath,
Vital breath, live virtue showing
    'Neath the ribs of death.
Dost thou see the fountain flowing?
    That is Brahma's blood,
Lucid blood–the same is glowing
    In the purpling bud.

Brahma's Eyes look forth divining
From the welkin's brow,
Full bright eyes–the same are shining
In the sacred cow.
Air, and Fire, and running River,
And the procreant clod,
Are but faces changing ever
Of one changeless God.
When thy wingèd thought ascendeth
Where high thoughts are free,
This is Brahma when he lendeth
Half the God to thee.
Brahma is the great Creator,
Life a mystic drama;
Heaven, and Earth, and living Nature
Are but masks of Brahma.

ROBERT BROWNING

1812-1889

From 'Pauline'

O GOD, where does this tend–these struggling aims?
What would I have? What is this 'sleep', which seems
To bound all? can there be a 'waking' point
Of crowning life? The soul would never rule–
It would be first in all things–it would have
Its utmost pleasure filled,–but that complete
Commanding for commanding sickens it.
The last point I can trace is, rest beneath
Some better essence than itself–in weakness;
This is 'myself'–not what I think should be
And what is that I hunger for but God?

My God, my God! let me for once look on thee
As tho' nought else existed: we alone.
And as creation crumbles, my soul's spark
Expands till I can say, 'Even from myself
I need thee, and I feel thee, and I love thee;
I do not plead my rapture in thy works
For love of thee–or that I feel as one
Who cannot die–but there is that in me
Which turns to thee, which loves, or which should love.'

Why have I girt myself with this hell-dress?
Why have I laboured to put out my life?
Is it not in my nature to adore,
And e'en for all my reason do I not
Feel him, and thank him, and pray to him–now?
Can I forgo the trust that he loves me?
Do I not feel a love which only ONE . . .
O thou pale form, so dimly seen, deep-eyed,
I have denied thee calmly–do I not
Pant when I read of thy consummate deeds,
And burn to see thy calm pure truths out-flash
The brightest gleams of earth's philosophy?
Do I not shake to hear aught question thee?
If I am erring save me, madden me,
Take from me powers and pleasures–let me die.
Ages, so I see thee: I am knit round
As with a charm, by sin and lust and pride,
Yet tho' my wandering dreams have seen all shapes
Of strange delight, oft have I stood by thee–
Have I been keeping lonely watch with thee
In the damp night by weeping Olivet,
Or leaning on thy bosom, proudly less–
Or dying with thee on the lonely cross–
Or witnessing thy bursting from the tomb!

From 'Paracelsus'

I

TRUTH is within ourselves; it takes no rise
From outward things, whate'er you may believe.
There is an inmost centre in us all,
Where truth abides in fullness; and around,
Wall upon wall, the gross flesh hems it in,
This perfect, clear perception–which is truth.
A baffling and perverting carnal mesh
Binds it, and makes all error: and, to KNOW,
Rather consists in opening out a way
Whence the imprisoned splendour may escape,
Than in effecting entry for a light
Supposed to be without.

II

I knew, I felt, (perception unexpressed,
Uncomprehended by our narrow thought,
But somehow felt and known in every shift
And change in the spirit,–nay, in every pore
Of the body, even,)–what God is, what we are
What life is–how God tastes an infinite joy
In infinite ways–one everlasting bliss,
From whom all being emanates, all power
Proceeds; in whom is life for evermore,
Yet whom existence in its lowest form
Includes; where dwells enjoyment there is he:
With still a flying point of bliss remote,
A happiness in store afar, a sphere
Of distant glory in full view; thus climbs
Pleasure its heights for ever and for ever.
The centre-fire heaves underneath the earth,
And the earth changes like a human face;

The molten ore bursts up among the rocks,
Winds into the stone's heart, outbranches bright
In hidden mines, spots barren river-beds,
Crumbles into fine sand where sunbeams bask–
God joys therein! The wroth sea's waves are edged
With foam, white as the bitten lip of hate,
When, in the solitary waste, strange groups
Of young volcanos come up, cyclops-like,
Staring together with their eyes on flame–
God tastes a pleasure in their uncouth pride.
Then all is still; earth is a wintry clod:
But spring-wind, like a dancing psaltress, passes
Over its breast to waken it, rare verdure
Buds tenderly upon rough banks, between
The withered tree-roots and the cracks of frost,
Like a smile striving with a wrinkled face;
The grass grows bright, the boughs are swoln with blooms
Like chrysalids impatient for the air,
The shining dorrs are busy, beetles run
Along the furrows, ants make their ado;
Above, birds fly in merry flocks, the lark
Soars up and up, shivering for very joy;
Afar the ocean sleeps; white fishing-gulls
Flit where the strand is purple with its tribe
Of nested limpets; savage creatures seek
Their loves in wood and plain–and God renews
His ancient rapture. Thus He dwells in all,
From life's minute beginnings, up at last
To man–the consummation of this scheme
Of being, the completion of this sphere
Of life: whose attributes had here and there
Been scattered o'er the visible world before,
Asking to be combined, dim fragments meant
To be united in some wondrous whole,

Imperfect qualities throughout creation,
Suggesting some one creature yet to make,
Some point where all those scattered rays should meet
Convergent in the faculties of man.

From 'Saul'

I HAVE gone the whole round of Creation: I saw and I spoke!
I, a work of God's hand for that purpose, received in my brain
And pronounced on the rest of His handwork–returned Him again
His creation's approval or censure: I spoke as I saw.
I report, as a man may of God's work–all's love, yet all's law.
Now I lay down the judgeship He lent me. Each faculty tasked
To perceive Him, has gained an abyss, where a dewdrop was asked.
Have I knowledge? confounded it shrivels at Wisdom laid bare.
Have I forethought? how purblind, how blank, to the Infinite Care!
Do I task any faculty highest, to image success?
I but open my eyes,–and perfection, no more and no less,
In the kind I imagined, full-fronts me, and God is seen God
In the star, in the stone, in the flesh, in the soul and the clod.
And thus looking within and around me, I ever renew
(With that stoop of the soul which in bending upraises it too)

The submission of Man's nothing-perfect to God's All-
Complete,
As by each new obeisance in spirit, I climb to His feet!
Yet with all this abounding experience, this Deity known,
I shall dare to discover some province, some gift of my own.
There's a faculty pleasant to exercise, hard to hoodwink,
I am fain to keep still in abeyance, (I laugh as I think)
Lest, insisting to claim and parade in it, wot ye, I worst
E'en the Giver in one gift. –Behold! I could love if I durst!
But I sink the pretension as fearing a man may o'ertake
God's own speed in the one way of love: I abstain for
love's sake.
–What, my soul? see thus far and no farther? when
doors great and small,
Nine-and-ninety flew ope at our touch, should the
hundredth appal?
In the least things have faith, yet distrust in the
greatest of all?
Do I find love so full in my nature, God's ultimate gift,
That I doubt His own love can compete with it? here,
the parts shift?
Here, the creature surpass the Creator, the end, what
Began?
Would I fain in my impotent yearning do all for this man,
And dare doubt He alone shall not help him, who yet
alone can?
Would it ever have entered my mind, the bare will, much
less power,
To bestow on this Saul what I sang of, the marvellous
dower
Of the life he was gifted and filled with? to make such
a soul,
Such a body, and then such an earth for insphering the
whole?

And doth it not enter my mind (as my warm tears attest)
These good things being given, to go on, and give one more, the best?
Ay, to save and redeem and restore him, maintain at the height
This perfection–succeed with life's dayspring, death's minute of night?
Interpose at the difficult minute, snatch Saul, the mistake,
Saul, the failure, the ruin he seems now–and bid him awake
From the dream, the probation, the prelude, to find himself set
Clear and safe in new light and new life,–a new harmony yet
To be run, and continued, and ended–who knows?– or endure!
The man taught enough by life's dream, of the rest to make sure;
By the pain-throb, triumphantly winning intensified bliss,
And the next world's reward and repose, by the struggles in this.

I believe it! 'tis Thou, God, that givest, 'tis I who receive:
In the first is the last, in Thy will is my power to believe.
All's one gift: Thou canst grant it moreover, as prompt to my prayer
As I breathe out this breath, as I open these arms to the air.
From Thy will, stream the worlds, life and nature, thy dread Sabaoth:
I will?–the mere atoms despise me! why am I not loth

To look that, even that in the face too? why is it I dare
Think but lightly of such impuissance? what stops my despair?
This;–'tis not what man Does which exalts him, but what man Would do!
See the King–I would help him but cannot, the wishes fall through.
Could I wrestle to raise him from sorrow, grow poor to enrich,
To fill up his life, starve my own out, I would–knowing which,
I know that my service is perfect. Oh, speak through me now!
Would I suffer for him that I love? So wouldst Thou–so wilt Thou!
So shall crown Thee the topmost, ineffablest, uttermost crown–
And Thy love fill infinitude wholly, nor leave up nor down
One spot for the creature to stand in! It is by no breath,
Turn of eye, wave of hand, that salvation joins issue with death!
As Thy Love is discovered almighty, almighty be proved
Thy power, that exists with and for it, of being Beloved!
He who did most, shall bear most; the strongest shall stand the most weak.
'Tis the weakness in strength, that I cry for! my flesh, that I seek
In the Godhead! I seek and I find it. O Saul, it shall be
A Face like my face that receives thee; a Man like to me,
Thou shalt love and be loved by, for ever: a Hand like this hand
Shall throw open the gates of new life to thee! See the Christ stand!

From 'Easter Day'

HE stood there. Like the smoke
Pillared o'er Sodom, when day broke,–
I saw Him. One magnific pall
Mantled in massive fold and fall
His dread, and coiled in snaky swathes
About His feet: night's black, that bathes
All else, broke, grizzled with despair,
Against the soul of blackness there.
A gesture told the mood within–
That wrapped right hand which based the chin.
That intense meditation fixed
On His procedure,–pity mixed
With the fulfilment of decree.
Motionless, thus, He spoke to me,
Who fell before His feet, a mass,
No man now.

'All is come to pass.
Such shows are over for each soul
They had respect to. In the roll
Of Judgement which convinced mankind
Of sin, stood many, bold and blind,
Terror must burn the truth into:
Their fate for them!–thou hadst to do
With absolute omnipotence,
Able its judgements to dispense
To the whole race, as every one
Were its sole object. Judgement done,
God is, thou art,–the rest is hurled
To nothingness for thee. This world,

This finite life, thou hast preferred,
In disbelief of God's own word,
To Heaven and to Infinity.
Here the probation was for thee,
To show thy soul the earthly mixed
With heavenly, it must choose betwixt.
The earthly joys lay palpable,–
A taint, in each, distinct as well;
The heavenly flitted, faint and rare,
Above them, but as truly were
Taintless, so, in their nature, best.
Thy choice was earth: thou didst attest
'Twas fitter spirit should subserve
The flesh, than flesh refine to nerve
Beneath the spirit's play. Advance
No claim to their inheritance
Who chose the spirit's fugitive
Brief gleams, and yearned, "This were to live
Indeed, if rays, completely pure
From flesh that dulls them, could endure,–
Not shoot in meteor-light athwart
Our earth, to show how cold and swart
It lies beneath their fire, but stand
As stars do, destined to expand,
Prove veritable worlds, our home."
Thou saidst,–"Let spirit star the dome
Of sky, that flesh may miss no peak,
No nook of earth,–I shall not seek
Its service further!" Thou art shut
Out of the heaven of spirit: glut
Thy sense upon the world: 'tis thine
For ever–take it!'

'How? Is mine,
The world?' (I cried, while my soul broke
Out in a transport.) 'Hast Thou spoke
Plainly in that? Earth's exquisite
Treasures of wonder and delight,
For me?'

The austere voice returned,–
'So soon made happy? Hadst thou learned
What God accounteth happiness,
Thou wouldst not find it hard to guess
What hell may be His punishment
For those who doubt if God invent
Better than they. Let such men rest
Content with what they judged the best.
Let the unjust usurp at will:
The filthy shall be filthy still:
Miser, there waits the gold for thee!
Hater, indulge thine enmity!
And thou, whose heaven self-ordained
Was, to enjoy earth unrestrained,
Do it! Take all the ancient show!
The woods shall wave, the rivers flow,
And men apparently pursue
Their works, as they were wont to do,
While living in probation yet.
I promise not thou shalt forget
The Past, now gone to its account;
But leave thee with the old amount
Of faculties, nor less nor more,
Unvisited, as heretofore,
By God's free spirit, that makes an end.
So, once more, take thy world! expend
Eternity upon its shows,–
Flung thee as freely as one rose

Out of a summer's opulence,
Over the Eden-barrier whence
Thou art excluded. Knock in vain!'
I sat up. All was still again.
I breathed free: to my heart, back fled
The warmth. 'But, all the world!'–I said.
I stooped and picked a leaf of fern,
And recollected I might learn
From books, how many myriad sorts
Of fern exist, to trust reports,
Each as distinct and beautiful
As this, the very first I cull.
Think, from the first leaf to the last!
Conceive, then, earth's resources! Vast
Exhaustless beauty, endless change
Of wonder! And this foot shall range
Alps, Andes,–and this eye devour
The bee-bird and the aloe-flower?

Then the Voice, 'Welcome so to rate
The arras-folds that variegate
The earth, God's antechamber, well!
The wise, who waited there, could tell
By these, what royalties in store
Lay one step past the entrance-door.
For whom, was reckoned, not too much,
This life's munificence? For such
As thou,–a race, whereof scarce one
Was able, in a million,
To feel that any marvel lay
In objects round his feet all day;
Scarce one, in many millions more,
Willing, if able, to explore

The secreter, minuter charm!
–Brave souls, a fern-leaf could disarm
Of power to cope with God's intent,–
Or scared if the south firmament
With north-fire did its wings refledge!
All partial beauty was a pledge
Of beauty in its plenitude:
But since the pledge sufficed thy mood,
Retain it! plenitude be theirs
Who looked above!'

Though sharp despairs
Shot through me, I held up, bore on.
'What matter though my trust were gone
From natural things? Henceforth my part
Be less with nature than with Art!
For Art supplants, gives mainly worth
To Nature; 'tis Man stamps the earth–
And I will seek his impress, seek
The statuary of the Greek,
Italy's painting–there my choice
Shall fix!'

'Obtain it!' said the voice,
–'The one form with its single act,
Which sculptors laboured to abstract,
The one face, painters tried to draw,
With its one look, from throngs they saw. . .
. . . 'But through
Life pierce,–and what has earth to do,
Its utmost beauty's appanage,
With the requirement of next stage?
Did God pronounce earth "very good"?
Needs must it be, while understood
For man's preparatory state;

Nothing to heighten nor abate:
Transfer the same completeness here,
To serve a new state's use–and drear
Deficiency gapes every side!
The good, tried once, were bad, retried.
See the enwrapping rocky niche,
Sufficient for the sleep, in which
The lizard breathes for ages safe:
Split the mould–and as this would chafe
The creature's new world-widened sense,
One minute after day dispense
The thousand sounds and sights that broke
In on him at the chisel's stroke,–
So, in God's eye, the earth's first stuff
Was, neither more nor less, enough
To house man's soul, man's need fulfil.
Man reckoned it immeasurable?
So thinks the lizard of his vault!
Could God be taken in default,
Short of contrivances, by you–
Or reached, ere ready to pursue
His progress through eternity?
That chambered rock, the lizard's world,
Your easy mallet's blow has hurled
To nothingness for ever; so,
Has God abolished at a blow
This world, wherein His saints were pent–
Who, though found grateful and content,
With the provision there, as thou,
Yet knew He would not disallow
Their spirit's hunger, felt as well,–
Unsated,–not unsatable,
As Paradise gives proof. Deride
Their choice now, thou who sit'st outside!

I cried in anguish, 'Mind, the mind,
So miserably cast behind,
To gain what had been wisely lost!
Oh, let me strive to make the most
Of the poor stinted soul, I nipped
Of budding wings, else now equipt
For voyage from summer isle to isle!
And though she needs must reconcile
Ambition to the life on ground,
Still, I can profit by late found
But precious knowledge. Mind is best–
I will seize mind, forgo the rest,
And try how far my tethered strength
May crawl in this poor breadth and length.
Let me, since I can fly no more,
At least spin dervish-like about
(Till giddy rapture almost doubt
I fly) through circling sciences,
Philosophies and histories!
Should the whirl slacken there, then verse,
Fining to music, shall asperse
Fresh and fresh fire-dew, till I strain
Intoxicate, half-break my chain!
Not joyless, though more favoured feet
Stand calm, where I want wings to beat
The floor. At least earth's bond is broke!'

Then (sickening even while I spoke),
'Let me alone! No answer, pray,
To this! I know what Thou wilt say!
All still is earth's–to know, as much
As feel its truths, which if we touch
With sense, or apprehend in soul,
What matter? I have reached the goal–

"Whereto does Knowledge serve!" will burn
My eyes, too sure, at every turn!
I cannot look back now, nor stake
Bliss on the race, for running's sake.
The goal's a ruin like the rest!'
– 'And so much worse thy latter quest,'
(Added the voice) 'that even on earth–
Whenever, in man's soul, had birth
Those intuitions, grasps of guess,
That pull the more into the less,
Making the finite comprehend
Infinity,–the bard would spend
Such praise alone, upon his craft,
As, when wind-lyres obey the waft,
Goes to the craftsman who arranged
The seven strings, changed them and rechanged–
Knowing it was the South that harped.
He felt his song, in singing, warped;
Distinguished his and God's part: whence
A world of spirit as of sense
Was plain to him, yet not too plain,
Which he could traverse, not remain
A guest in:–else were permanent
Heaven on earth which its gleams were meant
To sting with hunger for full light–
Made visible in verse, despite
The veiling weakness,–truth by means
Of fable, showing while it screens,–
Since highest truth, man e'er supplied,
Was ever fable on outside.
Such gleams made bright the earth an age;
Now, the whole sun's his heritage!
Take up thy world, it is allowed,
Thou who hast entered in the cloud!'

Then I–'Behold, my spirit bleeds,
Catches no more at broken reeds,–
But lilies flower those reeds above:
I let the world go, and take love!
Love survives in me, albeit those
I love be henceforth masks and shows,
Not loving men and women: still
I mind how love repaired all ill,
Cured wrong, soothed grief, made earth amends
With parents, brothers, children, friends!
Some semblance of a woman yet
With eyes to help me to forget,
Shall live with me; and I will match
Departed love with love, attach
Its fragments to my whole, nor scorn
The poorest of the grains of corn
I save from shipwreck on this isle,
Trusting its barrenness may smile
With happy foodful green one day,
More precious for the pains. I pray,
For love, then, only!'

At the word,
The form, I looked to have been stirred
With pity and approval, rose
O'er me, as when the headsman throws
Axe over shoulder to make end–
I fell prone, letting Him expend
His wrath, while, thus, the inflicting voice
Smote me. 'Is this thy fiinal choice?
Love is the best? 'Tis somewhat late!
And all thou dost enumerate
Of power and beauty in the world,
The mightiness of love was curled

Inextricably round about.
Love lay within it and without,
To clasp thee–but in vain! Thy soul
Still shrunk from Him who made the whole,
Still set deliberate aside
His love!–Now take love! Well betide
Thy tardy conscience! Haste to take
The show of love for the name's sake,
Remembering every moment Who,
Beside creating thee unto
These ends, and these for thee, was said
To undergo death in thy stead
In flesh like thine: so ran the tale.
What doubt in thee could countervail
Belief in it? Upon the ground
"That in the story had been found
Too much love! How could God love *so*?'
He who in all His works below
Adapted to the needs of man,
Made love the basis of the plan,–
Did love, as was demonstrated:
While man, who was so fit instead
To hate, as every day gave proof–
Man thought man, for his kind's behoof,
Both could and did invent that scheme
Of perfect love–'twould well beseem
Cain's nature thou wast wont to praise,
Not tally with God's usual ways!'

And I cowered deprecatingly–
'Thou Love of God! Or let me die,
Or grant what shall seem Heaven almost!
Let me not know that all is lost,
Though lost it be–leave me not tied

To this despair, this corpse-like bride!
Let that old life seem mine–no more–
With limitation as before,
With darkness, hunger, toil, distress:
Be all the earth a wilderness!
Only let me go on, go on,
Still hoping ever and anon
To reach one eve the Better Land!'

Then did the form expand, expand–
I knew Him through the dread disguise,
As the whole God within his eyes
Embraced me.

Abt Vogler

(After he has been extemporizing upon the musical instrument of his invention)

WOULD that the structure brave, the manifold
music I build,
Bidding my organ obey, calling its keys to their work,
Claiming each slave of the sound, at a touch, as when
Solomon willed
Armies of angels that soar, legions of demons that
lurk,
Man, brute, reptile, fly,–alien of end and of aim,
Adverse, each from the other heaven-high, hell-deep
removed,–
Should rush into sight at once as he named the ineffable
Name,
And pile him a palace straight, to pleasure the princess
he loved!

Would it might tarry like his, the beautiful building of
mine,
This which my keys in a crowd pressed and importuned
to raise!
Ah, one and all, how they helped, would dispart now and
now combine,
Zealous to hasten the work, heighten their master his
praise!
And one would bury his brow with a blind plunge down
to hell,
Burrow awhile and build, broad on the roots of things,
Then up again swim into sight, having based me my
palace well,
Founded it, fearless of flame, flat on the nether springs.

And another would mount and march, like the excellent
minion he was,
Ay, another and yet another, one crowd but with many
a crest,
Raising my rampired walls of gold as transparent as glass,
Eager to do and die, yield each his place to the rest:
For higher still and higher (as a runner tips with fire,
When a great illumination surprises a festal night–
Outlining round and round Rome's dome from space to
spire)
Up, the pinnacled glory reached, and the pride of my
soul was in sight.

In sight? Not half! for it seemed, it was certain, to
match man's birth,
Nature in turn conceived, obeying an impulse as I;
And the emulous heaven yearned down, made effort to
reach the earth,
As the earth had done her best, in my passion, to scale
the sky:

Novel splendours burst forth, grew familiar and dwelt with mine,
Not a point nor peak but found and fixed its wandering star;
Meteor-moons, balls of blaze: and they did not pale nor pine,
For earth had attained to heaven, there was no more near nor far.

Nay more; for there wanted not who walked in the glare and glow,
Presences plain in the place; or, fresh from the Protoplast,
Furnished for ages to come, when a kindlier wind should blow,
Lured now to begin and live, in a house to their liking at last;
Or else the wonderful Dead who have passed through the body and gone,
But were back once more to breathe in an old world worth their new:
What never had been, was now; what was, as it shall be anon;
And what is,–shall I say, matched both? for I was made perfect too.

All through my keys that gave their sounds to a wish of my soul,
All through my soul that praised as its wish flowed visibly forth,
All through music and me! For think, had I painted the whole,
Why, there it had stood, to see, nor the process so wonder-worth:

Had I written the same, made verse–still, effect proceeds from cause,
Ye know why the forms are fair, ye hear how the tale is told;
It is all triumphant art, but art in obedience to laws,
Painter and poet are proud in the artist-list enrolled:–

But here is the finger of God, a flash of the will that can,
Existent behind all laws, that made them and, lo, they are!
And I know not if, save in this, such gift be allowed to man,
That out of three sounds he frame, not a fourth sound, but a star.
Consider it well: each tone of our scale in itself is nought;
It is everywhere in the world–loud, soft, and all is said:
Give it to me to use! I mix it with two in my thought:
And, there! Ye have heard and seen: consider and bow the head!

Well, it is gone at last, the palace of music I reared;
Gone! and the good tears start, the praises that come too slow;
For one is assured at first, one scarce can say that he feared,
That he even gave it a thought, the gone thing was to go.
Never to be again! But many more of the kind
As good, nay, better perchance: is this your comfort to me?
To me, who must be saved because I cling with my mind
To the same, same self, same love, same God: ay, what was, shall be.

Therefore to whom turn I but to Thee, the ineffable Name?
Builder and maker, Thou, of houses not made with hands!
What, have fear of change from Thee who art ever the same?
Doubt that Thy power can fill the heart that Thy power expands?
There shall never be one lost good! What was, shall live as before;
The evil is null, is nought, is silence implying sound;
What was good, shall be good, with, for evil, so much good more;
On the earth the broken arcs; in the heaven, a perfect round.

All we have willed or hoped or dreamed of good, shall exist;
Not its semblance, but itself; no beauty, nor good, nor power
Whose voice has gone forth, but each survives for the melodist
When eternity affirms the conception of an hour.
The high that proved too high, the heroic for earth too hard,
The passion that left the ground to lose itself in the sky,
Are music sent up to God by the lover and the bard;
Enough that He heard it once: we shall hear it by and by.

And what is our failure here but a triumph's evidence
For the fullness of the days? Have we withered or agonized?

Why else was the pause prolonged but that singing might
issue thence?
Why rushed the discords in, but that harmony should
be prized?
Sorrow is hard to bear, and doubt is slow to clear,
Each sufferer says his say, his scheme of the weal and
woe:
But God has a few of us whom He whispers in the
ear;
The rest may reason and welcome: 'tis we musicians
know.

Well, it is earth with me; silence resumes her reign:
I will be patient and proud, and soberly acquiesce.
Give me the keys. I feel for the common chord
again,
Sliding by semitones, till I sink to the minor,–yes,
And I blunt it into a ninth, and I stand on alien
ground,
Surveying awhile the heights I rolled from into the
deep;
Which, hark, I have dared and done, for my resting-place
is found,
The C Major of this life: so, now I will try to sleep.

Rabbi Ben Ezra

GROW old along with me!
The best is yet to be,
The last of life, for which the first was made:
Our times are in His hand
Who saith 'A whole I planned,
Youth shows but half; trust God: see all, nor be afraid!'

Not that, amassing flowers,
Youth sighed 'Which rose make ours,
Which lily leave and then as best recall?'
Not that, admiring stars,
It yearned 'Nor Jove, nor Mars;
Mine be some figured flame which blends, transcends
them all!'

Not for such hopes and fears
Annulling youth's brief years,
Do I remonstrate: folly wide the mark!
Rather I prize the doubt
Low kinds exist without,
Finished and finite clods, untroubled by a spark.

Poor vaunt of life indeed,
Were man but formed to feed
On joy, to solely seek and find and feast:
Such feasting ended, then
As sure an end to men;
Irks care the crop-full bird? Frets doubt the maw-
crammed beast?

Rejoice we are allied
To That which doth provide
And not partake, effect and not receive!
A spark disturbs our clod;
Nearer we hold of God
Who gives, than of His tribes that take, I must believe.

Then, welcome each rebuff
That turns earth's smoothness rough,
Each sting that bids nor sit nor stand but go!
Be our joys three-parts pain!
Strive, and hold cheap the strain;
Learn, nor account the pang; dare, never grudge the throe!

For thence,–a paradox
Which comforts while it mocks,–
Shall life succeed in that it seems to fail:
What I aspired to be,
And was not, comforts me:
A brute I might have been, but would not sink i' the scale

What is he but a brute
Whose flesh hath soul to suit,
Whose spirit works lest arms and legs want play?
To man, propose this test–
Thy body at its best,
How far can that project thy soul on its lone way?

Yet gifts should prove their use:
I own the Past profuse
Of power each side, perfection every turn:
Eyes, ears took in their dole,
Brain treasured up the whole;
Should not the heart beat once 'How good to live and learn?'

Not once beat 'Praise be Thine!
I see the whole design,
I, who saw Power, see now Love perfect too:
Perfect I call Thy plan:
Thanks that I was a man!
Maker, remake, complete,–I trust what Thou shalt do!'

For pleasant is this flesh;
Our soul, in its rose-mesh
Pulled ever to the earth, still yearns for rest:
Would we some prize might hold
To match those manifold
Possessions of the brute,–gain most, as we did best!

Let us not always say
'Spite of this flesh to-day
I strove, made head, gained ground upon the whole!'
As the bird wings and sings,
Let us cry 'All good things
Are ours, nor soul helps flesh more, now, than flesh helps
soul!'

Therefore I summon age
To grant youth's heritage,
Life's struggle having so far reached its term:
Thence shall I pass, approved
A man, for ay removed
From the developed brute; a God though in the germ.

And I shall thereupon
Take rest, ere I be gone
Once more on my adventure brave and new:
Fearless and unperplexed,
When I wage battle next,
What weapons to select, what armour to indue.

Youth ended, I shall try
My gain or loss thereby;
Leave the fire ashes, what survives is gold:
And I shall weigh the same,
Give life its praise or blame:
Young, all lay in dispute; I shall know, being old

For note, when evening shuts,
A certain moment cuts
The deed off, calls the glory from the grey:
A whisper from the west
Shoots–'Add this to the rest,
Take it and try its worth: here dies another day.'

So, still within this life,
Though lifted o'er its strife,
Let me discern, compare, pronounce at last,
'This rage was right i' the main,
That acquiescence vain:
The Future I may face now I have proved the Past.'

For more is not reserved
To man, with soul just nerved
To act to-morrow what he learns to-day:
Here, work enough to watch
The Master work, and catch
Hints of the proper craft, tricks of the tool's true play.

As it was better, youth
Should strive, through acts uncouth,
Toward making, than repose on aught found made;
So, better, age, exempt
From strife, should know, than tempt
Further. Thou waitedst age; wait death nor be afraid!

Enough now, if the Right
And Good and Infinite
Be named here, as thou callest thy hand thine own,
With knowledge absolute,
Subject to no dispute
From fools that crowded youth, nor let thee feel alone.

Be there, for once and all,
Severed great minds from small,
Announced to each his station in the Past!
Was I, the world arraigned,
Were they, my soul disdained,
Right? Let age speak the truth and give us peace at last!

Now, who shall arbitrate?
Ten men love what I hate,
Shun what I follow, slight what I receive;
Ten, who in ears and eyes
Match me: we all surmise,
They, this thing, and I, that: whom shall my soul believe?

Not on the vulgar mass
Called 'work', must sentence pass,
Things done, that took the eye and had the price;
O'er which, from level stand,
The low world laid its hand,
Found straightway to its mind, could value in a trice:

But all, the world's coarse thumb
And finger failed to plumb,
So passed in making up the main account;
All instincts immature,
All purposes unsure,
That weighed not as his work, yet swelled the man's
amount:

Thoughts hardly to be packed
Into a narrow act,
Fancies that broke through language and escaped;
All I could never be,
All, men ignored in me,
This, I was worth to God, whose wheel the pitcher shaped.

Ay, note that Potter's wheel,
That metaphor! and feel
Why time spins fast, why passive lies our clay,–
Thou, to whom fools propound,
When the wine makes its round,
'Since life fleets, all is change; the Past gone, seize
to-day!'

Fool! All that is, at all,
Lasts ever, past recall;
Earth changes, but thy soul and God stand sure:
What entered into thee,
That was, is, and shall be:
Times's wheel runs back or stops: Potter and clay endure.

He fixed thee mid this dance
Of plastic circumstance,
This Present, thou, forsooth, wouldst fain arrest:
Machinery just meant
To give thy soul its bent,
Try thee and turn thee forth, sufficiently impressed.

What though the earlier grooves
Which ran the laughing loves
Around thy base, no longer pause and press?
What though, about thy rim,
Skull-things in order grim
Grow out, in graver mood, obey the sterner stress?

Look not thou down but up!
To uses of a cup,
The festal board, lamp's flash and trumpet's peal,
The new wine's foaming flow,
The Master's lips aglow!
Thou, heaven's consummate cup, what need'st thou
with earth's wheel?

But I need, now as then,
Thee, God, who mouldest men;
And since, not even while the whirl was worst,
Did I,–to the wheel of life
With shapes and colours rife,
Bound dizzily,–mistake my end, to slake Thy thirst:

So, take and use Thy work!
Amend what flaws may lurk,
What strain o' the stuff, what warpings past the aim!
My times be in Thy hand!
Perfect the cup as planned!
Let age approve of youth, and death complete the same!

WILLIAM BELL SCOTT

1812-1890

Pebbles in the Stream

HERE on this little bridge in this warm day
We rest us from our idle sauntering walk.
Over our shadows its continuous talk
The stream maintains, while now and then a stray
Dry leaf may fall where the still waters play
In endless eddies, through whose clear brown deep
The gorgeous pebbles quiver in their sleep.
The stream still hastes but cannot pass away.

Could I but find the words that would reveal
The unity in multiplicity,
And the profound strange harmony I feel
With those dead things, God's garments of to-day,
The listener's soul with mine they would anneal,
And make us one within eternity.

From 'The Year of the World'

GIVE reverence, O man, to mystery,
Keep your soul patient, and with closed eye hear.
Know that the Good is in all things, the whole
Being by him pervaded and upheld.

He is the will, the thwarting circumstance,
The two opposing forces equal both–
Birth, Death, are one. Think not the Lotus flower
Or tulip is more honoured than the grass,
The bindweed, or the thistle. He who kneels
To Cama, kneeleth unto me; the maid
Who sings to Ganga sings to me; I am
Wisdom unto the wise, and cunning lore
Unto the subtle. He who knows his soul,
And from thence looketh unto mine; who sees
All underneath the moon regardlessly,
Living on silent, as a shaded lamp
Burns with steady flame:–he sure shall find me–
He findeth wisdom, greatness, happiness.

Know, further, the Great One delighteth not
In him who works, and strives, and is against
The nature of the present. Not the less
Am I the gladness of the conqueror–
And the despair of impotence that fails.
I am the ultimate, the tendency
Of all things to *their* nature, which is *mine.*
Put round thee garments of rich softness, hang
Fine gold about thine ankles, hands, and ears,
Set the rich ruby and rare diamond
Upon thy brow.–I made them, I also
Made them be sought by thee; thou lack'st them not?
Then throw them whence they came, and leave with them
The wish to be aught else than nature forms.

Know that the great Good in the age called First,
Beheld a world of mortals, 'mong whom none
Enquired for Truth, because no falsehood was:
Nature was Truth; man held whate'er he wished:

No will was thwarted, and no deed was termed,
Good, Evil. In much wisdom is much grief.
He who increases knowledge sorrow also
Takes with it, till he rises unto me,
Knowing that I am in all, still the same:
Knowing that I am Peace in the contented.
I, Great, revealed unto the Seer, how man
Had wandered, and he gave a name and form
To my communings and he called it Veda.
To him who understands it is great gain–
Who understandeth not, to him the Sign
And ritual is authority and guide,
A living and expiring confidence.

CHRISTOPHER PEARSE CRANCH

1813-1892

So far, so near

THOU, so far, we grope to grasp thee–
Thou, so near, we cannot clasp thee–
Thou, so wise, our prayers grow heedless–
Thou, so loving, they are needless!
In each human soul thou shinest,
Human-best is thy divinest.
In each deed of love thou warmest;
Evil into good transformest.
Soul of all, and moving centre
Of each moment's life we enter.
Breath of breathing–light of gladness–
Infinite antidote of sadness;–
All-preserving ether flowing
Through the worlds, yet past our knowing.
Never past our trust and loving,
Nor from thine our life removing.

Still creating, still inspiring,
Never of thy creatures tiring;
Artist of thy solar spaces;
And thy humble human faces;
Mighty glooms and splendours voicing;
In thy plastic work rejoicing;
Through benignant law connecting
Best with best–and all perfecting,
Though all human races claim thee,
Thought and language fail to name thee,
Mortal lips be dumb before thee,
Silence only may adore thee!

From 'Ormuzd and Ahriman'

Satan speaks

THERE were no shadows till the worlds were made;
No evil and no sin till finite souls,
Imperfect thence, conditioned in free-will,
Took form, projected by eternal law
Through co-existent realms of time and space.
Naught evil, though it were the Prince of evil,
Hath being in itself. For God alone
Existeth in Himself, and Good, which lives
As sunshine lives, born of the Parent Sun.
I am the finite shadow of that Sun,
Opposite, not opposing, only seen
Upon the nether side.
No personal will am I, no influence bad
Or good. I symbolize the wild and deep
And unregenerated wastes of life,
Dark with transmitted tendencies of race
And blind mischance; all crude mistakes of will–

Proclivity unbalanced by due weight
Of favouring circumstance; all passion blown
By wandering winds; all surplusage of force
Piled up for use, but slipping from its base
Of law and order; all undisciplined
And ignorant mutiny against the wise
Restraint of rules by centuries old endorsed,
And proved the best so long it needs no proof;–
All quality o'erstrained until it cracks:–
Yet but a surface crack; the Eternal Eye
Sees underneath the soul's sphere, as above,
And knows the deep foundations of the world
Will not be jarred or loosened by the stress
Of sun and wind and rain upon the crust
Of upper soil. Nay, let the earthquake split
The mountains into steep and splintered chasms–
Down deeper than the shock the adamant
Of ages stands, symbol no less divine
Of the eternal Law than heaven above.

FREDERICK WILLIAM FABER

1814-1863

From 'The Eternal Word'

I

AMID the eternal silences
    God's endless Word was spoken;
None heard but He who always spake,
    And the silence was unbroken.
        Oh marvellous! O worshipful!
            No song or sound is heard,
        But everywhere and every hour,
        In love, in wisdom, and in power,
The Father speaks His dear Eternal Word!

II

For ever in the eternal land
The glorious Day is dawning;
For ever is the Father's Light
Like an endless outspread morning.
Oh marvellous! Oh worshipful!
No song or sound is heard,
But everywhere and every hour,
In love, in wisdom, and in power,
The Father speaks His dear Eternal Word!

III

From the Father's vast tranquillity,
In light co-equal glowing
The kingly consubstantial Word
Is unutterably flowing.
Oh marvellous! Oh worshipful!
No song or sound is heard,
But everywhere and every hour,
In love, in wisdom, and in power,
The Father speaks His dear Eternal Word!

IV

For ever climbs that Morning Star
Without ascent or motion;
For ever is its daybreak shed
On the Spirit's boundless ocean.
Oh marvellous! Oh worshipful!
No song or sound is heard,
But everywhere and every hour,
In love, in wisdom, and in power,
The Father speaks His dear Eternal Word

207

EDWARD CASWALL

1814-1878

The Order of Pure Intuition

HAIL, sacred Order of eternal Truth!
That deep within the soul,
In axiomatic majesty sublime,
One undivided whole,–

Up from the underdepth unsearchable
Of primal Being springs,
An inner world of thought, co-ordinate
With that of outward things!

Hail, Intuition pure! whose essences
The central core supply
Of conscience, language, science, certitude,
Art, beauty, harmony!

Great God! I thank Thy majesty supreme,
Whose all-creative grace
Not in the sentient faculties alone
Has laid my reason's base;

Not in abstractions thin by slow degrees
From grosser forms refin'd;
Not in tradition, nor the broad consent
Of conscious humankind;–

But in th' essential Presence of Thyself,
Within the soul's abyss;
Thyself, alike of her intelligence
The fount, as of her bliss;

Thyself, by nurture, meditation, grace,
Reflexively reveal'd;
Yet ever acting on the springs of thought,
E'en when from thought conceal'd!

AUBREY THOMAS DE VERE

1814-1902

Implicit Faith

OF all great Nature's tones that sweep
Earth's resonant bosom, far or near,
Low-breathed or loudest, shrill or deep,
How few are grasped by mortal ear.

Ten octaves close our scale of sound:
Its myriad grades, distinct or twined,
Transcend our hearing's petty bound,
To us as colours to the blind.

In Sound's unmeasured empire thus
The heights, the depths alike we miss;
Ah, but in measured sound to us
A compensating spell there is!

In holy music's golden speech
Remotest notes to notes respond:
Each octave is a world; yet each
Vibrates to worlds its own beyond.

Our narrow pale the vast resumes;
Our sea-shell whispers of the sea:
Echoes are ours of angel-plumes
That winnow far infinity!

–Clasp thou of Truth the central core!
Hold fast that centre's central sense!
An atom there shall fill thee more
Than realms on Truth's circumference.

That cradled Saviour, mute and small,
Was God–is God while worlds endure!
Who holds Truth truly holds it all
In essence, or in miniature.

Know what thou know'st! He knoweth much
Who knows not many things: and he
Knows most whose knowledge hath a touch
Of God's divine simplicity.

PHILIP JAMES BAILEY

1816-1902

Knowledge

THE knowledge of God is the wisdom of man–
This is the end of Being, wisdom; this
Of wisdom, action; and of action, rest;
And of rest, bliss; that by experience sage
Of good and ill, the diametric powers
Which thwart the world, the thrice-born might discern
That death divine alone can perfect both,
The mediate and initiate; that between
The Deity and nothing, nothing is.

The Atlantean axis of the world
And all the undescribed circumference,
Where earth's thick breath thins off to blankest space
Uniting with inanity, this truth
Confess, the sun-sire and the death-world too,
And undeflected spirit pure from Heaven,
That He who makes, destroying, saves the whole.
The Former and Re-Former of the world
In wisdom's holy spirit all renew.

To know this, is to read the runes of old,
Wrought in the time-outlasting rock; to see
Unblinded in the heart of light; to feel
Keen through the soul, the same essential strain,
Which vivifies the clear and fire-eyed stars,
Still harping their serene and silvery spell

In the perpetual presence of the skies,
And of the world-cored calm, where silence sits
In secret light all hidden; this to know–
Brings down the fiery unction from on high,
The spiritual chrism of the sun,
Which hallows and ordains the regnant soul–
Transmutes the splendid fluid of the frame
Into a fountain of divine delight,
And renovative nature;–shows us earth,
One with the great galactic line of life
Which parts the hemispheral palm of Heaven;
This with all spheres of Being makes concord
As at the first creation, in that peace,
Premotional, pre-elemental, prime,
Which is the hope of earth, the joy of Heaven,
The choice of the elect, the grace of life,
The blessing and the glory of our God.
And–as the vesper hymn of time precedes
The starry matins of Eternity,
And daybreak of existence in the Heavens,–
To know this, is to know we shall depart
Into the storm-surrounding calm on high,
The sacred cirque, the all-central infinite
Of that self-blessedness wherein abides
Our God, all-kind, all-loving, all-beloved;–
To feel life one great ritual, and its laws,
Writ in the vital rubric of the blood,
Flow in, obedience, and flow out, command,
In sealike circulation; and be here
Accepted as a gift by Him who gives
An empire as an alms, nor counts it aught,
So long as all His creatures joy in Him,
The great Rejoicer of the Universe,
Whom all the boundless spheres of Being bless.

From 'The Mystic'

GOD was, alone in unity. He willed
The infinite creation; and it was.
That the creation might exist, His Son,
And that it might return to Him, the Spirit
Disclosed themselves within Him; thus triune
But as the all-made must of necessity
Inferior be to its creator, thus
Arose the infinite imperfect, time,
The spirit-host angelic, heavenly race,
Brute life and vegetive, electric light,
Matter and fleshly form; to human souls
Nine generations from aeternity.
But God, who is Love, decreed it should return
By pure regeneration unto God;
Wherefore was need that He from whom came life
Should taste death, but in tasting swallow up;
That commune with all creatures might be made,
On this hand, and on that, with Deity.
Thus death and evil expiate ends divine;
The Spirit the imperfect hallowing, death
The Son; the soul regenerate hies to God;
And as in radial union with the point
Infinite, both in greatness, place, and power.
Lives with the maker and the all-made in love.

From 'Festus'

I

GOD is the sole and self-subsistent one;
From Him, the sun-creator, nature was
Aethereal essences, all elements,
The souls therein indigenous, and man

Symbolic of all being. Out of earth
The matron moon was moulded, and the sea
Filled up the shining chasm; both now fulfil
One orbit and one nature, and all orbs
With them one fate, one universal end.
From light's projective moment, in the earth
The moon was, even as earth i' the sun; the sun
A fiery incarnation of the heavens.
When sun, earth, moon again make one, resumes
Nature her heavenly state; is glorified.'
As, to the sleepless eye, form forth, at last,
The long immeasurable layers of light,
And beams of fire enormous in the east,
The broad foundations of the heaven-domed day
All fineless as the future, so uprose
On mine the great celestial certainty.
The mask of matter fell off, I beheld,
Void of all seeming, the sole substance mind,
The actualized ideal of the world.
An absolutest essence filled my soul;
And superseding all its modes and powers,
Gave to the spirit a consciousness divine;
A sense of vast existence in the skies;
Boundless commune with spiritual light, and proof
Self-shown, of heaven commensurate with all life.
And I to the light of the great spirit's eyes
Mine hungry eyes returned which, past the first
Intensifying blindness, clearlier saw
The words she uttered of triumphant truth.
For truly, and as my vision heightened, lo!
The universal volume of the heavens,
Star-lettered in celestial characters,
Moved musically into words her breath framed
forth,

And varied momently; and I perceived
That thus she spake of God: I silent still
And hearkening to the sea-swell of her voice:
'From one divine, all permanent unity comes
The many and infinite; from God all just
To himself and others, who to all is love,
Earth and the moon, like syllables of light,
Uttered by him, were with all creatures blessed
By him, and with a sevenfold blessing sealed
To perfect rest, celestial order; all
The double-tabled book of heaven and earth,
Despite such due deficiency as cleaves
Inevitably to soul, till God resume,
Progressive aye, possessing too all bliss
Elect and universal in the heavens.'

II

And none can truly worship but who have
The earnest of their glory from on high,
God's nature in them. It is the love of God,
The ecstatic sense of oneness with all things,
And special worship towards himself that thrills
Through life's self-conscious chord, vibrant in him,
Harmonious with the universe, which makes
Our sole fit claim to being immortal; that
Wanting nor willing, the world cannot worship.
And whether the lip speak, or in inspired
Silence, we clasp our hearts as a shut book
Of song unsung, the silence and the speech
Is each his; and as coming from and going
To him, is worthy of him and his love.
Prayer is the spirit speaking truth to truth;
The expiration of the thing inspired.
Above the battling rock-storm of this world

Lies heaven's great calm, through which as through a bell,
Tolleth the tongue of God eternally,
Calling to worship. Whoso hears that tongue
Worships. The spirit enters with the sound,
Preaching the one and universal word,
The God-word, which is spirit, life, and light;
The written word to one race, the unwrit
Revealment to the thousand-peopled world.
The ear which hears is pre-attuned in heaven,
The eye which sees prevision hath ere birth.
But the just future shall to many give
Gifts which the partial present doles to few;
To all the glory of obeying God.

EMILY BRONTË

1819-1848

The Visionary

SILENT is the house: all are laid asleep:
One alone looks out o'er the snow-wreaths deep,
Watching every cloud, dreading every breeze
That whirls the wildering drift, and bends the groaning
trees.

Cheerful is the hearth, soft the matted floor;
Not one shivering gust creeps through pane or door;
The little lamp burns straight, its rays shoot strong and
far:
I trim it well, to be the wanderer's guiding-star.

Frown, my haughty sire! chide, my angry dame!
Set your slaves to spy; threaten me with shame:
But neither sire nor dame nor prying serf shall know,
What angel nightly tracks that waste of frozen snow.

What I love shall come like visitant of air,
Safe in secret power from lurking human snare;
What loves me, no word of mine shall e'er betray,
Though for faith unstained my life must forfeit pay.

Burn, then, little lamp; glimmer straight and clear–
Hush! a rustling wing stirs, methinks, the air:
He for whom I wait, thus ever comes to me;
Strange Power! I trust thy might; trust thou my
  constancy.

Last Lines

NO coward soul is mine,
No trembler in the world's storm-troubled sphere:
  I see Heaven's glories shine,
And faith shines equal, arming me from fear.

  O God within my breast,
Almighty, ever-present Diety!
  Life–that in me has rest,
As I–undying Life–have power in Thee!

  Vain are the thousand creeds
That move men's hearts: unutterably vain;
  Worthless as withered weeds,
Or idlest froth amid the boundless main,

  To waken doubt in one
Holding so fast by thine infinity;
  So surely anchor'd on
The steadfast rock of immortality.

  With wide-embracing love
Thy Spirit animates eternal years,
  Pervades and broods above,
Changes, sustains, dissolves, creates, and rears.

Though earth and man were gone,
And suns and universes ceased to be,
And Thou were left alone,
Every existence would exist in Thee.
There is not room for Death,
Nor atom that his might could render void:
Thou–THOU art Being and Breath,
And what THOU art may never be destroy'd.

WALT WHITMAN[1]

1819-1892

From the 'Song of the Open Road'

I

FROM this hour I ordain myself loos'd of limits and imaginary lines,
Going where I list, my own master, total and absolute,
Listening to others, and considering well what they say,
Pausing, searching, receiving, contemplating,
Gently, but with undeniable will, divesting myself of the holds that would hold me.
I inhale great draughts of space,
The east and the west are mine, and the north and the south are mine.
I am larger, better than I thought,
I did not know I held so much goodness.
All seems beautiful to me;
I can repeat over to men and women, You have done such good to me, I would do the same to you,
I will recruit for myself and you as I go;
I will scatter myself among men and women as I go;
I will toss the new gladness and roughness among them;

[1] *By permission of Messrs. Appleton & Co., New York.*

Whoever denies me, it shall not trouble me;
Whoever accepts me, he or she shall be blessed, and shall
bless me.

II

Here is the efflux of the Soul;
The efflux of the Soul comes from within, through em-
bower'd gates, ever provoking questions;
These yearnings, why are they? These thoughts in the
darkness, why are they?
Why are there men and women that while they are nigh
me, the sunlight expands my blood?
Why, when they leave me, do my pennants of joy sink
flat and lank?
Why are there trees I never walk under, but large and
melodious thoughts descend upon me?
(I think they hang there winter and summer on those
trees, and always drop fruit as I pass;)
What is it I interchange so suddenly with strangers?
What with some driver, as I ride on the seat by his side?
What with some fisherman, drawing his seine by the shore,
as I walk by, and pause?
What gives me to be free to a woman's or man's good-will?
What gives them to be free to mine?

The efflux of the Soul is happiness–here is happiness;
I think it pervades the open air, waiting at all times;
Now it flows unto us–we are rightly charged.

Here rises the fluid and attaching character;
The fluid and attaching character is the freshness and
sweetness of man and woman;
(The herbs of the morning sprout no fresher and sweeter
every day out of the roots of themselves, than it
sprouts fresh and sweet continually out of itself.)

Toward the fluid and attaching character exudes the
sweat of the love of young and old;
From it falls distill'd the charm that mocks beauty and
attainments;
Toward it heaves the shuddering longing ache of contact.

Allons! whoever you are, come travel with me!
Travelling with me, you find what never tires.

The earth never tires;
The earth is rude, silent, incomprehensible at first–
Nature is rude and incomprehensible at first;
Be not discouraged–keep on–there are divine things,
well envelop'd;
I swear to you there are divine things more beautiful
than words can tell.

Allons! we must not stop here!
However sweet these laid-up stores–however convenient
this dwelling, we cannot remain here;
However shelter'd this port, and however calm these
waters, we must not anchor here;
However welcome the hospitality that surrounds us, we
are permitted to receive it but a little while.

III

All parts away for the progress of souls;
All religion, all solid things, arts, governments–all that
was or is apparent upon this globe or any globe, falls
into niches and corners before the procession of souls
along the grand roads of the universe.
Of the progress of the souls of men and women along the
grand roads of the universe, all other progress is the
needed emblem and sustenance.

From 'Passage to India'

O VAST Rondure, swimming in space,
Cover'd all over with visible power and beauty,
Alternate light and day and the teeming spiritual darkness,
Unspeakable high processions of sun and moon and countless stars above,
Below, the manifold grass and waters, animals, mountains, trees,
With inscrutable purpose, some hidden prophetic intention,
Now first it seems my thought begins to span thee.

Down from the gardens of Asia descending radiating,
Adam and Eve appear, then their myriad progeny after them,
Wandering, yearning, curious, with restless explorations,
With questionings, baffled, formless, feverish, with never-happy hearts,
With that sad incessant refrain, *Wherefore unsatisfied soul?* and *Whither O mocking life?*

Ah, who shall soothe these feverish children?
Who justify these restless explorations?
Who speak the secret of impassive earth?
Who bind it to us? what is this separate Nature so unnatural?
What is this earth to our affections? (unloving earth, without a throb to answer ours,
Cold earth, the place of graves.)

Yet soul be sure the first intent remains, and shall be carried out,
Perhaps even now the time has arrived.

After the seas are all cross'd, (as they seem already cross'd,)
After the great captains and engineers have accomplish'd
their work,
After the noble inventors, after the scientists, the chemist,
the geologist, ethnologist,
Finally shall come the poet worthy that name,
The true son of God shall come singing his songs.

Then not your deeds only O voyagers, O scientists and
inventors, shall be justified;
All these hearts as of fretted children shall be sooth'd,
All affection shall be fully responded to, the secret shall
be told,
All these separations and gaps shall be taken up and
hook'd and link'd together,
The whole earth, this cold, impassive, voiceless earth,
shall be completely justified,
Trinitas divine shall be gloriously accomplish'd and
compacted by the true son of God, the poet,
(He shall indeed pass the straits and conquer the mountains,
He shall double the cape of Good Hope to some purpose,)
Nature and Man shall be disjoin'd and diffused no more,
The true son of God shall absolutely fuse them. . . .

Passage indeed O soul to primal thought,
Not lands and seas alone, thy own clear freshness,
The young maturity of brood and bloom,
To realms of budding bibles.

O soul, repressless, I with thee and thou with me,
Thy circumnavigation of the world begin,
Of man, the voyage of his mind's return,
To reason's early paradise,
Back, back to wisdom's birth, to innocent intuitions,
Again with fair creation.

O we can wait no longer,
We too take ship O soul
Joyous we too launch out on trackless seas,
Fearless for unknown shores on waves of ecstasy to sail,
Amid the wafting winds, (thou pressing me to thee, I thee
    to me, O soul,)
Caroling free, singing our song of God,
Chanting our chant of pleasant exploration.

With laugh and many a kiss,
(Let others deprecate, let others weep for sin, remorse,
    humiliation,)
O soul thou pleasest me, I thee.

Ah more than any priest O soul we too believe in God,
But with the mystery of God we dare not dally.

O soul thou pleasest me, I thee,
Sailing these seas or on the hills, or waking in the night,
Thoughts, silent thoughts, of Time and Space and Death,
    like waters flowing,
Bear me indeed as through the regions infinite,
Whose air I breathe, whose ripples hear, lave me all over,
Bathe me O God in thee, mounting to thee,
I and my soul to range in range of thee.

O Thou transcendent,
Nameless, the fibre and the breath,
Light of the light, shedding forth universes, thou centre
    of them,
Thou mightier centre of the true, the good, the loving,
Thou moral, spiritual fountain–affection's source–thou
    reservoir,
(O pensive soul of me–O thirst unsatisfied–waitest not
    there?

Waitest not haply for us somewhere there the Comrade
perfect?)
Thou pulse–thou motive of the stars, suns, systems,
That, circling, move in order, safe, harmonious,
Athwart the shapeless vastnesses of space,
How should I think, how breathe a single breath, how
speak, if, out of myself,
I could not launch, to those, superior universes?

Swiftly I shrivel at the thought of God,
At Nature and its wonders, Time and Space and Death,
But that I, turning, call to thee O soul, thou actual
Me,
And lo, thou gently masterest the orbs,
Thou matest Time, smilest content at Death,
And fillest, swellest full the vastnesses of Space.

Greater than stars or suns,
Bounding O soul thou journeyest forth;
What love than thine and ours could wider amplify?
What aspirations, wishes, outvie thine and ours O soul?
What dreams of the ideal? what plans of purity, per-
fection, strength?
What cheerful willingness for others' sake to give up all?
For others' sake to suffer all?

Reckoning ahead O soul, when thou, the time achiev'd,
The seas all cross'd, weather'd the capes, the voyage
done,
Surrounded, copest, frontest God, yieldest, the aim
attain'd,
As fill'd with friendship, love complete, the Elder Brother
found,
The Younger melts in fondness in his arms.

Passage to more than India!
Are thy wings plumed indeed for such far flights?
O soul, voyagest thou indeed on voyages like those?
Disportest thou on waters such as those?
Soundest below the Sanscrit and the Vedas?
Then have thy bent unleash'd.

Passage to you, your shores, ye aged fierce enigmas!
Passage to you, to mastership of you, ye strangling problems!
You, strew'd with the wrecks of skeletons, that, living, never reach'd you.

Passage to more than India!
O secret of the earth and sky!
Of you O waters of the sea! O winding creeks and rivers!
Of you O woods and fields! of you strong mountains of my land!
Of you O prairies! of you gray rocks!
O morning red! O clouds! O rain and snows!
O day and night, passage to you!

O sun and moon and all you stars! Sirius and Jupiter!
Passage to you!

Passage, immediate passage! the blood burns in my veins!
Away O soul! hoist instantly the anchor!
Cut the hawsers–haul out–shake out every sail!
Have we not stood here like trees in the ground long enough?
Have we not grovel'd here long enough, eating and drinking like mere brutes?
Have we not darken'd and dazed ourselves with books long enough?

Sail forth—steer for the deep waters only,
Reckless, O soul, exploring, I with thee, and thou with me,
For we are bound where mariner has not yet dared to go,
And we will risk the ship, ourselves and all.

O my brave soul!
O farther farther sail!
O daring joy, but safe! are they not all the seas of God?
O farther, farther, farther sail!

Chanting the Square Deific

CHANTING the square deific, out of the One advancing, out of the sides,
Out of the old and new, out of the square entirely divine,
Solid, four-sided, (all the sides needed,) from this side Jehovah am I,
Old Brahm I, and I Saturnius am;
Not Time affects me—I am Time, old, modern as any,
Unpersuadable, relentless, executing righteous judgements,
As the Earth, the Father, the brown old Kronos, with laws,
Aged beyond computation, yet ever new, ever with those mighty laws rolling,
Relentless, I forgive no man—whoever sins dies—I will have that man's life;
Therefore let none expect mercy—have the seasons, gravitation, the appointed days, mercy? no more have I,
But as the seasons and gravitation, and as all the appointed days that forgive not,
I dispense from this side judgements inexorable without the least remorse.

Consolator most mild, the promis'd one advancing,
With gentle hand extended, the mightier God am I,
Foretold by prophets and poets in their most rapt
 prophecies and poems,
From this side, lo! the Lord Christ gazes–lo! Hermes
 I–lo! mine is Hercules' face,
All sorrow, labour, suffering, I, tallying it, absorb in
 myself,
Many times have I been rejected, taunted, put in prison,
 and crucified, and many times shall be again,
All the world have I given up for my dear brothers' and
 sisters' sake, for the soul's sake,
Wending my way through the homes of men, rich or
 poor, with the kiss of affection,
For I am affection, I am the cheer-bringing God, with
 hope and all-enclosing charity,
With indulgent words as to children, with fresh and sane
 words, mine only,
Young and strong I pass knowing well I am destin'd
 myself to an early death;
But my charity has no death–my wisdom dies not,
 neither early nor late,
And my sweet love bequeath'd here and elsewhere never
 dies.

Aloof, dissatisfied, plotting revolt,
Comrade of criminals, brother of slaves,
Crafty, despised, a drudge, ignorant,
With sudra face and worn brow, black, but in the depths
 of my heart, proud as any,
Lifted now and always against whoever scorning assumes
 to rule me,
Morose, full of guile, full of reminiscences, brooding,
 with many wiles,

(Though it was thought I was baffled and dispel'd, and
my wiles done, but that will never be,)
Defiant, I, Satan, still live, still utter words, in new lands
duly appearing, (and old ones also,)
Permanent here from my side, warlike, equal with any,
real as any,
Nor time nor change shall ever change me or my words.

Santa Spirita, breather, life,
Beyond the light, lighter than light,
Beyond the flames of hell, joyous, leaping easily above
hell,
Beyond Paradise, perfumed solely with mine own perfume,
Including all life on earth, touching, including God,
including Saviour and Satan,
Ethereal, pervading all (for without me what were all?
what were God?),
Essence of forms, life of the real identities, permanent,
positive, (namely the unseen,)
Life of the great round world, the sun and stars, and of
man, I, the general soul,
Here the square finishing, the solid, I the most solid,
Breathe my breath also through these songs.

All is Truth

O ME, man of slack faith so long,
Standing aloof–denying portions so long;
Only aware to-day of compact, all-diffused truth;
Discovering to-day there is no lie, or form of lie, and can
be none, but grows as inevitably upon itself as the
truth does upon itself,
Or as any law of the earth, or any natural production of
the earth does.

(This is curious, and may not be realized immediately–
But it must be realized;
I feel in myself that I represent falsehoods equally with the rest,
And that the universe does.)

Where has fail'd a perfect return, indifferent of lies or the truth?
Is it upon the ground, or in water or fire? or in the spirit of man? or in the meat and blood?

Meditating among liars, and retreating sternly into myself, I see that there are really no liars or lies after all,
And nothing fails its perfect return–And that what are called lies are perfect returns,
And that each thing exactly represents itself, and what has preceded it,
And that the truth includes all, and is compact, just as much as space is compact,
And that there is no law or vacuum in the amount of the truth–but that all is truth without exception;
And henceforth I will go celebrate anything I see or am,
And sing and laugh, and deny nothing.

Grand is the Seen

GRAND is the seen, the light, to me–grand are the sky and stars,
Grand is the earth, and grand are lasting time and space,
And grand their laws, so multiform, puzzling, evolutionary;
But grander far the unseen soul of me, comprehending, endowing all those,

Lighting the light, the sky and stars, delving the earth,
 sailing the sea,
(What were all those, indeed, without thee, unseen soul?
 of what amount without thee?)
More evolutionary, vast, puzzling, O my soul!
More multiform far–more lasting thou than they.

DORA GREENWELL

1821-1882

The Blade of Grass

'A sword shall go through thine own heart.'–*Prophecy of Zacharias*

OH! little blade of grass,
 A little sword thou art,
That in thy haste to pass
 Hast pierced thy mother's heart!

Oh! little blade of grass,
 A little tongue thou art
Of cleaving flame,–alas!
 Thou hast cleft thy mother's heart.

Oh! little blade, upcurled
 Leaf, sword, or fiery dart,
To win thy Father's world
 Thou must break thy mother's heart!

MATTHEW ARNOLD

1822-1888

Progress

THE Master stood upon the mount, and taught.
 He saw a fire in his disciples' eyes;
'The old law', they said, 'is wholly come to naught!
 Behold the new world rise!'

'Was it', the Lord then said, 'with scorn ye saw
The old law observed by Scribes and Pharisees?
I say unto you, see *ye* keep that law
More faithfully than these!

'Too hasty heads for ordering worlds, alas!
Think not that I to annul the law have will'd;
No jot, no tittle from the law shall pass,
Till all hath been fulfill'd.'

So Christ said eighteen hundred years ago.
And what then shall be said to those to-day,
Who cry aloud to lay the old world low
To clear the new world's way?

'Religious fervours! ardour misapplied!
Hence, hence,' they cry, 'ye do but keep man blind!
But keep him self-immersed, preoccupied,
And lame the active mind!'

Ah! from the old world let some one answer give:
'Scorn ye this world, their tears, their inward cares?
I saw unto you, see that *your* souls live
A deeper life than theirs!

'Say ye: The spirit of man has found new roads,
And we must leave the old faiths, and walk therein?–
Leave then the Cross as ye have left carved gods,
But guard the fire within!

'Bright, else, and fast the stream of life may roll,
And no man may the other's hurt behold;
Yet each will have one anguish–his own soul
Which perishes of cold.'

Here let that voice make end; then let a strain,
From a far lonelier distance, like the wind
Be heard, floating through heaven, and fill again
    These men's profoundest mind:

'Children of men! the unseen Power, whose eye
For ever doth accompany mankind,
Hath looked on no religion scornfully
    That men did ever find.

'Which has not taught weak wills how much they can?
Which has not fall'n on the dry heart like rain?
Which has not cried to sunk, self-weary man:
    Thou must be born again!

'Children of men! not that your age excel
In pride of life the ages of your sires,
But that *you* think clear, feel deep, bear fruit well,
    The Friend of man desires.'

From 'The Buried Life'

FATE, which foresaw
How frivolous a baby man would be,
By what distractions he would be possess'd,
How he would pour himself in every strife,
And well-nigh change his own identity–
That it might keep from his capricious play
His genuine self, and force him to obey
Even in his own despite, his being's law,
Bade through the deep recesses of our breast
The unregarded River of our Life
Pursue with indiscernible flow its way;
And that we should not see
The buried stream, and seem to be

Eddying about in blind uncertainty,
Though driving on with it eternally.

But often, in the world's most crowded streets,
But often, in the din of strife,
There rises an unspeakable desire
After the knowledge of our buried life,
A thirst to spend our fire and restless force
In tracking out our true, original course;
A longing to inquire
Into the mystery of this heart that beats
So wild, so deep in us, to know
Whence our thoughts come and where they go.
And many a man in his own breast then delves,
But deep enough, alas, none ever mines!
And we have been on many thousand lines,
And we have shown, on each, spirit and power,
But hardly have we, for one little hour,
Been on our own line, have we been ourselves;
Hardly had skill to utter one of all
The nameless feelings that course through our breast,
But they course on for ever unexpress'd.
And long we try in vain to speak and act
Our hidden self, and what we say and do
Is eloquent, is well–but 'tis not true!
And then we will no more be rack'd
With inward striving, and demand
Of all the thousand nothings of the hour
Their stupefying power;
Ah yes, and they benumb us at our call:
Yet still, from time to time, vague and forlorn,
From the soul's subterranean depth upborne
As from an infinitely distant land,
Come airs, and floating echoes, and convey
A melancholy into all our day.

Only–but this is rare–
When a belovèd hand is laid in ours,
When, jaded with the rush and glare
Of the interminable hours,
Our eyes can in another's eyes read clear,
When our world-deafen'd ear
Is by the tones of a loved voice caress'd–
A bolt is shot back somewhere in our breast,
And a lost pulse of feeling stirs again:
The eye sinks inward, and the heart lies plain,
And what we mean, we say, and what we would, we know.
A man becomes aware of his life's flow,
And hears its winding murmur, and he sees
The meadows where it glides, the sun, the breeze.

And there arrives a lull in the hot race
Wherein he doth for ever chase
That flying and elusive shadow, Rest.
An air of coolness plays upon his face,
And an unwonted calm pervades his breast.
And then he thinks he knows
The Hills where his life rose,
And the Sea where it goes.

From 'Lines Written in Kensington Gardens'

CALM soul of all things! make it mine
To feel, amid the city's jar,
That there abides a peace of thine,
Man did not make, and cannot mar!

The will to neither strive nor cry,
The power to feel with others give!
Calm, calm me more! nor let me die
Before I have begun to live.

From 'Empedocles on Aetna'

TO the elements it came from
Everything will return.
Our bodies to earth,
Our blood to water,
Heat to fire,
Breath to air.
They were well born, they will be well entomb'd!
But mind? . . .

And we might gladly share the fruitful stir
Down in our mother earth's miraculous womb!
Well might it be
With what roll'd of us in the stormy main!
We might have joy, blent with the all-bathing air,
Or with the nimble radiant life of fire!

But mind–but thought–
If these have been the master part of us–
Where will *they* find their parent element?
What will receive *them*, who will call *them* home?
But we shall still be in them, and they in us,
And we shall be the strangers of the world,
And they will be our lords, as they are now;
And keep us prisoners of our consciousness,
And never let us clasp and feel the All
But through their forms, and modes, and stifling veils.
And we shall be unsatisfied as now;
And we shall feel the agony of thirst,
The ineffable longing for the life of life
Baffled for ever: and still thought and mind
Will hurry us with them on their homeless march,

Over the unallied unopening earth,
Over the unrecognizing sea; while air
Will blow us fiercely back to sea and earth,
And fire repel us from its living waves.
And then we shall unwillingly return
Back to this meadow of calamity,
This uncongenial place, this human life;
And in our individual human state
Go through the sad probation all again,
To see if we will poise our life at last,
To see if we will now at last be true
To our own only true, deep-buried selves,
Being one with which we are one with the whole world;
Or whether we will once more fall away
Into some bondage of the flesh or mind,
Some slough of sense, or some fantastic maze
Forg'd by the imperious lonely thinking-power.
And each succeeding age in which we are born
Will have more peril for us than the last;
Will goad our senses with a sharper spur,
Will fret our minds to an intenser play,
Will make ourselves harder to be discern'd.
And we shall struggle awhile, gasp and rebel;
And we shall fly for refuge to past times,
Their soul of unworn youth, their breath of greatness;
And the reality will pluck us back,
Knead us in its hot hand, and change our nature.
And we shall feel our powers of effort flag,
And rally them for one last fight, and fail;
And we shall sink in the impossible strife,
And be astray for ever.

Slave of sense
I have in no wise been; but slave of thought?–

And who can say: I have been always free,
Lived ever in the light of my own soul?–
I cannot! I have lived in wrath and gloom,
Fierce, disputatious, ever at war with man,
Far from my own soul, far from warmth and light.
But I have not grown easy in these bonds–
But I have not denied what bonds these were!
Yea, I take myself to witness,
That I have loved no darkness,
Sophisticated no truth,
Nursed no delusion,
Allow'd no fear!

And therefore, O ye elements, I know–
Ye know it too–it hath been granted me
Not to die wholly, not to be all enslav'd.
I feel it in this hour! The numbing cloud
Mounts off my soul; I feel it, I breathe free!

Is it but for a moment?
Ah, boil up, ye vapours!
Leap and roar, thou sea of fire!
My soul glows to meet you.
Ere it flag, ere the mists
Of despondency and gloom
Rush over it again,
Receive me! Save me!

(*He plunges into the crater.*)

COVENTRY KERSEY DIGHTON PATMORE

1823-1896

Life of Life

WHAT'S that, which, ere I spake, was gone!
So joyful and intense a spark
That, whilst o'erhead the wonder shone,
The day, before but dull, grew dark?
I do not know; but this I know,
That, had the splendour lived a year,
The truth that I some heavenly show
Did see, could not be now more clear.
This know I too: might mortal breath
Express the passion then inspired,
Evil would die a natural death,
And nothing transient be desired;
And error from the soul would pass,
And leave the senses pure and strong
As sunbeams. But the best, alas,
Has neither memory nor tongue!

Vesica Piscis

IN strenuous hope I wrought,
And hope seem'd still betray'd;
Lastly I said,
'I have labour'd through the Night, nor yet
Have taken aught;
But at Thy word I will again cast forth the net!'
And, lo, I caught
(Oh, quite unlike and quite beyond my thought,)
Not the quick, shining harvest of the Sea,
For food, my wish,
But Thee!

Then, hiding even in me,
As hid was Simon's coin within the fish,
Thou sigh'd'st, with joy, 'Be dumb,
Or speak but of forgotten things to far-off times to come.'

Sponsa Dei

WHAT is this maiden fair,
The laughing of whose eye
Is in man's heart renew'd virginity;
Who yet sick longing breeds
For marriage which exceeds
The inventive guess of Love to satisfy
With hope of utter binding, and of loosing endless dear despair?
What gleams about her shine,
More transient than delight and more divine!
If she does something but a little sweet,
As gaze towards the glass to set her hair,
See how his soul falls humbled at her feet!
Her gentle step, to go or come,
Gains her more merit than a martyrdom;
And, if she dance, it doth such grace confer
As opes the heaven of heavens to more than her,
And makes a rival of her worshipper.
To die unknown for her were little cost!
So is she without guile,
Her mere refused smile
Makes up the sum of that which may be lost!
Who is this Fair
Whom each hath seen,
The darkest once in this bewailed dell,
Be he not destin'd for the glooms of hell?
Whom each hath seen

And known, with sharp remorse and sweet, as Queen
And tear-glad Mistress of his hopes of bliss,
Too fair for man to kiss?
Who is this only happy She,
Whom, by a frantic flight of courtesy,
Born of despair
Of better lodging for his Spirit fair,
He adores as Margaret, Maude, or Cecily?
And what this sigh,
That each one heaves for Earth's last lowlihead
And the Heaven high
Ineffably lock'd in dateless bridal-bed?
Are all, then, mad, or is it prophecy?
'Sons now we are of God,' as we have heard,
'But what we shall be hath not yet appear'd.'
O, Heart, remember thee,
That Man is none,
Save One.
What if this Lady be thy Soul, and He
Who claims to enjoy her sacred beauty be,
Not thou, but God; and thy sick fire
A female vanity,
Such as a Bride, viewing her mirror'd charms,
Feels when she sighs, 'All these are for his arms!'
A reflex heat
Flash'd on thy cheek from His immense desire,
Which waits to crown, beyond thy brain's conceit,
Thy nameless, secret, hopeless longing sweet,
Not by and by, but now,
Unless deny Him thou!

To the Body

CREATION'S and Creator's crowning good;
Wall of infinitude;
Foundation of the sky,
In Heaven forecast
And long'd for from eternity,
Though laid the last;
Reverberating dome,
Of music cunningly built home
Against the void and indolent disgrace
Of unresponsive space;
Little, sequester'd pleasure-house
For God and for His Spouse;
Elaborately, yea, past conceiving, fair,
Since, from the graced decorum of the hair,
Ev'n to the tingling, sweet
Soles of the simple, earth-confiding feet,
And from the inmost heart
Outwards unto the thin
Silk curtains of the skin,
Every least part
Astonish'd hears
And sweet replies to some like region of the spheres;
Form'd for a dignity prophets but darkly name,
Lest shameless men cry 'Shame!'
So rich with wealth conceal'd
That Heaven and Hell fight chiefly for this field;
Clinging to everything that pleases thee
With indefectible fidelity;
Alas, so true
To all thy friendships that no grace
Thee from thy sin can wholly disembrace;
Which thus 'bides with thee as the Jebusite,

That, maugre all God's promises could do,
The chosen People never conquer'd quite;
Who therefore lived with them,
And that by formal truce and as of right,
In metropolitan Jerusalem.
For which false fealty
Thou needs must, for a season, lie
In the grave's arms, foul and unshriven,
Albeit, in Heaven,
Thy crimson-throbbing Glow
Into its old abode aye pants to go,
And does with envy see
Enoch, Elijah, and the Lady, she
Who left the lilies in her body's lieu.
O, if the pleasures I have known in thee
But my poor faith's poor first-fruits be,
What quintessential, keen, ethereal bliss
Then shall be his
Who has thy birth-time's consecrating dew
For death's sweet chrism retain'd,
Quick, tender, virginal, and unprofaned!

AUGUSTA THEODOSIA DRANE

1823-1894

Forgotten among the Lilies

I fainted away abandoned;
And amid the lilies forgotten
Threw all my cares away.
(*St. John of the Cross. The Obscure Night*, Stanza viii)

THROUGH the dark night I wander on alone,
And, as one blinded, grope my weary way,
Without a lamp to shed its guiding ray;
I wander on unseen, and seeing none,
And caring to behold but only One.

I see not, yet my heart will give me light,
And safer than the noonday sun will guide
To where the Bridegroom waiteth for the Bride;
So walking on in faith and not by sight,
I cannot fear but He will guide me right. . . .

Forgotten 'mid the lilies; for I feel
Their gentle blossoms wave above my head;
I breathe the magic perfume which they shed,
As though my bleeding wounds they fain would heal,
And from my heart its aching sorrow steal.

A sad, sweet lot–I needs must call it sweet;
My cares, like withered buds, I cast aside,
And reck but little what may next betide;
The days and years fly past on pinions fleet,
Amid these lilies crushed beneath His feet.

Forgotten and abandoned;–yet withal
Leaning my heart upon my only Love:
Nay, raise me not, I do not care to move;
Soon I shall hear His gentle footstep fall,
And lift my eyes, and answer to His call.

Till then among the lilies let me lie;
See, I have cast my idle cares away:
Howe'er it be, I am content to stay
Until once more the Bridegroom passes by,
And hither turns His gracious, pitying eye.

Blame not my folly, for I know full well
My words can nought but idle babbling seem,
The madness of a fond and foolish dream:
Bear with my folly, for the thoughts that swell
This burning heart, I cannot, dare not tell.

Know only this–I suffer, yet I rest;
For all my cares and fears are cast away,
And more than this I know not how to say;
Forgotten though I be, I own it best
And 'mid the lilies lie in perfect rest.

What the Soul Desires

There Thou wilt show me what my soul desired;
There Thou wilt give at once, O my Life, what Thou gavest me the other day!
(*St. John of the Cross. Spiritual Canticle,* Stanza xxxviii)

THERE is a rapture that my soul desires,
There is a something that I cannot name;
I know not after what my soul aspires,
Nor guess from whence the restless longing came;
But ever from my childhood have I felt it,
In all things beautiful and all things gay,
And ever has its gentle, unseen presence
Fallen, like a shadow-cloud, across my way

It is the melody of all sweet music,
In all fair forms it is the hidden grace;
In all I love, a something that escapes me,
Flies my pursuit, and ever veils its face.
I see it in the woodland's summer beauty,
I hear it in the breathing of the air;
I stretch my hands to feel for it, and grasp it,
But ah! too well I know, it is not there.

In sunset-hours, when all the earth is golden,
And rosy clouds are hastening to the west,
I catch a waving gleam, and then 'tis vanished,
And the old longing once more fills my breast.

It is not pain, although the fire consumes me,
Bound up with memories of my happiest years;
It steals into my deepest joys–O mystery!
It mingles, too, with all my saddest tears.

Once, only once, there rose the heavy curtain,
The clouds rolled back, and for too brief a space
I drank in joy as from a living fountain,
And seemed to gaze upon it, face to face:
But of that day and hour who shall venture
With lips untouched by seraph's fire to tell?
I saw Thee, O my Life! I heard, I touched Thee,–
Then o'er my soul once more the darkness fell.

The darkness fell, and all the glory vanished;
I strove to call it back, but all in vain:
O rapture! to have seen it for a moment!
O anguish! that it never came again!
That lightning-flash of joy that seemed eternal,
Was it indeed but wandering fancy's dream?
Ah, surely no! that day the heavens opened,
And on my soul there fell a golden gleam.

O Thou, my Life, give me what then Thou gavest!
No angel vision do I ask to see,
I seek no ecstasy of mystic rapture,
Naught, naught, my Lord, my Life, but only Thee!
That golden gleam hath purged my sight, revealing,
In the fair ray reflected from above,
Thyself, beyond all sight, beyond all feeling,
The hidden Beauty, and the hidden Love.

As the hart panteth for the water-brooks,
And seeks the shades whence cooling fountains burst;
Even so for Thee, O Lord, my spirit fainteth,
Thyself alone hath power to quench its thirst.

Give me what then Thou gavest, for I seek it
No longer in Thy creatures, as of old;
I strive no more to grasp the empty shadow,
The secret of my life is found and told!

GEORGE MAC DONALD

1824-1905

A Prayer for the Past

ALL sights and sounds of day and year,
All groups and forms, each leaf and gem,
Are thine, O God, nor will I fear
To talk to Thee of them.

Too great Thy heart is to despise,
Whose day girds centuries about;
From things which we name small, Thine eyes
See great things looking out.

Therefore the prayerful song I sing
May come to Thee in ordered words:
Though lowly born, it needs not cling
In terror to its chords.

I think that nothing made is lost;
That not a moon has ever shone,
That not a cloud my eyes hath crossed
But to my soul is gone.

That all the lost years garnered lie
In this Thy casket, my dim soul;
And Thou wilt, once, the key apply,
And show the shining whole.

But were they dead in me, they live
In Thee, Whose Parable is–Time,
And Worlds, and Forms–all things that give
Me thoughts, and this my rime.

• • • • • •

Father, in joy our knees we bow:
This earth is not a place of tombs:
We are but in the nursery now;
They in the upper rooms.

For are we not at home in Thee,
And all this world a visioned show;
That, knowing what Abroad is, we
What Home is too may know?

Approaches

WHEN thou turn'st away from ill,
Christ is this side of thy hill.

When thou turnest toward good,
Christ is walking in thy wood.

When thy heart says, 'Father, pardon!'
Then the Lord is in thy garden.

When stern Duty wakes to watch,
Then His hand is on the latch.

But when Hope thy song doth rouse,
Then the Lord is in the house.

When to love is all thy wit,
Christ doth at thy table sit.

When God's will is thy heart's pole,
Then is Christ thy very soul.

De Profundis

WHEN I am dead unto myself, and let,
O Father, Thee live on in me,
Contented to do naught but pay my debt,
And leave the house to Thee,

Then shall I be Thy ransomed–from the cark
Of living, from the strain for breath,
From tossing in my coffin strait and dark,
At hourly strife with death!

Have mercy! in my coffin! and awake!
A buried temple of the Lord!
Grow, Temple, grow! Heart, from thy cerements break!
Stream out, O living Sword!

When I am with Thee as thou art with me,
Life will be self-forgetting power;
Love, ever conscious, buoyant, clear, and free,
Will flame in darkest hour.

Where now I sit alone, unmoving, calm,
    With windows open to Thy wind,
Shall I not know Thee in the radiant psalm
    Soaring from heart and mind?

The body of this death will melt away,
    And I shall know as I am known;
Know Thee my Father, every hour and day,
    As Thou know'st me Thine Own!

Lost and Found

I MISSED him when the sun began to bend;
I found him not when I had lost his rim;
With many tears I went in search of him,
Climbing high mountains which did still ascend,
And gave me echoes when I called my friend;
Through cities vast and charnel-houses grim,
And high cathedrals where the light was dim,
Through books and arts and works without an end,
But found him not–the friend whom I had lost.
And yet I found him–as I found the lark,
A sound in fields I heard but could not mark;
I found him nearest when I missed him most;
I found him in my heart, a life in frost,
A light I knew not till my soul was dark.

248

WILLIAM ALEXANDER
ARCHBISHOP OF ARMAGH

1824-1911

Sonnets

Suggested by St. Augustine

I

WHAT love I when I love Thee, O my God?
Not corporal beauty, nor the limb of snow,
Nor of loved light the white and pleasant flow,
Nor manna showers, nor streams that flow abroad,
Nor flowers of Heaven, nor small stars of the sod:
Not these, my God, I love, who love Thee so;
Yet love I something better than I know:–
A certain light on a more golden road;
A sweetness, not of honey or the hive;
A beauty, not of summer or the spring;
A scent, a music, and a blossoming
Eternal, timeless, placeless, without gyve,
Fair, fadeless, undiminish'd, ever dim,–
This, this is what I love in loving Him.

II

This, this is what I love, and what is this?
I ask'd the beautiful earth, who said–'not I'.
I ask'd the depths, and the immaculate sky
And all the spaces said–'not He but His.'
And so, like one who scales a precipice,
Height after height, I scaled the flaming ball
Of the great universe, yea, pass'd o'er all
The world of thought, which so much higher is.

Then I exclaimed, 'To whom is mute all murmur
  Of phantasy, of nature, and of art,
He, than articulate language hears a firmer
  And grander meaning in his own deep heart.
No sound from cloud or angel.' Oh, to win
That voiceless voice–'My servant, enter in'!

FRANCIS TURNER PALGRAVE

1825-1897

The City of God

Ἰδοὺ γὰρ, ἡ βασιλέια τοῦ Θεοῦ *ἐντὸς ὑμῶυ ἐστί.*

O THOU not made with hands,
Not throned above the skies,
Nor wall'd with shining walls,
Nor framed with stones of price,
  More bright than gold or gem,
  God's own Jerusalem!

Where'er the gentle heart
Finds courage from above;
Where'er the heart forsook
Warms with the breath of love;
  Where faith bids fear depart,
  City of God! thou art.

Thou art where'er the proud
In humbleness melts down;
Where self itself yields up;
Where martyrs win their crown;
  Where faithful souls possess
  Themselves in perfect peace.

Where in life's common ways
With cheerful feet we go;
When in His steps we tread
Who trod the way of woe;
    Where He is in the heart,
    City of God! thou art.

Not throned above the skies,
Nor golden-wall'd afar,
But where Christ's two or three
In His name gather'd are,
    Be in the midst of them,
    God's own Jerusalem!

DINAH MARIA (MULOCK) CRAIK

1826-1887

The Human Temple

'Know ye not that ye are the temple of God, and that the spirit of God dwelleth in you?'

The Temple in Darkness

DARKNESS broods upon the temple,
    Glooms along the lonely aisles,
Fills up all the orient window,
    Whence, like little children's wiles,
Shadows–purple, azure, golden–
    Broke upon the floor in smiles.

From the great heart of the organ
    Bursts no voice of chant or psalm;
All the air, by music-pulses
    Stirred no more, is deathly calm;
And no precious incense rising,
    Falls, like good men's prayer, in balm.

Not a sound of living footstep
    Echoes on the marble floor;
Not a sigh of stranger passing
    Pierces through the closèd door;
Quenched the light upon the altar:
    Where the priest stood, none stands more.

Lord, why hast Thou left Thy temple
    Scorned of man, disowned by Thee?
Rather let Thy right hand crush it,
    None its desolation see!
List–'He who the temple builded
    Doth His will there. Let it be!'

A Light in the Temple

Lo, a light within the temple!
    Whence it cometh no man knows;
Barred the doors: the night-black windows
    Stand apart in solemn rows,
All without seems gloom eternal,
    Yet the glimmer comes and goes–

As if silent-footed angels
    Through the dim aisles wandered fair,
Only traced amid the darkness,
    By the glory in their hair,
Till at the forsaken altar
    They all met, and praised God there.

Now the light grows–fuller, clearer;
    Hark, the organ 'gins to sound,
Faint, like broken spirit crying
    Unto Heaven from the ground;
While the chorus of the angels
    Mingles everywhere around.

See, the altar shines all radiant,
Though no mortal priest there stands,
And no earthly congregation
Worships with uplifted hands:
Yet they gather, slow and saintly,
In innumerable bands.

And the chant celestial rises
Where the human prayers have ceased:
No tear-sacrifice is offered,
For all anguish is appeased,
Through its night of desolation,
To His temple comes the Priest.

DANTE GABRIEL ROSSETTI

1828-1882

The Sea-Limits

CONSIDER the sea's listless chime:
Time's self it is, made audible,–
The murmur of the earth's own shell.
Secret continuance sublime
Is the sea's end: our sight may pass
No furlong farther. Since time was,
This sound hath told the lapse of time.

No quiet, which is death's,–it hath
The mournfulness of ancient life,
Enduring always at dull strife.
As the world's heart of rest and wrath,
Its painful pulse is in the sands.
Last utterly, the whole sky stands,
Grey and not known, along its path.

Listen alone beside the sea,
    Listen alone among the woods;
    Those voices of twin solitudes
Shall have one sound alike to thee:
    Hark where the murmurs of thronged men
    Surge and sink back and surge again,–
Still the one voice of wave and tree.

Gather a shell from the strown beach
    And listen at its lips: they sigh
    The same desire and mystery,
The echo of the whole sea's speech
    And all mankind is thus at heart
    Not anything but what thou art:
And Earth, Sea, Man, are all in each.

The Monochord

IS it the moved air or the moving sound
That is Life's self and draws my life from me,
    And by instinct ineffable decree
Holds my breath quailing on the bitter bound?
Nay, is it Life or Death, thus thunder-crowned,
    That 'mid the tide of all emergency
    Now notes my separate wave, and to what sea
Its difficult eddies labour in the ground?

Oh! what is this that knows the road I came,
The flame turned cloud, the cloud returned to flame,
    The lifted shifted steeps and all the way?–
That draws round me at last this wind-warm space,
And in regenerate rapture turns my face
    Upon the devious coverts of dismay?

GEORGE MEREDITH

1828-1909

Outer and Inner

FROM twig to twig the spider weaves
    At noon his webbing fine.
So near to mute the zephyrs flute
    That only leaflets dance.
The sun draws out of hazel leaves
    A smell of woodland wine.
I wake a swarm to sudden storm
    At any step's advance.

Along my path is bugloss blue,
    The star with fruit in moss;
The foxgloves drop from throat to top
    A daily lesser bell.
The blackest shadow, nurse of dew,
    Has orange skeins across;
And keenly red is one thin thread
    That flashing seems to swell.

My world I note ere fancy comes,
    Minutest hushed observe:
What busy bits of motioned wits
    Through antlered mosswork strive.
But now so low the stillness hums,
    My springs of seeing swerve,
For half a wink to thrill and think
    The woods with nymphs alive.

I neighbour the invisible
    So close that my consent
Is only asked for spirits masked
    To leap from trees and flowers.

And this because with them I dwell
    In thought, while calmly bent
To read the lines dear Earth designs
    Shall speak her life on ours.

Accept, she says; it is not hard
    In woods; but she in towns
Repeats, accept; and have we wept,
    And have we quailed with fears,
Or shrunk with horrors, sure reward
    We have whom knowledge crowns;
Who see in mould the rose unfold,
    The soul through blood and tears.

HENRY NUTCOMBE OXENHAM

1829-1888

The Child-Christ on the Cross

'Dolor meus in conspectu meo semper.'

VICTIM of love, in manhood's prime
    Thou wilt ascend the Cross to die:
Why hangs the Child before His time
    Stretched on that bed of agony?

'No thorn-wreath crowns My boyish brow,
    No scourge has dealt its cruel smart,
In hands and feet no nail-prints show,
    No spear is planted in My heart.

'They have not set Me for a sign,
    Hung bare beneath the sunless sky;
Nor mixed the draught of gall and wine
    To mock My dying agony.

'The livelong night, the livelong day,
My child, I travail for thy good,
And for thy sake I hang alway
Self-crucified upon the Rood.

'To witness to the living Truth,
To keep thee pure from sin's alloy,
I cloud the sunshine of My youth;
The Man must suffer in the Boy.

'Visions of unrepented sin,
The forfeit crown, the eternal loss,
Lie deep my sorrowing soul within,
And nail My body to the Cross.

'The livelong night, the livelong day,
A Child upon that Cross I rest;
All night I for My children pray,
All day I woo them to My breast.

'Long years of toil and pain are Mine,
Ere I be lifted up to die,
Where cold the Paschal moonbeams shine
At noon on darkened Calvary.

'Then will the thorn-wreath pierce My brow,
The nails will fix Me to the tree;
But I shall hang as I do now,
Self-crucified for love of thee!'

CHRISTINA GEORGINA ROSSETTI

1830-1894

Hymn, after Gabriele Rossetti

MY Lord, my Love! in pleasant pain
How often have I said,
'Blessèd that John who on Thy breast
Laid down his head.'
It was that contact all divine
Transformed him from above,
And made him amongst men the man
To show forth holy love.

Yet shall I envy blessèd John?
Nay not so verily,
Now that Thou, Lord, both Man and God,
Dost dwell in me:
Upbuilding with Thy Manhood's might
My frail humanity;
Yea, Thy Divinehood pouring forth,
In fullness filling me.

Me, Lord, Thy temple consecrate,
Even me to Thee alone;
Lord, reign upon my willing heart
Which is Thy throne:
To Thee the Seraphim fall down
Adoring round Thy house;
For which of them hath tasted Thee
My Manna and my Spouse?

Now that Thy life lives in my soul
And sways and warms it through,
I scarce seem lesser than the world,
Thy temple too.

O God, who dwellest in my heart,
    My God who fillest me,
The broad immensity itself
    Hath not encompassed Thee.

After Communion

WHY should I call Thee Lord, Who art my God?
    Why should I call Thee Friend, Who art my Love?
    Or King, Who art my very Spouse above?
Or call Thy Sceptre on my heart Thy rod?
    Lo now Thy banner over me is love,
All heaven flies open to me at Thy nod:
For Thou hast lit Thy flame in me a clod,
    Made me a nest for dwelling of Thy Dove.
    What wilt Thou call me in our home above,
Who now hast called me friend? how will it be
    When Thou for good wine settest forth the best?
Now Thou dost bid me come and sup with Thee,
    Now Thou dost make me lean upon Thy breast:
How will it be with me in time of love?

THOMAS EDWARD BROWN

1830-1897

Pain

THE man that hath great griefs I pity not;
    'Tis something to be great
    In any wise, and hint the larger state,
Though but in shadow of a shade, God wot!

Moreover, while we wait the possible,
    This man has touched the fact,
    And probed till he has felt the core, where, packed
In pulpy folds, resides the ironic ill.

And while we others sip the obvious sweet–
    Lip-licking after-taste
    Of glutinous rind, lo! this man hath made haste,
And pressed the sting that holds the central seat.

For thus it is God stings us into life,
    Provoking actual souls
    From bodily systems, giving us the poles
That are His own, not merely balanced strife.

Nay, the great passions are His veriest thought,
    Which whoso can absorb,
    Nor, querulous halting, violate their orb,
In him the mind of God is fullest wrought.

Thrice happy such an one! Far other he
    Who dallies on the edge
    Of the great vortex, clinging to a sedge
Of patent good, a timorous Manichee;

Who takes the impact of a long-breathed force,
    And fritters it away
    In eddies of disgust, that else might stay
His nerveless heart, and fix it to the course.

For there is threefold oneness with the One;
    And he is one, who keeps
    The homely laws of life; who, if he sleeps,
Or wakes, in his true flesh God's will is done.

And he is one, who takes the deathless forms,
    Who schools himself to think
    With the All-thinking, holding fast the link,
God-riveted, that bridges casual storms.

But tenfold one is he, who feels all pains
    Not partial, knowing them
    As ripples parted from the gold-beaked stem,
Wherewith God's galley onward ever strains.

To him the sorrows are the tension-thrills
    Of that serene endeavour,
    Which yields to God for ever and for ever
The joy that is more ancient than the hills.

My Garden

A GARDEN is a lovesome thing, God wot!
Rose plot,
Fringed pool,
Ferned grot–
The veriest school
Of peace; and yet the fool
Contends that God is not–
Not God! in gardens! when the eve is cool?
Nay, but I have a sign;
'Tis very sure God walks in mine.

Disguises

HIGH stretched upon the swinging yard,
I gather in the sheet;
But it is hard
And stiff, and one cries haste.
Then He that is most dear in my regard
Of all the crew gives aidance meet;
But from His hands, and from His feet,
A glory spreads wherewith the night is starred:

Moreover of a cup most bitter-sweet
With fragrance as of nard,
And myrrh, and cassia spiced,
He proffers me to taste.
Then I to Him:–'Art Thou the Christ?'
He saith–'Thou say'st.'

Like to an ox
That staggers 'neath the mortal blow,
She grinds upon the rocks:–
Then straight and low
Leaps forth the levelled line, and in our quarter locks
The cradle's rigged; with swerving of the blast
We go,
Our Captain last–
Demands
'Who fired that shot?' Each silent stands–
Ah, sweet perplexity!
This too was He.

I have an arbour wherein came a toad
Most hideous to see–
Immediate, seizing staff or goad,
I smote it cruelly.
Then all the place with subtle radiance glowed–
I looked, and it was He!

Land, Ho!

I KNOW 'tis but a loom of land,
Yet is it land, and so I will rejoice,
I know I cannot hear His voice
Upon the shore, nor see Him stand;
Yet is it land, ho! land.

The land! the land! the lovely land!
'Far off,' dost say? *Far off*–ah, blessèd home!
Farewell! farewell! thou salt sea-foam!
Ah, keel upon the silver sand–
Land, ho! land.

You cannot see the land, my land,
You cannot see, and yet the land is there–
My land, my land, through murky air–
I did not say 'twas close at hand–
But–land, ho! land.

Dost hear the bells of my sweet land,
Dost hear the kine, dost hear the merry birds?
No voice, 'tis true, no spoken words,
No tongue that thou may'st understand–
Yet is it land, ho! land.

It's clad in purple mist, my land,
In regal robe it is apparellèd,
A crown is set upon its head,
And on its breast a golden band–
Land, ho! land.

Dost wonder that I long for land?
My land is not a land as others are–
Upon its crest there beams a star,
And lilies grow upon the strand–
Land, ho! land.

Give me the helm! there is the land!
Ha! lusty mariners, she takes the breeze!
And what my spirit sees it sees–
Leap, bark, as leaps the thunderbrand–
Land, ho! land.

Specula

WHEN He appoints to meet thee, go thou forth–
It matters not
If south or north,
Bleak waste or sunny plot.
Nor think, if haply He thou seek'st be late,
He does thee wrong.
To stile or gate
Lean thou thy head, and long!
It may be that to spy thee He is mounting
Upon a tower,
Or in thy counting
Thou hast mista'en the hour.
But, if He comes not, neither do thou go
Till Vesper chime
Belike thou then shalt know
He hath been with thee all the time.

JEAN INGELOW

1830-1897

From 'Scholar and Carpenter'

'GRAND is the leisure of the earth;
She gives her happy myriads birth,
And after harvest fears not dearth,
But goes to sleep in snow-wreaths dim.
Dread is the leisure up above
The while He sits whose name is Love,
And waits, as Noah did, for the dove,
To wit if she would fly to him.

'He waits for us, while, houseless things,
We beat about with bruisèd wings
On the dark floods and water-springs,
    The ruined world, the desolate sea;
With open windows from the prime
All night, all day, He waits sublime,
Until the fullness of the time
    Decreed from His eternity.

'Where is OUR leisure?–Give us rest.
Where is the quiet we possessed?
We must have had it once–were blest
    With peace whose phantoms yet entice.
Sorely the mother of mankind
Longed for the garden left behind;
For we still prove some yearnings blind
    Inherited from Paradise.'

'Hold, heart!' I cried; 'for trouble sleeps,
I hear no sound of aught that weeps;
I will not look into thy deeps–
    I am afraid, I am afraid!'
'Afraid!' she saith; 'and yet 'tis true
That what man dreads he still should view–
Should do the thing he fears to do,
    And storm the ghosts in ambuscade!'

'What good!' I sigh. 'Was reason meant
To straighten branches that are bent,
Or soothe an ancient discontent,
    The instinct of a race dethroned?
Ah! doubly should that instinct go,
Must the four rivers cease to flow,
Nor yield those rumours sweet and low
    Wherewith man's life is undertoned.'

'Yet had I but the past,' she cries,
'And it was lost, I would arise
And comfort me some other wise.
    But more than loss about me clings:
I am but restless with my race;
The whispers from a heavenly place,
Once dropped among us, seem to chase
    Rest with their prophet-visitings.

'The race is like a child, as yet
Too young for all things to be set
Plainly before him, with no let
    Or hindrance meet for his degree;
But ne'ertheless by much too old
Not to perceive that men withhold
More of the story than is told,
    And so infer a mystery.

'If the Celestials daily fly
With messages on missions high,
And float, our nests and turrets nigh,
    Conversing on Heaven's great intents;
What wonder hints of coming things,
Whereto men's hope and yearning clings,
Should drop like feathers from their wings
    And give us vague presentiments.

'And as the waxing moon can take
The tidal waters in her wake,
And lead them round and round, to break
    Obedient to her drawings dim;
So may the movements of His mind,
The first Great Father of mankind,
Affect with answering movements blind,
    And draw the souls that breathe by Him.

'We had a message long ago
That like a river peace should flow,
And Eden bloom again below.
We heard, and we began to wait:
Full soon that message men forgot;
Yet waiting is their destined lot,
And, waiting for they know not what,
They strive with yearnings passionate.'

SIR EDWIN ARNOLD

1832-1904

From 'The Light of Asia'

OM, AMITAYA! measure not with words
Th' Immeasurable; nor sink the string of thought
Into the Fathomless. Who asks doth err,
Who answers, errs. Say nought!

The Books teach Darkness was, at first of all,
And Brahm, sole meditating in that Night:
Look not for Brahm and the Beginning there!
Nor him, nor any light

Shall any gazer see with mortal eyes,
Or any searcher know by mortal mind;
Veil after veil will lift–but there must be
Veil upon veil behind.

Stars sweep and question not. This is enough
That life and death and joy and woe abide;
And cause and sequence, and the course of time,
And Being's ceaseless tide,

Which, ever changing, runs, linked like a river
By ripples following ripples, fast or slow–
The same yet not the same–from far-off fountain
To where its waters flow

Into the seas. These, steaming to the Sun,
Give the lost wavelets back in cloudy fleece
To trickle down the hills, and glide again;
Having no pause or peace.

This is enough to know, the phantasms are;
The Heavens, Earths, Worlds, and changes changing them,
A mighty whirling wheel of strife and stress
Which none can stay or stem. . . .

If ye lay bound upon the wheel of change,
And no way were of breaking from the chain,
The Heart of boundless Being is a curse,
The Soul of Things fell Pain.

Ye are not bound! the Soul of Things is sweet,
The Heart of Being is celestial rest;
Stronger than woe is will: that which was Good
Doth pass to Better–Best.

I, Buddh, who wept with all my brothers' tears,
Whose heart was broken by a whole world's woe,
Laugh and am glad, for there is Liberty!
Ho! ye who suffer! know

Ye suffer from yourselves. None else compels,
None other holds you that ye live and die,
And whirl upon the wheel, and hug and kiss
Its spokes of agony,

Its tire of tears, its nave of nothingness.
 Behold, I show you Truth! Lower than hell,
Higher than Heaven, outside the utmost stars,
 Farther than Brahm doth dwell,

Before beginning, and without an end,
 As space eternal and as surety sure,
Is fixed a Power divine which moves to good,
 Only its laws endure. . . .

That which ye sow ye reap. See yonder fields!
 The sesamum was sesamum, the corn
Was corn. The Silence and the Darkness knew!
 So is a man's fate born. . . .

If he shall day by day dwell merciful,
 Holy and just and kind and true; and rend
Desire from where it clings with bleeding roots,
 Till love of life have end:

He–dying–leaveth as the sum of him
 A life-count closed, whose ills are dead and quit,
Whose good is quick and mighty, far and near,
 So that fruits follow it.

No need hath such to live as ye name life;
 That which began in him when he began
Is finished: he hath wrought the purpose through
 Of what did make him Man.

Never shall yearnings torture him, nor sins
 Stain him, nor ache of earthly joys and woes
Invade his safe eternal peace; nor deaths
 And lives recur. He goes

Unto NIRVÂNA. He is one with Life,
Yet lives not. He is blest, ceasing to be.
OM, MANI PADME, OM! the Dewdrop slips
Into the shining sea! . . .

AH! BLESSED LORD ! OH, HIGH DELIVERER!
FORGIVE THIS FEEBLE SCRIPT,
WHICH DOTH THEE WRONG,
MEASURING WITH LITTLE WIT THY LOFTY LOVE.
AH! LOVER! BROTHER! GUIDE! LAMP OF THE LAW!
I TAKE MY REFUGE IN THY NAME AND THEE!
I TAKE MY REFUGE IN THY LAW OF GOOD!
I TAKE MY REFUGE IN THY ORDER! *OM* !
THE DEW IS ON THE LOTUS!—RISE, GREAT SUN!
AND LIFT MY LEAF AND MIX ME WITH THE WAVE.
OM MANI PADME HUM, THE SUNRISE COMES !
THE DEWDROP SLIPS INTO THE SHINING SEA !

SIR LEWIS MORRIS

1833-1907

A Heathen Hymn

O LORD, the Giver of my days,
My heart is ready, my heart is ready;
I dare not hold my peace, nor pause,
For I am fain to sing Thy praise.

I praise Thee not, with impious pride,
For that Thy partial hand has given
Bounties of wealth or form or brain,
Good gifts to other men denied.

Nor weary Thee with blind request,
For fancied goods Thy hand withholds;
I know not what to fear or hope,
Nor aught but that Thy will is best.

Not whence I come, nor whither I go,
Nor wherefore I am here, I know;
Nor if my life's tale ends on earth,
Or mounts to bliss, or sinks to woe.

Nor know I aught of Thee, O Lord;
Behind the veil Thy face is hidden:
We faint, and yet Thy face is hidden;
We cry,–Thou answerest not a word.

But this I know, O Lord, Thou art,
And by Thee I too live and am;
We stand together, face to face,
Thou the great whole, and I the part.

We stand together, soul to soul,
Alone amidst Thy waste of worlds;
Unchanged, though all creation fade,
And Thy swift suns forget to roll.

Wherefore, because my life is Thine,
Because, without Thee I were not;
Because, as doth the sea, the sun,
My nature gives back the Divine.

Because my being with ceaseless flow
Sets to Thee as the brook to the sea;
Turns to Thee, as the flower to the sun,
And seeks what it may never know.

Because, without me Thou hadst been
For ever, seated midst Thy suns;
Marking the soulless cycles turn,
Yet wert Thyself unknown, unseen.

I praise Thee, everlasting Lord.
In life and death, in heaven and hell:
What care I, since indeed Thou art,
And I the creature of Thy word.

Only if such a thing may be:
When all Thy infinite will is done,
Take back the soul Thy breath has given,
And let me lose myself in Thee.

A New Orphic Hymn

THE peaks, and the starlit skies, the deeps of the fathomless seas,
Immanent is He in all, yet higher and deeper than these.

The heart, and the mind, and the soul, the thoughts and the yearnings of Man,
Of His essence are one and all, and yet define it who can?

The love of the Right, tho' cast down, the hate of victorious Ill,
All are sparks from the central fire of a boundless beneficent Will.

Oh, mystical secrets of Nature, great Universe undefined,
Ye are part of the infinite work of a mighty ineffable Mind.

Beyond your limitless Space, before your measureless Time,
Ere Life or Death began was this changeless Essence sublime.

In the core of eternal calm He dwelleth unmoved and alone
'Mid the Universe He has made, as a monarch upon his throne.

And the self-same inscrutable Power which fashioned
the sun and the star
Is Lord of the feeble strength of the humblest creatures
that are.

The weak things that float or creep for their little life
of a day,
The weak souls that falter and faint, as feeble and futile
as they;

The malefic invisible atoms unmarked by man's purblind
eye
That beleaguer our House of Life, and compass us till
we die;

All these are parts of Him, the indivisible One,
Who supports and illumines the many, Creation's Pillar
and Sun!

Yea, and far in the depths of Being, too dark for a mortal
brain,
Lurk His secrets of Evil and Wrong, His creatures of
Death and of Pain.

A viewless Necessity binds, a determinate Impetus drives
To a hidden invisible goal the freightage of numberless lives.

The waste, and the pain, and the wrong, the abysmal
mysteries dim,
Come not of themselves alone, but are seed and issue of Him.

And Man's spirit that spends and is spent in mystical
questionings,
Oh, the depths of the fathomless deep, oh, the riddle and
secret of things,
And the voice through the darkness heard, and the rush
of winnowing wings!

273

RICHARD WATSON DIXON

1833-1900

Rapture: An Ode

I

WHAT is this?
The white and crumbling clouds leave bare the blue;
Shines out the central sun with golden hue;
And all the fruit-trees, rolling blossom-boughed,
Are white and billowy as the rolling cloud.
The warm beam bedded sleeps upon the trees,
The springing thickets and the gorse-bound leas;
Sleeps where I lie at ease,
Pulling the ruby orchis and the pale
Half-withered cowslip from the hill-side grass,
Midway the brow that overhangs the vale,
Where the sleepy shadows pass,
And the sunbeam sleeps till all is grown
Into one burning sapphire stone,
All air, all earth, each violet-deepened zone.

II

It sleeps and broods upon the moss-mapped stone,
The thready mosses and the plumy weeds;
Numbers the veined flowers one after one,
Their colours and their leaves and ripening seeds:
Above, around, its influence proceeds;
It tracks in gleams the stream through crowding bush,
And beds of sworded flags and bearded rush,
Where slow it creeps along the lower ground;
The ridges far above are all embrowned,
The golden heavens over all are ploughed
In furrows of fine tissue that abound,
And melting fragments of the whitest cloud.

III

Ah, what is this, that now with sated eyes
And humming ears the soul no more descries?
Drawn back upon the spirit all the sense
Becomes intelligence;
And to be doubly now unfolded feels
That which itself reveals;
Double the world of all that may appear
To eye or hand or ear;
Double the soul of that which apprehends
By that which sense transcends.

IV

For deep the cave of human consciousness;
The thoughts, like light, upon its depths may press,
Seeking and finding wonders numberless;
But never may they altogether pierce
The hollow gloom so sensitive and fierce
Of the deep bosom: far the light may reach,
There is a depth unreached; in clearest speech
There is an echo from an unknown place:
And in the dim, unknown, untrodden space
Our life is hidden; were we all self-known,
No longer should we live; a wonder shown
Is wonderful no more; and being flies
For ever from its own self-scrutinies.
Here is the very effort of the soul
To keep itself unmingled, safe, and whole
In changes and the flitting feints of sense:
Here essence holds a calm and sure defence;
It is a guarded shrine and sacred grove,
A fountain hidden where no foot may rove,
A further depth within a sounded sea;
A mirror 'tis from hour to hour left free

By things reflected: and because 'tis so,
Therefore the outer world and all its show
Is as the music of the upper wave
To the deep Ocean in his sunken cave;
A part of its own self, yet but its play,
Which doth the sunbeam and the cloud convey
To central deeps, where in awful shade
The stormless heart receives the things conveyed,
Knowing the cloud by darkness, and the light
By splendours dying through the infinite.

V

And being such the soul doth recognize
The doubleness of nature, that there lies
A soul occult in Nature, hidden deep
As lies the soul of man in moveless sleep.
And like a dream
Broken in circumstance and foolish made,
Through which howe'er the future world doth gleam,
And floats a warning to the gathered thought,
Like to a dream,
Through sense and all by sense conveyed,
Into our soul the shadow of that soul
Doth float.
Then are we lifted up erect and whole
In vast confession to that universe
Perceived by us: our soul itself transfers
Thither by instinct sure; it swiftly hails
The mighty spirit similar; it sails
In the divine expansion; it perceives
Tendencies glorious, distant; it enweaves
Itself with excitations more than thought
Unto that soul unveiled and yet unsought.

VI

Ye winds and clouds of light,
  Ye lead the soul to God;
The new-born soul that height
With rapturous foot hath trod,
And is received of God:
God doth the soul receive
Which mounts toward Him, and alone would dwell
With Him; though finite with the Infinite,
Though finite, rising with a might
Like to infinitude.
Gently receiving such He doth dispel
All solitary horror with delight,
Honouring the higher mood.

VII

For though the soul pants with fierce ecstasy
The unattainable to grasp, to be
For ever mingled with infinity;
And this in vain, since God Himself withdraws
From human knowledge, e'en as its own laws
Seclude the soul from sense;
Yet not from love He hies;
From love God never flies.
Love is the soul's best sense, which God descries,
Which bares the covert of intelligence:
And, honouring in love the higher mood,
With lovely joys He fills the solitude
Of His own presence, whither trusting Him
The soul hath mounted: lo, it might have found
Utter destruction on this higher ground,
Tenuity of air and swooning dim

For lack of breath; but now it finds hereby
A lovely vesture of infinity,
And ecstasies that nourish ecstasy.
God giveth love to love, and ministers
Substance to substance; life to life He bears.

VIII

Therefore, ye winds and ye
High moving clouds of light,
Ye rivers running free,
Thou glory of the sea,
Thou glory of the height,
The gleam beside the bush,
The tremble of the rush,
To me made manifest,
The beauty of the flower
In summer's sunny power,
Portions of entity supreme ye be,
And motions massed upon eternal rest.

IX

Broad breezes, clouds of light,
Thither ye lead the soul,
To this most sacred height
Above the sacred whole:
The azure world is not so fair,
The azure world and all the circling air,
As that true spiritual kingdom known
Unto the spirit only and alone;
Thither the soul ye bear,
Oh winds and clouds of light.

X

Ye winds and clouds of light,
    That bear the soul to God;
The new-born soul that height
    By ecstasy hath trod.

RODEN BERKELEY WRIOTHESLEY NOEL

1834-1894

From 'Pan'

AH! Nature, would that I before I pass
Might thrill with joy of thy communion
One childlife only knowing thee from far!
Love we may well, for surely one were nought
Without the other, intermarrying breath;
Nature the systole, thought the diastole
Of one Divine forever-beating Heart.
Feeding from her maternal breast we grow
Full to our height of stately dominance,
And yet create, yea dower as we grow
Her with all colour, form and comeliness.
Nature the heaving of a tender breast
Revealing inspiration from within,
Sweet rending of a calyx, telling clear
Expansion of the spirit's folded flower,
Nature the lake where looking long we fall
With our own likeness tremulous in love.

. . . .

And shall we climb, ascension infinite,
From star to star? explore from world to world–
Gods reigning yonder in the tranquil stars?
Death! what is Death? a turning-point of Life

Winding so sharp the way dips out of sight,
Seeming to end, yet winding on for ever
Through teeming glories of the Infinite.
Look with bold eyes unquailing in the face
Of that foul haunting phantom, it will fade,
Melt to the face of some familiar friend. . . .[1]

One selfsame Spirit breathing evermore
Rouses in each the momentary wave,
One water and one motion and one wind,
Now feeble undulation myriadfold,
Now headlong mountain thunder-clothed and crowned
With foamy lightning; such we name Zerduscht,
Dante, Spinoza, or Napoleon–
The motion travels, and the wave subsides. . . .[1]

May cold ascetic hard, ill-favoured, crude,
Ever persuade me vision and fond play
Of sense about fair fleshly loveliness
Of youth in man or woman is accurst–
Since God hath made the spirit, but a fiend
Hath mocked it with a syren phantom-flesh?–
Nay, to mine ear 'tis rankest blasphemy!
For is not flesh the shadow of the soul,
Her younger sister, both alike Divine?
Yea verily! for when I love a friend
How may I sunder body from the soul?
Few win my love, but they who win it seem
Ever well-favoured to me, and I greet
All comeliness of colour and of form,
Mere side reverse of spiritual grace.
Yea, limbs well turned and bodies almond-smooth
Full fair and white in maiden or in youth,
With what sense-thrillings may attend on these;

[1] These dots are the author's, and do not mark omissions.

All lusty might of supple athletic men;
Are surely worthy reverence like flowers,
Or like the culminating heart and soul.
Only to each one yield his very own:
Yield to young sense his toy of fantasy,
And never frown until he glides to steal
The royal sceptre from Intelligence,
Or crown of light from spiritual Love.
Nor dare to maim lives infinite Divine
Seeking to graft one pale monotonous flower;
For is not Being thirsting to exhaust
His all exhaustless capability?
Evil mere vantage-ground for an advance,
If not for thee, yet for the universe,
And so for thee as member of the whole.

From 'De Profundis'

THE Spirit grows the form for self-expression,
And for a hall where she may hold high session
With sister souls, who, allied with her, create
Her fair companion, her espousèd mate.
Ever the hidden Person will remould
For all our lives fresh organs manifold,
Gross for the earthly, for the heavenly fine,
Ethereal woof, wherein their graces shine.
And there be secret avenues, with doors
Yielding access to inmost chamber floors
Of the soul's privacy; all varying frames,
Responsive to the several spirit-flames.
The vital form our lost now animate
Is one with what in their low mortal state
They made their own; the corse mere ashes, waste,

For all grand uses of the world replaced.
A larva needs no more the unliving husk,
When soaring winged he rends the dwelling dusk.

A rabble rout of Sense light-headed pours
Into the holy Spirit-temple doors,
Where many a grave and stately minister
His place and function doth on each confer.
These Forms inhabiting the sacred gloom,
Whose name is legion, Present, Past, To Come,
One, Many, Same, or Different, evolve
Sweet concord from confusion; they resolve
The Babel dissonance to a choral song,
Till in divine societies a throng
Sets with one will toward the inmost shrine,
To feed there upon mystic Bread and Wine.
The Bacchanals are sobered, and grow grave,
In solemn silence treading the dim nave:
On their light hearts bloom-pinioned angels lay
Calm, hushful hands of married night and day.

It is a changing scene within the pile:
New shows arrive, and tarry for a while:
But if one living Spirit-fane could fall,
His ruin were the knell of doom for all.
Their being blended each with every one,
If any failed, the universe were gone.
These conscious forms inhabit every mind;
All selves in one organic self they bind;
The bloomy beams, and all the shadowy blooms
Are pure white Light eternal that illumes
A universal conscious Spirit-whole,
Fair modulated in each several soul
To many-functioned organs of one Will,
Whose sovran Being who prevails to kill?

We may expand our being to embrace,
And mirror all therein of every race;
Each is himself by universal grace.
Dying is self-fulfilment; and we cherish
His life, who, wanting ours, would wholly perish.
The Father may not be without the Son;
No love, will, knowledge, were for Him alone.
And change is naught
Save at the bar of a sole personal thought,
Enthroned for judgment, summoning past time
With present, hearing now concordant rhyme,
Now variance among voices vanishing,
That so win semblance of substantial thing.
But how conceive that there may ever be
Change in the nerve of change, our known identity?

If we, poor worms, involved in our own cloud,
Deem the wide world lies darkling in a shroud,
Raving the earth holds no felicity,
One child's clear laughter may rebuke the lie,
A lark's light rapture soaring in the blue,
Or rainbow radiant from a drop of dew!

Nor let a low-born Sense usurp the rule,
Who is but handmaid in a loftier school,
Where Love and Conscience a lore not of earth
Impart to Wisdom, child of heavenly birth.
O Thou unknown, inscrutable Divine!
I deem that I am Thine, and Thou art mine;
And though I may not gaze into Thy face,
I feel that all are clasped in Thine embrace.
The Christ is with us, and He points to Thee:
When we have grown into Him we shall see;
Behold the Father in the perfect Son,
And feel, with Him, Thy holy will be done!

Love may not compass her full harmony,
Wanting the deep dread note of those who die.
And as with master-hand He sweeps the grand awakening chords,
Our wailing sighs leap winged, live talismanic words,
Dull woes and errors tempered to seraphic swords,
Love's colour-chorus flames with glorious morning-red,
His alchemy transmuting the poured heart's blood of our dead,
And lurid bale from murderous eyes of souls who inly bled!

Whose mortal mind may sail around the ocean of Thy might,
Billowing away in awful gloom to issues infinite?
Bind Thee with his poor girdle? Surveying all thy shore!
His daring sinks confounded, foundering evermore,
In his dazed ear reverberating a tempestuous roar!
. . .Who sounds the abyss of Thine immense design? We rest,
Aware that Thou art better than our best.

SIR ALFRED COMYN LYALL

1835-1911

From 'Sîva"

'Mors Janua Vitae.'

I AM the God of the sensuous fire
That moulds all Nature in forms divine;
The symbols of death and of man's desire,
The springs of change in the world, are mine;
The organs of birth and the circlet of bones,
And the light loves carved on the temple stones.

I am the lord of delights and pain,
    Of the pest that killeth, of fruitful joys;
I rule the currents of heart and vein;
    A touch gives passion, a look destroys;
In the heat and cold of my lightest breath
Is the might incarnate of Lust and Death.

If a thousand altars stream with blood
    Of the victims slain by the chanting priest,
Is a great God lured by the savoury food?
    I reck not of worship, or song, or feast;
But that millions perish, each hour that flies,
Is the mystic sign of my sacrifice.

Ye may plead and pray for the millions born;
    They come like dew on the morning grass;
Your vows and vigils I hold in scorn,
    The soul stays never, the stages pass;
All life is the play of the power that stirs
In the dance of my wanton worshippers.

And the strong swift river my shrine below
    It runs, like man, its unending course
To the boundless sea from eternal snow;
    Mine is the Fountain–and mine the Force
That spurs all nature to ceaseless strife;
And my image is Death at the gates of Life.

In many a legend and many a shape,
    In the solemn grove and the crowded street,
I am the Slayer, whom none escape;
    I am Death trod under a fair girl's feet;
I govern the tides of the sentient sea
That ebbs and flows to eternity.

And the sum of the thought and the knowledge of man
Is the secret tale that my emblems tell;
Do ye seek God's purpose, or trace his plan?
Ye may read your doom in my parable:
For the circle of life in its flower and its fall
Is the writing that runs on my temple wall. . . .

Let my temples fall, they are dark with age,
Let my idols break, they have stood their day;
On their deep hewn stones the primeval sage
Has figured the spells that endure alway;
My presence may vanish from river and grove,
But I rule for ever in Death and Love.

FRANCES RIDLEY HAVERGAL

1836-1879

From 'The Thoughts of God'

THEY say there is a hollow, safe and still,
A point of coolness and repose
Within the centre of a flame, where life might dwell
Unharmed and unconsumed, as in a luminous shell,
Which the bright walls of fire enclose
In breachless splendour, barrier that no foes
Could pass at will.

There is a point of rest
At the great centre of the cyclone's force,
A silence at its secret source;–
A little child might slumber undistressed,
Without the ruffle of one fairy curl,
In that strange central calm amid the mighty whirl.

So in the centre of these thoughts of God,
Cyclones of power, consuming glory-fire,–
As we fall o'erawed
Upon our faces, and are lifted higher
By His great gentleness, and carried nigher
Than unredeemèd angels, till we stand
Even in the hollow of His hand,–
Nay more! we lean upon His breast–
There, there we find a point of perfect rest
And glorious safety. There we see
His thoughts to us-ward, thoughts of peace
That stoop to tenderest love; that still increase
With increase of our need; that never change,
That never fail, or falter, or forget.
O pity infinite!
O royal mercy free!
O gentle climax of the depth and height
Of God's most precious thoughts, most wonderful, most
strange!
'For I am poor and needy, yet
The Lord Himself, Jehovah, *thinketh upon me!'*

ALGERNON CHARLES SWINBURNE

1837-1909

Hertha

I AM that which began;
Out of me the years roll;
Out of me God and man;
I am equal and whole;
God changes, and man, and the form of them bodily;
I am the soul.

Before ever land was,
Before ever the sea,
Or soft hair of the grass,
Or fair limbs of the tree,
Or the flesh-coloured fruit of my branches, I was, and thy soul was in me.

First life on my sources
First drifted and swam;
Out of me are the forces
That save it or damn;
Out of me man and woman, and wild-beast and bird:
Before God was, I am.

Beside or above me
Naught is there to go;
Love or unlove me,
Unknow me or know,
I am that which unloves me and loves ; I am stricken, and I am the blow.

I the mark that is missed
And the arrows that miss,
I the mouth that is kissed
And the breath in the kiss,
The search, and the sought, and the seeker, the soul and the body that is.

I am that thing which blesses
My spirit elate;
That which caresses
With hands uncreate
My limbs unbegotten that measure the length of the measure of fate.

But what thing dost thou now,
Looking Godward, to cry
'I am I, thou art thou,
I am low, thou art high'?
I am thou, whom thou seekest to find him; find thou but
thyself, thou art I.

I the grain and the furrow,
The plough-cloven clod
And the ploughshare drawn thorough,
The germ and the sod,
The deed and the doer, the seed and the sower, the dust
which is God.

Hast thou known how I fashioned thee,
Child, underground?
Fire that impassioned thee,
Iron that bound,
Dim changes of water, what thing of all these hast thou
known of or found?

Canst thou say in thine heart
Thou hast seen with thine eyes
With what cunning of art
Thou wast wrought in what wise,
By what force of what stuff thou wast shapen, and shown
on my breast to the skies?

Who hath given, who hath sold it thee,
Knowledge of me?
Hath the wilderness told it thee?
Hast thou learnt of the sea?
Hast thou communed in spirit with night? have the
winds taken counsel with thee?

Have I set such a star
To show light on thy brow
That thou sawest from afar
What I show to thee now?
Have ye spoken as brethren together, the sun and the mountains and thou?

What is here, dost thou know it?
What was, hast thou known?
Prophet nor poet
Nor tripod nor throne
Nor spirit nor flesh can make answer, but only thy mother alone.

Mother, not maker,
Born, and not made;
Though her children forsake her,
Allured or afraid,
Praying prayers to the God of their fashion, she stirs not for all that have prayed.

A creed is a rod,
And a crown is of night;
But this thing is God,
To be man with thy might,
To grow straight in the strength of thy spirit, and live out thy life as the light.

I am in thee to save thee,
As my soul in thee saith,
Give thou as I gave thee,
Thy life-blood and breath,
Green leaves of thy labour, white flowers of thy thought, and red fruit of thy death.

Be the ways of thy giving
As mine were to thee;
The free life of thy living,
Be the gift of it free;
Not as servant to lord, nor as master to slave, shalt thou give thee to me.

O children of banishment,
Souls overcast,
Were the lights ye see vanish meant
Alway to last,
Ye would know not the sun overshining the shadows and stars overpast.

I that saw where ye trod
The dim paths of the night
Set the shadow called God
In your skies to give light;
But the morning of manhood is risen, and the shadowless soul is in sight.

The tree many-rooted
That swells to the sky
With frondage red-fruited,
The life-tree am I;
In the buds of your lives is the sap of my leaves: ye shall live and not die.

But the Gods of your fashion
That take and that give,
In their pity and passion
That scourge and forgive,
They are worms that are bred in the bark that falls off; they shall die and not live.

My own blood is what stanches
The wounds in my bark;
Stars caught in my branches
Make day of the dark,
And are worshipped as suns till the sunrise shall tread out
their fires as a spark.

Where dead ages hide under
The live roots of the tree,
In my darkness the thunder
Makes utterance of me;
In the clash of my boughs with each other ye hear the
waves sound of the sea.

That noise is of Time,
As his feathers are spread
And his feet set to climb
Through the boughs overhead,
And my foliage rings round him and rustles, and branches
are bent with his tread.

The storm-winds of ages
Blow through me and cease,
The war-wind that rages,
The spring-wind of peace,
Ere the breath of them roughen my tresses, ere one of
my blossoms increase.

All sounds of all changes,
All shadows and lights
On the world's mountain-ranges
And stream-riven heights,
Whose tongue is the wind's tongue and language of
storm-clouds on earth-shaking nights;

All forms of all faces,
All works of all hands
In unsearchable places
Of time-stricken lands,
All death and all life, and all reigns and all ruins, drop
through me as sands.

Though sore be my burden
And more than ye know,
And my growth have no guerdon
But only to grow,
Yet I fail not of growing for lightnings above me or
deathworms below.

These too have their part in me,
As I too in these;
Such fire is at heart in me,
Such sap is this tree's,
Which hath in it all sounds and all secrets of infinite lands
and of seas.

In the spring-coloured hours
When my mind was as May's,
There brake forth of me flowers
By centuries of days,
Strong blossoms with perfume of manhood, shot out
from my spirit as rays.

And the sound of them springing
And smell of their shoots
Were as warmth and sweet singing
And strength to my roots;
And the lives of my children made perfect with freedom
of soul were my fruits.

I bid you but be;
I have need not of prayer;
I have need of you free
As your mouths of mine air;
That my heart may be greater within me, beholding the fruits of me fair.

More fair than strange fruit is
Of faiths ye espouse;
In me only the root is
That blooms in your boughs;
Behold now your God that ye made you, to feed him with faith of your vows.

In the darkening and whitening
Abysses adored,
With dayspring and lightning
For lamp and for sword,
God thunders in heaven, and his angels are red with the wrath of the Lord.

O my sons, O too dutiful
Toward Gods not of me,
Was not I enough beautiful?
Was it hard to be free?
For behold, I am with you, am in you and of you; look forth now and see.

Lo, winged with world's wonders,
With miracles shod,
With the fires of his thunders
For raiment and rod,
God trembles in heaven, and his angels are white with the terror of God.

For his twilight is come on him,
His anguish is here;
And his spirits gaze dumb on him,
Grown grey from his fear;
And his hour taketh hold on him stricken, the last of his infinite year.

Thought made him and breaks him,
Truth slays and forgives;
But to you, as time takes him,
This new thing it gives,
Even love, the beloved Republic, that feeds upon freedom and lives.

For truth only is living,
Truth only is whole,
And the love of his giving
Man's polestar and pole;
Man, pulse of my centre, and fruit of my body, and seed of my soul.

One birth of my bosom;
One beam of mine eye;
One topmost blossom
That scales the sky;
Man, equal and one with me, man that is made of me, man that is I.

A Nympholept

SUMMER, and noon, and a splendour of silence, felt,
Seen, and heard of the spirit within the sense.
Soft through the frondage the shades of the sunbeams melt,
Sharp through the foliage the shafts of them, keen and dense,
Cleave, as discharged from the string of the God's bow, tense
As a war-steed's girth, and bright as a warrior's belt.
Ah, why should an hour that is heaven for an hour pass hence?

I dare not sleep for delight of the perfect hour,
Lest God be wroth that his gift should be scorned of man.
The face of the warm bright world is the face of a flower,
The word of the wind and the leaves that the light winds fan
As the word that quickened at first into flame, and ran,
Creative and subtle and fierce with invasive power,
Through darkness and cloud, from the breath of the one God, Pan.

The perfume of earth possessed by the sun pervades
The chaster air that he soothes but with sense of sleep.
Soft, imminent, strong as desire that prevails and fades,
The passing noon that beholds not a cloudlet weep
Imbues and impregnates life with delight more deep
Than dawn or sunset or moonrise on lawns or glades
Can shed from the skies that receive it and may not keep.

The skies may hold not the splendour of sundown fast;
It wanes into twilight as dawn dies down into day.
And the moon, triumphant when twilight is overpast,
Takes pride but awhile in the hours of her stately sway.
But the might of the noon, though the light of it pass away,
Leaves earth fulfilled of desires and of dreams that last;
But if any there be that hath sense of them none can say.

For if any there be that hath sight of them, sense, or trust
Made strong by the might of a vision, the strength of a dream,
His lips shall straiten and close as a dead man's must,
His heart shall be sealed as the voice of a frost-bound stream.
For the deep mid mystery of light and of heat that seem
To clasp and pierce dark earth, and enkindle dust,
Shall a man's faith say what it is? or a man's guess deem?

Sleep lies not heavier on eyes that have watched all night
Than hangs the heat of the noon on the hills and trees.
Why now should the haze not open, and yield to sight
A fairer secret than hope or than slumber sees?
I seek not heaven with submission of lips and knees,
With worship and prayer for a sign till it leap to light:
I gaze on the gods about me, and call on these.

I call on the gods hard by, the divine dim powers
Whose likeness is here at hand, in the breathless air,
In the pulseless peace of the fervid and silent flowers,
In the faint sweet speech of the waters that whisper there.
Ah, what should darkness do in a world so fair?
The bent-grass heaves not, the couch-grass quails not or cowers;
The wind's kiss frets not the rowan's or aspen's hair.

But the silence trembles with passion of sound suppressed,
And the twilight quivers and yearns to the sunward, wrung
With love as with pain; and the wide wood's motionless breast
Is thrilled with a dumb desire that would fain find tongue
And palpitates, tongueless as she whom a man-snake stung,
Whose heart now heaves in the nightingale, never at rest
Nor satiated ever with song till her last be sung.

Is it rapture or terror that circles me round, and invades
Each vein of my life with hope–if it be not fear?
Each pulse that awakens my blood into rapture fades,
Each pulse that subsides into dread of a strange thing near
Requickens with sense of a terror less dread than dear.
Is peace not one with light in the deep green glades
Where summer at noonday slumbers? Is peace not here?

The tall thin stems of the firs, and the roof sublime
That screens from the sun the floor of the steep still wood,
Deep, silent, splendid, and perfect and calm as time,
Stand fast as ever in sight of the night they stood,
When night gave all that moonlight and dewfall could.
The dense ferns deepen, the moss glows warm as the thyme:
The wild heath quivers about me: the world is good.

Is it Pan's breath, fierce in the tremulous maidenhair,
That bids fear creep as a snake through the woodlands, felt
In the leaves that it stirs not yet, in the mute bright air,
In the stress of the sun? For here has the great God dwelt:
For hence were the shafts of his love or his anger dealt.
For here has his wrath been fierce as his love was fair,
When each was as fire to the darkness its breath bade melt.

Is it love, is it dread, that enkindles the trembling noon,
That yearns, reluctant in rapture that fear has fed,
As man for woman, as woman for man? Full soon,
If I live, and the life that may look on him drop not dead,
Shall the ear that hears not a leaf quake hear his tread,
The sense that knows not the sound of the deep day's tune
Receive the God, be it love that he brings or dread.

The naked noon is upon me: the fierce dumb spell,
The fearful charm of the strong sun's imminent might,
Unmerciful, steadfast, deeper than seas that swell,
Pervades, invades, appals me with loveless light,
With harsher awe than breathes in the breath of night.
Have mercy, God who art all! For I know thee well,
How sharp is thine eye to lighten, thine hand to smite.

The whole wood feels thee, the whole air fears thee: but fear
So deep, so dim, so sacred, is wellnigh sweet.
For the light that hangs and broods on the woodlands here,
Intense, invasive, intolerant, imperious, and meet
To lighten the works of thine hands and the ways of thy feet,
Is hot with the fire of the breath of thy life, and dear
As hope that shrivels or shrinks not for frost or heat.

Thee, thee the supreme dim godhead, approved afar,
Perceived of the soul and conceived of the sense of man
We scarce dare love, and we dare not fear: the star
We call the sun, that lit us when life began
To brood on the world that is thine by his grace for
a span,
Conceals and reveals in the semblance of things that are
Thine immanent presence, the pulse of thy heart's life,
Pan.

The fierce mid noon that wakens and warms the snake
Conceals thy mercy, reveals thy wrath: and again
The dew-bright hour that assuages the twilight brake
Conceals thy wrath and reveals thy mercy: then
Thou art fearful only for evil souls of men
That feel with nightfall the serpent within them wake,
And hate the holy darkness on glade and glen.

Yea, then we know not and dream not if ill things be,
Or if aught of the work of the wrong of the world be thine.
We hear not the footfall of terror that treads the sea,
We hear not the moan of winds that assail the pine:
We see not if shipwreck reign in the storm's dim shrine;
If death do service and doom bear witness to thee
We see not,–know not if blood for thy lips be wine.

But in all things evil and fearful that fear may scan,
As in all things good, as in all things fair that fall,
We know thee present and latent, the lord of man;
In the murmuring of doves, in the clamouring of winds
that call
And wolves that howl for their prey; in the mid-
night's pall,
In the naked and nymph-like feet of the dawn, O Pan,
And in each life living, O thou the God who art all.

Smiling and singing, wailing and wringing of hands,
  Laughing and weeping, watching and sleeping, still
Proclaim but and prove but thee, as the shifted sands
  Speak forth and show but the strength of the sea's
    wild will
  That sifts and grinds them as grain in the storm-
    wind's mill.
In thee is the doom that falls and the doom that stands:
  The tempests utter thy word, and the stars fulfil.

Where Etna shudders with passion and pain volcanic
  That rend her heart as with anguish that rends a man's,
Where Typho labours, and finds not his thews Titanic,
  In breathless torment that ever the flame's breath fans,
  Men felt and feared thee of old, whose pastoral clans
Were given to the charge of thy keeping; and soundless panic
  Held fast the woodland whose depths and whose
    heights were Pan's.

And here, though fear be less than delight, and awe
  Be one with desire and with worship of earth and thee,
So mild seems now thy secret and speechless law,
  So fair and fearless and faithful and godlike she,
  So soft the spell of thy whisper on stream and sea,
Yet man should fear lest he see what of old men saw
  And withered: yet shall I quail if thy breath smite me.

Lord God of life and of light and of all things fair,
  Lord God of ravin and ruin and all things dim,
Death seals up life, and darkness the sunbright air,
  And the stars that watch blind earth in the deep night
    swim
  Laugh, saying, 'What God is your God, that ye call
    on him?
What is man, that the God who is guide of our way
    should care
  If day for a man be golden, or night be grim?'

But thou, dost thou hear? Stars too but abide for
a span,
Gods too but endure for a season; but thou, if thou be
God, more than shadows conceived and adored of man,
Kind Gods and fierce, that bound him or made him free,
The skies that scorn us are less in thy sight than we,
Whose souls have strength to conceive and perceive thee,
Pan,
With sense more subtle than senses that hear and see.

Yet may it not say, though it seek thee and think to find
One soul of sense in the fire and the frost-bound clod,
What heart is this, what spirit alive or blind,
That moves thee: Only we know that the ways we trod
We tread, with hands unguided, with feet unshod,
With eyes unlightened; and yet, if with steadfast mind,
Perchance may we find thee and know thee at last for
God.

Yet then should God be dark as the dawn is bright,
And bright as the night is dark on the world–no more.
Light slays not darkness, and darkness absorbs not light;
And the labour of evil and good from the years of yore
Is even as the labour of waves on a sunless shore.
And he who is first and last, who is depth and height,
Keeps silence now, as the sun when the woods wax hoar.

The dark dumb godhead innate in the fair world's life
Imbues the rapture of dawn and of noon with dread,
Infects the peace of the star-shod night with strife,
Informs with terror the sorrow that guards the dead.
No service of bended knee or of humbled head
May soothe or subdue the God who has change to wife:
And life with death is as morning with evening weds.

And yet, if the light and the life in the light that here
Seem soft and splendid and fervid as sleep may seem
Be more than the shine of a smile or the flash of a tear,
Sleep, change, and death are less than a spell-struck dream,
And fear than the fall of a leaf on a starlit stream.
And yet, if the hope that hath said it absorb not fear,
What helps it man that the stars and the waters gleam?

What helps it man, that the noon be indeed intense,
The night be indeed worth worship? Fear and pain
Were lords and masters yet of the secret sense,
Which now dares deem not that light is as darkness, fain
Though dark dreams be to declare it, crying in vain.
For whence, thou God of the light and the darkness, whence
Dawns now this vision that bids not the sunbeams wane?

What light, what shadow, diviner than dawn or night,
Draws near, makes pause, and again–or I dream–draws near?
More soft than shadow, more strong that the strong sun's light,
More pure than moonbeams–yea, but the rays run sheer
As fire from the sun through the dusk of the pinewood, clear
And constant; yea, but the shadow itself is bright
That the light clothes round with love that is one with fear.

Above and behind it the noon and the woodland lie,
Terrible, radiant with mystery, superb and subdued,

Triumphant in silence; and hardly the sacred sky
Seems free from the tyrannous weight of the dumb fierce mood
Which rules as with fire and invasion of beams that brood
The breathless rapture of earth till its hour pass by
And leave her spirit released and her peace renewed.

I sleep not: never in sleep has a man beholden
This. From the shadow that trembles and yearns with light
Suppressed and elate and reluctant–obscure and golden
As water kindled with presage of dawn or night–
A form, a face, a wonder to sense and sight,
Grows great as the moon through the month; and her eyes embolden
Fear, till it change to desire, and desire to delight.

I sleep not: sleep would die of a dream so strange;
A dream so sweet would die as a rainbow dies,
As a sunbow laughs and is lost on the waves that range
And reck not of light that flickers or spray that flies.
But the sun withdraws not, the woodland shrinks not or sighs,
No sweet thing sickens with sense or with fear of change;
Light wounds not, darkness blinds not, my steadfast eyes.

Only the soul in my sense that receives the soul
Whence now my spirit is kindled with breathless bliss
Knows well if the light that wounds it with love makes whole,
If hopes that carol be louder than fears that hiss,
If truth be spoken of flowers and of waves that kiss,
Of clouds and stars that contend for a sunbright goal.
And yet may I dream that I dream not indeed of this?

An earth-born dreamer, constrained by the bonds of birth,
 Held fast by the flesh, compelled by his veins that beat
And kindle to rapture or wrath, to desire or to mirth,
 May hear not surely the fall of immortal feet,
 May feel not surely if heaven upon earth be sweet;
And here is my sense fulfilled of the joys of earth,
 Light, silence, bloom, shade, murmur of leaves that meet.

Bloom, fervour, and perfume of grasses and flowers aglow,
 Breathe and brighten about me: the darkness gleams,
The sweet light shivers and laughs on the slopes below,
 Made soft by leaves that lighten and change like dreams;
 The silence thrills with the whisper of secret streams
That well from the heart of the woodland: these I know:
 Earth bore them, heaven sustained them with showers
  and beams.

I lean my face to the heather, and drink the sun
 Whose flame-lit odour satiates the flowers: mine eyes
Close, and the goal of delight and of life is one:
 No more I crave of earth or her kindred skies.
 No more? But the joy that springs from them smiles
  and flies:
The sweet work wrought of them surely, the good work
  done,
 If the mind and the face of the season be loveless, dies.

Thee, therefore, thee would I come to, cleave to, cling,
 If haply thy heart be kind and thy gifts be good,
Unknown sweet spirit, whose vesture is soft in spring,
 In summer splendid, in autumn pale as the wood
 That shudders and wanes and shrinks as a shamed thing
  should,
In winter bright as the mail of a war-worn king
 Who stands where foes fled far from the face of him stood.

My spirit or thine is it, breath of thy life or of mine,
Which fills my sense with a rapture that casts out fear?
Pan's dim frown wanes, and his wild eyes brighten as thine,
Transformed as night or as day by the kindling year.
Earth-born, or mine eye were withered that sees, mine ear
That hears were stricken to death by the sense divine,
Earth-born I know thee: but heaven is about me here.

The terror that whispers in darkness and flames in light,
The doubt that speaks in the silence of earth and sea,
The sense, more fearful at noon than in midmost night,
Of wrath scarce hushed and of imminent ill to be,
Where are they? Heaven is as earth, and as heaven to me
Earth: for the shadows that sundered them here take flight;
And naught is all, as am I, but a dream of thee.

JOHN ADDINGTON SYMONDS

1840-1893

The Vanishing Point

THERE are who, when the bat on wing transverse
Skims the swart surface of some neighbouring mere,
Catch that thin cry too fine for common ear:
Thus the last joy-note of the universe
Is borne to those few listeners who immerse
Their intellectual hearing in no clear
Paean, but pierce it with the thin-edged spear
Of utmost beauty which contains a curse.
Dead on their sense fall marches hymeneal,
Triumphal odes, hymns, symphonies sonorous;
They crave one shrill vibration, tense, ideal,
Transcending and surpassing the world's chorus;
Keen, fine, ethereal, exquisitely real,
Intangible as star's light quivering o'er us.

The Prism of Life

ALL that began with God, in God must end:
All lives are garnered in His final bliss:
All wills hereafter shall be one with His:
When in the sea we sought, our spirits blend.
Rays of pure light, which one frail prism may rend
Into conflicting colours, meet and kiss
With manifold attraction, yet still miss
Contentment, while their kindred hues contend.
Break but that three-edged glass:–inviolate
The sundered beams resume their primal state,
Weaving pure light in flawless harmony.
Thus decomposed, subject to love and strife,
God's thought, made conscious through man's mortal life,
Resumes through death the eternal unity.

Adventante Deo

LIFT up your heads, gates of my heart, unfold
Your portals to salute the King of kings!
Behold Him come, borne on cherubic wings
Engrained with crimson eyes and grail of gold!
Before His path the thunder-clouds withhold
Their stormy pinions, and the desert sings:
He from His lips divine and forehead flings
Sunlight of peace unfathomed, bliss untold.
O soul, faint soul, disquieted how long!
Lift up thine eyes, for lo, thy Lord is near,
Lord of all loveliness and strength and song,
The Lord who brings heart-sadness better cheer,
Scattering those midnight dreams that dote on wrong,
Purging with heaven's pure rays love's atmosphere!

An Invocation

TO God, the everlasting, who abides,
One Life within things infinite that die:
To Him whose unity no thought divides:
Whose breath is breathèd through immensity.

Him neither eye hath seen, nor ear hath heard;
Nor reason, seated in the souls of men,
Though pondering oft on the mysterious word,
Hath e'er revealed His Being to mortal ken.

Earth changes, and the starry wheels roll round;
The seasons come and go, moons wax and wane;
The nations rise and fall, and fill the ground,
Storing the sure results of joy and pain:

Slow knowledge widens toward a perfect whole,
From that first man who named the name of heaven,
To him who weighs the planets as they roll,
And knows what laws to every life are given.

Yet He appears not. Round the extreme sphere
Of science still thin ether floats unseen:
Darkness still wraps Him round; and ignorant fear
Remains of what we are, and what have been.

Only we feel Him; and in aching dreams,
Swift intuitions, pangs of keen delight,
The sudden vision of His glory seems
To sear our souls, dividing the dull night:

And we yearn toward Him. Beauty, Goodness, Truth;
These three are one; one life, one thought, one being;
One source of still rejuvenescent youth;
One light for endless and unclouded seeing.

Mere symbols we perceive–the dying beauty,
The partial truth that few can comprehend,
The vacillating faith, the painful duty,
The virtue labouring to a dubious end.

O God, unknown, invisible, secure,
Whose being by dim resemblances we guess,
Who in man's fear and love abidest sure,
Whose power we feel in darkness and confess!

Without Thee nothing is, and Thou art nought
When on Thy substance we gaze curiously:
By Thee impalpable, named Force and Thought,
The solid world still ceases not to be.

Lead Thou me God, Law, Reason, Duty, Life!
All names for Thee alike are vain and hollow–
Lead me, for I will follow without strife;
Or, if I strive, still must I blindly follow.

309

ELLEN MARY CLERKE

1840-1906

The Building and Pinnacle of the Temple

NOT made with hands, its walls began to climb
From roots in Life's foundations deeply set,
Far down amid primaeval forms, where yet
Creation's Finger seemed to grope in slime.
Yet not in vain passed those first-born of Time,
Since each some presage gave of structure met
In higher types, lest these the bond forget
That links Earth's latest to the fore-world's prime
And living stone on living stone was laid,
In scale ascending ever, grade on grade,
To that which in its Maker's eyes seemed good–
The Human Form: and in that shrine of thought,
By the long travail of the ages wrought,
The Temple of the Incarnation stood.

Through all the ages since the primal ray,
Herald of life, first smote the abysmal night
Of elemental Chaos, and the might
Of the Creative Spark informed the clay,
From worm to brute, from brute to man–its way
The Shaping Thought took upward, flight on flight,
By stages which Earth's loftiest unite
Unto her least, made kin to such as they.
As living link, or prophecy, or type
Of purpose for fulfilment yet unripe,
Each has its niche in the supreme design;
Converging to one Pinnacle, whereat
Sole stands Creation's Masterpiece–and that
Which was through her–the Human made Divine.

HENRY BERNARD CARPENTER

1840-1887

From 'Liber Amoris'

I

OH, there are moments in man's mortal years
When for an instant that which long has lain
Beyond our reach is on a sudden found
In things of smallest compass, and we hold
The unbounded shut in one small minute's space,
And worlds within the hollow of our hand,–
A world of music in one word of love,
A world of love in one quick wordless look,
A world of thought in one translucent phrase,
A world of memory in one mournful chord,
A world of sorrow in one little song.
Such moments are man's holiest,–the divine
And first-sown seeds of Love's eternity.
And such were those last moments when I sat
Beside my long-lost friend, soft-laid again
In what no longer was his lair of death,
But now his bed of glory. Life, all life,
Its terrors and its tumults and its tears,
Its hopes, its agonies and its ecstasies,
Its nights of sorrow and its dawns of joy,
Its visionary raptures and its dull
Death-darkened hours, its longings, losses, gains,
Curses and cries and lamentations loud,
Sins, frenzies, and despairs, the monstrous births
Of thought and action groping for the light,
The false, the true, the night's red underworld
Of nadir darkness, and the zenith stars
Lost in their spheral music beating time
To every heart that hates or loves or mourns, –

These now were one, and I was one with these,
And these with me through Love's transfusing power
That passed upon me then. There as we sat,–
My brother and I, my brother made anew,
My brother thrice made mine, for ever mine,
Made one and equal with me through Love's might,–
We felt all space was ours, all time was ours;
We were as those that reign above the worlds;
And in our souls we saw the light round which
All multiformal things grow uniform,
The many sing as one. And we were one,
Calm-seated in the heaven that overflows
With the world's music of perpetual peace.

II

And then I thought that He whom we name God
Was not perhaps some unit of cold thought
Such as Greek sages gave to Christian saints,
A primal number, lone, creationless;
But now He came to me, as oft before,
The everlasting Twofold, ever one,
The man and woman still inseparable.
And as the absolute can never live
Without its relative; as silent space
Knows nothing, never sees or hears itself
Without time's measuring music; as cold form
Lies blind and blank till colour comes with kiss
And warmth outpoured upon it, such as once
Elisha poured upon the lifeless child,–
So God was now no longer unto me
A lonely masculine might above the worlds,
But as the man and woman, twofold life,
Its married Law and Love, and these were one.

And from their wedded love sprang forth a child,
Their first-begotten-son, whose name was Love,–
Love their great heir, the lord of life and death,
The holder of the keys to all we know
And all the secrets of the unsearchable,
The chalice-bearer of the world's life-wine,
Bringer of light and steersman of the stars.

HARRIET ELEANOR HAMILTON-KING

b.1840

The Bride Reluctant

'LEAVE the romance before the end;
  Leave the late roses to their fall;
Dismiss the nurselings thou dost tend;
  I hear another, closer call.
'Tis I, thy Guardian, give thee word,
  Thy Bridegroom seeketh thee, O sweet!
Thy Bridegroom comes,–His step I heard–
  Within thy chamber thee to meet.'

'Another day, another time!
  'Tis pleasant in the outer room;
I love the airy summer clime,
  And not the inner chamber's gloom.
And this year's roses will not come
  Again; but betwixt us the bond
Is fixed, and fast, and wearisome;
  For one is fickle, one is fond.'

'Come to thy chamber, for He stands
  Tearful, and seeking only, thee;
With ravished eyes, and outstretched hands,
  And He commands resistlessly.

Come to thy chamber, though it be
    Narrow, and dark, and full of pain;
He paid a heavy price for thee,
        And can He let thee go again?'

'My Bridegroom's bed is cold and hard,
    My Bridegroom's kiss is ice and fire,
My Bridegroom's clasp is iron-barred,
    I am consumed in His desire:
My Bridegroom's touch is as a sword
    That pierces every nerve and limb;
"Depart from me," I moan, "O Lord!"
    All the night long I spend with Him.'

'Oh! heart of woman holdeth not
    The passion of His love for thee;
He sees thee perfect, without spot,
    Crowned with celestial jewelry.
The doors of Heaven could not hold
    His feet from hasting to thy side;
The ardours of the Suns are cold
    To His for thee, His hard-won bride.'

'Rather am I His bondmaiden,
    Compelled by law and not by love.
Oh, would I were enfranchised; then
    With wings of silver, like a dove–
Then would I flee, past heaven's far bound,
    The unendurable embrace;
Then would I hide in earth's profound
    From the strange terror of His Face!'

'Enter, to keep thy Bridegroom's tryst!
    Liking or loth I thee have led:
He is thine own, albeit He wist
    That thy half-hearted love was dead.

What though His Bride with Him must share
  A couch of thorns without repose?
Thousands this moment death would dare
  To know one word of all she knows.'

'I pine, on haunted hills to muse,
  To face the open sunrise skies;
I pine for friends that I might choose;
  I pine for little children's eyes;
For free and fearless limbs–to move
  Breasting the wave, breasting the breeze:
But jealous love is cruel love,
  And He denies me all of these.'

'Child, take thy roses, take thy toys,
  Take back thy life and liberty;
Thy days shall flow in simple joys,
  And undisturbed thy nights shall be.
Thy Bridegroom does thee no more wrong,
  Poor child, the victim of His Heart:
Look but on Him once more,–one long
  Last look, and then from Him depart.

'Farewell–one look. But oh! this lone
  Bare desert, where I might be free!
Thy Face I see–Thy Face, my own,
  And naught in heaven or earth but Thee!
But O my Lord, my Life, my Love,
  Thou knowest all my weakness best;
Take back into the ark Thy dove,
  And comfort me upon Thy breast!'

From 'The Disciples'

WE suffer. Why we suffer,–that is hid
With God's foreknowledge in the clouds of Heaven.
The first book written sends that human cry
Out of the clear Chaldean pasture-lands
Down forty centuries; and no answer yet
Is found, nor will be found, while yet we live
In limitations of Humanity.
But yet one thought has often stayed by me
In the night-watches, which has brought at least
The patience for the hour, and made the pain
No more a burden which I groaned to leave,
But something precious which I feared to lose.
–How shall I show it, but by parables?

The sculptor, with his Psyche's wings half-hewn,
May close his eyes in weariness, and wake
To meet the white cold clay of his ideal
Flushed into beating life, and singing down
The ways of Paradise. The husbandman
May leave the golden fruitage of his groves
Ungarnered, and upon the Tree of Life
Will find a richer harvest waiting him.
The soldier dying thinks upon his bride,
And knows his arms shall never clasp her more,
Until he first the face of his unborn child
Behold in heaven: for each and all of life,
In every phase of action, love, and joy,
There is fulfilment only otherwhere.–

But if, impatient, thou let slip thy cross,
Thou wilt not find it in this world again,
Nor in another; here, and here alone
Is given thee to suffer for God's sake.

In other worlds we shall more perfectly
Serve Him and love Him, praise Him, work for Him,
Grow near and nearer Him with all delight;
But then we shall not any more be called
To suffer, which is our appointment here.
Canst thou not suffer then one hour,–or two?
If He should call thee from thy cross to-day,
Saying, It is finished!–that hard cross of thine
From which thou prayest for deliverance,
Thinkest thou not some passion of regret
Would overcome thee? Thou wouldst say, 'So soon?
Let me go back, and suffer yet awhile
More patiently;–I have not yet praised God.'
And He might answer to thee,–'Never more.
All pain is done with.' Whensoe'er it comes,
That summons that we look for, it will seem
Soon, yea too soon. Let us take heed in time
That God may now be glorified in us;
And while we suffer, let us set our souls
To suffer perfectly: since this alone,
The suffering, which is this world's special grace,
May here be perfected and left behind.

–But in obedience and humility;–
Waiting on God's hand, not forestalling it.
Seek not to snatch presumptuously the palm
By self-election; poison not thy wine
With bitter herbs if He has made it sweet;
Nor rob God's treasuries because the key
Is easy to be turned by mortal hands.
The gifts of birth, death, genius, suffering,
Are all for His hand only to bestow.
Receive thy portion, and be satisfied.
Who crowns himself a king is not the more

Royal; nor he who mars himself with stripes
The more partaker of the Cross of Christ.

But if Himself He come to thee, and stand
Beside thee, gazing down on thee with eyes
That smile, and suffer; that will smite thy heart,
With their own pity, to a passionate peace;
And reach to thee Himself the Holy Cup
(With all its wreathen stems of passion-flowers
And quivering sparkles of the ruby stars),
Pallid and royal, saying 'Drink with Me';
Wilt thou refuse? Nay, not for Paradise!
The pale brow will compel thee, the pure hands
Will minister unto thee; thou shalt take
Of that communion through the solemn depths
Of the dark waters of thine agony,
With heart that praises Him, that yearns to Him
The closer through that hour. Hold fast His hand,
Though the nails pierce thine too! take only care
Lest one drop of the sacramental wine
Be spilled, of that which ever shall unite
Thee, soul and body to thy living Lord!

Therefore gird up thyself, and come, to stand
Unflinching under the unfaltering hand,
That waits to prove thee to the uttermost.
It were not hard to suffer by His hand,
If thou couldst see His face;–but in the dark!
That is the one last trial:–be it so.
Christ was forsaken, so must thou be too:
How couldst thou suffer but in seeming, else?
Thou wilt not see the face nor feel the hand,
Only the cruel crushing of the feet,
When through the bitter night the Lord comes down
To tread the winepress.–Not by sight, but faith,
Endure, endure,–be faithful to the end!

SARAH WILLIAMS

1841-1868

Deep-sea Soundings

MARINER, what of the deep?
This of the deep:
Twilight is there, and solemn, changeless calm;
Beauty is there, and tender healing balm–
Balm with no root in earth, or air, or sea,
Poised by the finger of God, it floateth free,
And, as it threads the waves, the sound doth rise,–
Hither shall come no further sacrifice;
Never again the anguished clutch at life,
Never again great Love and Death in strife;
He who hath suffered all, need fear no more,
Quiet his portion now, for evermore.

Mariner, what of the deep?
This of the deep:
Solitude dwells not there, though silence reign;
Mighty the brotherhood of loss and pain;
There is communion past the need of speech,
There is a love no words of love can reach;
Heavy the waves that superincumbent press,
But as we labour here with constant stress,
Hand doth hold out to hand not help alone,
But the deep bliss of being fully known.
There are no kindred like the kin of sorrow,
There is no hope like theirs who fear no morrow.

Mariner, what of the deep?
This of the deep:
Though we have travelled past the line of day,
Glory of night doth light us on our way,

Radiance that comes we know not how nor whence,
Rainbows without the rain, past duller sense,
Music of hidden reefs and waves long past,
Thunderous organ tones from far-off blast,
Harmony, victrix, throned in state sublime,
Couched on the wrecks be-gemmed with pearls of time;
Never a wreck but brings some beauty here;
Down where the waves are stilled the sea shines clear;
Deeper than life the plan of life doth lie,
He who knows all, fears naught. Great Death shall die.

ROBERT BUCHANAN

1841-1901

The Tree of Life

THE Master said:
'I have planted the Seed of a Tree,
It shall be strangely fed
With white dew and with red,
And the Gardeners shall be three–
Regret, Hope, Memory!'

The Master smiled:
For the Seed that He had set
Broke presently thro' the mould,
With a glimmer of green and gold,
And the Angels' eyes were wet–
Hope, Memory, Regret.

The Master cried:
'It liveth–breatheth–see!
Its soft lips open wide–
It looks from side to side–
How strange they gleam on me,
The little dim eyes of the Tree!'

The Master said:
    'After a million years,
The Seed I set and fed
To itself hath gatherèd
    All the world's smiles and tears–
    How mighty it appears!'

The Master said:
    'At last, at last, I see
A Blossom, a Blossom o' red
From the heart of the Tree is shed.
    'Tis fairer certainly
    Than the Tree, or the leaves of the Tree.'

The Master cried:
    'O Angels, that guard the Tree,
A Blossom, a Blossom divine
Grows on this greenwood of mine:
    What may this Blossom be?
    Name this Blossom to me!'

The Master smiled;
    For the Angels answered thus:
'Our tears have nourish'd the same,
We have given it a name
    That seemeth fit to us–
    We have called it *Spiritus*.'

The Master said:
    'This Flower no Seed shall bear;
But hither on a day
My beautiful Son shall stray,
    And shall snatch it unaware,
    And wreath it in his hair.'

The Master smiled:
    'The Tree shall never bear–
Seedless shall perish the Tree,
But the Flower my Son's shall be;
    He will pluck the Flower and wear,
    Till it withers in his hair!'

From 'The City of Dream'

THE Woof that I weave not
    Thou wearest and weavest,
The Thought I conceive not
    Thou darkly conceivest;
The wind and the rain,
    The night and the morrow,
The rapture of pain
    Fading slowly to sorrow,
The dream and the deed,
    The calm and the storm,
The flower and the seed,
    Are thy Thought and thy Form.
I die, yet depart not,
    I am bound, yet soar free,
Thou art and thou art not,
    and ever shalt be!

From 'The City of Dream'
The Man

YONDER the veil'd Musician sits, His feet
Upon the pedals of dark formless suns,
His fingers on the radiant spheric keys,
His face, that it is death to look upon,

Misted with incense rising nebulous
Out of abysmal chaos and cohering
Into the golden flames of Life and Being!
And underneath his touch Music itself
Grows living, heard as far as thought can creep
Or dream can soar; or that Creation stirs,
And drinks the sound, and sings!–So far away
He sits, the Mystery, wrapt for ever round
With brightness and with awe and melody;
Yet even here, on these low-lying shores,
Lower than is the footstool of His throne,
We hear Him and adore Him, nay, can feel
His breath as vapour round our mouths, inhaling
That soul within the soul whereby we live
From that divine for-ever-beating Heart
Which thrills the universe with Light and Love!

The Pilgrim

So far away He dwells, my soul indeed
Scarcely discerns Him, and in sooth I seek
A gentler presence and a nearer Friend.

The Man

So far? O blind, He broods beside thee now
Here in this silence, with His eyes on thine!
O deaf, His voice is whispering in thine ears
Soft as the breathing of the slumberous seas!

The Pilgrim

I see not and I hear not; but I see
Thine eyes burn dimly, like a corpse-light seen
Flickering amidst the tempest; and I hear
Only the elemental grief and pain
Out of whose shadow I would creep for ever.

The Man

Thou canst not, brother; for these, too, are God!

The Pilgrim

How? Is my God, then, as a homeless ghost
Blown this way, that way, with the elements?

The Man

He is without thee, and within thee too;
Thy living breath, and that which drinks thy breath:
Thy being, and the bliss beyond thy being.

The Pilgrim

So near, so far? He shapes the farthest sun
New-glimmering on the farthest fringe of space,
Yet stoops and with a leaf-light finger-touch
Reaches my heart and makes it come and go!

The Man

Yea; and He is thy heart within thy heart,
And thou a portion of His Heart Divine!

JAMES RHOADES

b.1841

O Soul of Mine!

AGAIN that Voice, which on my listening ears
Falls like star-music filtering through the spheres:
'Know this, O Man, sole root of sin in thee
Is *not* to know thine own divinity!'

And the Voice said:
'Awake, thou drunken and yet not with wine!
Arise and shine!
Uplift thee from the dead!

Cast off the clinging cerements of sin
Fool-sense hath swathed thee in!
Though drugged and dulled
With every evil anodyne
From the rank soil of the world's waste-heap culled,
Thou crown and pattern of the eternal Plan,
Awake, O Soul of Man!
O Soul of Mine,
Awake, I say, and know thyself divine!

'Behold, behold!
Thou art not that thou deemest,
Or to thy fellows seemest
In death-bound body hearsed:
But, like a silver summit
Enshrouded
And o'er-clouded
With earth-born vapour vainest,
So gross no eye may plumb it,
E'en as of old
From out My Heart all-seeing–
Ere yet in body dressed,
Best of the best,
And of most holy holiest–
Thou soared'st into being,
So, godlike as at first
I made thee, thou remainest.

'What look of wonder dawns within thine eyes,
O soul of Mine?
Hast utterly forgot from whence art risen?
That essence rare can walls of space imprison,
Or time with dull decrepitude surprise?

Nay now
From every chain thy self hath forged for thee
Thy Self can set thee free:
Let the sea burn,
Let fire to water turn,
But thou
Cleave to thy birthright and thy Royal Line!

'For lo! thou hast within thee to dispel
This haunting hell
Of error-teemèd night
That hides thy height,
And the dread rumour and malefic breath
Of thy doomed enemy, Death,
Whose birth-lair, ignorance, like a stagnant pool,
Of its accursèd kind
Breeds ague of unfaith, and terrors blind
Hatched in the darkened hollows of the mind;
Whence too arise
Hallucinations, lurid phantasies,
And gross desires, with every vice that springs
From false imaginings,
And vain reliance upon visible things–
The mad misrule
Of creeds and deeds idolatrous, whereof
Love were sworn hater, an she were not Love.

'These in their hidden dens
Behoves thee with pure thoughts to cleave or cleanse,
Aye, and unmask those counterfeits of bliss,
Which to believe thy deep undoing is–
Joys which but lure to leave thee,
And leave to grieve thee,

Not of the fine-spun stuff
That from the eternal spool
My Hands would weave thee!
Enough, enough!
How long shall they deceive thee,
And thou still dote
Importuning high Heaven
That more be given
With cries monotonous as the wry-neck's note?

'Such pleasures and such pain
Alike are vain.
Not while the chords of thought are keyed to these
Shalt thou find rest or ease,
Seeing that thyself art tuned eternally
To That which only is without alloy
Pure Life and Joy.
Ah! would thy throbbing shell
Awake the Spirit's whispered harmonies,
Bethink thee well
That every trembling hidden string must be
Vibrant of Me
Who am the Truth, and at thy centre dwell–
The very Breath of God made visible!
For know the myriad miseries of mankind,
And the long reign of sin,
Came but of questing outward, for to find
That which abides within.

'But what hast thou to do with sinning,
O Soul of Mine,
Or what with dying,
Sorrow and sighing,
Who hast nor ending nor beginning,

Nor power from thy perfection to decline?–
Who canst not guess
From the gaunt shadow cast
On folly's fog-belt, but shalt learn at last,
Thine own inalienable loveliness;
Whom sinless, deathless, I created
Of elements so fine,
That with my Being sated,
In glorious garments dight
Of Life and Light,
Lowly, yet unafraid,
With an eternity of joy sufficed,
The Spirit's Self might love thee
And brood above thee,
Pure Maid
And Mother of the indwelling Christ!

'Hereby thou comest at last unto thine own,
The Heaven of Heaven!
Self-wittingly at one
With Him who hath the Universe for throne,
Who wieldeth the stars seven;
Who only is
The Mystery of Mysteries
Ineffable, My Son,
My sole-begotten ere the worlds began,
Made manifest as Man.

'And the grim Nothingness thou namest Death,
With all his shadowy peers–
Angers, and lusts, and fears–
The which so long against thy peace did plot,
Shall be remembered not,
Or, shrivelling at a breath,

Be known as naught;
Yea, that they never were
Save in the realm of things that but appear,
Creations of thine unillumined thought.

'Then deem not Heaven a place,
As though 'twere measurable in terms of sense–
Length, breadth, circumference,
Or spread throughout illimitable space.
It is the enthronization of the soul
Upon the heights of Being; it is to know;
It is the rapture that I AM is so,
Whatever clouds of ignorance up-roll.
It is the joy of joys,
To thrill co-operant with the primal cause
Of the unswerving laws
Which hold in everlasting equipoise
Those balances of God,
The visible and invisible Universe;
Wherein, couldst thou but measure with His rod–
With undistorted sight
Couldst read aright–
Nor better is, nor worse,
But only best;
'Tis from thy centre to thine utmost bound
To feel that thou hast found–
That thou too art
From all to all eternity a part
Of that which never was in speech expressed,
The unresting Order which is more than rest.

'Who is he prateth of Original Sin?
I am thine Origin,
And I thy Kingdom waiting thee within!

Seek Me, and thou hast found it,
My seas of Life surround it,
My Love's o'er-arching splendour
For canopy hath crowned it.
All that nor eye nor ear
Can hear or see
Lies stored within its boundless empery.
Not there, O Soul of Mine,
Shalt thou surrender,
Torn from thy tortured breast,
Those whom thou heldest here
In bonds so tender.
Death cannot quell
Their residue divine.
Seek, then, within, but spurn the unhallowed spell:
In light unutterable alive they shine,
Leave thou to Me the rest!
Have I not said?
And shall not they that mourn be comforted?

'Yet these for whom thou pinest,
Thy dearest and divinest,
Are but rills from out the river
Of the all-and-only Giver:
Why tarry, then, thy thirst in Him to slake
Who flowed through earthen channels for thy sake,
From death-drought to deliver?
Hadst thou but eyes for seeing
The wells of thine own being,
What draughts of living water wouldst thou take!

'Ever, then, singly, and all aims above,–
For That I AM is thine,–
Think Oneness, and think Worship, and think Love;

The which, translated to thine outward need
(Sith every thought must still creative prove),
Shall limn their likeness with invisible hand–
As the sea-ripples write them on the sand–
In bodily form and deed.
So shalt thou make for thine eternal Meed;
So shalt thou fashion thee, O Soul of Mine,
A glorious shrine
Wherein to house thee, and wherethrough to shine–
Or here, or in My Mansions crystalline–
Serenely changeless, dazzlingly divine!'

From 'Out of the Silence'

LO! in the vigils of the night, ere sped
The first bright arrows from the Orient shed,
The heart of Silence trembled into sound,
And out of Vastness came a Voice, which said:

I AM alone; thou only art in Me:
I am the stream of Life that flows through thee:
I comprehend all substance, fill all space:
I am pure Being, by whom all things be.

I am thy Dawn, from darkness to release:
I am the Deep, wherein thy sorrows cease:
Be still! be still! and know that I am God:
Acquaint thyself with Me, and be at peace!

I am the Silence that is more than sound:
If therewithin thou lose thee, thou art found:
The stormless, shoreless Ocean, which is I–
Thou canst not breathe, but in its bosom drowned.

I am all Love: there is naught else but I:
I am all Power: the rest is phantasy:
Evil, and anguish, sorrow, death, and hell–
These are the fear-flung shadows of a lie.

Arraign not Mine Omnipotence, to say
That aught beside in earth or heaven hath sway!
The powers of darkness are not: that which is
Abideth: these but vaunt them for a day.

Know thou thyself: as thou hast learned of Me,
I made thee three in one, and one in three–
Spirit and Mind and Form, immortal Whole,
Divine and undivided Trinity.

Seek not to break the triple bond assigned:
Mind sees by Spirit: Body moves by Mind:
Divorced from Spirit, both way-wildered fall–
Leader and led, the blindfold and the blind.

Look not without thee: thou hast that within,
Makes whole thy sickness, impotent thy sin:
Survey thy forces, rally to thyself:
That which thou would'st not hath no power to win.

I, God, enfold thee like an atmosphere:
Thou to thyself wert never yet more near:
Think not to shun Me: whither would'st thou fly?
Nor go not hence to seek Me: I am here.

FREDERICK WILLIAM HENRY MYERS

1843-1901

Sunrise

LOOK, O blinded eyes and burning,
Think, O heart amazed with yearning,
Is it yet beyond thine earning,
        That delight that was thine all?–
Wilful eyes and undiscerning,
Heart ashamed of bitter learning,
It is flown beyond returning,
        It is lost beyond recall.

Who with prayers has overtaken
Those glad hours when he would waken
To the sound of branches shaken
        By an early song and wild,–
When the golden leaves would flicker,
And the loving thoughts come thicker,
And the thrill of life beat quicker
        In the sweet heart of the child?

Yet my soul, tho' thou forsake her,
Shall adore thee, till thou take her,
In the morning, O my Maker,
        For thine oriflamme unfurled:
For the lambs beneath their mothers
For the bliss that is another's ,
For the beauty of my brothers,
        For the wonder of the world.

From above us and from under,
In the ocean and the thunder,
Thou preludest to the wonder
        Of the Paradise to be:
For a moment we may guess thee
From thy creatures that confess thee
When the morn and even bless thee,
        And thy smile is on the sea.

Then from something seen or heard,
Whether forests softly stirred,
Or the speaking of a word,
Or the singing of a bird,
        Cares and sorrows cease:
For a moment on the soul
Falls the rest that maketh whole,
        Falls the endless peace.

O the hush from earth's annoys!
O the heaven, O the joys
Such as priest and singing-boys
        Cannot sing or say!
There is no more pain and crying,
There is no more death and dying,
As for sorrow and for sighing,–
        These shall flee away.

A Cosmic Outlook

BACKWARD!–beyond this momentary woe!–
Thine was the world's dim dawn, the prime emprize;
Eternal aeons gaze thro' these sad eyes,
And all the empyreal sphere hath shaped thee so.
Nay! all is living, all is plain to know!
This rock has drunk the ray from ancient skies;
Strike! and the sheen of that remote sunrise
Gleams in the marble's unforgetful glow.
Thus hath the cosmic light endured the same
Ere first that ray from Sun to Sirius flew;
Aye, and in heaven I heard the mystic Name
Sound, and a breathing of the Spirit blew;
Lit the long Past, bade shine the slumbering flame
And all the Cosmorama blaze anew.

Onward! thro' baffled hope, thro' bootless prayer,
With strength that sinks, with high task half begun,
Things great desired, things lamentable done,
Vows writ in water, blows that beat the air.
On! I have guessed the end; the end is fair.
Not with these weak limbs is thy last race run;
Not all thy vision sets with this low sun;
Not all thy spirit swoons in this despair.
Look how thine own soul, throned where all is well,
Smiles to regard thy days disconsolate;
Yea; since herself she wove the worldly spell,
Doomed thee for lofty gain to low estate;–
Sown with thy fall a seed of glory fell;
Thy heaven is in thee, and thy will thy fate.

Inward! aye, deeper far than love or scorn,
Deeper than bloom of virtue, stain of sin,
Rend thou the veil and pass alone within,
Stand naked there and feel thyself forlorn!
Nay! in what world, then, Spirit, wast thou born?
Or to what World-Soul art thou entered in?
Feel the Self fade, feel the great life begin,
With Love re-rising in the cosmic morn.
The inward ardour yearns to the inmost goal;
The endless goal is one with the endless way;
From every gulf the tides of Being roll,
From every zenith burns the indwelling day;
And life in Life has drowned thee and soul in Soul;
And these are God, and thou thyself art they.

From 'Saint Paul'

LO as some bard on isles of the Aegean
Lovely and eager when the earth was young,
Burning to hurl his heart into a paean,
Praise of the hero from whose loins he sprung;–

He, I suppose, with such a care to carry,
Wandered disconsolate and waited long,
Smiting his breast, wherein the notes would tarry,
Chiding the slumber of the seed of song:

Then in the sudden glory of a minute
Airy and excellent the proëm came,
Rending his bosom, for a god was in it,
Waking the seed, for it had burst in flame.

So even I athirst for his inspiring,
 I who have talked with Him forget again,
Yes, many days with sobs and with desiring
 Offer to God a patience and a pain;

Then thro' the mid complaint of my confession,
 Then thro' the pang and passion of my prayer,
Leaps with a start the shock of his possession,
 Thrills me and touches, and the Lord is there.

Lo if some pen should write upon your rafter
 Mene and mene in the folds of flame,
Think you could any memories thereafter
 Wholly retrace the couplet as it came?

Lo if some strange intelligible thunder
 Sang to the earth the secret of a star,
Scarce could ye catch, for terror and for wonder,
 Shreds of the story that was pealed so far:–

Scarcely I catch the words of his revealing,
 Hardly I hear Him, dimly understand,
Only the Power that is within me pealing
 Lives on my lips and beckons to my hand.

Whoso has felt the Spirit of the Highest
 Cannot confound nor doubt Him nor deny:
Yea with one voice, O world, tho' thou deniest,
 Stand thou on that side, for on this am I.

Rather the earth shall doubt when her retrieving
 Pours in the rain and rushes from the sod,
Rather than he for whom the great conceiving
 Stirs in his soul to quicken into God.

Aye, tho' thou then shouldst strike him from his glory
    Blind and tormented, maddened and alone,
Even on the cross would he maintain his story,
    Yes and in hell would whisper, I have known.

A Last Appeal

O SOMEWHERE, somewhere, God unknown,
    Exist and be!
I am dying; I am all alone;
    I must have Thee!

God! God! my sense, my soul, my all,
    Dies in the cry:–
Saw'st thou the faint star flame and fall?
    Ah! it was I.

EDWARD DOWDEN

1843-1913

By the Window

STILL deep into the West I gazed; the light
Clear, spiritual, tranquil as a bird
Wide-winged that soars on the smooth gale and sleeps,
Was it from sun far-set or moon unrisen?
Whether from moon, or sun, or angel's face
It held my heart from motion, stayed my blood,
Betrayed each rising thought to quiet death
Along the blind charm'd way to nothingness,
Lull'd the last nerve that ached. It was a sky
Made for a man to waste his will upon,

To be received as wiser than all toil,
And much more fair. And what was strife of men?
And what was time?

Then came a certain thing.
Are intimations for the elected soul
Dubious, obscure, of unauthentic power
Since ghostly to the intellectual eye,
Shapeless to thinking? Nay, but are not we
Servile to words and an usurping brain,
Infidels of our own high mysteries,
Until the senses thicken and lose the world,
Until the imprisoned soul forgets to see,
And spreads blind fingers forth to reach the day,
Which once drank light, and fed on angels' food?

It happened swiftly, came and straight was gone.

One standing on some aery balcony
And looking down upon a swarming crowd
Sees one man beckon to him with finger-tip
While eyes meet eyes; he turns and looks again–
The man is lost, and the crowd sways and swarms.
Shall such an one say, 'Thus 'tis proved a dream,
And no hand beckoned, no eyes met my own?'
Neither can I say this. There was a hint,
A thrill, a summons faint yet absolute,
Which ran across the West; the sky was touch'd,
And failed not to respond. Does a hand pass
Lightly across your hair? you feel it pass
Not half so heavy as a cobweb's weight,
Although you never stir; so felt the sky
Not unaware of the Presence, so my soul
Scarce less aware. And if I cannot say

The meaning and monition, words are weak
Which will not paint the small wing of a moth,
Nor bear a subtile odour to the brain,
And much less serve the soul in her large needs.
I cannot tell the meaning, but a change
Was wrought in me; it was not the one man
Who came to the luminous window to gaze forth,
And who moved back into the darkened room
With awe upon his heart and tender hope;
From some deep well of life tears rose; the throng
Of dusty cares, hopes, pleasures, prides fell off,
And from a sacred solitude I gazed
Deep, deep into the liquid eyes of Life.

Awakening

WITH brain o'erworn, with heart a summer clod,
With eye so practised in each form around,–
And all forms mean,–to glance above the ground
Irks it, each day of many days we plod,
Tongue-tied and deaf, along life's common road.
But suddenly, we know not how, a sound
Of living streams, an odour, a flower crowned
With dew, a lark upspringing from the sod,
And we awake. O joy and deep amaze!
Beneath the everlasting hills we stand,
We hear the voices of the morning seas,
And earnest prophesyings in the land,
While from the open heaven leans forth at gaze
The encompassing great cloud of witnesses.

Communion

LORD, I have knelt and tried to pray to-night,
But Thy love came upon me like a sleep,
And all desire died out; upon the deep
Of Thy mere love I lay, each thought in light
Dissolving like the sunset clouds, at rest
Each tremulous wish, and my strength weakness, sweet
As a sick boy with soon o'erwearied feet
Finds, yielding him unto his mother's breast
To weep for weakness there. I could not pray,
But with closed eyes I felt Thy bosom's love
Beating toward mine, and then I would not move
Till of itself the joy should pass away;
At last my heart found voice,–'Take me, O Lord,
And do with me according to Thy word.'

A New Hymn for Solitude

I FOUND Thee in my heart, O Lord,
  As in some secret shrine;
I knelt, I waited for Thy word,
I joyed to name Thee mine.

I feared to give myself away
  To that or this; beside
Thy altar on my face I lay,
  And in strong need I cried.

Those hours are past. Thou art not mine,
  And therefore I rejoice,
I wait within no holy shrine,
  I faint not for the voice.

In Thee we live; and every wind
Of heaven is Thine; blown free
To west, to east, the God unshrined
Is still discovering me.

The Secret of the Universe

AN ODE

(By a Western Spinning Dervish)

I SPIN, I spin, around, around,
And close my eyes,
And let the bile arise
From the sacred region of the soul's Profound;
Then gaze upon the world; how strange! how new!
The earth and heaven are one,
The horizon-line is gone,
The sky how green! the land how fair and blue!
Perplexing items fade from my large view,
And thought which vexed me with its false and true
Is swallowed up in Intuition; this,
This is the sole true mode
Of reaching God,
And gaining the universal synthesis
Which makes All–One; while fools with peering eyes
Dissect, divide, and vainly analyse.
So round, and round, and round again!
How the whole globe swells within my brain,
The stars inside my lids appear,
The murmur of the spheres I hear
Throbbing and beating in each ear;
Right in my navel I can feel
The centre of the world's great wheel.

Ah peace divine, bliss dear and deep,
No stay, no stop,
Like any top
Whirling with swiftest speed, I sleep.
O ye devout ones round me coming,
Listen! I think that I am humming;
No utterance of the servile mind
With poor chop-logic rules agreeing
Here shall ye find,
But inarticulate burr of man's unsundered being.
Ah, could we but devise some plan,
Some patent jack by which a man
Might hold himself ever in harmony
With the great whole, and spin perpetually,
As all things spin
Without, within,
As Time spins off into Eternity,
And Space into the inane Immensity,
And the Finite into God's Infinity,
Spin, spin, spin, spin.

The Initiation

UNDER the flaming wings of cherubim
I moved toward that high altar. O, the hour!
And the light waxed intenser, and the dim
Low edges of the hills and the grey sea
Were caught and captur'd by the present Power,
My sureties and my witnesses to be.

Then the light drew me in. Ah, perfect pain!
Ah, infinite moment of accomplishment!
Thou terror of pure joy, with neither wane
Nor waxing, but long silence and sharp air

As womb-forsaking babes breathe. Hush! the event
    Let him who wrought Love's marvellous things declare.

Shall I who fear'd not joy, fear grief at all?
    I on whose mouth Life laid his sudden lips
Tremble at Death's weak kiss, and not recall
    That sundering from the flesh, the flight from time,
The judgements stern, the clear apocalypse,
    The lightnings, and the Presences sublime.

How came I back to earth? I know not how,
    Nor what hands led me, nor what words were said.
Now all things are made mine,–joy, sorrow; now
    I know my purpose deep, and can refrain;
I walk among the living, not the dead;
    My sight is purged; I love and pity men.

Love's Lord

WHEN weight of all the garner'd years
    Bows me, and praise must find relief
In harvest-song, and smiles and tears
    Twist in the band that binds my sheaf;

Thou known Unknown, dark, radiant sea
    In whom we live, in whom we move,
My spirit must lose itself in Thee,
    Crying a name–Life, Light, or Love.

FREDERICK WILLIAM ORDE WARD

b. 1843

The Beatific Vision

BETWIXT the dawning and the day it came
Upon me like a spell,
While tolled a distant bell,
A wondrous vision but without a name
In pomp of shining mist and shadowed flame,
Exceeding terrible;
Before me seemed to open awful Space,
And sheeted tower and spire
With forms of shrounded 'tire
Arose and beckoned with unearthly grace,
I felt a Presence through I saw no face
But the dark rolling fire.

And then a Voice as sweet and soft as tears
But yet of gladness part,
Thrilled through my inmost heart,
Which told the secret of the solemn years
And swept away the clouds of gloomy fears,
The riddles raised by art ;
Till all my soul was bathed with trembling joy
And lost in dreadful bliss,
As at God's very kiss,
While the earth shrivelled up its broken toy,
And like a rose the heavens no longer coy
Laid bare their blue abyss.

The giant wheels and all the hidden springs
Of this most beauteous globe,
Which man may never probe,
Burst on me with a blaze of angel wings
And each bright orb that like a diamond clings
To the veiled Father's robe;

I saw with vision that was more than sight,
The levers and the laws
That fashion stars as straws
And link with perfect loveliness of right,
In the pure duty that is pure delight
And to one Centre draws.

I knew with sudden insight all was best,
The passion and the pain,
The searchings that seem vain
But lead if by dim blood-stained steps to Rest,
And only are the beatings of God's Breast
Beneath the iron chain;
I knew each work was blessèd in its place,
The eagle and the dove,
While Nature was the glove
Of that dear Hand which everywhere we trace,
I felt a Presence though I saw no face,
And it was boundless Love.

Redemption

ALL living creatures' pain,
The sufferings of the lowliest thing that creeps
Or flies a moment ere it sinks and sleeps,
Are too Redemption's tears and not in vain–
For nothing idly weeps.
Earth is through these fulfilling that it must
As in Christ's own eternal Passion chain,
And flowering from the dust.

The driven and drudging ass
Crushed by the bondage of its bitter round,
Repeats the Gospel in that narrow bound;
God is reflected in the blade of grass,

And *there* is Calvary's ground.
O not an insect or on leaf or sod
But in its measure is a looking-glass,
And shows Salvation's God.

All thus are carrying on,
And do work out, the one Redemption's tale;
Each is a little Christ on hill or dale,
The hell where Mercy's light has never shone
Is with that Mercy pale,
And though flesh turns from agony they dread,
Even as they groan and travail it is gone–
Love riseth from the dead.

ARTHUR WILLIAM EDGAR O'SHAUGHNESSY

1844-1881

The Lover

I WAS not with the rest at play;
My brothers laughed in joyous mood:
But I–I wandered far away
    Into the fair and silent wood;
    And with the trees and flowers I stood,
As dumb and full of dreams as they:
  –For One it seemed my whole heart knew,
    Or One my heart had known long since,
Was peeping at me through the dew;
And with bright laughter seemed to woo
    My beauty, like a Fairy prince.

Oh, what a soft enchantment filled
    The lonely paths and places dim!
It was as though the whole wood thrilled,
    And a dumb joy, because of him,
    Weighed down the lilies tall and slim,
And made the roses blush, and stilled

The great wild voices in half fear:
  It was as though his smile did hold
  All things in trances manifold;
And in each place as he drew near
  The leaves were touched and turned to gold. . .

But more and more he seemed to seek
  My heart: till, dreaming of all this,
I thought one day to hear him speak,
  Or feel, indeed, his sudden kiss
  Bind me to some great unknown bliss:
Then there would stay upon my cheek
  Full many a light and honied stain,
  That told indeed how I had lain
Deep in the flowery banks all day;
  And round me too there would remain
Some strange wood-blossom's scent alway. . . .

–O, the incomparable love
  Of him, my Lover!–O, to tell
Its way and measure were above
  The throbbing chords of speech that swell
  Within me!–Doth it not excel
All other, sung or written of?
Yea now, O all ye fair mankind–
Consider well the gracious line
Of those your lovers; call to mind
Their love of you, and ye shall find
  Not one among them all like mine.

It seems as though, from calm to calm,
  A whole fair age had passed me by,
Since first this Lover, through a charm
  Of flowers, wooed so tenderly,
  I had no fear of drawing nigh,
Nor knew, indeed, that–with an arm

Closed round and holding me–he led
    My eager way from sight to sight
    Of all the summer magic–right
To where himself had surely spread
    Some pleasant snare for my delight.

And now, in an eternal sphere,
    Beneath one flooding look of his–
Wherein, all beautiful and dear,
    That endless melting gold that is
    His love, with flawless memories
Grows ever richer and more clear–
    My life seems held, as some faint star
    Beneath its sun: and through the far
Celestial distances for miles,
    To where vast mirage futures are,
I trace the gilding of his smiles. . . .

For, one by one, e'en as I rise,
    And feel the pure Ethereal
Refining all before my eyes:
    Whole beauteous worlds material
    Are seen to enter gradual
The great transparent paradise
Of this my dream; and, all revealed,
    To break upon me more and more
Their inward singing souls, and yield
A wondrous secret half concealed
    In all their loveliness before.

And so, when, through unmeasured days,
    The far effulgence of the sea
Is holding me in long amaze,
    And stealing with strange ecstasy
    My heart all opened silently;–
There reach me, from among the sprays,

Ineffable faint words that sing
    Within me,–how, for me alone,
One who is lover–who is King,
    Hath dropt, as 'twere a precious stone,
    That sea–a symbol of his throne. . . .

And, through the long charmed solitude
    Of throbbing moments, whose strong link
Is one delicious hope pursued
    From trance to trance, the while I think
    And know myself upon the brink
Of His eternal kiss,–endued
With part of him, the very wind
    Hath power to ravish me in sips
Or long mad wooings that unbind
My hair,–wherein I truly find
    The magic of his unseen lips.

And, so almighty is the thrill
    I feel at many a faintest breath
Or stir of sound–as 'twere a rill
    Of joy traversing me, or death
    Dissolving all that hindereth
My thought from power to fulfil
Some new embodiment of bliss,–
    I do consume with the immense
Delight as of some secret kiss,
    And am become like one whose sense
    Is used with raptures too intense! . . .

Yea, mystic consummation! yea,
    O wondrous suitor,–whosoe'er
Thou art; that in such mighty way,
    In distant realms, athwart the air
    And lands and seas, with all things fair
Hast wooed me even till this day;–

It seems thou drawest near to me;
Or I, indeed, so nigh to thee,
I catch rare breaths of a delight
From thy most glorious country, see
Its distant glow upon some height. . . .

O thou my Destiny! O thou
My own–my very Love–my Lord!
Whom from the first day until now
My heart, divining, hath adored
So perfectly it hath abhorred
The tie of each frail human vow–
O I would whisper in thine ear–
Yea, may I not, once, in the clear
Pure night, when, only, silver shod
The angels walk?–thy name, I fear
And love, and tremble saying–GOD!

En Soph

Prayer of the Soul on entering Human Life

EN SOPH, uncomprehended in the thought
Of man or angel, having all that is
In one eternity of Being brought
Into a moment: yet with purposes,
Whence emanate those lower worlds of Time,
And Force, and Form, where man, with one wing caught
In clogging earth, angels in freer clime,
From partial blindness into partial sight,
Strive, yearn, and, with an inward hope sublime,
Rise ever; or, mastered by down-dragging might,
And groping weakly with an ill-trimmed light,
Sink, quenched;

En Soph was manifest, as dim
And awful as upon Egyptian throne
Osiris sits; but splendour covered Him;
And circles of the Sephiroth tenfold,
Vast and mysterious, intervening rolled.

And lo! from all the outward turning zones,
Before Him came the endless stream of souls
Unborn, whose destiny is to descend
And enter by the lowest gate of being.
And each one coming, saw, on written scrolls
And semblances that he might comprehend,
The things of Life and Death and Fate–which seeing,
Each little soul, as quivering like a flame
It paled before that splendour, stood and prayed
A piteous, fervent prayer against the shame
And ill of living, and would so have stayed
A flame-like emanation as before,
Unsullied and untried. Then, as he ceased
The tremulous supplication, full of sore
Foreboding agony to be released
From going on the doubtful pilgrimage
Of earthly hope and sorrow, for reply
A mighty angel touched his sight, to close,
Or nearly close, his spiritual eye,
So he should look on luminous things like those
No more till he had learned to live and die.

And when the pure bright flame, my soul, at last
Passed there in turn, it flickered like them all;
But oh! with some surpassing sad forecast
Of more than common pains that should befall
The man whose all too human heart has bled
With so much love and anguish until now,

And has not broken yet, and is not dead,
    And shaken as a leaf in autumn late,
Tormented by the wind, my soul somehow
    Found speech and prayed like this against my Fate:

The pure flame pent within the fragile form
    Will writhe with inward torments; blind desires,
Seizing, will whirl me in their frenzied storm,
    Clutching at shreds of heaven and phantom fires.
A voice, in broken ecstasies of song,
    Awakening mortal ears with its high pain,
Will leave an echoing agony along
    The stony ways and o'er the sunless plain,
While men stand listening in a silent throng.

And all the silences of life and death,
    Like doors closed on the thing my spirit seeks,
Importuning each in turn, will freeze the breath
    Upon my lips, appal the voice that speaks;
Until the silence of a human heart
    At length, when I have wept there all my tears,
Poured out my passion, given my stainless part
    Of heaven to hear what maybe no man hears,
Will work a woe that never can depart.

Oh, let me not be parted from the light,
    Oh, send me not to where the outer stars
Tread their uncertain orbits, growing less bright,
    Cycle by cycle; where, through narrowing bars,
The soul looks up and scarcely sees the throne
    It fell from; where the stretched-out Hand that guides
On to the end, in that dull slackening zone
    Reaches but feebly; and where man abides,
And finds out heaven with his heart alone.

I fear to live the life that shall be mine
Down in the half lights of that wandering world,
Mid ruined angels' souls that cease to shine,
Where fragments of the broken stars are hurled,
Quenched to the ultimate dark. Shall I believe,
Remembering, as of some exalted dream,
The life of flame, the splendour that I leave?
For, between life and death, shall it not seem
The fond false hope my shuddering soul would weave?. . .

So prayed I, feeling even as I prayed
Torments and fever of a strange unrest
Take hold upon my spirit, fain to have stayed
In the eternal calm, and ne'er essayed
The perilous strife, the all too bitter test
Of earthly sorrows, fearing–and ah! too well–
To be quite ruined in some grief below,
And ne'er regain the heaven from which I fell.
But then the angel smote my sight–'twas so
I woke into this world of love and woe.

GERARD MANLEY HOPKINS

1844-1889

The Habit of Perfection

ELECTED Silence, sing to me
And beat upon my whorlèd ear,
Pipe me to pastures still and be
The music that I care to hear.

Shape nothing, lips; be lovely-dumb:
It is the shut, the curfew sent
From there where all surrenders come
Which only makes you eloquent.

Be shellèd, eyes, with double dark
And find the uncreated light:
This ruck and reel which you remark
Coils, keeps, and teases simple sight.

Palate, the hutch of tasty lust,
Desire not to be rinsed with wine:
The can must be so sweet, the crust
So fresh that come in fasts divine!

Nostrils, your careless breath that spend
Upon the stir and keep of pride,
What relish shall the censers send
Along the sanctuary side!

O feel-of-primrose hands, O feet
That want the yield of plushy sward,
But you shall walk the golden street,
And you unhouse and house the Lord.

And, Poverty, be thou the bride
And now the marriage feast begun,
And lily-coloured clothes provide
Your spouse not laboured-at, nor spun.

God's Grandeur

THE world is charged with the grandeur of God.
It will flame out, like shining from shook foil,
It gathers to a greatness like the ooze of oil
Crushed. Why do men then now not reck His rod?
Generations have trod, have trod, have trod;
And all is seared with trade; bleared, smeared with toil;
And bears man's smudge, and shares man's smell; the soil
Is bare now, nor can foot feel being shod.
And for all this, nature is never spent;
There lives the dearest freshness deep down things;
And though the last lights from the black west went,
Oh, morning at the brown brink eastwards springs–
Because the Holy Ghost over the bent
World broods with warm breast, and with, ah, bright wings.

Mary Mother of Divine Grace, compared to the Air we breathe

WILD air, world-mothering air,
Nestling me everywhere,
That each eyelash or hair
Girdles; goes home betwixt
The fleeciest, frailest-flixed
Snow-flake; that's fairly mixed
With riddles, and is rife
In every least thing's life;
This needful, never spent
And nursing element;

My more than meat and drink,
My meal at every wink;
This air which by life's law
My lung must draw and draw
Now, but to breathe its praise,–
Minds me in many ways
Of her who not only
Gave God's infinity,
Dwindled to infancy,
Welcome in womb and breast,
Birth, milk, and all the rest,
But mothers each new grace
That does now reach our race,
Mary Immaculate,
Merely a woman, yet
Whose presence, power is
Great as no goddess's
Was deemèd, dreamèd; who
This one work has to do–
Let all God's glory through,
God's glory, which would go
Thro' her and from her flow
Off, and no way but so.
I say that we are wound
With mercy round and round
As if with air: the same
Is Mary, more by name,
She, wild web, wondrous robe,
Mantles the guilty globe.
Since God has let dispense
Her prayers His providence.
Nay, more than almoner,
The sweet alms' self is her
And men are meant to share
Her life as life does air.

If I have understood,
She holds high motherhood
Towards all our ghostly good,
And plays in grace her part
About man's beating heart,
Laying like air's fine flood
The death-dance in his blood;
Yet no part but what will
Be Christ our Saviour still.
Of her flesh He took flesh:
He does take, fresh and fresh,
Though much the mystery how,
Not flesh but spirit now,
And wakes, O marvellous!
New Nazareths in us,
Where she shall yet conceive
Him, morning, noon, and eve;
New Bethlems, and He born
There, evening, noon and morn.
Bethlem or Nazareth,
Men here may draw like breath
More Christ, and baffle death;
Who, born so, comes to be
New self, and nobler me
In each one, and each one
More makes, when all is done,
Both God's and Mary's son.
Again look overhead
How air is azurèd.
O how! Nay do but stand
Where you can lift your hand
Skywards: rich, rich it laps
Round the four finger-gaps.
Yet such a sapphire-shot

Charged, steepèd sky will not
Stain light. Yea, mark you this:
It does no prejudice.
The glass-blue days are those
When every colour glows,
Each shape and shadow shows.
Blue be it: this blue heaven
The seven or seven times seven
Hued sunbeam will transmit
Perfect, nor alter it.
Or if there does some soft
On things aloof, aloft,
Bloom breathe, that one breath more
Earth is the fairer for.
Whereas did air not make
This bath of blue and slake
This fire, the sun would shake
A blear and blinding ball
With blackness bound, and all
The thick stars round him roll,
Flashing like flecks of coal,
Quartz-fret, or sparks of salt
In grimy vasty vault.
    So God was God of old;
A mother came to mould
Those limbs like ours which are,
What must make our daystar
Much dearer to mankind:
Whose glory bare would blind
Or less would win man's mind.
Through her we may see Him
Made sweeter, not made dim,
And her hand leaves His light
Sifted to suit our sight.

Be thou, then, O thou dear
Mother, my atmosphere
My happier world wherein
To wend and meet no sin;
Above me, round me lie
Fronting my froward eye
With sweet and scarless sky;
Stir in my ears, speak there
Of God's love, O live air,
Of patience, penance, prayer;
World-mothering air, air wild,
Wound with thee, in thee isled,
Fold home, fast fold thy child.

EDWARD CARPENTER

b.1844

By the Shore

ALL night by the shore.
The obscure water, the long white lines of advancing foam, the rustle and thud, the panting sea-breaths, the pungent sea-smell,
The great slow air moving from the distant horizon, the immense mystery of space, and the soft canopy of the clouds!

The swooning thuds go on–the drowse of ocean goes on:
The long inbreaths–the short sharp outbreaths–the silence between.

I am a bit of the shore: the waves feed upon me, they come pasturing over me;
I am glad, O waves, that you come pasturing over me.

I am a little arm of the sea: the same tumbling
swooning dream goes on–I feel the waves all
around me, I spread myself through them.
How delicious! I spread and spread. The waves
tumble through and over me–they dash through
my face and hair.
The night is dark overhead: I do not see them, but
I touch them and hear their gurgling laughter.

The play goes on!
The strange expanding indraughts go on!
Suddenly I am the Ocean itself: the great soft wind
creeps over my face.
I am in love with the wind–I reach my lips to its kisses.
How delicious! all night and ages and ages long to
spread myself to the gliding wind!
But now (and ever) it maddens me with its touch,
I arise and whirl in my bed, and sweep my arms
madly along the shores.

I am not sure any more which my own particular bit
of shore is;
All the bays and inlets know me: I glide along in and
out under the sun by the beautiful coast-line;
My hair floats leagues behind me; millions together
my children dash against my face;
I hear what they say and am marvellously content.

All night by the shore;
And the sea is a sea of faces.

The long white lines come up–face after face comes
and falls past me–
Thud after thud. Is it pain or joy?
Face after face–endless!

I do not know; my sense numbs; a trance is on me–
    I am becoming detached!
I am a bit of the shore:
The waves feed upon me, they pasture all over me, my
    feeling is strangely concentrated at every point
    where they touch me;
I am glad O waves that you come pasturing over me.

I am detached, I disentangle myself from the shore;
    I have become free–I float out and mingle with
    the rest.
The pain, the acute clinging desire, is over–I feel
    beings like myself all around me, I spread myself
    through and through them, I am merged in a sea
    of contact.
Freedom and equality are a fact. Life and joy seem
    to have begun for me.

The play goes on!
Suddenly I am the great living Ocean itself–the awful
    Spirit of Immensity creeps over my face.

I am in love with it. All night and ages and ages long
    and for ever I pour my soul out to it in love.
I spread myself out broader and broader for ever, that
    I may touch it and be with it everywhere.
There is no end. But ever and anon it maddens me
    with its touch. I arise and sweep away my bounds.

I know but I do not care any longer which my own
    particular body is–all conditions and fortunes
    are mine.
By the ever-beautiful coast-line of human life, by all
    shores, in all climates and countries, by every
    secluded nook and inlet,

Under the eye of my beloved Spirit I glide:
O joy! for ever, ever, joy!
I am not hurried–the whole of eternity is mine;
With each one I delay, with each one I dwell–with you
I dwell.
The warm breath of each life ascends past me;
I take the thread from the fingers that are weary, and
go on with the work;
The secretest thoughts of all are mine, and mine are
the secretest thoughts of all.

All night by the shore;
And the fresh air comes blowing with the dawn.
The mystic night fades–but my joy fades not.
I arise and cast a stone into the water (O sea of faces
I cast this poem among you)–and turn landward
over the rustling beach.

Love's Vision

AT night in each other's arms,
Content, overjoyed, resting deep deep down in
the darkness,
Lo! the heavens opened and He appeared–
Whom no mortal eye may see,
Whom no eye clouded with Care,
Whom none who seeks after this or that, whom none
who has not escaped from self.

There–in the region of Equality, in the world of
Freedom no longer limited,
Standing as a lofty peak in heaven above the clouds,
From below hidden, yet to all who pass into that region
most clearly visible–
He the Eternal appeared.

Over the Great City

OVER the great city,
Where the wind rustles through the parks and
gardens,
In the air, the high clouds brooding,
In the lines of street perspective, the lamps, the traffic,
The pavements and the innumerable feet upon them,
I Am: make no mistake–do not be deluded.

Think not because I do not appear at the first glance–
because the centuries have gone by and there is
no assured tidings of me–that therefore I am not
there.
Think not because all goes its own way that therefore
I do not go my own way through all.
The fixed bent of hurrying faces in the street–each
turned towards its own light, seeing no other–
yet I am the Light towards which they all look.
The toil of so many hands to such multifarious ends,
yet my hand knows the touch and twining of them
all.

All come to me at last.
There is no love like mine;
For all other love takes one and not another;
And other love is pain, but this is joy eternal.

So Thin a Veil

SO thin a veil divides
Us from such joy, past words,
Walking in daily life—the business of the hour, each
  detail seen to;
Yet carried, rapt away, on what sweet floods of other
  Being:
Swift streams of music flowing, light far back through
  all Creation shining,
Loved faces looking—
Ah! from the true, the mortal self
So thin a veil divides!

The World-Spirit

LIKE soundless summer lightning seen afar,
  A halo o'er the grave of all mankind,
O undefinèd dream-embosomed star,
  O charm of human love and sorrow twined:

Far, far away beyond the world's bright streams,
  Over the ruined spaces of the lands,
Thy beauty, floating slowly, ever seems
  To shine most glorious; then from out our hands

To fade and vanish, evermore to be
  Our sorrow, our sweet longing sadly borne,
Our incommunicable mystery
  Shrined in the soul's long night before the morn.

Ah! in the far fled days, how fair the sun
  Fell sloping o'er the green flax by the Nile,
Kissed the slow water's breast, and glancing shone
  Where laboured men and maidens, with a smile

Cheating the laggard hours; o'er them the doves
Sailed high in evening blue; the river-wheel
Sang, and was still; and lamps of many loves
Were lit in hearts, long dead to woe or weal.

And, where a shady headland cleaves the light
That like a silver swan floats o'er the deep
Dark purple-stained Aegean, oft the height
Felt from of old some poet-soul upleap,

As in the womb a child before its birth,
Foreboding higher life. Of old, as now,
Smiling the calm sea slept, and woke with mirth
To kiss the strand, and slept again below.

So, from of old, o'er Athens' god-crowned steep
Or round the shattered bases of great Rome,
Fleeting and passing, as in dreamful sleep,
The shadow-peopled ages go and come:

Sounds of a far-awakened multitude,
With cry of countless voices intertwined,
Harsh strife and stormy roar of battle rude,
Labour and peaceful arts and growth of mind.

And yet, o'er all, the One through many seen,
The phantom Presence moving without fail,
Sweet sense of closelinked life and passion keen
As of the grass waving before the gale.

What art Thou, O that wast and art to be?
Ye forms that once through shady forest-glade
Or golden light-flood wandered lovingly,
What are ye? Nay, though all the past do fade

Ye are not therefore perished, ye whom erst
    The eternal Spirit struck with quick desire,
And led and beckoned onward till the first
    Slow spark of life became a flaming fire.

Ye are not therefore perished: for behold
    To-day ye move about us, and the same
Dark murmur of the past is forward rolled
    Another age, and grows with louder fame

Unto the morrow: newer ways are ours,
    New thoughts, new fancies, and we deem our lives
New-fashioned in a mould of vaster powers;
    But as of old with flesh the spirit strives,

And we but head the strife. Soon shall the song
    That rolls all down the ages blend its voice
With our weak utterance and make us strong;
    That we, borne forward still, may still rejoice,

Fronting the wave of change. Thou who alone
    Changeless remainest, O most mighty Soul,
Hear us before we vanish! O make known
    Thyself in us, us in thy living whole.

367

SAMUEL WADDINGTON

b.1844

A Persian Apologue

LOVE came to crave sweet love, if love might be;
To the Belovëd's door he came, and knocked:–
'And who art thou?' she asked,– 'we know not thee!'
Then shyly listened, nor the door unlocked.
Love answered, 'It is I!' 'Nay, thee and me
This house will never hold.'–'Twas thus she mocked
His piteous quest; and, weeping, home went he,
While thro' the night the moaning plane-tree rocked.
Three seasons sped, and lo, again Love came;
Again he knocked; again in simple wise,
'Pray, who is there?' she asked,–'What is thy name?'
But Love had learnt the magic of replies,–
'It is Thyself!' he whispered, and behold,
The door was opened, and love's mystery told.

JOHN BANNISTER TABB

1845-1909

The Life-tide

EACH wave that breaks upon the strand,
How swift soe'er to spurn the sand
And seek again the sea,
Christ-like, within its lifted hand
Must bear the stigma of the land
For all eternity.

Communion

ONCE when my heart was passion-free
To learn of things divine,
The soul of nature suddenly
Outpoured itself in mine.

I held the secrets of the deep,
And of the heavens above;
I knew the harmonies of sleep,
The mysteries of love.

And for a moment's interval
The earth, the sky, the sea–
My soul encompassed, each and all,
As now they compass me.

To one in all, to all in one–
Since Love the work began–
Life's ever widening circles run,
Revealing God and man.

An Interpreter

WHAT, O Eternity,
Is Time to thee?–
What to the boundless All
My portion small?

Lift up thine eyes, my soul!
Against the tidal roll
Stands many a stone,
Whereon the breakers thrown
Are dashed to spray–
Else were the Ocean dumb.

So, in the way
Of tides eternal, thou
Abidest now;
And God Himself doth come
A suppliant to thee,
Love's prisoned thought to free.

Christ and the Pagan

I HAD no God but these,
The sacerdotal Trees,
And they uplifted me.
'I hung upon a Tree.'

The sun and moon I saw,
And reverential awe
Subdued me day and night.
'I am the perfect Light.'

Within a lifeless Stone–
All other gods unknown–
I sought Divinity.
'The Corner-Stone am I.'

For sacrificial feast,
I slaughtered man and beast,
Red recompense to gain.
'So I, a Lamb, was slain.

'Yea; such My hungering Grace
That wheresoe'er My face
Is hidden, none may grope
Beyond eternal Hope.'

All in All

WE know Thee, each in part–
A portion small;
But love Thee, as Thou art–
The All in all:
For Reason and the rays thereof
Are starlight to the noon of Love.

EMILY HENRIETTA HICKEY

b.1845

'The Greatest of these is Charity'

I

THERE came one day a leper to my door:
I shrank from him in loathing and in dread,
But yet, remembering how old legends said
That Jesus Christ so often heretofore
Came in such guise to try His saints of yore,
I brought him in, and clothed, and warmed, and fed;
Yea, brake my box of precious nard, to pour
Its costly fragrancy upon his feet.
And when the house was filled with odour sweet,
I looked to see the loveliest face,–but o'er
The leper came no change divine to greet
My eager soul, which did such change entreat.
And then I bowed my head, and wept full sore–
Ah! the times change; such visions come no more!

II

With tear-dimmed eyes I went upon my way,
Passed from the city to the April wood,
Where the young trees in trembling gladness stood;
And once again my grievèd heart grew gay.
Then did I see a little child at play;
All the sweet April fountain of his blood
Tossed out in joy, that brake in laughter-spray;
And all my heart it loved him; so I bent
To kiss his sunny mouth. Then through me went
That which I may not tell, nor can, to-day.
When was such healing with such wounding blent?
Such pain supreme with such supreme content?
The fires of God comfort as well as slay,
Else had I surely died, who am but clay.

371

GEORGE BARLOW

b.1847

The Immortal and the Mortal

OH where the immortal and the mortal meet
In union than of wind and wave more sweet,
Meet me, O God–
Where Thou hast trod
I follow, along the blood-print of Thy feet.

Oh, though the austere ensanguined road be hard
And all the blue skies shine through casemates barred,
I follow Thee–
Show Thou to me
Thy face, the speechless face divinely marred.

Lo! who will love and follow to the end,
Shall he not also to hell's depths descend?
Shall he not find
The whole world blind,
Searching among the lone stars for a friend?

Lo! who will follow love throughout the way,
From crimson morning flush till twilight grey?
Who fears not chains,
Anguish and pains,
If love wait at the ending of the day?

If at the ending of the day life's bride
Be near our hearts in vision glorified:
If at the end
God's hand extend
That far triumphant boon for which we sighed.

Oh, where the immortal to our mortal flows,
Flushing our grey clay heart to its own rose,
Spirit supreme
Upon me gleam;
Make me Thine own; I reckon not the throes.

I would pour out my heart in one long sigh
Of speechless yearning towards Thine home on high:
I would be pure,
Suffer, endure,
Pervade with ceaseless wings the unfathomed sky.

Oh, at the point where God and man are one,
Meet me, Thou God; flame on me like the sun;
I would be part
Of Thine own heart,
That by my hands Thy love-deeds may be done:

That by my hands Thy love-truths may be shown
And far lands know me for Thy very own;
That I may bring
The dead world spring:–
The flowers awake, Lord, at Thy word alone.

Oh, to the point where man and God unite,
Raise me, Thou God; transfuse me with Thy light;
Where I would go
Thou, God, dost know;
For Thy sake I will face the starless night.

The night is barren, black, devoid of bloom,
Scentless and waste, a wide appalling tomb;
Dark foes surround
The soul discrowned
And strange shapes lower and threaten through the gloom.

But where Thou art with me Thy mortal, one,
God, mine immortal, my death-conquering sun,
        Meet me and show
        What path to go
Till the last work of deathless love be done.

DIGBY MACKWORTH DOLBEN

1848-1867

'Strange, all-absorbing Love'

STRANGE, all-absorbing Love, who gatherest
Unto Thy glowing all my pleasant dew,
Then delicately my garden waterest,
Drawing the old, to pour it back anew:

In the dim glitter of the dawning hours
'Not so,' I said, 'but still those drops of light,
Heart-shrined among the petals of my flowers,
Shall hold the memory of the starry night

'So fresh, no need of showers shall there be.'–
Ah, senseless gardener! must it come to pass
That 'neath the glaring noon thou shouldest see
Thine earth become as iron, His heavens as brass?

Nay rather, O my Sun, I will be wise,
Believe in Love which may not yet be seen,
Yield Thee my earth-drops, call Thee from the skies,
In soft return, to keep my bedding green.

So when the bells at Vesper-tide shall sound,
And the dead ocean o'er my garden flows,
Upon the Golden Altar may be found
Some scarlet berries and a Christmas rose.

Flowers for the Altar

I

TELL us, tell us, holy shepherds,
    What at Bethlehem you saw.–
'Very God of Very God
    Asleep amid the straw.'

Tell us, tell us, all ye faithful,
    What this morning came to pass
At the awful elevation
    In the Canon of the Mass.–
'Very God of Very God,
    By whom the worlds were made,
In silence and in helplessness
    Upon the altar laid.'

Tell us, tell us, wondrous Jesu,
    What has drawn Thee from above
To the manger and the altar.–
    All the silence answers–Love.

II

Through the roaring streets of London
    Thou art passing, hidden Lord,
Uncreated, Consubstantial,
    In the seventh heaven adored.

As of old the ever-Virgin
    Through unconscious Bethlehem
Bore Thee, not in glad procession,
    Jewelled robe and diadem;

Not in pomp and not in power,
  Onward to Nativity,
Shrined but in the tabernacle
  Of her sweet Virginity.

Still Thou goest by in silence,
  Still the world cannot receive,
Still the poor and weak and weary
  Only, worship and believe.

CHRISTINA CATHERINE FRASER-TYTLER (MRS. EDWARD LIDDELL)

b.1848

In Summer Fields

SOMETIMES, as in the summer fields
I walk abroad, there comes to me
So strange a sense of mystery,
My heart stands still, my feet must stay,
I am in such strange company.

I look on high–the vasty deep
Of blue outreaches all my mind;
And yet I think beyond to find
Something more vast–and at my feet
The little bryony is twined.

Clouds sailing as to God go by,
Earth, sun, and stars are rushing on;
And faster than swift time, more strong
Than rushing of the worlds, I feel
A something Is, of name unknown.

And turning suddenly away,
Grown sick and dizzy with the sense
Of power, and mine own impotence,
I see the gentle cattle feed
In dumb unthinking innocence.

The great Unknown above; below,
The cawing rooks, the milking-shed;
God's awful silence overhead;
Below, the muddy pool, the path
The thirsty herds of cattle tread.

Sometimes, as in the summer fields
I walk abroad, there comes to me
So wild a sense of mystery,
My senses reel, my reason fails,
I am in such strange company.

Yet somewhere, dimly, I can feel
The wild confusion dwells in me,
And I, in no strange company,
Am the lost link 'twixt Him and these,
And touch Him through the mystery.

WILLIAM ERNEST HENLEY

1849-1903

I am the Reaper

I AM the Reaper.
All things with heedful hook
Silent I gather.
Pale roses touched with the spring,
Tall corn in summer,

Fruits rich with autumn, and frail winter blossoms–
Reaping, still reaping–
All things with heedful hook
Timely I gather.

I am the Sower.
All the unbodied life
Runs through my seed-sheet.
Atom with atom wed,
Each quickening the other,
Fall through my hands, ever changing, still changeless.
Ceaselessly sowing,
Life, incorruptible life,
Flows from my seed-sheet.

Maker and breaker,
I am the ebb and the flood,
Here and Hereafter,
Sped through the tangle and coil
Of infinite nature,
Viewless and soundless I fashion all being.
Taker and giver,
I am the womb and the grave,
The Now and the Ever.

EDMUND GOSSE

b.1849

The Tide of Love

LOVE, flooding all the creeks of my dry soul,
From which the warm tide ebbed when I was born,
Following the moon of destiny, doth roll
    His slow rich wave along the shore forlorn,
To make the ocean–God–and me, one whole.

So, shuddering in its ecstasy, it lies,
    And, freed from mire and tangle of the ebb,
Reflects the waxing and the waning skies,
    And bears upon its panting breast the web
Of night and her innumerable eyes.

Nor can conceive at all that it was blind,
    But trembling with the sharp approach of love,
That, strenuous, moves without one breath of wind,
    Gasps, as the wakening maid, on whom the Dove
With folded wings of deity declined.

She in the virgin sweetness of her dream
    Thought nothing strange to find her vision true;
And I thus bathed in living rapture deem
    No moveless drought my channel ever knew,
But rustled always with the murmuring stream.

Old and New

I. B.C.

COME, Hesper, and ye Gods of mountain waters,
    Come, nymphs and Dryades,
Come, silken choir of soft Pierian daughters,
    And girls of lakes and seas,
Evoë! and evoë Io! crying,
    Fill all the earth and air;
Evoë! till the quivering words, replying,
    Shout back the echo there!

All day in soundless swoon or heavy slumber,
    We lay among the flowers,
But now the stars break forth in countless number
    To watch the dewy hours;

And now Iacchus, beautiful and glowing,
  Adown the hill-side comes,
Mid tabrets shaken high, and trumpets blowing,
  And resonance of drums.

The leopard-skin is round his smooth white shoulders,
  The vine-branch round his hair,
Those eyes that rouse desire in maid-beholders
  Are glittering, glowworm-fair;
Crowned king of all the provinces of pleasure,
  Lord of a wide domain,
He comes, and brings delight that knows no measure,
  A full Saturnian reign.

Take me, too, Maenads, to your fox-skin chorus,
  Rose-lipped like volute-shells,
For I would follow where your host canorous
  Roars down the forest-dells;
The sacred frenzy rends my throat and bosom!
  I shout, and whirl where He,
Our Vine-God, tosses like some pale blood-blossom
  Swept on a stormy sea.

Around his car, with streaming hair, and frantic,
  The Maenads and wild gods
And shaggy fauns and wood-girls corybantic
  Toss high the ivy-rods;
Brown limbs with white limbs madly intertwining
  Whirl in a fiery dance,
Till, when at length Orion is declining,
  We glide into a trance.

The satyr's heart is faintly, faintly beating,
  The choir of nymphs is mute;
Iacchus up the western slope is fleeting,
  Uncheered by horn or flute;

Hushed, hushed are all the shouting and the singing,
 The frenzy, the delight,
Since out into the cold grey air upspringing,
 The morning-star shines bright.

II. A.D.

Not with a choir of angels without number,
 And noise of lutes and lyres,
But gently, with the woven veil of slumber
 Across Thine awful fires,
We yearn to watch Thy face, serene and tender,
 Melt, smiling, calm and sweet,
Where round the print of thorns, in thornlike splendour,
 Transcendent glories meet.

We have no hopes if Thou art close beside us,
 And no profane despairs,
Since all we need is Thy great hand to guide us,
 Thy heart to take our cares;
For us is no to-day, to-night, to-morrow,
 No past time nor to be,
We have no joy but Thee, there is no sorrow,
 No life to live but Thee.

The cross, like pilgrim-warriors, we follow,
 Led by our eastern star;
The wild crane greets us, and the wandering swallow
 Bound southward for Shinar;
All night that single star shines bright above us;
 We go with weary feet,
But in the end we know are they who love us,
 Whose pure embrace is sweet.

Most sweet of all, when dark the way and moonless,
To feel a touch, a breath,
And know our weary spirits are not tuneless,
Our unseen goal not Death;
To know that Thou, in all Thy old sweet fashion,
Are near us to sustain!
We praise Thee, Lord, by all Thy tears and passion,
By all Thy cross and pain!

For when this night of toil and tears is over,
Across the hills of spice,
Thyself wilt meet us, glowing like a lover
Before Love's Paradise;
There are the saints, with palms and hymns and roses,
And better still than all,
The long, long day of bliss that never closes,
Thy marriage festival!

EDMOND GORE ALEXANDER HOLMES

b.1850

The Creed of My Heart

A FLAME in my heart is kindled by the might of the
morn's pure breath;
A passion beyond all passion; a faith that eclipses faith;
A joy that is more than gladness; a hope that outsoars
desire;
A love that consumes and quickens; a soul-transfiguring fire.
My life is possessed and mastered: my heart is inspired
and filled.
All other visions have faded: all other voices are stilled.
My doubts are vainer than shadows: my fears are idler
than dreams:
They vanish like breaking bubbles, those old soul-
torturing themes.

The riddles of life are cancelled, the problems that bred
 despair:
I cannot guess them or solve them, but I know that they
 are not there.
They are past, they are all forgotten, the breeze has blown
 them away;
For life's inscrutable meaning is clear as the dawn of day.
It is there–the secret of Nature–there in the morning's
 glow;
There in the speaking stillness; there in the rose-flushed
 snow.
It is here in the joy and rapture; here in my pulsing breast:
I feel what has ne'er been spoken: I know what has ne'er
 been guessed.

The rose-lit clouds of morning; the sun-kissed mountain
 heights;
The orient streaks and flushes; the mingling shadows and
 lights;
The flow of the lonely river; the voice of its distant
 stream;
The mists that rise from the meadows, lit up by the sun's
 first beam;–
They mingle and melt as I watch them; melt and mingle
 and die.
The land is one with the water: the earth is one with the sky.
The parts are as parts no longer: Nature is All and One:
Her life is achieved, completed: her days of waiting are
 done.

I breathe the breath of the morning. I am one with the
 one World-Soul.
I live my own life no longer, but the life of the living
 Whole.

I am more than self: I am selfless: I am more than self:
I am I.
I have found the springs of my being in the flush of the eastern sky.
I–the true self, the spirit, the self that is born of death–
I have found the flame of my being in the morn's ambrosial breath.
I lose my life for a season: I lose it beyond recall:
But I find it renewed, rekindled, in the life of the One, the All.
I look not forward or backward: the abysses of time are nought.
From pole to pole of the heavens I pass in a flash of thought.
I clasp the world to my bosom: I feel its pulse in my breast,–
The pulse of measureless motion, the pulse of fathomless rest.
Is it motion or rest that thrills me? Is it lightning or moonlit peace?
Am I freer than waves of ether, or prisoned beyond release?
I know not; but through my spirit, within me, around, above,
The world-wide river is streaming, the river of life and love.
Silent, serene, eternal, passionless, perfect, pure;–
I may not measure its windings, but I know that its aim is sure.
In its purity seethes all passion: in its silence resounds all song:
Its strength is builded of weakness: its right is woven of wrong.

I am borne afar on its bosom; yet its source and its goal
are mine,
From the sacred springs of Creation to the ocean of love
Divine.
I have ceased to think or to reason: there is nothing to
ponder or prove:
I hope, I believe no longer: I am lost in a dream of love.

Nirvana

COULD my heart but see Creation as God sees it,–
from within;
See His grace behind its beauty, see His will behind its
force;
See the flame of life shoot upward when the April days
begin;
See the wave of life rush outward from its pure eternal
source;

Could I see the summer sunrise glow with God's tran-
scendent hope;
See His peace upon the waters in the moonlit summer
night;
See Him nearer still when, blinded, in the depths of gloom
I grope,–
See the darkness flash and quiver with the gladness of
His light;

Could I see the red-hot passion of His love resistless burn
Through the dumb despair of winter, through the
frozen lifeless clod;–
Could I see what lies around me as God sees it, I should learn
That its outward life is nothing, that its inward life
is God.

Vain the dream! To spirit only is the spirit-life revealed:
God alone can see God's glory: God alone can feel God's love.
By myself the soul of Nature from myself is still concealed;
And the earth is still around me, and the skies are still above.

Vain the dream! I cannot mingle with the all-sustaining soul:
I am prisoned in my senses; I am pinioned by my pride;
I am severed by my selfhood from the world-life of the Whole;
And my world is near and narrow, and God's world is waste and wide.

Vain the dream! Yet in the morning, when the eastern skies are red,
When the dew is on the meadows, when the lark soars up and sings,–
Leaps a sudden flame within me from its ashes pale and dead,
And I see God's beauty burning through the veil of outward things.

Brighter grows the veil and clearer, till, beyond all fear and doubt,
I am ravished by God's splendour into oneness with His rest;
And I draw the world within me, and I send my soul without;
And God's pulse is in my bosom, and I lie upon God's breast.

Dies the beatific vision in the moment of its birth;
 Dies, but in its death transfigures all the sequence of my days;
Dies, but dying crowns with triumph all the travail of the earth,
 Till its harsh discordant murmurs swell into a psalm of praise.

Then a yearning comes upon me to be drawn at last by death,
 Drawn into the mystic circle in which all things live and move,
Drawn into the mystic circle of the love which is God's breath,–
 Love creative, love receptive, love of loving, love of love.

God! the One, the All of Being! let me lose my life in Thine;
 Let me be what Thou hast made me, be a quiver of Thy flame.
Purge my self from self's pollution; burn it into life divine;
 Burn it till it dies triumphant in the firespring whence it came.

La Vie Profonde

HEMMED in by petty thoughts and petty things,
 Intent on toys and trifles all my years,
Pleased by life's gauds, pained by its pricks and stings,
 Swayed by ignoble hopes, ignoble fears;
Threading life's tangled maze without life's clue,
 Busy with means, yet heedless of their ends,
Lost to all sense of what is real and true,
 Blind to the goal to which all Nature tends:–
Such is my surface self: but deep beneath,
 A mighty actor on a world-wide stage,
Crowned with all knowledge, lord of life and death,
 Sure of my aim, sure of my heritage,–
I–the true self–live on, in self's despite,
That 'life profound' whose darkness is God's light.

The God Within

LIFE of my life! soul of my inmost soul!
 Pure central point of everlasting light!
Creative splendour! Fountain-head and goal
 Of all the rays that make the darkness bright–
  And pierce the gloom of nothing more and more
 And win new realms from the abyss of night!
  O God, I veil my eyes and kneel before
  Thy shrine of love and tremble and adore.

The unfathomable past is but the dawn
 Of thee triumphant rising from the tomb;
And could we deem thy lamp of light withdrawn,
 Back in an instant into primal gloom

All things that are, all things that time has wrought,
All that shall ever yet unseal the womb
Of elemental Chaos, swift as thought
Would melt away and leave a world of nought.

We gaze in wonder on the starry face
Of midnight skies, and worship and aspire,
Yet all the kingdoms of abysmal space
Are less than thy one point of inmost fire:
We dare not think of time's unending way,
Yet present, past, and future would expire,
And all eternity would pass away
In thy one moment of intensest day.

Of old our fathers heard thee when the roll
Of midnight thunder crashed across the sky:
I hear thee in the silence of the soul–
Its very stillness is the majesty
Of thy mysterious voice, that moves me more
Than wrath of tempest as it rushes by,
Or booming thunder, or the surging roar
Of seas that storm a never-trodden shore.

And they beheld thee when the lightning shone,
And tore the leaden slumber of the storm
With vivid flame that was and then was gone,
Whose blaze made blind, whose very breath was warm:–
But I, if I would see thee, pray for grace
To veil my eyes to every outward form,
And in the darkness for a moment's space
I see the splendour of thy cloudless face.

In thought I climb to Being's utmost brink
And pass beyond the last imagined star,
And tremble and grow dizzy while I think–
But thou art yet more infinitely far,

O God, from me who breathe the air of sin,
And I am doomed to traverse worlds that are
More fathomless to fancy ere I win
The central altar of the soul within.

How shall I worship thee? With speechless awe
Of guilt that shrinks when innocence is near
And veils its face: with faith, that ever saw
Most when its eyes were clouded with a tear:
With hope, the breath of spirits that aspire:
Lastly, with love–the grave of every fear,
The fount of faith, the triumph of desire,
The burning brightness of thine own white fire. . . .

O God that dwellest in transcendent light
Beyond our dreams, who grope in darkness here,
Beyond imagination's utmost flight,–
I bless thee most that sometimes when a tear
Of tender yearning rises unrepressed,
Lo! for an instant thou art strangely near–
Nearer to my own heart than I who rest
In speechless adoration on thy breast.

FRANCIS WILLIAM BOURDILLON

b.1852

The Chantry of the Cherubim

O CHANTRY of the Cherubim,
Down-looking on the stream!
Beneath thy boughs the day grows dim;
Through windows comes the gleam;
A thousand raptures fill the air,
Beyond delight, beyond despair.

I will not name one flower that clings
 In cluster at my feet!
I will not hail one bird that sings
 Its anthem loud or sweet!
This is the floor of Heaven, and these
The angels that God's ear do please.

I walk as one unclothed of flesh,
 I wash my spirit clean;
I see old miracles afresh,
 And wonders yet unseen.
I will not leave Thee till Thou give
Some word whereby my soul may live!

I listened–but no voice I heard;
 I looked–no likeness saw;
Slowly the joy of flower and bird
 Did like a tide withdraw;
And in the heaven a silent star
Smiled on me, infinitely far.

I buoyed me on the wings of dream,
 Above the world of sense;
I set my thought to sound the scheme,
 And fathom the Immense;
I tuned my spirit as a lute
To catch wind-music wandering mute.

Yet came there never voice nor sign;
 But throught my being stole
Sense of a Universe divine,
 And knowledge of a soul
Perfected in the joy of things,
The star, the flower, the bird that sings.

Nor I am more, nor less, than these;
    All are one brotherhood;
I and all creatures, plants, and trees,
    The living limbs of God;
And in an hour, as this, divine,
I feel the vast pulse throb in mine.

WILLIAM JAMES DAWSON

b. 1854

Inspirations

SOMETIMES, I know not why, nor how, nor whence,
    A change comes over me, and then the task
  Of common life slips from me. Would you ask
What power is this which bids the world go hence?
  Who knows? I only feel a faint perfume
Steal through the rooms of life; a saddened sense
Of something lost; a music as of brooks
That babble to the sea; pathetic looks
  Of closing eyes that in a darkened room
  Once dwelt on mine: I feel the general doom
Creep nearer, and with God I stand alone.
  O mystic sense of sudden quickening!
Hope's lark-song rings, or life's deep undertone
  Wails through my heart–and then I needs must sing.

EDITH MATILDA THOMAS

b. 1854

Patmos

ALL around him Patmos lies,
Who hath spirit-gifted eyes,
Who his happy sight can suit
To the great and the minute.
Doubt not but he holds in view
A new earth and heaven new;
Doubt not but his ear doth catch
Strain nor voice nor reed can match:
Many a silver, sphery note
Shall within his hearing float.

All around him Patmos lies,
Who unto God's priestess flies:
Thou, O Nature, bid him see,
Through all guises worn by thee,
A divine apocalypse.
Manifold his fellowships:
Now the rocks their archives ope;
Voiceless creatures tell their hope
In a language symbol-wrought;
Groves to him sigh out their thought;
Musings of the flower and grass
Through his quiet spirit pass.
'Twixt new earth and heaven new
He hath traced and holds the clue,
Number his delights ye may not;
Fleets the year but these decay not.
Now the freshets of the rain,
Bounding on from hill to plain,
Show him earthly streams have rise
In the bosom of the skies.

Now he feels the morning thrill,
As upmounts, unseen and still,
Dew the wing of evening drops.
Now the frost, that meets and stops
Summer's feet in tender sward,
Greets him, breathing heavenward.
Hieroglyphics writes the snow,
Through the silence falling slow;
Types of star and petaled bloom
A white missal-page illume.
By these floating symbols fine,
Heaven-truth shall be divine.

All around him Patmos lies,
Who hath spirit-gifted eyes;
He need not afar remove,
He need not the times reprove,
Who would hold perpetual lease
Of an isle in seas of peace.

Spirit to Spirit

DEAD? Not to thee, thou keen watcher,–not silent, not viewless, to thee,
Immortal still wrapped in the mortal! I, from the mortal set free,
Greet thee by many clear tokens thou smilest to hear and to see.

For I, when thou wakest at dawn, to thee am the entering morn;
And I, when thou walkest abroad, am the dew on the leaf and the thorn,
The tremulous glow of the noon, the twilight on harvests of corn.

I am the flower by the wood-path,–thou bendest to look
in my eyes;
The bird in its nest in the thicket,–thou heedest my
love-laden cries;
The planet that leads the night legions,–thou liftest thy
gaze to the skies.

And I am the soft-dropping rain, the snow with its flutter-
ing swarms;
The summer-day cloud on the hilltops, that showeth thee
manifold forms;
The wind from the south and the west, the voice that
sings courage in storms!

Sweet was the earth to thee ever, but sweeter by far to
thee now:
How hast thou room for tears, when all times marvelest
thou,
Beholding who dwells with God in the blossoming sward
and the bough!

Once as a wall were the mountains, once darkened between
us the sea;
No longer these thwart and baffle, forbidding my passage
to thee:
Immortal still wrapped in the mortal, I linger till thou
art set free!

OSCAR WILDE

1856-1900

E Tenebris

COME down, O Christ, and help me! reach thy hand,
For I am drowning in a stormier sea
Than Simon on thy lake of Galilee:
The wine of life is spilt upon the sand,
My heart is as some famine-murdered land
Whence all good things have perished utterly,
And well I know my soul in Hell must lie
If I this night before God's throne should stand.
'He sleeps perchance, or rideth to the chase,
Like Baal, when his prophets howled that name
From morn to noon on Carmel's smitten height.'
Nay, peace, I shall behold, before the night,
The feet of brass, the robe more white than flame,
The wounded hands, the weary human face.

From 'Panthea'

WE are resolved into the supreme air,
We are made one with what we touch and see,
With our heart's blood each crimson sun is fair,
With our young lives each spring-impassioned tree
Flames into green, the wildest beasts that range
The moor our kinsmen are, all life is one, and all is change.

With beat of systole and of diastole
One grand great life throbs through earth's giant heart,
And mighty waves of single Being roll
From nerveless germ to man, for we are part
Of every rock and bird and beast and hill,
One with the things that prey on us, and one with what
we kill. . . .

And we two lovers shall not sit afar,
    Critics of nature, but the joyous sea
Shall be our raiment, and the bearded star
    Shoot arrows at our pleasure! We shall be
Parts of the mighty universal whole,
And through all aeons mix and mingle with the Kosmic Soul!

We shall be notes in that great Symphony
    Whose cadence circles through the rhythmic spheres,
And all the live World's throbbing heart shall be
    One with our heart; the stealthy creeping years
Have lost their terrors now, we shall not die,
The Universe itself shall be our Immortality!

From 'Humanitad'

TO make the Body and the Spirit one
    With all right things, till no thing live in vain
From morn to noon, but in sweet unison
    With every pulse of flesh and throb of brain
The Soul in flawless essence high enthroned,
Against all outer vain attack invincibly bastioned,

Mark with serene impartiality
    The strife of things, and yet be comforted,
Knowing that by the chain causality
    All separate existences are wed
Into one supreme whole, whose utterance
Is joy, or holier praise! ah! surely this were governance

Of Life in most august omnipresence,
    Through which the rational intellect would find
In passion its expression, and mere sense,
    Ignoble else, lend fire to the mind,
And being joined with it in harmony
More mystical than that which binds the stars planetary,

Strike from their several tones one octave chord
    Whose cadence being measureless would fly
Through all the circling spheres, then to its Lord
    Return refreshed with its new empery
And more exultant power,–this indeed
Could we but reach it were to find the last, the perfect creed.

• • • • • •

O smitten mouth! O forehead crowned with thorn!
    O chalice of all common miseries!
Thou for our sakes that loved thee not hast borne
    An agony of endless centuries,
And we were vain and ignorant nor knew
That when we stabbed thy heart it was our own real
        hearts we slew.

Being ourselves the sowers and the seeds,
    The night that covers and the lights that fade,
The spear that pierces and the side that bleeds,
    The lips betraying and the life betrayed;
The deep hath calm: the moon hath rest: but we
Lords of the natural world are yet our own dread enemy.

Is this the end of all that primal force
    Which, in its changes being still the same,
From eyeless Chaos cleft its upward course,
    Through ravenous seas and whirling rocks and flame,
Till the suns met in heaven and began
Their cycles, and the morning stars sang, and the Word
        was Man!

Nay, nay, we are but crucified, and though
    The bloody sweat falls from our brows like rain,
Loosen the nails–we shall come down I know,
    Stanch the red wounds–we shall be whole again,
No need have we of hyssop-laden rod,
That which is purely human, that is Godlike, that is God.

WILLIAM SHARP

1856-1902

The Valley of Silence

IN the secret Valley of Silence
No breath doth fall;
No wind stirs in the branches;
No bird doth call:
As on a white wall
A breathless lizard is still,
So silence lies on the valley
Breathlessly still.

In the dusk-grown heart of the valley
An altar rises white:
No rapt priest bends in awe
Before its silent light:
But sometimes a flight
Of breathless words of prayer
White-wing'd enclose the altar,
Eddies of prayer.

Desire

THE desire of love, Joy:
The desire of life, Peace:
The desire of the soul, Heaven:
The desire of God–a flame-white secret for ever.

The White Peace

IT lies not on the sunlit hill
Nor on the sunlit plain:
Nor ever on any running stream
Nor on the unclouded main–

But sometimes, through the Soul of Man,
Slow moving o'er his pain,
The moonlight of a perfect peace
Floods heart and brain.

The Rose of Flame

OH, fair immaculate rose of the world, rose of my dream, my Rose!
Beyond the ultimate gates of dream I have heard thy mystical call:
It is where the rainbow of hope suspends and the river of rapture flows–
And the cool sweet dews from the wells of peace for ever fall.

And all my heart is aflame because of the rapture and peace,
And I dream, in my waking dreams and deep in the dreams of sleep,
Till the high sweet wonderful call that shall be the call of release
Shall ring in my ears as I sink from gulf to gulf and from deep to deep–

Sink deep, sink deep beyond the ultimate dreams of all desire–
Beyond the uttermost limit of all that the craving spirit knows:
Then, then, oh then I shall be as the inner flame of thy fire,
O fair immaculate rose of the world, Rose of my dream, my Rose!

The Mystic's Prayer

LAY me to sleep in sheltering flame,
O Master of the Hidden Fire!
Wash pure my heart, and cleanse for me
My soul's desire.

In flame of sunrise bathe my mind,
O Master of the Hidden Fire,
That, when I wake, clear-eyed may be
My soul's desire.

Triad

FROM the Silence of Time, Time's Silence borrow.
In the heart of To-day is the word of To-morrow.
The Builders of Joy are the Children of Sorrow.

MARGARET DELAND

b.1857

Life

BY one great Heart the Universe is stirred:
By Its strong pulse, stars climb the darkening blue;
It throbs in each fresh sunset's changing hue,
And thrills through low sweet song of every bird:

By It, the plunging blood reds all men's veins;
Joy feels that heart against his rapturous own,
And on It, Sorrow breathes her sharpest groan;
It bounds through gladnesses and deepest pains.

Passionless beating through all Time and Space,
Relentless, calm, majestic in Its march,
Alike, though Nature shake heaven's endless arch,
Or man's heart break, because of some dead face!

'Tis felt in sunshine greening the soft sod,
In children's smiling, as in mother's tears;
And, for strange comfort, through the aching years,
Men's hungry souls have named that great Heart, God!

AGNES MARY FRANCES DUCLAUX (ROBINSON-DARMESTETER)

1857

Rhythm

O BEAT and pause that count the life of man,
Throb of the pulsing heart!
Ripple of tides and stars beyond our scan!
Rhythm o' the ray o' the sun and the red o' the rose!
Thrill of the lightning's dart!
All, all are one beyond this world of shows.

Neither with eyes that see nor ears that hear
May we discern thee here,
Nor comprehend, O Life of life, thy laws,
But all our idols praise the perfect whole;
And I have worshipped thee, O rhythmic soul,
Chiefly in beat and pause.

O beat and pause that count the life of man,
Throb of the pulsing heart!
Ripple of tides and stars beyond our scan!
Rhythm o' the ray o' the sun and the red o' the rose!
Thrill of the lightning's dart!
Yea, all are one behind our world of shows.

The Idea

BENEATH this world of stars and flowers
That rolls in visible deity,
I dream another world is ours
And is the soul of all we see.

It hath no form, it hath no spirit;
It is perchance the Eternal Mind;
Beyond the sense that we inherit
I feel it dim and undefined.

How far below the depth of being,
How wide beyond the starry bound
It rolls unconscious and unseeing,
And is as Number or as Sound.

And through the vast fantastic visions
Of all this actual universe,
It moves unswerved by our decisions,
And is the play that we rehearse.

Antiphon to the Holy Spirit

Men and Women sing.

Men.

O THOU that movest all, O Power
That bringest life where'er Thou art,
O Breath of God in star and flower,
Mysterious aim of soul and heart;
Within the thought that cannot grasp Thee
In its unfathomable hold,
We worship Thee who may not clasp Thee,
O God, unreckoned and untold!

Women.

O Source and Sea of Love, O Spirit
That makest every soul akin,
O Comforter whom we inherit,
We turn and worship Thee within!
To give beyond all dreams of giving,
To lose ourselves as Thou in us,
We long; for Thou, O Fount of living,
Art lost in Thy creation thus!

Men.

The mass of unborn matter knew Thee,
And lo! the splendid silent sun
Sprang out to be a witness to Thee
Who art the All, who art the One;
The airy plants unseen that flourish
Their floating strands of filmy rose,
Too small for sight, are Thine to nourish;
For Thou art all that breathes and grows.

Women.

Thou art the ripening of the fallows,
The swelling of the buds in rain;
Thou art the joy of birth that hallows
The rending of the flesh in twain;
O Life, O Love, how undivided
Thou broodest o'er this world of Thine,
Obscure and strange, yet surely guided
To reach a distant end divine!

Men.

We know Thee in the doubt and terror
That reels before the world we see;
We know Thee in the faiths of error;
We know Thee most who most are free.

This phantom of the world around Thee
  Is vast, divine, but not the whole:
We worship Thee, and we have found Thee
  In all that satisfies the soul!

Men and Women.

How shall we serve, how shall we own Thee,
  O breath of Love and Life and Thought?
How shall we praise, who are not shown Thee?
  How shall we serve, who are as nought?
Yet, though Thy worlds maintain unbroken
  The silence of their awful round,
A voice within our souls hath spoken,
  And we who seek have more than found.

MAY PROBYN

The Beloved

WHEN the storm was in the sky,
  And the west was black with showers,
My Beloved came by
  With His Hands full of flowers–
  Red burning flowers,
Like flame that pulsed and throbbed–
  And beyond in the rain-smitten bowers
The turtle-dove sobbed.

(Sweet in the rough weather
  The voice of the turtle-dove–
'Beautiful altogether
  Is my Love.
  His Hands are open spread for love
And full of jacinth stones–
  As the apple-tree among trees of the grove
Is He among the sons.'

The voice of the turtle-dove
    Sweet in the wild weather–
'Until the daybreak dwells my Love
    Among the hills of Bether.
    Among the lilied lawns of Bether,
As a young hart untired–
    Chosen out of thousands,–altogether
To be desired.')

When the night was in the sky,
    And heavily went the hours,
My Beloved drew nigh
    With His Hands full of flowers–
    Burning red flowers
Like cups of scented wine–
    And He said, 'They are all ours,
Thine and Mine.

'I gathered them from the bitter Tree–
    Why dost thou start?
I gathered the Five of them for thee,
    Child of My Heart.
    These are they that have wrung my Heart,
And with fiercest pangs have moved Me–
    I gathered them–why dost thou shrink apart?
In the house of them that loved Me.'

(Sweet through the rain-swept blast
    The moan of the turtle-dove–
'You, that see Him go past,
    Tell Him I languish with love.
    Thou hast wounded my heart, O my Love!
With but one look of Thine eyes,
    While yet the boughs are naked above
And winter is in the skies.')

'Honey-laden flowers
For the children nursed on the knee,
Who sow not bramble among their bowers–
But what' He said 'for thee?
Not joys of June for thee,
Not lily, no, nor rose–
For thee the blossom of the bitter Tree,
More sweet than ought that blows.'

(The voice of the turtle-dove–
'How shall my heart be fed
With pleasant apples of love,
When the winter time has fled.
The rain and the winter fled,
How all His gifts shall grace me,
When His Left Hand is under my head,
And His Right Hand doth embrace me.')

SIR JAMES RENNELL RODD

b. 1858

From 'In Excelsis'

BY those heights we dare to dare,
By the greatness of our prayer,
Ever growing, loftier reaching
To a royaller beseeching,
By the olden woes washed painless, white and stainless in the tears of bitter price,
By the strength of our assurance to endurance of the need of sacrifice,
Not by dreaming but by using,
Not by claiming but refusing,
Then shall dawn on eyes unsealing the revealing of a self that knows and grows,
And the stream of thy devotion find the ocean when its meaning overflows.

So take the thread that seemed so frail,
Have faith to hope and never quail,
For all the weary woes of earth
And all the hollowness of mirth,
Accept but this divine in man
Believe I ought to means I can,
And comprehend the perfect plan.

Lift thee o'er thy 'here' and 'now',
Look beyond thine 'I' and 'thou',
Every effort points the next,
And the way grows unperplexed
To wider ranges, larger scope,
All things possible to hope!
Till thou feel the breath of morning shadow scorning
and on spirit wings unfurled
Win the way to realms of wonder,
Rolling starward with the thunder,
Flashing earthwards with the lightning to the brightening
the dark edges of the world,
Till the vastness shall absorb thee,
And the light of lights enorb thee,
And the wings on which thou soarest
Thou wilt need to shade thine eyes,
For the radiance thou adorest,
For the nearness of sunrise;
Then thy strongest strength shall be
In thine own humility,
Wrapt into the holiest holy
In thy worship vastly aisled,
Bend the knee and whisper lowly
'Our Father' with the child!

VICTOR JAMES DALEY

1858-1905

The Voice of the Soul

IN Youth, when through our veins runs fast
The bright red stream of life,
The Soul's Voice is a trumpet-blast
That calls us to the strife.

The Spirit spurns its prison-bars,
And feels with force endued
To scale the ramparts of the stars
And storm Infinitude.

Youth passes; like a dungeon grows
The Spirit's house of clay:
The voice that once in music rose
In murmurs dies away.

But in the day when sickness sore
Smites on the body's walls,
The Soul's Voice through the breach once more
Like to a trumpet calls.

Well shall it be with him who heeds
The mystic summons then!
His after-life with loving deeds
Shall blossom amongst men.

He shall have gifts–the gift that feels
The germ within the clod,
And hears the whirring of the wheels
That turn the mills of God!

The gift that sees with glance profound
    The secret soul of things,
And in the silence hears the sound
    Of vast and viewless wings!

The veil of Isis sevenfold
    To him as gauze shall be,
Wherethrough, clear-eyed, he shall behold
    The Ancient Mystery.

He shall do battle for the True,
    Defend till death the Right,
With Shoes of Swiftness Wrong pursue,
    With Sword of Sharpness smite.

And, dying, he shall haply hear,
    Like golden trumpets blown
For joy, far voices sweet and clear–
    Soul-voices like his own.

FRANCIS THOMPSON

1859-1907

The Hound of Heaven

I FLED Him, down the nights and down the days;
I fled Him, down the arches of the years;
I fled Him, down the labyrinthine ways
        Of my own mind; and in the mist of tears
I hid from Him, and under running laughter.
                Up vistaed hopes I sped;
                And shot, precipitated,
Adown Titanic glooms of chasmèd fears,
    From those strong Feet that followed, followed after.

But with unhurrying chase,
And unperturbèd pace,
Deliberate speed, majestic instancy,
They beat–and a Voice beat
More instant than the Feet–
'All things betray thee, who betrayest Me.'

I pleaded, outlaw-wise,
By many a hearted casement, curtained red,
Trellised with intertwining charities;
(For, though I knew His love Who followèd,
Yet was I sore adread
Lest, having Him, I must have naught beside).
But, if one little casement parted wide,
The gust of His approach would clash it to.
Fear wist not to evade, as Love wist to pursue.
Across the margent of the world I fled,
And troubled the gold gateways of the stars,
Smiting for shelter on their clangèd bars;
Fretted to dulcet jars
And silvern chatter the pale ports o' the moon.
I said to Dawn: Be sudden–to Eve: Be soon;
With thy young skiey blossoms heap me over
From this tremendous Lover–
Float thy vague veil about me, lest He see!
I tempted all His servitors, but to find
My own betrayal in their constancy,
In faith to Him their fickleness to me,
Their traitorous trueness, and their loyal deceit.
To all swift things for swiftness did I sue;
Clung to the whistling mane of every wind.
But whether thy swept, smoothly fleet,
The long savannahs of the blue;
Or whether, Thunder-driven,
They clanged his chariot 'thwart a heaven,

Plashy with flying lightnings round the spurn o' their
feet:–
Fear wist not to evade as Love wist to pursue.
Still with unhurrying chase,
And unperturbèd pace,
Deliberate speed, majestic instancy,
Came on the following Feet,
And a Voice above their beat–
'Naught shelters thee, who wilt not shelter Me.'

I sought no more that after which I strayed
In face of man or maid;
But still within the little children's eyes
Seems something, something that replies,
They at least are for me, surely for me!
I turned me to them very wistfully;
But just as their young eyes grew sudden fair
With dawning answers there,
Their angel plucked them from me by the hair.
'Come then, ye other children, Nature's–share
With me' (said I) 'your delicate fellowship;
Let me greet you lip to lip,
Let me twine with you caresses,
Wantoning
With our Lady-Mother's vagrant tresses,
Banqueting
With her in her wind-walled palace,
Underneath her azured daïs,
Quaffing, as your taintless way is,
From a chalice
Lucent-weeping out of the dayspring.'
So it was done:
I in their delicate fellowship was one–
Drew the bolt of Nature's secrecies.
I knew all the swift importings

On the wilful face of skies;
I knew how the clouds arise
Spumèd of the wild sea-snortings;
All that's born or dies
Rose and drooped with; made them shapers
Of mine own moods, or wailful or divine;
With them joyed and was bereaven.
I was heavy with the even,
When she lit her glimmering tapers
Round the day's dead sanctities.
I laughed in the morning's eyes.
I triumphed and I saddened with all weather,
Heaven and I wept together,
And its sweet tears were salt with mortal mine;
Against the red throb of its sunset-heart
I laid my own to beat,
And share commingling heat;
But not by that, by that, was eased my human smart.
In vain my tears were wet on Heaven's grey cheek.
For ah! we know not what each other says,
These things and I; in sound *I* speak–
Their sound is but their stir, they speak by silences.
Nature, poor stepdame, cannot slake my drouth;
Let her, if she would owe me,
Drop yon blue bosom-veil of sky, and show me
The breasts o' her tenderness:
Never did any milk of hers once bless
My thirsting mouth.
Nigh and nigh draws the chase,
With unperturbèd pace,
Deliberate speed, majestic instancy;
And past those noisèd Feet
A voice comes yet more fleet–
'Lo! naught contents thee, who content'st not Me!'

Naked I wait Thy love's uplifted stroke!
My harness piece by piece Thou hast hewn from me,
And smitten me to my knee;
I am defenceless utterly.
I slept, methinks, and woke,
And, slowly gazing, find me stripped in sleep.
In the rash lustihead of my young powers,
I shook the pillaring hours
And pulled my life upon me; grimed with smears,
I stand amid the dust o' the mounded years–
My mangled youth lies dead beneath the heap.
My days have crackled and gone up in smoke,
Have puffed and burst as sun-starts on a stream.
Yea, faileth now even dream
The dreamer, and the lute the lutanist;
Even the linked fantasies, in whose blossomy twist
I swung the earth a trinket at my wrist,
Are yielding; cords of all too weak account
For earth with heavy griefs so overplussed.
Ah! is Thy love indeed
A weed, albeit an amaranthine weed,
Suffering no flowers except its own to mount?
Ah! must–
Designer infinite!–
Ah! must Thou char the wood ere Thou canst limn
with it?
My freshness spent its wavering shower i' the dust;
And now my heart is as a broken fount,
Wherein tear-drippings stagnate, spilt down ever
From the dank thoughts that shiver
Upon the sighful branches of my mind.
Such is; what is to be?
The pulp so bitter, how shall taste the rind?
I dimly guess what Time in mists confounds;

Yet ever and anon a trumpet sounds
From the hid battlements of Eternity;
Those shaken mists a space unsettle, then
Round the half-glimpsèd turrets slowly wash again.
        But not ere him who summoneth
        I first have seen, enwound
With glooming robes purpureal, cypress-crowned;
His name I know, and what his trumpet saith.
Whether man's heart or life it be which yields
        Thee harvest, must Thy harvest-fields
        Be dunged with rotten death?

            Now of that long pursuit
            Comes on at hand the bruit;
        That Voice is round me like a bursting sea:
            'And is thy earth so marred,
            Shattered in shard on shard?
        Lo, all things fly thee, for thou fliest Me!
        Strange, piteous, futile thing!
Wherefore should any set thee love apart?
Seeing none but I makes much of naught' (He said),
'And human love needs human meriting:
        How hast thou merited–
Of all man's clotted clay the dingiest clot?
        Alack, thou knowest not
How little worthy of any love thou art!
Whom wilt thou find to love ignoble thee,
        Save Me, save only Me?
All which I took from thee I did but take,
        Not for thy harms,
But just that thou might'st seek it in My arms.
        All which thy child's mistake
Fancies as lost, I have stored for thee at home:
        Rise, clasp My hand, and come!'

Halts by me that footfall:
Is my gloom, after all,
Shade of His hand, outstretched caressingly?
'Ah, fondest, blindest, weakest,
I am He Whom thou seekest!
Thou dravest love from thee, who dravest Me.'

From 'The Mistress of Vision'

WHERE is the land of Luthany,
Where is the tract of Elenore?
I am bound therefor.

'Pierce thy heart to find the key;
With thee take
Only what none else would keep;
Learn to dream when thou dost wake,
Learn to wake when thou dost sleep.
Learn to water joy with tears,
Learn from fears to vanquish fears;
To hope, for thou dar'st not despair,
Exult, for that thou dar'st not grieve;
Plough thou the rock until it bear;
Know, for thou else couldst not believe;
Lose, that the lost thou may'st receive;
Die, for none other way canst live.
When earth and heaven lay down their veil,
And that apocalypse turns thee pale;
When thy seeing blindeth thee
To what thy fellow-mortals see;
When their sight to thee is sightless;
Their living, death; their light, most lightless;
Search no more–
Pass the gates of Luthany, tread the region Elenore.'

Where is the land of Luthany,
And where the region Elenore?
I do faint therefor.

'When to the new eyes of thee
All things by immortal power,
Near or far,
Hiddenly
To each other linkèd are,
That thou canst not stir a flower
Without troubling of a star;
When thy song is shield and mirror
To the fair snake-curlèd Pain,
Where thou dar'st affront her terror
That on her thou may'st attain
Perséan conquest; seek no more,
O seek no more!
Pass the gates of Luthany, tread the region Elenore.'

Orient Ode

LO, in the sanctuaried East,
Day, a dedicated priest
In all his robes pontifical exprest,
Lifteth slowly, lifteth sweetly,
From out its Orient tabernacle drawn,
Yon orbèd sacrament confest
Which sprinkles benediction through the dawn;
And when the grave procession's ceased,
The earth with due illustrious rite
Blessed,–ere the frail fingers featly
Of twilight, violet-cassocked acolyte,
His sacerdotal stoles unvest–

Sets, for high close of the mysterious feast,
The sun in august exposition meetly
Within the flaming monstrance of the West. . . .

To thine own shape
Thou round'st the chrysolite of the grape,
Bind'st thy gold lightnings in his veins;
Thou storest the white garners of the rains.
Destroyer and preserver, thou
Who medicinest sickness, and to health
Art the unthankèd marrow of its wealth;
To those apparent sovereignties we bow
And bright appurtenances of thy brow!
Thy proper blood dost thou not give,
That Earth, the gusty Maenad, drink and dance?
Art thou not life of them that live?
Yea, in glad twinkling advent, thou dost dwell
Within our body as a tabernacle!
Thou bittest with thine ordinance
The jaws of Time, and thou dost mete
The unsustainable treading of his feet.
Thou to thy spousal universe
Art Husband, she thy Wife and Church;
Who in most dusk and vidual curch,
Her Lord being hence,
Keeps her cold sorrows by thy hearse.
The heavens renew their innocence
And morning state
But by thy sacrament communicate;
Their weeping night the symbol of our prayers,
Our darkened search,
And sinful vigil desolate.
Yea, biune in imploring dumb,
Essential Heavens and corporal Earth await;

The Spirit and the Bride say: Come!
Lo, of thy Magians I the least
Haste with my gold, my incenses and myrrhs,
To thy desired epiphany, from the spiced
Regions and odorous of Song's traded East.
Thou, for the life of all that live
The victim daily born and sacrificed;
To whom the pinion of this longing verse
Beats but with fire which first thyself did give,
To thee, O Sun–or is't perchance, to Christ?

Ay, if men say that on all high heaven's face
The saintly signs I trace
Which round my stolèd altars hold their solemn place,
Amen, amen! For oh, how could it be,–
When I with wingèd feet had run
Through all the windy earth about,
Quested its secret of the sun,
And heard what thing the stars together shout,–
I should not heed thereout
Consenting counsel won:–
'By this, O Singer, know we if thou see.
When men shall say to thee: Lo! Christ is here,
When men shall say to thee: Lo! Christ is there,
Believe them: yea, and this–then art thou seer,
When all thy crying clear
Is but: Lo here! lo there!–ah me, lo everywhere!'

Assumpta Maria

'MORTALS, that behold a Woman
Rising 'twixt the Moon and Sun;
Who am I the heavens assume? an
All am I, and I am one.

'Multitudinous ascend I,
Dreadful as a battle arrayed,
For I bear you whither tend I;
Ye are I: be undismayed!
I, the Ark that for the graven
Tables of the Law was made;
Man's own heart was one; one, Heaven;
Both within my womb were laid.
For there Anteros with Eros,
Heaven with man, conjoinèd was,–
Twin-stone of the Law, *Ischyros,*
Agios Athanatos.

'I, the flesh-girt Paradises
Gardenered by the Adam new,
Daintied o'er with dear devices
Which He loveth, for He grew.
I, the boundless strict savannah
Which God's leaping feet go through;
I, the heaven whence the Manna,
Weary Israel, slid on you!
He the Anteros and Eros,
I the body, He the Cross;
He upbeareth me, *Ischyros,*
Agios Athanatos!

'I am Daniel's mystic Mountain,
    Whence the mighty stone was rolled;
I am the four Rivers' Fountain,
    Watering Paradise of old;
Cloud down-raining the Just One am,
    Danae of the Shower of Gold;
I the Hostel of the Sun am;
    He the Lamb, and I the Fold.
        He the Anteros and Eros,
            I the body, He the Cross;
        He is fast to me, *Ischyros,*
            Agios Athanatos!

'I, the presence-hall where Angels
    Do enwheel their placèd King–
Even my thoughts which, without change else,
    Cyclic burn and cyclic sing.
To the hollow of Heaven transplanted,
    I a breathing Eden spring,
Where with venom all outpanted
    Lies the slimed Curse shrivelling.
        For the brazen Serpent clear on
            That old fangèd knowledge shone;
        I to Wisdom rise, *Ischyron,*
            Agion Athanaton!

'Then commanded and spake to me
    He who framed all things that be;
And my Maker entered through me,
    In my tent His rest took He.
Lo! He standeth, Spouse and Brother,
    I to Him, and He to me,
Who upraised me where my mother
    Fell, beneath the apple-tree.

Risen 'twixt Anteros and Eros,
  Blood and Water, Moon and Sun,
He upbears me, He *Ischyros,*
  I bear Him, the *Athanaton!'*

Where is laid the Lord arisen?
  In the light we walk in gloom;
Though the Sun has burst his prison,
  We know not his biding-room.
Tell us where the Lord sojourneth,
  For we find an empty tomb.
'Whence He sprung, there He returneth,
  Mystic Sun,–the Virgin's Womb.'
    Hidden Sun, His beams so near us,
      Cloud enpillared as He was
    From of old, there He, *Ischyros,*
      Waits our search, *Athanatos.*

'Who will give Him me for brother,
  Counted of my family,
Sucking the sweet breasts of my Mother?–
  I His flesh, and mine is He;
To my Bread myself the bread is,
  And my Wine doth drink me: see,
His left hand beneath my head is.
  His right hand embraceth me!'
    Sweetest Anteros and Eros,'
      Lo, her arms He learns across;
    Dead that we die not, stooped to rear us,
      Thanatos Athanatos.

Who is She, in candid vesture.
  Rushing up from out the brine?
Treading with resilient gesture
  Air, and with that Cup divine?
She in us and we in her are,
  Beating Godward; all that pine,
Lo, a wonder and a terror–
  The Sun hath blushed the Sea to Wine!
    He the Anteros and Eros,
      She the Bride and Spirit; for
    Now the days of promise near us,
      And the Sea shall be no more.

Open wide thy gates, O Virgin,
  That the King may enter thee!
At all gates the clangours gurge in,
  God's paludament lightens, see!
Camp of Angels! Well we even
  Of this thing may doubtful be,–
If thou art assumed to Heaven,
  Or is Heaven assumed to thee!
    Consummatum. Christ the promised,
      Thy maiden realm, is won, O Strong!
    Since to such sweet Kingdom comest,
      Remember me, poor Thief of Song!

Cadent fails the stars along:–
  Mortals, that behold a Woman
    Rising 'twixt the Moon and Sun;
  Who am I the heavens assume? an
    All am I, and I am one.

The Veteran of Heaven

O CAPTAIN of the wars, whence won Ye so great scars?
In what fight did Ye smite, and what manner was the foe?
Was it on a day of rout they compassed Thee about,
Or gat Ye these adornings when Ye wrought their overthrow?

' 'Twas on a day of rout they girded Me about,
They wounded all My brow, and they smote Me through the side:
My hand held no sword when I met their armèd horde,
And the conqueror fell down, and the Conquered bruised his pride.'

What is this, unheard before, that the Unarmed make war,
And the Slain hath the gain, and the Victor hath the rout?
What wars, then, are these, and what the enemies,
Strange Chief, with the scars of Thy conquest trenched about?

'The Prince I drave forth held the Mount of the North,
Girt with the guards of flame that roll round the pole.
I drave him with My wars from all his fortress-stars,
And the sea of death divided that My march might strike its goal.

'In the keep of Northern Guard, many a great daemonian
sword
Burns as it turns round the Mount occult, apart:
There is given him power and place still for some certain
days,
And his name would turn the Sun's blood back upon
its heart.'

What is *Thy* Name? Oh, show!–'My Name ye may
not know;
'Tis a going forth with banners, and a baring of much
swords:
But My titles that are high, are they not upon My thigh?
"King of Kings!" are the words, "Lord of Lords!"
It is written "King of Kings, Lord of Lords".'

Desiderium Indesideratum

O GAIN that lurk'st ungainèd in all gain!
O love we just fall short of in all love!
O height that in all heights art still above!
O beauty that dost leave all beauty pain!
Thou unpossessed that mak'st possession vain,
See these strained arms which fright the simple air,
And say what ultimate fairness holds thee, Fair!
They girdle Heaven, and girdle Heaven in vain;
They shut, and lo! but shut in their unrest.
Thereat a voice in me that voiceless was:–
'Whom seekest thou through the unmarged arcane,
And not discern'st to thine own bosom prest?'
I looked. My claspèd arms athwart my breast
Framed the august embraces of the Cross.

The Kingdom of God

O WORLD invisible, we view thee,
O world intangible, we touch thee,
O world unknowable, we know thee,
Inapprehensible, we clutch thee!

Does the fish soar to find the ocean,
The eagle plunge to find the air–
That we ask of the stars in motion
If they have rumour of thee there?

Not where the wheeling systems darken,
And our benumbed conceiving soars!–
The drift of pinions, would we hearken,
Beats at our own clay-shuttered doors.

The angels keep their ancient places;–
Turn but a stone, and start a wing!
'Tis ye, 'tis your estrangèd faces,
That miss the many-splendoured thing.

But (when so sad thou canst not sadder)
Cry;–and upon thy so sore loss
Shall shine the traffic of Jacob's ladder
Pitched betwixt Heaven and Charing Cross.

Yea, in the night, my Soul, my daughter,
Cry,–clinging Heaven by the hems;
And lo, Christ walking on the water
Not of Gennesareth, but Thames!

HENRY CHARLES BEECHING

b.1859

The Tree of Life

Recognition in four Seasons

ARGUMENT

A prophet, desiring to recover for men the fruit of the Tree of Life, seems to find Paradise by certain traditional signs of beauty in nature. He is further persuaded by observing the beauty and innocence of children. By and by he comes upon the Tree of Knowledge, whose fruit, now old, he discerns to be evil; but from which, to his desire, new is brought forth, which is good. At each recognition one of the Guardian Angels of the Tree of Life is withdrawn, until there is left only the Angel of Death, in the light of whose sword he perceives it. The Angels' songs are not heard by the prophet.

I. SPRING

Prophet

O TREE of life, blissful tree,
Old as the world, still springing green,
Planted, watered by God; whose fruit
Hath year by year fallen about the root,
And century by century;
Grant me that I thy glory unseen
At last attain to see!

Chorus of Angels

The flame of our eyes still hideth
The fatal tree:
Which God in charge confideth
That none may see,
Till 'gainst our light advances
A purer ray,
And melts with fervid glances
Our swords of day.

Prophet

Conside- rate lilia agri quomodo crescunt.

This garden I consider: if not the wise
Repute it Paradise,
The wise may err and ancient fame be lost;
As Ophir on the swart Arabian coast,–
Whence she, of Saba queen,
In silk raiment and gold,
Bearing spices manifold,
Not unlike this lily's purer sheen,
Came a weary way to salute Solomon,
Fainting to see, and fainted having seen,
Such wisdom dazzled from his throne,–
Now Ophir lies unknown;
Yet stumbling haply on gold, a man shall say
Who feeds his flock by the well,
'Lo Ophir!' what if I to-day
A like token recover, and tell.

Chorus of Angels

The fire of our heart presages
(And gins to dim,)
That though through ageless ages
We wait for him
He comes; our glory retires,
And shrinks from strife,
Folding in closer fires
The Tree of Life.

Prophet

Goeth up a mist,
To water the ground from the four streams at even;
Wrapt in a veil of amethyst

The trees and thickets wait for Spring to appear,
An angel out of heaven,
Bringing apparel new for the new year;
In the soft light the birds
Reset to the loved air the eternal words,
And in the woods primroses peer.

Angel of the Spring

He hath seen me with eyes of wonder
And named my name,
My shield is riven in sunder,
And quencht my flame:
My task is done, and rewarded
If faithfully;
By others now is guarded
The mystic tree.

II. SUMMER

Prophet

O tree of life, blessed tree,
When shall I thy beauty attain to see?
New fledged ev'n now, new canopied with
green,
(Not darkening ever as these in brooding heat,)
To beasts of the field a screen,
A shadowy bower for weary eyes and feet:
Tree by tree musing, I find not thee.

Sinite parvulos, &c.

See, in the rippling water the children at play,
Flashing hither and thither, diamonded with
spray;
Lithe and fair their limbs, their hearts light
and gay–
As fair as they of Niobe;

Divinely fair, but too divinely famed;
  Not so now let it be.
Children of Adam these by birth proclaimed,
Clasping a mother's breast, a father's knee,
  By father's father named.
  Ay, but see, but see,
Their mien how high, how free their spirit!
  They are naked and not ashamed
Of that translucent veil, that symmetry.
  How they shout for glee!
It is the primal joy, and not the curse, they
      inherit.
  A child of Adam, a child of God can he be?
  O look, look and see!

The Angels of Children

His ear through nature's noises,
  Where'er he trod,
Could hear in the children's voices
  The praise of God.
Our task is done, and rewarded
  If faithfully,
By others now is guarded
  The mystic tree.

III. AUTUMN

Prophet

Say who are ye upon this bank reclining
  At random laid,
Where loaded boughs a diaper intertwining
  Of fragrant shade,
Stretch down their fruits to cheer the heart's
  repining.

Dicit enim Vetus melius est.

They hear me not, asleep, or drunken, or (ah!)
 dead.
O Tree of Knowledge, 'tis thou, tree divine
Of good and ill:–trembling, I view thee.
To me, as them, thy golden apples incline,
Able to slake my thirst, or else undo me.
Which shall I pluck, which dread
Of all their goodlihead?
If roots be twain, from which there flows
To these elixir, poison to those,
How can I track their currents through the
 stem
Which bears and buries them?
Nay, but it cannot be the tree of good;
'Tis utter evil; to nearer view
The fruit dislustres, dull of hue,
All its ripe vermilion vanished,
Dead fruit, not human food;
And these mistaking souls from life are banished.
But see,–a wonder,–lo, on each branch swells
A new fruit ruddy-rinded, that smells
Freshly, and from their places in decay
The old shrivel and drop away.
The ripeness allures to taste, O what should
 stay me?
Ill was the old, but the new is goodly and
 sweet:
A blessing is in it, desire to greet,
Not a curse to slay me;
(O divine the taste!)
Of the blind to open the eyes,
Deaf ears to unstop, make wise
The feeble-hearted, and to-day (O haste!)
For these poor dead the tree of life display!

Angel of the Tree of Divine Knowledge

The old fruit which evil bringeth
He hath eschewed;
I breathe, and a new fruit springeth;
He saw it good.
My task is done, and rewarded
If faithfully;
By others now is guarded
The mystic tree.

IV. WINTER

Prophet

I had thought ere this to have blest mine eyes
With thy vision benign, immortal tree;
For since that fruit, more than with Euphrasy,
My spirits are all alert, my sense more keen.
Nor is the north that chides with the stript boughs
An enemy, if it shows
All these but mortal, though in Paradise.
But thou, O still unseen,
Come into sight; not yet I faint, but abide
And ever abide, yearning thee to behold.
Thee following, this girdling forest wide,
My heart by hope made bold,
I have laboured through, and now emerge at length
Torn by the briers, spent my strength;
But branches wintry-bare deny the sheen
Of the amaranthine leaves and fruit of gold.
Till now at last the light
Fails from my hope as from the heaven,

Where marshal the clouds, blown up with
 boisterous breath;
The trees strain from the blast of death
Shrieking convulsed, so fierce the hail is driven
 Across the vault of night.
And now the waving brand
Of a cherub lightens down
And rends the air with crashing din;
Ah, if it be by God's command
To show light in the darkness of nature's frown
Qui per- That I my purpose win!
diderit It flashes and still flashes, and now I see
animam Beyond the blaze glooming a tree, a tree,
suam Stately and large,–(O light deceive not,
inveniet. O weary eyes not now believe not!)–
Unseen before; to that I press,
Despite the tempest and limbs' tardiness.
Lighten, O sword divine, to clear my way,
And thou, O happy heart, upstay
Steps that falter and swerve, since few
Remain; come light again, I shall win through.

Angel of Death

My flame he hath not abhorred,
 Nor nature's strife,
But lightened through my sword
 Hath passed to Life.
My task is done, and rewarded
 If faithfully;
Henceforth no more is guarded
 The mystic tree.

433

ARTHUR EDWARD WAITE

b. 1860

At the End of Things

THE world uprose as a man to find Him–
    Ten thousand methods, ten thousand ends–
Some bent on treasure; the more on pleasure;
    And some on the chaplet which fame attends:
But the great deep's voice in the distance dim
Said: Peace, it is well; they are seeking Him.

When I heard that all the world was questing,
    I look'd for a palmer's staff and found,
By a reed-fringed pond, a fork'd hazel-wand
    On a twisted tree, in a bann'd waste-ground;
But I knew not then what the sounding strings
Of the sea-harps say at the end of things.

They told me, world, you were keen on seeking;
    I cast around for a scrip to hold
Such meagre needs as the roots of weeds–
    All weeds, but one with a root of gold;
Yet I knew not then how the clangs ascend
When the sea-horns peal and the searchings end.

An old worn wallet was that they gave me,
    With twelve old signs on its seven old skins;
And a star I stole for the good of my soul,
    Lest the darkness came down on my sins;
For I knew not who in their life had heard
Of the sea-pipes shrilling a secret word.

I join'd the quest that the world was making,
  Which follow'd the false ways far and wide,
While a thousand cheats in the lanes and streets
  Offer'd that wavering crowd to guide;
But what did they know of the sea-reed's speech
When the peace-words breathe at the end for each?

The fools fell down in the swamps and marshes;
  The fools died hard on the crags and hills;
The lies which cheated, so long repeated,
  Deceived, in spite of their evil wills,
Some knaves themselves at the end of all–
Though how should they hearken when sea-flutes call?

But me the scrip and the staff had strengthen'd;
  I carried the star; that star led me:
The paths I've taken, of most forsaken,
  Do surely lead to an open sea:
As a clamour of voices heard in sleep,
Come shouts through the dark on the shrouded deep.

Now it is noon; in the hush prevailing
  Pipes, harps and horns into flute-notes fall;
The sea, conceding my star's true leading,
  In tongues sublime at the end of all
Gives resonant utterance far and near:–
'Cast away fear;
Be of good cheer;
He is here,
Is here!'

And now I know that I sought Him only
  Even as child, when for flowers I sought;
In the sins of youth, as in search for truth,
  To find Him, hold Him alone I wrought.

The knaves too seek Him, and fools beguiled–
So speak to them also, sea-voices mild!

Which then was wisdom and which was folly?
    Did my star more than the cozening guide?
The fool, as I think, at the chasm's brink,
    Prone by the swamp or the marsh's side,
Did, even as I, in the end rejoice,
Since the voice of death must be His true voice.

A Ladder of Life

FROM age to age in the public place,
        With the under steps in view,
The stairway stands, having earth for base,
    But the heavens it passes through.

O height and deep,
And the quests, in sleep,
Yet the Word of the King says well,
That the heart of the King is unsearchable.

Of the utmost steps there are legends grand,
    And far stars shine as they roll;
But, of child or man in the wonderful land,
    Is there one who has scaled the whole?

Yet the great hope stirs,
Though His thoughts as yours
Are not, since the first man fell;
For the heart of the King is unsearchable.

A pulsing song of the stairway strange
  Sing, lark, dissolved in the sky!
But no, for it passes beyond the range
  Of thy song and thy soaring high.

The star is kin
To our soul within–
God orders His world so well:
Yet the heart of the King is unsearchable.

They say that the angels thereby come down,
  Thereby do the saints ascend,
And that God's light shining from God's own Town
  May be seen at the stairway's end:

For good and ill
May be mixed at will,
The false shew true by a spell,
But the heart of the King is unsearchable.

Now, the stairway stands by the noisy mart
  And the stairway stands by the sea;
About it pulses the world's great heart
  And the heart of yourself and me.

We may read amiss
Both in that and this,
And the truth we read in a well;
Since the heart of the King is unsearchable

For a few steps here and a few steps there
  It is fill'd with our voices loud,
But above these slumbers the silent air
  And the hush of a dreaming cloud.

In the strain and stress
Of that silentness,
Our hearts for the height may swell;
But the heart of the King is unsearchable.

Some few of us, fill'd with a holy fire,
The Cross and the Christ have kiss'd;
We have sworn to achieve our soul's desire
By mass and evangelist:

Of step the third
I can bring down word,
And you on the fifth may dwell;
Yet the heart of the King is unsearchable.

As each of us stands at his place assign'd
And ponders the things we love,
It is meet and right we should call to mind
That some must have pass'd above:

Yes, some there are
Who have pass'd so far,
They have never return'd to tell;
And the heart of the King is unsearchable.

Some glimpse at least of the end we glean,
Of the spiral curve and plan;
For stretch as it may through the worlds unseen,
They are ever the worlds of man;

And–with all spaces–
His mind embraces
The way of the stairs as well–
For his heart, like the King's, is unsearchable.

Restoration

I CAME into the world for love of Thee,
    I left Thee at Thy bidding;
I put off my white robes and shining crown
And came into this world for love of Thee.

I have lived in the grey light for love of Thee,
    In mean and darken'd houses:
The scarlet fruits of knowledge and of sin
Have stain'd me with their juice for love of Thee.

I could not choose but sin for love of Thee,
    From Thee so sadly parted;
I could not choose but put away my sin
And purge and scourge those stains for love of Thee.

My soul is sick with life for love of Thee,
    Nothing can ease or fill me:
Restore me, past the frozen baths of death,
My crown and robes, desired for love of Thee:

And take me to Thyself for love of Thee;
    My loss or gain counts little,
But Thou must need me since I need Thee so,
Crying through day and night for love of Thee!

How I came to the Sea

I

A VOICE in the dark imploring,
 A sweet flute play'd in the light,
An organ pealing and pouring
 Through the world's cathedral height–
And again the charge and the flight,
The clash and hurtle of fight.
O thou art grand, thou art lonely,
 In thy melody, in thy moan,
 With the sense of a world unknown
Filling the known world only!

Great voice, which invokes and urges
 The strenuous souls to strive,
Gather thy waves, thy surges;
 Thy breakers heap and drive,
 Thy long tides marshal and lead.
 The little ripple shall plead
In little whispers on golden sand;
And further out on the rocky strand,
Where white crests crumble and white spume scourges,
 Thy drums and tocsins and horns shall blow.
 Thy long reverberant beats shall come and go,
From where thy surf-line in sky-line merges
 To where, by sounding buffet and blow–
Blare of paeans and muffle of dirges–
 Capes which crumble and torn cliffs know
 The strength and stress of thine ebb and flow–
Waste and know thee and thee confess.
 We do not know thee, we own, we know;
But our soul's might in thy might rejoices,
Our hearts respond to thy wild vast voices!
Thought with its fleetness swift wings from the course
  of thee;

Tongues in the speech of thee;
Hope at the source of thee;
Fire from the gleams of thee, strength from the force
of thee;
Width through the reach of thee:
Depth from thy deepness, unfathom'd by plummet,
And height from thy night-sky's impervious summit–
Omen and sign!
These have we drawn from thee, these do we bring to thee;
Nature's great sacraments rise from and spring to thee.
All other ministries–sun, when 'tis shrouded,
Moon in the morning light meagre and pallid,
Stars overclouded–
All are invalid
For spaces and seasons; but thou,
Thy greatest ministry is always now.
O sacramental sea, terrible sea,
Thine are the words of the mystery–
Grand-word and Pass-Word and Number thine,
Grades and Degrees to the height advancing,
And the golden dawn and the glory glancing
Far and away to the secret shrine!

II

There shall be no more sea, they say,
On Nature's great coronation day,
When the Bridegroom comes to the Bride.
Shall earth then lose her sacraments of tide–
Motion, measures tremendous, echoing far and long–
Glister, sparkle and glow, ring of an endless song?
O words prophetic, ye princes and priests attend;
This is the Quest's end promised, the marvellous end
Of all our voyage and venture since time began.
To the Quest for ever the sea's voice calleth man;

And this in a mystery-world, by only the side-light
broken–
That a Quest there is and an end–is the single secret
spoken
All over that vibrant main:
Of the Quest for ever it tells, of the ends and dooms to gain.

I rise in the half-light early, I vest myself in haste;
I pass over highway and byway, the fielded land and the
waste;
As much as a man may prosper, all eager I climb and go
down,
For this day surely meseems that the Quest may receive
a crown.
To and fro in the search I hurry, and some men bid me
narrate
What means this fever, and why so eager, and whether
their help I wait;
Not as yet they know of the Quest, although they are
questing early and late.
And others, my brothers, the same great end pursuing,
Stop me and ask, What news? Fellow Craft, is there any-
thing doing?
Is there light in the East anywhere, some sign set forth
in a star,
Or a louder watchword utter'd from over the harbour bar?
And above the light swift music of all its fleeting joys
The world spreads daily through length and breadth, the
great Quest's rumour and noise.
Who sought it first, who longest, and who has attain'd
almost?
All this in town and in village its heralds proclaim and post;
But the sun goes down and the night comes on for a space
to quench endeavour,
While star after star through the spaces far shew the track
of the Quest for ever!

III

But still, in the hush and the haunting, I stand, even I,
by the shore,
And the sea in the sunshine crooning pervades me with
deep unrest,
For it speaks of the Quest, of the Quest–
With a torrent of tongues in a thousand tones
And a far-off murmur of viewless zones,
Old and new, new and old, of the Quest;
Amen, it speaks evermore!
The whole wide world of voice and of rushing sound
You may seek through vainly,
But never a voice is found
To search the soul with such deep unrest,
Or to speak of the Quest
So plainly.

Then surely thither the Quest's way lies
And a man shall not err therein;
Yet not on the surface surely seen with eyes,
For thence the swallow has come and thereon the sea-mew
flies;
And the haunting ships with tremulous sails, we learn,
For ever about it hover, pass to their place and return;
And over the wastes thereof the tempests ravage and burn,
Or the sea-spouts spin.
But not of these is the Quest;
In the deep, in the deep it lies–
Ah, let me plunge therein!

But the caves of the deep are silent, and the halls of the
deep are still;
Not there is the clarion bird
Or the wind's loud organ heard;
No blythe voice cries on the hill.

A sail, a sail for the seaman, sailing East and West;
And a horse for the rover when he goeth over the dappled
    down and road!
But a man may better remain in his own abode
Who is vow'd to the wonderful end which crowns the
    Quest;
For sail and compass, and coach and steed and the rest,
The king's highway, and the beaten track, and the great
    sea-road–
  Are these the way of the Quest?

Travel, travel and search, eyes that are eager glisten
  (To-day is perchance too late),
I stand on the marge and listen
  (To-morrow is stored with fate);
  I stand on the marge and wait.
I know that the deep, with its secret, is a sacramental
    hymn.
Enough that it speaks to me vaguely with meanings
    reserved and dim,
  Saga and rune of eld;
Enough that its volume and grandeur hint the great tale
    withheld;
While, far through the depth and the darkness, the echoing
    halls of the soul
  Reply to the roar and the roll,
    Themselves in the mystery-tongue,
    All the world over sung,
  As the sibyl awaking from dream
  In oracles hints at the theme
    That has never been spoken or spell'd.

Of Consummation

WISE, O heart, is the heart which loves; but what of the heart which refrains–
Not as if counting the cost, and preferring the ease to the pains,
But knowing how treasures of all are neither received nor given,
The aching void that is under love and above it the aching heaven?

Wise are the lips which have learn'd how long may linger the lips' caress,
But wiser they who the hungering lips can chasten and repress,
For that which our fain mouths burn to kiss and loving arms to embrace
Has never been given to lips or arms in the world of time and space.

Wise, therefore, and wise above all, is he who does not swerve aside,
But knows to his greatest need on earth is service of earth denied;
Who, least things asking of flesh and blood, and less than the least of rest,
Goes on demanding the perfect good and disdaining the second best.

After much conquest and toil no doubt, but high in his starry tracks,
Shall the greater ministers come to him burning the sacred flax,
Saying: So passes the world and so the glory and light expend;
But the High Term, follow'd unflinching, cries: I can repay at the end.

Διάγνωσις

The Morality of the Lost Word

WITH a measure of light and a measure of shade,
The world of old by the Word was made;
By the shade and light was the Word conceal'd,
And the Word in flesh to the world reveal'd
Is by outward sense and its forms obscured;
The spirit within is the long lost Word,
Besought by the world of the soul in pain
Through a world of words which are void and vain.
O never while shadow and light are blended
Shall the world's Word-Quest or its woe be ended,
And never the world of its wounds made whole
Till the Word made flesh be the Word made soul!

ARCHIBALD LAMPMAN

1861-1899

The Clearer Self

BEFORE me grew the human soul,
And after I am dead and gone,
Through grades of effort and control
The marvellous work shall still go on.

Each mortal in his little span
Hath only lived, if he have shown
What greatness there can be in man
Above the measured and the known;

How through the ancient layers of night,
In gradual victory secure,
Grows ever with increasing light
The Energy serene and pure:

The Soul that from a monstrous past,
From age to age, from hour to hour,
Feels upward to some height at last
Of unimagined grace and power.

Though yet the sacred fire be dull,
In folds of thwarting matter furled,
Ere death be nigh, while life is full,
O Master Spirit of the world,

Grant me to know, to seek, to find,
In some small measure though it be,
Emerging from the waste and blind,
The clearer self, the grander me!

Peccavi, Domine

O POWER to whom this earthly clime
Is but an atom in the whole,
O Poet-heart of Space and Time,
O Maker and immortal Soul,
Within whose glowing rings are bound,
Out of whose sleepless heart had birth
The cloudy blue, the starry round,
And this small miracle of earth:

Who liv'st in every living thing,
And all things are thy script and chart,
Who rid'st upon the eagle's wing,
And yearnest in the human heart;
O Riddle with a single clue,
Love, deathless, protean, secure,
The ever old, the ever new,
O Energy, serene and pure.

Thou, who art also part of me,
  Whose glory I have sometime seen,
O Vision of the Ought-to-be,
  O Memory of the Might-have-been,
I have had glimpses of thy way,
  And moved with winds and walked with stars,
But, weary, I have fallen astray,
  And, wounded, who shall count my scars?

O Master, all my strength is gone;
  Unto the very earth I bow;
I have no light to lead me on;
  With aching heart and burning brow,
I lie as one that travaileth
  In sorrow more than he can bear;
I sit in darkness as of death,
  And scatter dust upon my hair.

The God within my soul hath slept,
  And I have shamed the nobler rule;
O Master, I have whined and crept;
  O Spirit, I have played the fool.
Like him of old upon whose head
  His follies hung in dark arrears,
I groan and travail in my bed,
  And water it with bitter tears.

I stand upon thy mountain-heads,
  And gaze until mine eyes are dim;
The golden morning glows and spreads;
  The hoary vapours break and swim.
I see thy blossoming fields, divine,
  Thy shining clouds, thy blessèd trees–
And then that broken soul of mine–
  How much less beautiful than these!

O Spirit, passionless, but kind,
  Is there in all the world, I cry,
Another one so base and blind,
  Another one so weak as I?
O Power, unchangeable, but just,
  Impute this one good thing to me,
I sink my spirit to the dust
  In utter dumb humility.

MARY ELIZABETH COLERIDGE

1861-1907

'He came unto His own, and His own received Him not'

AS Christ the Lord was passing by,
  He came, one night, to a cottage door.
  He came, a poor man, to the poor;
He had no bed whereon to lie.

He asked in vain for a crust of bread,
  Standing there in the frozen blast.
  The door was locked and bolted fast.
'Only a beggar!' the poor man said.

Christ the Lord went further on,
  Until He came to a palace gate.
  There a king was keeping his state,
In every window the candles shone.

The king beheld Him out in the cold.
  He left his guests in the banquet-hall.
  He bade his servants tend them all.
'I wait on a Guest I know of old.'

' 'Tis only a beggar-man!' they said.
  'Yes,' he said; 'it is Christ the Lord.'
  He spoke to Him a kindly word,
He gave Him wine and he gave Him bread.

Now Christ is Lord of Heaven and Hell,
  And all the words of Christ are true.
  He touched the cottage, and it grew;
He touched the palace, and it fell.

The poor man is become a king.
  Never was man so sad as he.
  Sorrow and Sin on the throne make three,
He has no joy in mortal thing.

But the sun streams in at the cottage door
  That stands where once the palace stood,
  And the workman, toiling to earn his food,
Was never a king before.

Good Friday in my Heart

GOOD FRIDAY in my heart! Fear and affright!
  My thoughts are the Disciples when they fled,
My words the words that priest and soldier said,
My deed the spear to desecrate the dead.
And day, Thy death therein, is changed to night.

Then Easter in my heart sends up the sun.
My thoughts are Mary, when she turned to see.
My words are Peter, answering, 'Lov'st thou Me?'
My deeds are all Thine own drawn close to Thee,
And night and day, since Thou dost rise, are one.

After St. Augustine

SUNSHINE let it be or frost,
  Storm or calm, as Thou shalt choose;
Though Thine every gift were lost,
  Thee Thyself we could not lose.

BLISS CARMAN

b.1861

Veni Creator

Πνεῦμα κυρίου ἐπ' ἐμέ

I

LORD of the grass and hill,
Lord of the rain,
White Overlord of will,
Master of pain,

I who am dust and air
Blown through the halls of death,
Like a pale ghost of prayer,–
I am thy breath.

Lord of the blade and leaf,
Lord of the bloom,
Sheer Overlord of grief,
Master of doom,

Lonely as wind or snow,
Through the vague world and dim,
Vagrant and glad I go;
I am thy whim.

Lord of the storm and lull,
Lord of the sea,
I am thy broken gull,
Blown far alee.

Lord of the harvest dew,
Lord of the dawn,
Star of the paling blue
Darkling and gone,

Lost on the mountain height
Where the first winds are stirred,
Out of the wells of night
I am thy word.

Lord of the haunted hush,
Where raptures throng,
I am thy hermit thrush,
Ending no song.

Lord of the frost and cold ,
Lord of the North,
When the red sun grows old
And day goes forth,

I shall put off this girth,–
Go glad and free,
Earth to my mother earth,
Spirit to thee.

II

Lord of my heart's elation,
Spirit of things unseen,
Be thou my aspiration
Consuming and serene!

Bear up, bear out, bear onward
This mortal soul alone,
To selfhood or oblivion,
Incredibly thine own,–

As the foamheads are loosened
And blown along the sea,
Or sink and merge forever
In that which bids them be.

I, too, must climb in wonder,
Uplift at thy command,–
Be one with my frail fellows
Beneath the wind's stong hand.

A fleet and shadowy column
Of dust or mountain rain,
To walk the earth a moment
And be dissolved again.

Be thou my exaltation
Or fortitude of mien,
Lord of the world's elation
Thou breath of things unseen!

A Creature Catechism

I

Soul, what art thou in the tribes of the sea?

LORD, *said a flying fish,*
Below the foundations of storm
We feel the primal wish
Of the earth take form.

Through the dim green water-fire
We see the red sun loom,
And the quake of a new desire
Takes hold on us down in the gloom.

No more can the filmy drift
Nor draughty currents buoy
Our whim to its bent, nor lift
Our heart to the height of its joy.

When sheering down to the Line
Come polar tides from the North,
Thy silver folk of the brine
Must glimmer and forth.

Down in the crumbling mill
Grinding eternally,
We are the type of thy will
To the tribes of the sea.

II

Soul, what art thou in the tribes of the air?

Lord, *said a butterfly,*
Out of a creeping thing,
For days in the dust put by,
The spread of a wing

Emerges with pulvil of gold
On a tissue of green and blue,
And there is thy purpose of old
Unspoiled and fashioned anew.

Ephemera, ravellings of sky
And shreds of the Northern light,
We age in a heart-beat and die
Under the eaves of night.

What if the small breath quail,
Or cease at a touch of the frost?
Not a tremor of joy shall fail,
Nor a pulse be lost.

This fluttering life, never still,
Survives to oblivion's despair.
We are the type of thy will
To the tribes of the air.

III

Soul, what art thou in the tribes of the field?

Lord, *said a maple seed,*
Though well we are wrapped and bound,
We are the first to give heed,
When thy bugles give sound.

We banner thy House of the Hills
With green and vermilion and gold,
When the floor of April thrills
With the myriad stir of the mould,

And her hosts for migration prepare.
We too have the veined twin-wings,
Vans for the journey of air.
With the urge of a thousand springs

Pent for a germ in our side,
We perish of joy, being dumb,
That our race may be and abide
For aeons to come.

When rivulet answers to rill
In snow-blue valleys unsealed,
We are the type of thy will
To the tribes of the field.

IV

Soul, what art thou in the tribes of the ground?

Lord, when the time is ripe,
Said a frog through the quiet rain,
We take up the silver pipe
For the pageant again.

When the melting wind of the South
Is over meadow and pond,
We draw the breath of thy mouth,
Reviving the ancient bond.

Then must we fife and declare
The unquenchable joy of earth,–
Testify hearts still dare,
Signalize beauty's worth.

Then must we rouse and blow
On the magic reed once more,
Till the glad earth-children know
Not a thing to deplore.

When rises the marshy trill
To the soft spring night's profound,
We are the type of thy will
To the tribes of the ground.

V

Soul, what art thou in the tribes of the earth?

Lord, *said an artist born,*
We leave the city behind
For the hills of open morn,
For fear of our kind.

Our brother they nailed to a tree
For sedition; they bully and curse
All those whom love makes free.
Yet the very winds disperse

Rapture of birds and brooks,
Colours of sea and cloud,–
Beauty not learned of books,
Truth that is never loud.

We model our joy into clay,
Or help it with line and hue,
Or hark for its breath in stray
Wild chords and new.

For to-morrow can only fulfil
Dreams which to-day have birth;
We are the type of thy will
To the tribes of the earth.

On Love

TO the assembled folk
At great St. Kavin's spoke
Young Brother Amiel on Christmas Eve;
I give you joy, my friends,
That as the round year ends,
We meet once more for gladness by God's leave.

On other festal days
For penitence or praise
Or prayer we meet, or fullness of thanksgiving;
To-night we calendar
The rising of that star
Which lit the old world with new joy of living.

Ah, we disparage still
The Tidings of Good Will,
Discrediting Love's gospel now as then!
And with the verbal creed
That God is love indeed,
Who dares make Love his god before all men?

Shall we not, therefore, friends,
Resolve to make amends
To that glad inspiration of the heart;
To grudge not, to cast out
Selfishness, malice, doubt,
Anger and fear; and for the better part,

To love so much, so well,
The spirit cannot tell
The range and sweep of her own boundary!
There is no period
Between the soul and God;
Love is the tide, God the eternal sea. . . .

To-day we walk by love;
To strive is not enough,
Save against greed and ignorance and might.
We apprehend peace comes
Not with the roll of drums,
But in the still processions of the night.

And we perceive, not awe
But love is the great law
That binds the world together safe and whole.
The splendid planets run
Their courses in the sun;
Love is the gravitation of the soul.

In the profound unknown,
Illumined, fair, and lone,
Each star is set to shimmer in its place.
In the profound divine
Each soul is set to shine,
And its unique appointed orbit trace.

There is no near nor far,
Where glorious Algebar
Swings round his mighty circuit through the night,
Yet where without a sound
The winged seed comes to ground,
And the red leaf seems hardly to alight.

One force, one lore, one need
For satellite and seed,
In the serene benignity for all.
Letting her time-glass run
With star-dust, sun by sun,
In Nature's thought there is no great nor small.

There is no far nor near
Within the spirit's sphere.
The summer sunset's scarlet-yellow wings
Are tinged with the same dye
That paints the tulip's ply.
And what is colour but the soul of things?

(The earth was without form;
God moulded it with storm,
Ice, flood, and tempest, gleaming tint and hue;
Lest it should come to ill
For lack of spirit still,
He gave it colour,–let the love shine through.). . .

Of old, men said, 'Sin not;
By every line and jot
Ye shall abide; man's heart is false and vile.'
Christ said, 'By love alone
In man's heart is God known;
Obey the word no falsehood can defile.'. . .

And since that day we prove
Only how great is love,
Nor to this hour its greatness half believe.
For to what other power
Will life give equal dower,
Or chaos grant one moment of reprieve!

Look down the ages' line,
Where slowly the divine
Evinces energy, puts forth control;
See mighty love alone
Transmuting stock and stone,
Infusing being, helping sense and soul.

And what is energy,
In-working, which bids be
The starry pageant and the life of earth?
What is the genesis
Of every joy and bliss,
Each action dared, each beauty brought to birth?

What hangs the sun on high?
What swells the growing rye?
What bids the loons cry on the Northern lake?
What stirs in swamp and swale,
When April winds prevail,
And all the dwellers of the ground awake?. . .

What lurks in the deep gaze
Of the old wolf? Amaze,
Hope, recognition, gladness, anger, fear.
But deeper than all these
Love muses, yearns, and sees,
And is the self that does not change nor veer.

Not love of self alone,
Struggle for lair and bone,
But self-denying love of mate and young,
Love that is kind and wise,
Knows trust and sacrifice,
And croons the old dark universal tongue. . . .

And who has understood
Our brothers of the wood,
Save he who puts off guile and every guise
Of violence,–made truce
With panther, bear, and moose,
As beings like ourselves whom love makes wise?

For they, too, do love's will,
Our lesser clansmen still;
The House of Many Mansions holds us all;
Courageous, glad and hale,
They go forth on the trail,
Hearing the message, hearkening to the call. . . .

Open the door to-night
Within your heart, and light
The lantern of love there to shine afar.
On a tumultuous sea
Some straining craft, maybe,
With bearings lost, shall sight love's silver star.

ALICE MEYNELL

To a Daisy

SLIGHT as thou art, thou art enough to hide,
Like all created things, secrets from me,
And stand a barrier to eternity.
And I, how can I praise thee well and wide

From where I dwell–upon the hither side?
Thou little veil for so great mystery,
When shall I penetrate all things and thee,
And then look back? For this I must abide,

Till thou shalt grow and fold and be unfurled
Literally between me and the world.
Then shall I drink from in beneath a spring,

And from a poet's side shall read his book.
O daisy mine, what will it be to look
From God's side even of such a simple thing?

Via, et Veritas, et Vita

'YOU never attained to Him.' 'If to attain
Be to abide, then that may be.'
'Endless the way, followed with how much pain!'
'The way was He.'

The Unknown God

ONE of the crowd went up,
And knelt before the Paten and the Cup,
Received the Lord, returned in peace, and prayed
Close to my side; then in my heart I said:

'O Christ, in this man's life–
This stranger who is Thine–in all his strife,
All his felicity, his good and ill,
In the assaulted stronghold of his will,

'I do confess Thee here,
Alive within this life; I know Thee near
Within this lonely conscience, closed away
Within this brother's solitary day.

'Christ in his unknown heart,
His intellect unknown–this love, this art,
This battle and this peace, this destiny
That I shall never know, look upon me!

'Christ in his numbered breath,
Christ in his beating heart and in his death,
Christ in his mystery! From that secret place
And from that separate dwelling, give me grace.'

In Portugal, 1912

AND will they cast the altars down,
   Scatter the chalice, crush the bread?
In field, in village, and in town
   He hides an unregarded head;

Waits in the corn-lands far and near,
   Bright in His sun, dark in His frost,
Sweet in the vine, ripe in the ear–
   Lonely unconsecrated Host.

In ambush at the merry board
   The Victim lurks unsacrificed;
The mill conceals the harvest's Lord,
   The wine-press holds the unbidden Christ.

Christ in the Universe

WITH this ambiguous earth
   His dealings have been told us. These abide:
The signal to a maid, the human birth,
The lesson, and the young Man crucified.

   But not a star of all
The innumerable host of stars has heard
How He administered this terrestrial ball.
Our race have kept their Lord's entrusted Word.

   Of His earth-visiting feet
None knows the secret, cherished, perilous,
The terrible, shamefast, frightened, whispered, sweet,
Heart-shattering secret of His way with us.

No planet knows that this
Our wayside planet, carrying land and wave,
Love and life multiplied, and pain and bliss,
Bears, as chief treasure, one forsaken grave.

Nor, in our little day,
May His devices with the heavens be guessed,
His pilgrimage to thread the Milky Way
Or His bestowals there be manifest.

But in the eternities,
Doubtless we shall compare together, hear
A million alien Gospels, in what guise
He trod the Pleiades, the Lyre, the Bear.

O, be prepared, my soul!
To read the inconceivable, to scan
The myriad forms of God those stars unroll
When, in our turn, we show to them a Man.

KATHERINE TYNAN HINKSON

The Beloved

BLOW gently over my garden,
Wind of the Southern sea,
In the hour that my Love cometh
And calleth me!
My Love shall entreat me sweetly,
With voice like the wood-pigeon;
'I am here at the gate of thy garden,
Here in the dawn.'

Then I shall rise up swiftly
All in the rose and grey,
And open the gate to my Lover
At dawning of day.
He hath crowns of pain on His forehead,
And wounds in His hands and feet;
But here mid the dews of my garden
His rest shall be sweet.

Then blow not out of your forests,
Wind of the icy North;
But Wind of the South that is healing
Rise and come forth!
And shed your musk and your honey,
And spill your odours of spice,
For one who forsook for my garden
His Paradise!

The Flying Wheel

WHEN I was young the days were long,
Oh, long the days when I was young:
So long from morn to evenfall
As they would never end at all.

Now I grow old Time flies, alas!
I watch the years and seasons pass.
Time turns him with his fingers thin
A wheel that whirls while it doth spin.

There is no time to take one's ease,
For to sit still and be at peace:
Oh, whirling wheel of Time, be still,
Let me be quiet if you will!

Yet still it turns so giddily,
So fast the years and seasons fly,
Dazed with the noise and speed I run
And stay me on the Changeless One.

I stay myself on Him who stays
Ever the same through nights and days:
The One Unchangeable for aye,
That was and will be: the one Stay,

O'er whom Eternity will pass
But as an image in a glass;
To whom a million years are nought,–
I stay myself on a great Thought.

I stay myself on the great Quiet
After the noises and the riot;
As in a garnished chamber sit
Far from the tumult of the street.

Oh, wheel of Time, turn round apace!
But I have found a resting-place.
You will not trouble me again
In the great peace where I attain.

SIR HENRY NEWBOLT

b.1862

The Final Mystery

This myth, of Egyptian origin, formed part of the instruction given to those initiated in the Orphic mysteries, and written versions of it were buried with the dead.

HEAR now, O Soul, the last command of all–
When thou hast left thine every mortal mark,
And by the road that lies beyond recall
Won through the desert of the Burning Dark,

Thou shalt behold within a garden bright
A well, beside a cypress ivory-white.

Still is that well, and in its waters cool
White, white and windless, sleeps that cypress tree:
Who drinks but once from out her shadowy pool
Shall thirst no more to all eternity.
Forgetting all, by all forgotten clean,
His soul shall be with that which hath not been.

But thou, though thou be trembling with thy dread,
And parched with thy desire more fierce than flame,
Think on the stream wherefrom thy life was fed,
And that diviner fountain whence it came.
Turn thee and cry–behold, it is not far–
Unto the hills where living waters are.

'Lord, though I lived on earth, the child of earth,
Yet was I fathered by the starry sky:
Thou knowest I came not of the shadows' birth,
Let me not die the death that shadows die.
Give me to drink of the sweet spring that leaps
From Memory's fount, wherein no cypress sleeps.'

Then shalt thou drink, O Soul, and therewith slake
The immortal longing of thy mortal thirst;
So of thy Father's life shalt thou partake,
And be for ever that thou wert at first.
Lost in remembered loves, yet thou more thou
With them shalt reign in never-ending *Now*.

ARTHUR CHRISTOPHER BENSON

b. 1862

Prayer

MY sorrow had pierced me through; it throbbed in my heart like a thorn;
This way and that I stared, as a bird with a broken limb
Hearing the hound's strong feet thrust imminent through the corn,
So to my God I turned: and I had forgotten Him.

Into the night I breathed a prayer like a soaring fire;–
So to the windswept cliff the resonant rocket streams,–
And it struck its mark, I know; for I felt my flying desire
Strain, like a rope drawn home, and catch in the land of dreams.

What was the answer? This–the horrible depth of night,
And deeper, as ever I peer, the huge cliff's mountainous shade,
While the frail boat cracks and grinds, and never a star in sight,
And the seething waves smite fiercer;–and yet I am not afraid.

469

GEORGE SANTAYANA

b.1863

'O World, thou choosest not'

O WORLD, thou choosest not the better part!
It is not wisdom to be only wise,
And on the inward vision close the eyes,
But it is wisdom to believe the heart.
Columbus found a world, and had no chart,
Save one that faith deciphered in the skies;
To trust the soul's invincible surmise
Was all his science and his only art.
Our knowledge is a torch of smoky pine
That lights the pathway but one step ahead
Across a void of mystery and dread.
Bid, then, the tender light of faith to shine
By which alone the mortal heart is led
Unto the thinking of the thought divine.

'O Martyred Spirit'

O MARTYRED Spirit of this helpless Whole,
Who dost by pain for tyranny atone,
And in the star, the atom, and the stone,
Purgest the primal guilt, and in the soul;
Rich but in grief, thou dost thy wealth unroll,
And givest of thy substance to thine own,
Mingling the love, the laughter, and the groan
In the large hollow of the heaven's bowl.
Fill full my cup; the dregs and honeyed brim
I take from thy just hand, more worthy love
For sweetening not the draught for me or him.
What in myself I am, that let me prove;
Relent not for my feeble prayer, nor dim
The burning of thine altar for my hymn.

HERBERT TRENCH

b. 1865

Lindisfarne

OUR seer, the net-mender,
The day that he died
Looked out to the seaward
At ebb of the tide;
Gulls drove like the snow
Over bight, over barn,
As he sang to the ebb
On the rock Lindisfarne:
'Hail, thou blue ebbing!
The breakers are gone
From the stormy coast-islet
Bethundered and lone!
Hail, thou wide shrinking
Of foam and of bubble–
The reefs are laid bare
And far off is the trouble!
For through this retreating
As soft as a smile,
The isle of the flood
Is no longer an isle. . . .

By the silvery isthmus
Of sands that uncover,
Now feet as of angels
Come delicate over–
The fluttering children
Flee happily over!
To the beach of the mainland
Return is now clear,
The old travel thither
Dry-shod, without fear. . . .

And now, at the wane,
When foundations expand,
Doth the isle of the soul,
Lindisfarne, understand
She stretcheth to vastness
Made one with the land!'

I Seek Thee in the Heart Alone

FOUNTAIN of Fire whom all divide,
We haste asunder like the spray
But waneless doth Thy flame abide
Whom every torch can take away!

I seek Thee in the heart alone,
I shall not find in hill or plain;
Our rushing star must keep its moan,
Our nightly soul its homeward pain.

Song out of thought, Light out of power,
Even the consumings of this breast
Advance the clearness of that hour
When all shall poise, and be at rest.

It cracks at last–the glowing sheath,
The illusion, Personality;
Absorbed and interwound with death
The myriads are dissolved in Thee.

WILLIAM BUTLER YEATS

b. 1865

The Rose of Battle

ROSE of all Roses, Rose of all the World!
The tall thought-woven sails, that flap unfurled
Above the tide of hours, trouble the air,
And God's bell buoyed to be the water's care;
While hushed from fear, or loud with hope, a band
With blown, spray-dabbled hair gather at hand.
Turn if you may from battles never done,
I call, as they go by me one by one,
Danger no refuge holds, and war no peace,
For him who hears love sing and never cease,
Beside her clean-swept hearth, her quiet shade:
But gather all for whom no love hath made
A woven silence, or but came to cast
A song into the air, and singing past
To smile on the pale dawn; and gather you
Who have sought more than is in rain or dew
Or in the sun and moon, or on the earth,
Or sighs amid the wandering starry mirth,
Or comes in laughter from the sea's sad lips;
And wage God's battles in the long grey ships.
The sad, the lonely, the insatiable,
To these Old Night shall all her mystery tell;
God's bell has claimed them by the little cry
Of their sad hearts, that may not live nor die.

Rose of all Roses, Rose of all the World!
You, too, have come where the dim tides are hurled
Upon the wharves of sorrow, and heard ring
The bell that calls us on; the sweet far thing.

Beauty grown sad with its eternity
Made you of us, and of the dim grey sea.
Our long ships loose thought-woven sails and wait,
For God has bid them share an equal fate;
And when at last defeated in His wars,
They have gone down under the same white stars,
We shall no longer hear the little cry
Of our sad hearts, that may not live nor die.

To the Secret Rose

FAR off, most secret, and inviolate Rose,
Enfold me in my hour of hours; where those
Who sought thee at the Holy Sepulchre,
Or in the wine-vat, dwell beyond the stir
And tumult of defeated dreams; and deep
Among pale eyelids heavy with the sleep
Men have named beauty. Your great leaves enfold
The ancient beards, the helms of ruby and gold
Of the crowned Magi; and the king whose eyes
Saw the Pierced Hands and Rood of Elder rise
In druid vapour and make the torches dim;
Till vain frenzy awoke and he died; and him
Who met Fand walking among flaming dew,
By a grey shore where the wind never blew,
And lost the world and Emir for a kiss;
And him who drove the gods out of their liss
And till a hundred morns had flowered red
Feasted, and wept the barrows of his dead;
And the proud dreaming king who flung the crown
And sorrow away, and calling bard and clown
Dwelt among wine-stained wanderers in deep woods;
And him who sold tillage and house and goods,

And sought through lands and islands numberless years
Until he found with laughter and with tears
A woman of so shining loveliness,
That men threshed corn at midnight by a tress,
A little stolen tress. I too await
The hour of thy great wind of love and hate.
When shall the stars be blown about the sky,
Like the sparks blown out of a smithy, and die?
Surely thine hour has come, thy great wind blows,
Far off, most secret, and inviolate Rose?

ARTHUR SYMONS

b. 1865

The Ecstasy

WHAT is this reverence in extreme delight
That waits upon my kisses as they storm,
Vehemently, this height
Of steep and inaccessible delight;
And seems with newer ecstasy to warm
Their slackening ardour, and invite,
From nearer heaven, the swarm
Of hiving stars with mortal sweetness down?
Never before
Have I endured an exaltation
So exquisite in anguish, and so sore
In promise and possession of full peace.
Cease not, O nevermore
Cease,
To lift my joy, as upon windy wings,
Into that infinite ascension, where,
In baths of glittering air,
It finds a heaven and like an angel sings.

Heaven waits above,
There where the clouds and fastnesses of love
Lift earth into the skies;
And I have seen the glimmer of the gates,
And twice or thrice
Climbed half the difficult way,
Only to say
Heaven waits,
Only to fall away from paradise.
But now, O what is this
Mysterious and uncapturable bliss
That I have known, yet seems to be
Simple as breath, and easy as a smile,
And older than the earth?
Now but a little while
This ultimate ecstasy
Has parted from its birth,
Now but a little while been wholly mine,
Yet am I utterly possessed
By the delicious tyrant and divine
Child, this importunate guest.

Indian Meditation

WHERE shall this self at last find happiness?
O Soul, only in nothingness.
Does not the Earth suffice to its own needs?
And what am I but one of the Earth's weeds?
All things have been and all things shall go on
Before me and when I am gone;
This self that cries out for eternity
Is what shall pass in me:
The tree remains, the leaf falls from the tree.

I would be as the leaf, I would be lost
In the identity and death of frost,
Rather than draw the sap of the tree's strength
And for the tree's sake be cast off at length.
To be is homage unto being; cease
To be, and be at peace,
If it be peace for self to have forgot
Even that it is not.

The Turning Dervish

STARS in the heavens turn,
I worship like a star,
And in its footsteps learn
Where peace and wisdom are.

Man crawls as a worm crawls;
Till dust with dust he lies,
A crooked line he scrawls
Between the earth and skies.

Yet God, having ordained
The course of star and sun,
No creature hath constrained
A meaner course to run.

I, by his lesson taught,
Imaging his design,
Have diligently wrought
Motion to be divine.

I turn until my sense,
Dizzied with waves of air,
Spins to a point intense,
And spires and centres there.

There, motionless in speed,
I drink that flaming peace,
Which in the heavens doth feed
The stars with bright increase.

Some spirit in me doth move
Through ways of light untrod,
Till, with excessive love,
I drown, and am in God.

MADISON JULIUS CAWEIN

1865-1914

Sibylline

THERE is a glory in the apple boughs
  Of silver moonlight; like a torch of myrrh,
Burning upon an altar of sweet vows,
  Dropped from the hand of some wan worshipper:
And there is life among the apple blooms
  Of whisp'ring winds; as if a god addressed
The flamen from the sanctuary glooms
  With secrets of the bourne that hope hath guessed,
Saying: 'Behold! a darkness which illumes,
    A waking which is rest.'

There is a blackness in the apple trees
  Of tempest; like the ashes of an urn
Hurt hands have gathered upon blistered knees,
  With salt of tears, out of the flames that burn:
And there is death among the blooms, that fill
  The night with breathless scent,–as when, above
The priest, the vision of his faith doth will
  Forth from his soul the beautiful form thereof,–
Saying: 'Behold! a silence never still;
    The other form of love.'

The Watcher on the Tower

I

The Voice of a Man

WHAT of the Night, O Watcher?

The Voice of a Woman

Yea, what of it?

The Watcher

A star has risen; and a wind blows strong.

Voice of the Man

The Night is dark.

The Watcher

But God is there above it.

Voice of the Woman

The Night is dark; the Night is dark and long.

II

Voice of the Man

What of the Night, O Watcher?

Voice of the Woman

Night of Sorrow!

The Watcher

Out of the East there comes a sound, like song.

Voice of the Man

The Night is dark.

The Watcher

Have courage! There's To-morrow!

Voice of the Woman

The Night is dark; the Night is dark and long.

III

Voice of the Man

What of the Night, O Watcher?

Voice of the Woman

Is it other?

The Watcher

I see a gleam; a thorn of light; a thong.

Voice of the Man

The Night is dark.

The Watcher

The Morning comes, my Brother.

Voice of the Woman

The Night is dark; the Night is dark and long.

IV

Voice of the Man

What now, what now, O Watcher?

The Watcher

Red as slaughter
The Darkness dies. The Light comes swift and strong.

Voice of the Man

The Night was long.–What sayest thou, my Daughter?

Voice of the Woman

The Night was dark; the Night was dark and long.

Attainment

ON the Heights of Great Endeavour,–
Where Attainment looms forever,–
Toiling upward, ceasing never,
Climb the fateful Centuries:
Up the difficult, dark places,
Joy and anguish in their faces,
On they strive, the living races,
And the dead, that no one sees.

Shape by shape, with brow uplifted,
One by one, where night is rifted,
Pass the victors, many gifted,
Where the heaven opens wide:
While below them, fallen or seated,
Mummy-like, or shadow-sheeted,
Stretch the lines of the defeated,–
Scattered on the mountainside.

And each victor, passing wanly,
Gazes on that Presence lonely,
With unmoving eyes where only
Grow the dreams, for which men die:
Grow the dreams, the far, ethereal,
That on earth assume material
Attributes, and, vast imperial,
Rear their battlements on high.

Kingdoms, marble-templed, towered,
Where the Arts, the many-dowered,–
That for centuries have flowered,
Trampled under War's wild heel,–

Lift immortal heads and golden,
Blossoms of the times called olden,
Soul-alluring, earth-withholden,
Universal in appeal.

As they enter,–high and lowly,–
On the hush these words fall slowly:–
'Ye who kept your purpose holy,
Never dreamed your cause was vain,
Look!–Behold, through time abating,
How the long, sad days of waiting,
Striving, starving, hoping, hating,
Helped your spirit to attain.

'For to all who dream, aspire,
Marry effort to desire,
On the cosmic heights, in fire
Beaconing, my form appears:–
I am marvel, I am morning!
Beauty in man's heart and warning!–
On my face none looks with scorning,
And no soul attains who fears.'

WALTER LESLIE WILMSHURST

b.1866

Anima Naturae

SWIRL of the river aflow to the sea,
Aspen a-quiver all tremulously,
Skylark that shivereth song o'er the lea,
Shaft of the sun;
Snowflakes that sprinkle the wind-bitten wold,
Fireflies that twinkle with shimmer of gold,
Wavelets that wrinkle the sands where ye rolled,
Rivulet's ripple and run;

Lone mountain-meres that are silently dreaming
Of far-flashing spheres that enmirrored are beaming,
Clouds' crystal tears when the rainbow is gleaming,
I, also a son
Of the Mother, inherit the soul of her infinite throng,
See it and hear it my paths all about and among,
Throb with your spirit and sing with the manifold song
Of the infinite, manifold One.

Nox Nivosa

SNOWFLAKES downfloating from the void
Upon my face,
Spilth of the silent alchemy employed
In deeps of space
Where viewless everlasting fingers ply
The power whose secret is the mystery
That doth my world encase;

Power that with equal ease outshakes
Yon architrave
Of massy stars in heaven and these frail flakes
Earth's floor that pave;
Swings the flamed orbs with infinite time for dower
And strews these velvet jewels not an hour
Of sunshine that will brave;

Yet of whose clustered crystals none
But speaks the act
Of the hand that steers each ceaseless-wheeling sun
And to whose tact
Fire-wreath and spangled ice alike respond;
Thoughts from the void frozen to flower and frond,
Divinely all compact;

Snowflakes, of pureness unalloyed,
That in dark space
Are built, and spilt from out the teeming void
With prodigal grace,
Air-quarried temples though you fall scarce-felt
And all your delicate architecture melt
To tears upon my face,–

I too am such encrystalled breath
In the void planned
And bodied forth to surge of life and death;
And as I stand
Beneath this sacramental spilth of snow,
Crumbling, you whisper: 'Fear thou not to go
Back to the viewless hand;

'Thence to be moulded forth again
Through time and space
Till thy imperishable self attain
Such strength and grace
Through endless infinite refinement passed
By the eternal Alchemist that at last
Thou see Him face to face.'

The Mystery of Light

SOULS there be to whom 'tis given
Easily to enter heaven;
Scarce an effort on their part,
Without struggle, prayer, or art;
Sometimes utterly unknowing
Why such glory should be showing;
Wondering what the reason is
Of the inflaming ecstasies
That Christ giveth unto His.

Often they, not understanding,
Catch a rarer light expanding;
Doing but their daily task,
Falls away some filmy mask,
And before their eyes extended
Heaven with earth is interblended;
And beyond this outward strife
They see what hidden peace is rife
In God's great reservoirs of life.

Some in that rapt state elysian
Are accorded richer vision;
Watch the thronging angels pass
To a high celestial Mass;
See a veilèd, flaming Centre,
See a Great High Priest there enter,
Whence a Host he lifteth up
And a crimson-brimming Cup,
Which He bids all eat and sup.

Or a day falls, past relating,
When a Dove, divinely mating,
Stirs the sheltering leaves apart
O'er some deeply-nested heart;
And, Himself within interning,
Lo! the very bush is burning
With the blasonry of love
Of that far-descended Dove
In His bridal-mate's alcove.

Such things simple souls and holy
Often know, whilst men less lowly
Beat the breast and bend the brain
In their labour to attain;

Till from heaven, tired of crying,
They will turn, all heaven denying;
Seeking ways of lesser bliss
Which, in His large Mysteries,
Christ denieth not to His.

Let not me, who have no mission
Yet to see the shining Vision,
E'er forget that night and day
Are His strange vicarious way;
He by one prepares the other,
Glooming me to light my brother.
May I ever blinded be
If my disability
Help my fellow-man to see.

In this night of my unknowing
His symbol-light shall be my showing.
I'll know that at the rise of sun
High Mass, for all, in heaven's begun;
That when at noon-tide height it lingers
Christ lifts the Host in His pierc'd fingers;
And at its setting it shall tell
How He descendeth, loving well,
Even to me, His child in hell.

RICHARD LE GALLIENNE

b.1866

The Second Crucifixion

LOUD mockers in the roaring street
  Say Christ is crucified again:
Twice pierced His gospel-bearing feet,
  Twice broken His great heart in vain.

I hear, and to myself I smile,
For Christ talks with me all the while.

No angel now to roll the stone
    From off His unawaking sleep,
In vain shall Mary watch alone,
    In vain the soldiers vigil keep.

Yet while they deem my Lord is dead
My eyes are on His shining head.

Ah! never more shall Mary hear
    That voice exceeding sweet and low
Within the garden calling clear:
    Her Lord is gone, and she must go.

Yet all the while my Lord I meet
In every London lane and street.

Poor Lazarus shall wait in vain,
    And Bartimaeus still go blind;
The healing hem shall ne'er again
    Be touched by suffering humankind.

Yet all the while I see them rest,
The poor and outcast, in His breast.

No more unto the stubborn heart
    With gentle knocking shall He plead,
No more the mystic pity start,
    For Christ twice dead is dead indeed.

So in the street I hear men say,
Yet Christ is with me all the day.

487

LAURENCE HOUSEMAN

b.1865

The Continuing City

GOD, who made man out of dust,
Willed him to be
Not to known ends, but to trust
His decree.

This is our city, a soul
Walled within clay;
Separate hearts of one whole,
Bound we obey.

All that He meant us to be,
Could we discern,–
Life had no meaning,–or we
Had not to learn.

Thou, beloved, doubt not the truth
Eyesight makes dim!
All life, to age from youth,
Brings us to Him:

Him Whom thou hast not seen,
Canst not yet know:
Human hearts stand between,
His to foreshow.

Couldst thou possess thine own,
That were the key;
He, to Whom hearts are known,
Keeps it from thee.

Thou all thy days must live,
Thyself the quest;
Plucking the heart to give
From thine own breast.

Till thou, from other eyes,
At kindred calls,
Seest thine own towers arise,
And thine own walls,–

Where, conquering the wide air,
Peopling its waste,
Citadels everywhere
Like stars stand based:

Losing thy soul, thy soul
Again to find;
Rendering toward that goal
Thy separate mind.

The Mystery of the Incarnation

A DISPUTATION BETWEEN CHRIST AND THE HUMAN FORM

(For the Feast of the Nativity)

COMEST Thou peaceably, O Lord?
'Yea, I am Peace!
Be not so fearful to afford
Thy Maker room! for I am the Reward
To which all generations of increase
Looking did never cease.

'Down from amid dark wings of storm
I set My Feet
To earth. Will not My earth grow warm
To feel her Maker take the form
He made, when now, Creation's purpose meet,
Man's body is to be God's Mercy-seat?'

Lord, I am foul: there is no whole
Fair part in me
Where Thou canst deign to be!
This form is not Thy making, since it stole
Fruit from the bitter Tree.
'Yet still thou hast the griefs to give in toll
That I may test the sickness of man's soul.'

O Lord, my work is without worth!
I am afraid,
Lest I should mar the blissful Birth.
Quoth Christ, 'Ere seas had shores, or earth
Foundations laid,
My Cross was made!'

'Naught canst thou do that was not willed
By Love to be,
To bring the Work to pass through Me.
No knee
Stiffens, or bends before My Sov'reignty,
But from the world's beginning hath fulfilled
Its choice betwixt the valleyed and the hilled.
For both, at one decree,
My Blood was spilled.'

Yet canst Thou use these sin-stained hands?
'These hands,' quoth Christ,
'Of them I make My need:
Since they sufficed to forge the bands

Wherein I hunger, they shall sow the seed!
And with bread daily they shall feed
My Flesh till, bought and bound, It stands
A Sacrifice to bleed.'

Lord, let this house be swept and garnished first!
For fear lest sin
Do there look in,
Let me shut fast the windows: lest Thou thirst,
Make some pure inner well of waters burst:
For no sweet water can man's delving win–
Earth is so curst.
Also bar up the door: Thou wilt do well
To dwell, whilst with us, anchorite in Thy cell.

Christ said 'Let be: leave wide
All ports to grief!
Here when I knock I will not be denied
The common lot of all that here abide;
Were I so blinded, I were blind in chief:
How should I see to bring the blind relief?

Wilt Thou so make Thy dwelling? Then I fear
Man, after this, shall dread to enter here:
For all the inner courts will be so bright,
He shall be dazzled with excess of light,
and turn, and flee!
'But from his birth I will array him right,
And lay the temple open for his sight,
And say to help him, as I bid him see:
"This is for thee!" '

Love, the Tempter

(*Season of Lent*)

OH, tempt me not! I love too well this snare
Of silken cords.
Nay, Love, the flesh is fair;
So tempt me not! This earth affords
Too much delight;
Withdraw Thee from my sight,
Lest my weak soul break free
And throw me back to Thee!

Thy Face is all too marred. Nay, Love, not I–
I did not that! Doubtless Thou hadst to die:
Others did faint for Thee; but I faint not.
Only a little while hath sorrow got
The better of me now; for Thou art grieved,
Thinking I need Thee. Oh, Christ, lest I fall
Weeping between Thy Feet, and give Thee all:
Oh, Christ, lest love condemn me unreprieved
Into Thy bondage, be it not believed
That Thou hast need of *me*!

Dost Thou not know
I never turned aside to mock Thy Woe?
I had respect to Thy great love for men:
Why wilt Thou, then,
Question of each new lust–
'Are these not ashes, and is this not dust?'
Ah, Love, Thou hast not eyes
To see how sweet it is!
Each for himself be wise:
Mock not my bliss!

Ere Thou cam'st troubling, was I not content?
    Because I pity Thee, and would be glad
    To go mine own way, and not leave Thee sad,
Is all my comfort spent?

Go Thine own ways, nor dream Thou needest me!
Yet if, again, Thou on the bitter Tree
Wert hanging now, with none to succour Thee
    Or run to quench Thy sudden cry of thirst,
    Would not I be the first–
Ah, Love, the prize!–
To lift one cloud of suffering from Thine Eyes?

    Oh, Christ, let be!
Stretch not Thine ever-pleading Hands thus wide,
Nor with imperious gesture touch Thy Side!
Past is Thy Calvary. By the Life that died,
    Oh, tempt not me!

Nay, if Thou weepest, then must I weep too,
Sweet Tempter, Christ! Yet what can *I* undo,
    I, the undone, the undone,
    To comfort Thee, God's Son?
Oh, draw me near, and, for some lowest use,
    That I may be
    Lost and undone in Thee,
Me from mine own self loose!

A Prayer for the Healing of the Wounds of Christ

(For Advent)

IS not the work done? Nay, for still the Scars
Are open; still Earth's Pain stands deified,
With Arms spread wide:
And still, like falling stars,
Its Blood-drops strike the doorposts, where abide
The watchers with the Bride,
To wait the final coming of their kin,
And hear the sound of kingdoms gathering in.

While Earth wears wounds, still must Christ's Wounds
remain,
Whom Love made Life, and of Whom Life made Pain,
And of Whom Pain made Death.
No breath,
Without Him, sorrow draws; no feet
Wax weary, and no hands hard labour bear,
But He doth wear
The travail and the heat:
Also, for all things perishing, He saith,
'*My* grief, *My* pain, *My* death.'

O kindred Constellation of bright stars,
Ye shall not last for aye!
Far off there dawns a comfortable day
Of healing for those Scars:
When, faint in glory, shall be wiped away
Each planetary fire,
Now, all the aching way the balm of Earth's desire!

For from the healèd nations there shall come
The healing touch: the blind, the lamed, the dumb,
    With sight, and speed, and speech,
    And ardent reach
Of yearning hands shall cover up from sight
Those Imprints of a night
Forever past. And all the Morians' lands
Shall stretch out hands of healing to His Hands.
    While to His Feet
    The timid, sweet
Four-footed ones of earth shall come and lay,
Forever by, the sadness of their day:
And, they being healed, healing spring from them.
So for the Stem
And Rod of Jesse, roots and trees and flowers,
Touched with compassionate powers,
    Shall cause the thorny Crown
    To blossom down
        Laurel and bay.

            So lastly to His Side,
Stricken when, from the Body that had died,
Going down He saw sad souls being purified,
    Shall rise, out of the deeps no man
    Can sound or scan,
The morning star of Heaven that once fell
And fashioned Hell:–
    Now, star to star
    Mingling to melt where shadeless glories are.

O Earth, seek deep, and gather up thy soul,
And come from high and low, and near and far,
And make Christ whole!

495

GEORGE WILLIAM RUSSELL ('A.E.')

b. 1867

Star Teachers

EVEN as a bird sprays many-coloured fires,
The plumes of paradise, the dying light
Rays through the fevered air in misty spires
That vanish in the height.

These myriad eyes that look on me are mine;
Wandering beneath them I have found again
The ancient ample moment, the divine,
The God-root within men.

For this, for this the lights innumerable
As symbols shine that we the true light win:
For every star and every deep they fill
Are stars and deeps within.

Desire

WITH Thee a moment! Then what dreams have play!
Traditions of eternal toil arise,
Search for the high, austere and lonely way
The Spirit moves in through eternities.
Ah, in the soul what memories arise!

And with what yearning inexpressible,
Rising from long forgetfulness I turn
To Thee, invisible, unrumoured, still:
White for Thy whiteness all desires burn.
Ah, with what longing once again I turn!

The City

Full of Zeus the cities: full of Zeus the harbours: full of Zeus are all the ways of men.

WHAT domination of what darkness dies this hour,
And through what new, rejoicing, winged, ethereal power
O'erthrown, the cells opened, the heart released from fear?
Gay twilight and grave twilight pass. The stars appear
O'er the prodigious, smouldering, dusky, city flare.
The hanging gardens of Babylon were not more fair
Than these blue flickering glades, where childhood in its glee
Re-echoes with fresh voice the heaven-lit ecstasy.
Yon girl whirls like an eastern dervish. Her dance is
No less a god-intoxicated dance than his,
Though all unknowing the arcane fire that lights her feet,
What motions of what starry tribes her limbs repeat.
I, too, firesmitten, cannot linger: I know there lies
Open somewhere this hour a gate to Paradise,
Its blazing battlements with watchers thronged, O where?
I know not, but my flame-winged feet shall lead me there.
O, hurry, hurry, unknown shepherd of desires,
And with thy flock of bright imperishable fires
Pen me within the starry fold, ere the night falls
And I am left alone below immutable walls,
Or am I there already, and is it Paradise
To look on mortal things with an immortal's eyes?
Above the misty brilliance the streets assume
A night-dilated blue magnificence of gloom
Like many-templed Nineveh tower beyond tower;
And I am hurried on in this immortal hour.

Mine eyes beget new majesties: my spirit greets
The trams, the high-built glittering galleons of the streets
That float through twilight rivers from galaxies of light.
Nay, in the Fount of Days they rise, they take their flight,
And wend to the great deep, the Holy Sepulchre.
Those dark misshapen folk to be made lovely there
Hurry with me, not all ignoble as we seem,
Lured by some inexpressible and gorgeous dream.
The earth melts in my blood. The air that I inhale
Is like enchanted wine poured from the Holy Grail.
What was that glimmer then? Was it the flash of wings
As through the blinded mart rode on the King of Kings?
O stay, departing glory, stay with us but a day,
And burning seraphim shall leap from out our clay,
And plumed and crested hosts shall shine where men have
been,
Heaven hold no lordlier court than earth at College Green.
Ah, no, the wizardy is over; the magic flame
That might have melted all in beauty fades as it came.
The stars are far and faint and strange. The night draws
down.
Exiled from light, forlorn, I walk in Dublin Town.
Yet had I might to lift the veil, the will to dare,
The fiery rushing chariots of the Lord are there,
The whirlwind path, the blazing gates, the trumpets
blown,
The halls of heaven, the majesty of throne by throne,
Enraptured faces, hands uplifted, welcome sung
By the thronged gods, tall, golden-coloured, joyful, young.

Krishna

I PAUSED beside the cabin door and saw the King
of Kings at play,
Tumbled upon the grass I spied the little heavenly
runaway.
The mother laughed upon the child made gay by its
ecstatic morn,
And yet the sages spake of It as of the Ancient and
Unborn.
I heard the passion breathed amid the honeysuckle
scented glade,
And saw the King pass lightly from the beauty that he had
betrayed.
I saw him pass from love to love; and yet the pure
allowed His claim
To be the purest of the pure, thrice holy, stainless,
without blame.
I saw the open tavern door flash on the dusk a ruddy
glare,
And saw the King of Kings outcast reel brawling through
the starlit air.
And yet He is the Prince of Peace of whom the ancient
wisdom tells,
And by their silence men adore the lovely silence where
He dwells.
I saw the King of Kings again, a thing to shudder at and
fear,
A form so darkened and so marred that childhood fled
if it drew near.
And yet He is the Light of Lights whose blossoming is
Paradise,
That Beauty of the King which dawns upon the seers'
enraptured eyes.

I saw the King of Kings again, a miser with a heart
grown cold,
And yet He is the Prodigal, the Spendthrift of the Heavenly
Gold,
The largesse of whose glory crowns the blazing brows
of cherubim,
And sun and moon and stars and flowers are jewels
scattered forth by Him.
I saw the King of Kings descend the narrow doorway to
the dust
With all his fires of morning still, the beauty, bravery,
and lust.
And yet He is the life within the Ever-living Living Ones,
The ancient with eternal youth, the cradle of the infant
suns,
The fiery fountain of the stars, and He the golden urn
where all
The glittering spray of planets in their myriad beauty fall.

Unity

ONE thing in all things have I seen:
One thought has haunted earth and air:
Clangour and silence both have been
Its palace chambers. Everywhere

I saw the mystic vision flow
And live in men and woods and streams,
Until I could no longer know
The stream of life from my own dreams.

Sometimes it rose like fire in me
Within the depths of my own mind,
And spreading to infinity,
It took the voices of the wind:

It scrawled the human mystery–
Dim heraldry–on light and air;
Wavering along the starry sea
I saw the flying vision there.

Each fire that in God's temple lit
Burns fierce before the inner shrine,
Dimmed as my fire grew near to it
And darkened at the light of mine.

At last, at last, the meaning caught–
The spirit wears its diadem;
It shakes its wondrous plumes of thought
And trails the stars along with them.

Reconciliation

I BEGIN through the grass once again to be bound to the Lord;
I can see, through a face that has faded, the face full of rest
Of the earth, of the mother, my heart with her heart in accord,
As I lie 'mid the cool green tresses that mantle her breast
I begin with the grass once again to be bound to the Lord.

By the hand of a child I am led to the throne of the King
For a touch that now fevers me not is forgotten and far,
And His infinite sceptred hands that sway us can bring
Me in dreams from the laugh of a child to the song of a star.
On the laugh of a child I am borne to the joy of the King.

501

CHARLES WEEKES

b. 1867

That

. . . alone
From all eternity

WHAT is that beyond thy life,
And beyond all life around,
Which, when thy quick brain is still,
Nods to thee from the stars?
Lo, it says, thou hast found
Me, the lonely, lonely one.

DORA SIGERSON SHORTER

I am the World

I AM the song, that rests upon the cloud;
I am the sun;
I am the dawn, the day, the hiding shroud,
When dusk is done.

I am the changing colours of the tree;
The flower uncurled;
I am the melancholy of the sea;
I am the world.

The other souls that, passing in their place,
Each in his groove;
Outstretching hands that chain me and embrace,
Speak and reprove.

'O atom of that law, by which the earth
Is poised and whirled;
Behold! you hurrying with the crowd assert
You are the world.'

Am I not one with all the things that be
  Warm in the sun?
All that my ears can hear, or eyes can see,
  Till all be done.

Of song and shine, of changing leaf apart,
  Of bud uncurled:
With all the senses pulsing at my heart,
  I am the world.

One day the song that drifts upon the wind
  I shall not hear:
Nor shall the rosy shoots to eyes grown blind
  Again appear.

Deaf, in the dark, I shall arise and throw
  From off my soul
The withered world with all its joy and woe,
  That was my goal.

I shall arise, and like a shooting star
  Slip from my place;
So lingering see the old world from afar
  Revolve in space.

And know more things than all the wise may know
  Till all be done;
Till One shall come who, breathing on the stars,
  Blows out the sun.

JANE BARLOW

Beyond all Shores and Seas

LIES yet a well of wonder
All shores and seas beyond,
Where shines that dimness under,
More deep than in a dream,
Full many a diamond
With elfin gleam,

Glows up the glimmering water
Full many a ruby's fire:
If ever an earth-born daughter
Their wizard light behold,
She may no more desire
Our gems and gold.

Nay, some in sooth, who only
Adream thereon did gaze,
Thenceforth fare wandering lonely,
And seek with sorrow vain
The glory of such rays
To find again.

Oft, oft, high-heavenward turning
The quivering stars have conned,
Or watched the wide west burning
Nor shall their hearts appease,
Whose hope lies hid beyond
All shores and seas.

One and All

O'ER boundless fields of night, lo, near and far
Light, dewdrop's blink, and Light, Aeonian star.
Wan wraiths that flickering roam by marish ways;
Fierce surge of levin-bright foam where oceans blaze–
Fly's spark and flame gulfs dire, your fount is one,
Deep in the worlds' arch-fire of all suns' Sun.

A burning seed of strife Fate strews, and so
Life, men's grudged dole, and Life, gods' feast aglow.
Clod's captive, senses' thrall, oft grieved, soon slain;
Immortal, glad o'er all to range and reign–
Frail breath, and spirit eterne, beyond thought's seeing
Ye touch for one sole bourne all being's Being.

JAMES STEPHENS

The Seeker

I SAT me down and looked around
The little lamp-lit room, and saw
Where many pictures gloomed and frowned
In sad, still life, nor made a sound–
A many for one to draw:
Shadow and sea and ground
Held by the artist's law,
Beauty without a flaw,
All with a sense profound.

One teeming brain was wood and hill,
And sloping pastures wide and green,
And cool, deep seas where rivers spill
The snows of mountains far and chill,
Sad pools where the shadows lean.

Old trees that hang so still.
Fields which the reapers glean.
Plains where the wind is keen.
Each with a nerve to thrill.

Elusive figures swayed and yearned
By lake and misty greenwood dim,
Seeking in sorrow: they had learned
In one night's dream might be discerned,
A pace from the world's rim,
Wages their woe had earned,
Rest from the labour grim,
God and the peace of Him–
These in a frame interned.

. . . . .

On through the forest, one step on,
One step, O Powers, let me attain
This hard, dead step, let me be gone
Back where I and the morning shone,
Back ere the dream shall wane
When I and a star were one.
Seen through the veils of pain
Glory shall shine again:
God, has the vision gone?

The Fullness of Time

ON a rusty iron throne
Past the furthest star of space
I saw Satan sit alone,
Old and haggard was his face;
For his work was done and he
Rested in eternity.

And to him from out the sun
Came his father and his friend
Saying, now the work is done
Enmity is at an end:
And he guided Satan to
Paradises that he knew.

Gabriel without a frown,
Uriel without a spear,
Raphael came singing down
Welcoming their ancient peer,
And they seated him beside
One who had been crucified.

The Breath of Life

AND while they talked and talked, and while they sat
Changing their base minds into baser coin;
And telling–they! how truth and beauty join,
And how a certain this was good, but that
Was baser than the viper or the toad,
Or the blind beggar glaring down the road.

I turned from them in fury, and I ran
To where the moon shone out upon the height,
Down the long reaches of a summer night,
Stretching slim fingers, and the starry clan
Grew thicker than the flowers that we see
Clustered in quiet fields of greenery.

Around me was the night-time sane and cold,
The clouds that knew no care and no restraint
Swung through the silences, or drifted faint
To pale horizons, wreathing fold on fold,
The moon's sharp edge, each rolling cloud a sea,
A foam of silver shining gloriously.

The quietudes that sunder star from star,
The hazy distances of loneliness,
Where never eagle's wing or timid press
Of lark or wren could venture, and the far
Profundities untravelled and unstirred
By any act of man or thought or word.

These held me with amazement and delight:
I yearned up through the spaces of the sky,
Beyond the rolling clouds, beyond the high
And delicate white moon, and up the height,
And past the rocking stars, and out to where
The ether failed in spaces sharp and bare.

The breath that is the very breath of life
Throbbed close to me: I heard the pulses beat,
That lift the universes into heat:
The slow withdrawal, and the deeper strife
Of His wide respiration, like a sea
It ebbed and flooded through immensity.

His breath alone in wave on mighty wave!
O moon and stars swell to a raptured song!
Ye mountains toss the harmony along!
O little men with little souls to save
Swing up glad chantings, ring the skies above,
With boundless gratitude for boundless love!

Probing the ocean to its steepest drop;
Rejoicing in the viper and the toad,
And the blind beggar glaring down the road;
And they who talk and talk and never stop
Equally quickening; with a care to bend
The gnat's slant wing into a swifter end.

Searching the quarries of all life, the deep
Low crannies and shy places of the world,
To warm the smallest insect that is curled
In a deep root, or on the sun to heap
Fiercer combustion, spending love on all
In equal share, the mighty and the small.

. . . .

The silence clung about me like a gift,
The tender night-time folded me around
Protectingly, and in a peace profound
The clouds drooped slowly backward drift on drift
Into the darkness, and the moon was gone,
And soon the stars had vanished every one.

But on the sky, a handsbreadth in the west,
A faint cold brightness crept and soared and spread,
Until the rustling heavens overhead,
And the grey trees and grass were manifest:
Then through the chill a golden spear was hurled,
And the big sun tossed laughter on the world.

JOHN CHARLES EARLE

Onward and Upward

I PASS the vale. I breast the steep.
  I bear the cross: the cross bears me.
Light leads me on to light. I weep
  For joy at what I hope to see
When, scaled at last the arduous height,
  For every painful step I trod,
I traverse worlds on worlds of light,
  And pierce some deeper depth of God.

'Lo, I am with you always'

WIDE fields of corn along the valleys spread;
    The rain and dews mature the swelling vine;
I see the Lord is multiplying bread;
    I see Him turning water into wine;
    I see Him working all the works divine
He wrought when Salemward His steps were led;
    The selfsame miracles around Him shine;
He feeds the famished; He revives the dead;
    He pours the flood of light on darkened eyes;
He chases tears, diseases, fiends away;
    His throne is raised upon these orient skies;
His footstool is the pave whereon we pray.
    Ah, tell me not of Christ in Paradise,
For He is all around us here to-day.

'Found of them that sought Him not'

I WILL arise and to my Father go;
    This very hour the journey is begun.
I start to reach the blissful goal, and, lo,
    My spirit at one bound her race has run.
    For seeking God and finding Him are one.
He feeds the rillets that towards Him flow.
    It is the Father Who first seeks the son,
And moves all heavenward movement, swift or slow.
I dare not pride myself on finding Him.
    I dare not dream a single step was mine.
His was the vigour in the palsied limb–
    His the electric fire along the line–
When drowning, His the untaught power to swim
    Float o'er the surge, and grasp the rock divine.

Bodily Extension

THE body is not bounded by its skin;
Its effluence, like a gentle cloud of scent,
Is wide into the air diffused, and, blent
With elements unseen, its way doth win
To ether frontiers, where take origin
Far subtler systems, nobler regions meant
To be the area and the instrument
Of operations ever to begin
Anew and never end. Thus every man
Wears as his robe the garment of the sky–
So close his union with the cosmic plan,
So perfectly he pierces low and high–
Reaching as far in space as creature can,
And co-extending with immensity.

ARTHUR SHEARLY CRIPPS

b. 1869

Missa Viatoris
(In dread of Famine)

HERE, Pan, on grey rock slab we set for Thee
Thy Feast–the White Cake and the Red in Cup–
Shepherd and Lamb, we, lost goats, offer up
In pastoral wise Thine own Divinity.

The scared moon dips, the hardy sun comes up
To spy our Secret from yon cloudy hill:
O Pan that Thou by cloud and sun mayst fill
Our hills with food, we lift Thy Cake and Cup.

Heart of all good in men and beasts and earth,
Here on the hill our hearts, we lift them up:
Life-Blood and Flesh–White Cake and Red in Cup–
We break and pour Thee for our drought and dearth!

An Easter Hymn

(Easter in South Africa falls in Autumn)

HIS wide Hands fashioned us white grains and red
His Eyes weep rains to swell them in their bed,
Whereby the dust-grains of our lives are fed.
Alleluia!

In Earth our mother's bosom undecayed
The Seed-corn of the Flesh He took, He laid–
One white small Grain beneath a sealed rock's shade.
Alleluia!

How blind that Seed lay till this autumn morn
When forth it sprouted blade and flower and corn,
And with Its lifted Head the seal was torn!
Alleluia!

Hope of men's bodies' grains both red and white–
Shrivelled and sere and void of speech and sight,
Is that blind Seed Who burst His way to light.
Alleluia!

We, God's red millet grains, men hold so cheap,
Innumerable beneath our grey rocks sleep,
Yet He that cared to sow us cares to reap.
Alleluia!

The Black Christ

(At Easter in South Africa)

PILATE and Caïaphas
They have brought this thing to pass–
That a Christ the Father gave,
Should be guest within a grave.

Church and State have willed to last
This tyranny not over-past;
His dark southern Brows around
They a wreath of briars have bound,
In His dark despiséd Hands
Writ in sores their writing stands.

By strait starlit ways I creep,
Caring while the careless sleep,
Bearing balms, and flow'rs to crown
That poor Head the stone holds down,
Through some crack or crevice dim
I would reach my sweets to Him.

Easter suns they rise and set,
But that stone is steadfast yet:
Past my lifting 'tis but I
When 'tis lifted would be nigh.
I believe, whate'er they say,
The sun shall dance an Easter Day,
And I that through thick twilight grope
With balms of faith, and flow'rs of hope,
Shall lift mine eyes and see that stone
Stir and shake, if not be gone.

From 'The Death of St. Francis'

'WHAT art Thou, dearest Lord, and what am I,
Vile worm and worthless dust?'
He answered me.
On Holy Cross Day to my prayer there came
An Angel bearing in his rainbow wings
Nailed Hands and Feet, the Image of my Lord.

How can I tell it? The thing is sacred, dear,
O brothers mine, I give you all I can,
And yet I leave you but the husk of it,
The heart of it I selfish take away.
How can I tell? The thing is sacred, dear,–
Hands grew to hands, feet seemed to grow to feet,
His Hands to my hands, Feet of His to mine;
Exalted and extended on His cross,
I seemed in one great stab of eager pain
To feel His heart beating within my heart.

Brethren, this thing so sacred, and so dear,
I would that I could tell you, for it seems
Surely a sin to give God's poor my all,
And yet to keep Love's purest ingot back,
That fever-throb of His within my heart,
That moment's gold refined in sharpest fire,
And anguish of a crucifying world.

'What art Thou, dearest Lord, and what am I,
Vile worm and worthless servant?'
Answer came.
I felt His Heart to beat within my heart.
It seemed He lent His Sacred Heart to me:
One moment did I know His wish, His work,
As if mine own they were, and knew with them
The worm-like weakness of my wasted life,
My service worthless to win back His world.
(Sharp Sister Faintness knits dark brows at me,
And o'er her shoulder looks sweet Sister Death,
Holding a glass my last hour's sands run down.)

I cannot tell the half of it, yet hear
What rush of feeling still comes back to me,

From that proud torture hanging on His Cross,
From that gold rapture of His Heart in mine.

I knew in blissful anguish what it means
To be a part of Christ, and feel as mine
The dark distresses of my brother limbs,
To feel it bodily and simply true,
To feel as mine the starving of His poor,
To feel as mine the shadow of curse on all,
Hard words, hard looks, and savage misery,
And struggling deaths, unpitied and unwept.
To feel rich brothers' sad satieties,
The weary manner of their lives and deaths,
That want in love, and lacking love lack all.
To feel the heavy sorrow of the world
Thicken and thicken on to future hell,
To mighty cities with their miles of streets,
Where men seek work for days, and walk and starve,
Freezing on river-banks on winter nights,
And come at last to cord or stream or steel.

The horror of the things our brothers bear!
It was but naught to that which after came,
The woe of things we make our brothers bear,
Our brothers and our sisters! In my heart
Christ's Heart seemed beating, and the world's whole sin,–
Its crimson malice and grey negligence,–
Rose up and blackening hid the Face of God.

I that in Christ had tasted to the full
The nails and knotted scourges of the world,
Now felt the contrary and greater woe,–
The utmost ache of God's atoning grief,–
Their bitterness who scourge and drive the nails,

And bring upon themselves a darker pain
Than any felt by scourged or crucified.
Upon my heart gnawed, worse than sorrow of death,–
Sorrow of selfishness, and cursed my Cross
With black forsaking of the Face of Love.
My God, my God, Thou wast forsaking me! . . .

Ah! brothers mine, how any words are cold
To tell the agony of being part
Of every schism in the Crucified,
Of feeling hand smite out at fellow hand,
And foot spurn fellow foot, and breasts refuse
The milk of mercy to the lips that were
Flesh of their own flesh. The sucked and empty names
Of 'brother' and of 'sister' how they hissed,
Hissed through the savage teeth that tore the flesh,
Withered in mouths that kissed to endless shame.
No sob of Love but echoing fell away
In earthquake thunders of unthankfulness.

Vile worm and worthless servant, how I knew
My work, our work, as nothing in that tide
Of a vast world's refusal of the Cross
Setting toward that world's appointed doom!

The thing is very sacred, very dear,
Sweet Jesu, help me tell them, how my heart
Swelled near to breaking with the Love of Thine,
That felt it all and Loved and Loved and Loved.
I felt the Sacred Heart within my own,
And knew one pulse therein of purest strength,
That drove a cry of passion to my lips,
'Father, forgive, they know not what they do.'

Could I but tell you how that cry seemed truth–
The truest prayer my lips had ever made–
I had told you almost all! It may not be.

O Heart of Jesus, Sacred, Passionate,
Anguish it was, yet anguish that was bliss,
To love them heart to heart, each selfish heart,
To clasp them close, and pray in utter truth–
'Father, forgive, they know not what they do.'
One was the heart of him that ground the poor,
Poor weary heart, so blinded and misled!
One was the heart of her that reeked in shame,
Poor weary heart, so blinded and misled!
One was my heart that wasted half its years,
And knew so little how to use the rest
To God's sole glory, and the love of men,
Poor weary heart, so blinded and misled!

But O! that Sacred Heart rushed out to them
In veriest anguish and in veriest bliss,
Demanding, craving, in sure hope of them,
'Father, forgive, they know not what they do.'

And O! that Sacred Heart burnt up in Flame
Against that harsh misleader of our world,
And O! I felt an awful thrill of Love
As with one heart-beat of wild ecstasy
I set my heel upon that Serpent's head
In resolute anguish, watching how the fangs
Snapped at my heel, and gored it into blood,
My heel that yet shall grind his head to dust.
Was it I that did it? Nay, the Christ in me,
But when I woke His Prints were in my hands,
And in my feet, while in my side there showed
As it were the Heart-Wound from the soldier's lance.

517

ROBERT HUGH BENSON

1871-1914

The Teresian Contemplative

SHE moves in tumult; round her lies
  The silence of the world of grace;
The twilight of our mysteries
  Shines like high noonday on her face;
Our piteous guesses, dim with fears,
She touches, handles, sees, and hears.

In her all longings mix and meet;
  Dumb souls through her are eloquent;
She feels the world beneath her feet
  Thrill in a passionate intent;
Through her our tides of feeling roll
And find their God within her soul.

Her faith the awful Face of God
  Brightens and blinds with utter light;
Her footsteps fall where late He trod;
  She sinks in roaring voids of night;
Cries to her Lord in black despair,
And knows, yet knows not, He is there.

A willing sacrifice she takes
  The burden of our fall within;
Holy she stands; while on her breaks
  The lightning of the wrath of sin;
She drinks her Saviour's cup of pain,
And, one with Jesus, thirsts again.

From 'Christian Evidences'

NOW God forbid that Faith be blind assent,
Grasping what others know; else Faith were nought
But learning, as of some far continent
Which others sought,
And carried thence, better the tale to teach,
Pebbles and shells, poor fragments of the beach.

Now God forbid that Faith be built on dates,
Cursive or uncial letters, scribe or gloss,
What one conjectures, proves, or demonstrates:
This were the loss
Of all to which God bids that man aspire,
This were the death of life, quenching of fire.

Nay, but with Faith I see. Not even Hope,
Her glorious sister, stands so high as she.
For this but stands expectant on the slope
That leads where He
Her source and consummation sets His seat,
Where Faith dwells always to caress His Feet.

Nay, but with Faith I saw my Lord and God
Walk in the fragrant garden yesterday.
Ah! how the thrushes sang; and, where He trod
Like spikenard lay
Jewels of dew, fresh-fallen from the sky,
While all the lawn rang round with melody.

Nay, but with Faith I marked my Saviour go,
One August noonday, down the stifling street
That reeked with filth and man; marked from Him flow
Radiance so sweet,
The man ceased cursing, laughter lit the child,
The woman hoped again, as Jesus smiled.

Nay, but with Faith I sought my Lord last night,
And found Him shining where the lamp was dim;
The shadowy altar glimmered, height on height,
A throne for Him:
Seen as through lattice work His gracious Face
Looked forth on me and filled the dark with grace.

Nay then, if proof and tortured argument
Content thee–teach thee that the Lord is there,
Or risen again; I pray thee be content,
But leave me here
With eye unsealed by any proof of thine,
With eye unsealed to know the Lord is mine.

GILBERT KEITH CHESTERTON

b. 1873

The Holy of Holies

'ELDER father, though thine eyes
Shine with hoary mysteries,
Canst thou tell what in the heart
Of a cowslip blossom lies?

'Smaller than all lives that be,
Secret as the deepest sea,
Stands a little house of seeds,
Like an elfin's granary.

'Speller of the stones and weeds,
Skilled in Nature's crafts and creeds,
Tell me what is in the heart
Of the smallest of the seeds.'

'God Almighty, and with Him
Cherubim and Seraphim,
Filling all eternity–
Adonai Elohim.'

ALEISTER CROWLEY

The Quest

APART, immutable, unseen,
Being, before itself had been,
Became. Like dew a triple queen
Shone as the void uncovered:
The silence of deep height was drawn
A veil across the silver dawn
On holy wings that hovered.[1]

The music of three thoughts became
The beauty, that is one white flame,
The justice that surpasses shame,
The victory, the splendour,
The sacred fountain that is whirled
From depths beyond that older world
A new world to engender.[2]

The kingdom is extended.[3] Night
Dwells, and I contemplate the sight
That is not seeing, but the light
That secretly is kindled,

[1] A qabalistic description of Macroprosopus. 'Dew,' 'Deep Height,' &c., are his titles.

[2] Microprosopus.

[3] Malkuth, the Bride. In its darkness the Light may yet be found.

Though oft-time its most holy fire
Lacks oil, whene'er my own Desire
Before desire has dwindled.

I see the thin web binding me
With thirteen cords of unity [1]
Toward the calm centre of the sea.
(O thou supernal mother![2])
The triple light my path divides
To twain and fifty sudden sides[3]
Each perfect as each other.

Now backwards, inwards still my mind
Must track the intangible and blind,
And seeking, shall securely find
Hidden in secret places
Fresh feast for every soul that strives,
New life for many mystic lives,
And strange new forms and faces.

My mind still searches, and attains
By many days and many pains
To That which Is and Was and reigns
Shadowed in four and ten;[4]
And loses self in sacred lands,
And cries and quickens, and understands
Beyond the first Amen. [5]

[1] The Hebrew characters composing the name Achd, Unity, add up to 13.

[2] Binah, the Great Deep: the offended Mother who shall be reconciled to her daughter by Bn, the Son.

[3] Bn adds to 52.

[4] Jehovah, the name of 4 letters, 1+2+3+4=10

[5] The first Amen is =91 or 7 x 13. The second is the Inscrutable Amoun.

The Neophyte[1]

TO-NIGHT I tread the unsubstantial way
That looms before me, as the thundering night
Falls on the ocean: I must stop, and pray
One little prayer, and then–what bitter fight
Flames at the end beyond the darkling goal?
These are my passions that my feet must tread;
This is my sword, the fervour of my soul;
This is my Will, the crown upon my head.
For see! the darkness beckons: I have gone,
Before this terrible hour, towards the gloom,
Braved the wild dragon, called the tiger on
With whirling cries of pride, sought out the tomb
Where lurking vampires battened, and my steel
Has wrought its splendour through the gates of death.
My courage did not falter: now I feel
My heart beat wave-wise, and my throat catch breath
As if I choked; some horror creeps between
The spirit of my will and its desire,
Some just reluctance to the Great Unseen
That coils its nameless terrors, and its dire
Fear round my heart; a devil cold as ice
Breathes somewhere, for I feel his shudder take
My veins: some deadlier asp or cockatrice
Slimes in my senses: I am half awake,
Half automatic, as I move along
Wrapped in a cloud of blackness deep as hell,
Hearing afar some half-forgotten song
As of disruption; yet strange glories dwell
Above my head, as if a sword of light,
Rayed of the very Dawn, would strike within
The limitations of this deadly night
That folds me for the sign of death and sin–

[1] This poem describes the Initiation of the *true* 'Hermetic Order of the Golden Dawn' in its spiritual aspect.

O Light! descend! My feet move vaguely on
In this amazing darkness, in the gloom
That I can touch with trembling sense. There shone
Once, in my misty memory, in the womb
Of some unformulated thought, the flame
And smoke of mighty pillars; yet my mind
Is clouded with the horror of this same
Path of the wise men: for my soul is blind
Yet: and the foemen I have never feared
I could not see (if such should cross the way),
And therefore I am strange: my soul is seared
With desolation of the blinding day
I have come out from: yes, that fearful light
Was not the Sun: my life has been the death,
This death may be the life: my spirit sight
Knows that at last, at least. My doubtful breath
Is breathing in a nobler air; I know,
I know it in my soul, despite of this,
The clinging darkness of the Long Ago,
Cruel as death, and closer than a kiss,
This horror of great darkness. I am come
Into this darkness to attain the light:
To gain my voice I make myself as dumb:
That I may see I close my outer sight:
So, I am here. My brows are bent in prayer:
I kneel already in the Gates of Dawn;
And I am come, albeit unaware,
To the deep sanctuary: my hope is drawn
From wells profounder than the very sea.
Yea, I am come, where least I guessed it so,
Into the very Presence of the Three
That Are beyond all Gods. And now I know
What spiritual Light is drawing me
Up to its stooping splendour. In my soul

I feel the Spring, the all-devouring Dawn,
Rush with my Rising. There, beyond the goal,
The Veil is rent!
Yes: let the veil be drawn.

The Rose and the Cross

OUT of the seething cauldron of my woes,
Where sweets and salt and bitterness I flung;
Where charmèd music gathered from my tongue,
And where I chained strange archipelagoes
Of fallen stars; where fiery passion flows
A curious bitumen; where among
The glowing medley moved the tune unsung
Of perfect love: thence grew the Mystic Rose.

Its myriad petals of divided light;
Its leaves of the most radiant emerald;
Its heart of fire like rubies. At the sight
I lifted up my heart to God and called:
How shall I pluck this dream of my desire?
And lo! there shaped itself the Cross of Fire!

EVELYN UNDERHILL (MRS. STUART MOORE)

b. 1875

Immanence

I COME in the little things,
Saith the Lord:
Not borne on morning wings
Of majesty, but I have set My Feet
Amidst the delicate and bladed wheat
That springs triumphant in the furrowed sod.

There do I dwell, in weakness and in power;
Not broken or divided, saith our God!
In your strait garden plot I come to flower:
About your porch My Vine
Meek, fruitful, doth entwine;
Waits, at the threshold, Love's appointed hour.

I come in the little things,
Saith the Lord:
Yea! on the glancing wings
Of eager birds, the softly pattering feet
Of furred and gentle beasts, I come to meet
Your hard and wayward heart. In brown bright eyes
That peep from out the brake, I stand confest.
On every nest
Where feathery Patience is content to brood
And leaves her pleasure for the high emprize
Of motherhood–
There doth My Godhead rest.

I come in the little things,
Saith the Lord:
My starry wings
I do forsake,
Love's highway of humility to take:
Meekly I fit My stature to your need.
In beggar's part
About your gates I shall not cease to plead–
As man, to speak with man–
Till by such art
I shall achieve My Immemorial Plan,
Pass the low lintel of the human heart.

Introversion

WHAT do you seek within, O Soul, my Brother?
What do you seek within?
I seek a Life that shall never die,
Some haven to win
From mortality.

What do you find within, O Soul, my Brother?
What do you find within?
I find great quiet where no noises come.
Without, the world's din:
Silence in my home.

Whom do you find within, O Soul, my Brother?
Whom do you find within?
I find a friend that in secret came:
His scarred hands within
He shields a faint flame.

What would you do within, O Soul, my Brother?
What would you do within?
Bar door and window that none may see:
That alone we may be
(Alone! face to face,
In that flame-lit place!)
When first we begin
To speak one with another.

Uxbridge Road

THE Western Road goes streaming out to seek the cleanly wild,
It pours the city's dim desires towards the undefiled,
It sweeps betwixt the huddled homes about its eddies grown
To smear the little space between the city and the sown:
The torments of that seething tide who is there that can see?
There's one who walked with starry feet the western road by me!

He is the Drover of the soul; he leads the flock of men
All wistful on that weary track, and brings them back again.
The dreaming few, the slaving crew, the motley caste of life–
The wastrel and artificer, the harlot and the wife–
They may not rest, for ever pressed by one they cannot see:
The one who walked with starry feet the western road by me.

He drives them east, he drives them west, between the dark and light;
He pastures them in city pens, he leads them home at night.
The towery trams, the threaded trains, like shuttles to and fro
To weave the web of working days in ceaseless travel go.
How harsh the woof, how long the weft! who shall the fabric see?
The one who walked with starry feet the western road by me!

Throughout the living joyful year at lifeless tasks to strive,
And scarcely at the end to save gentility alive;
The villa plot to sow and reap, to act the villa lie,
Beset by villa fears to live, midst villa dreams to die;
Ah, who can know the dreary woe? and who the splendour see?
The one who walked with starry feet the western road by me.

Behold! he lent me as we went the vision of the seer;
Behold! I saw the life of men, the life of God shine clear.
I saw the hidden Spirit's thrust; I saw the race fulfil
The spiral of its steep ascent, predestined of the Will.
Yet not unled, but shepherded by one they may not see–
The one who walked with starry feet the western road by me!

Regnum Caelorum Vim Patitur

WHEN our five-angled spears, that pierced the world
And drew its life-blood, faint before the wall
Which hems its secret splendour–when we fall,
Lance broken, banner furled,
Before that calm invincible defence
Whereon our folly hurled
The piteous armies of intelligence–
Then, often-times, we know
How conquering mercy to the battle field
Comes through the darkness, freely to bestow
The prize for which we fought
Not knowing what we sought,
And salve the wounds of those who would not yield.

He loves the valiant foe; he comes not out to meet
The craven soul made captive of its fear:
Not these the victories that to him are sweet!
But the impetuous soldiery of truth,
And knighthood of the intellectual quest,
Who ask not for his ruth
Nor would desire his rest:
These are to him most dear,
And shall in their surrender yet prevail.
Yea! at the end of unrewarded days,
By swift and secret ways
As on a sudden moonbeam shining clear,
Soft through the night shall slide upon their gaze
The thrice-defended vision of the Grail:
And when his peace hath triumphed, these shall be
The flower of his celestial chivalry.

And did you think, he saith
As to and fro he goes the trenches through,
My heart impregnable, that you must bring
The ballisters of faith
Their burning bolts to fling,
And all the cunning intricate device
Of human wit,
One little breach to make
That so you might attain to enter it?
Nay, on the other side
Love's undefended postern is set wide:
But thus it is I woo
My dearest sons, that an ignoble ease
Shall never please,
Nor any smooth and open way entice.
Armed would I have them come
Against the mighty bastions of their home;

Out of high failure win
Their way within,
And from my conquering hand their birthright take.

Corpus Christi

COME, dear Heart!
The fields are white to harvest: come and see
As in a glass the timeless mystery
Of love, whereby we feed
On God, our bread indeed.
Torn by the sickles, see him share the smart
Of travailing Creation: maimed, despised,
Yet by his lovers the more dearly prized
Because for us he lays his beauty down–
Last toll paid by Perfection for our loss!
Trace on these fields his everlasting Cross,
And o'er the stricken sheaves the Immortal Victim's crown.

From far horizons came a Voice that said,
'Lo! from the hand of Death take thou thy daily bread.'
Then I, awakening, saw
A splendour burning in the heart of things:
The flame of living love which lights the law
Of mystic death that works the mystic birth.
I knew the patient passion of the earth,
Maternal, everlasting, whence there springs
The Bread of Angels and the life of man.

Now in each blade
I, blind no longer, see
The glory of God's growth: know it to be
An earnest of the Immemorial Plan.
Yea, I have understood

How all things are one great oblation made:
He on our altars, we on the world's rood.
Even as this corn,
Earth-born,
We are snatched from the sod;
Reaped, ground to grist,
Crushed and tormented in the Mills of God,
And offered at Life's hands, a living Eucharist.

ELLA DIETZ

Emanation

OUT of the depths of the Infinite Being eternal,
Out of the cloud more bright than the brightness
of sun,
Out of the inmost the essence of spirit supernal,
We issued as one.

First essence electric, concentric, revolving, subduing,
We throbbed through the ether, a part of the infinite germ,
Dissolving, resolving, absorbing, reforming, renewing,
The endless in term.

Through forms multifarious onward and ever advancing,
Progressing through ether from molecule to planet and star,
Forms infinitesimal revealed by the sunbeam while dancing,
Controlled from afar.

Then part of the elements swayed by invisible forces,
The spirit of flame interchangeably water and air,
And matter more gross, still moulded by stars in their
courses,
To forms new and rare.

Part of the salt of the sea–of the fathomless ocean–
Part of the growth of the earth, and the light hid within,
The Boundless and Endless revealed in each varying motion
Unknown yet to sin.

The breath of all life, harmonious, ductile, complying,
Obedient lapsed in the force of the Infinite Will,
Untiring, unresting, incessant, unknowing, undying,
Love's law we fulfil.

Spirit of growth in the rocks, and the ferns, and the mosses,
Spirit of growth in the trees, and the grasses, and flowers,
Rejoicing in life, unconscious of changes or losses,
Of days or of hours.

Spirit of growth in the bird and the bee, ever tending
To form more complex its beauty and use thus combined,
Adapted perfection, the finite and infinite blending,
One gleam from One Mind.

Thus spirally upward we come from the depths of creation,
The man and the woman–the garden of Eden have found,
And joined by the Lord in an endless and holy relation
Ensphered and made round.

The innermost law of their being fulfilling, obeying,
The King and the Queen, perfected, companioned, are crowned,
The Incomprehensible thus in expression conveying
Its ultimate bound.

Obedience still is the law of each fresh emanation,
The prayer to the Father, 'Not my will, but Thy will be done,'
Then deathless, immortal, we pass through all forms of creation,
The twain lost in One.

The King's Daughter

The Word, the Redeemed is such as needs to be washed, and cleansed, and clothed upon.
In her lives the Imrah, the Word which is distilled and purified.
The feminine Imrah, or seven times purified words of Elôhah and of Jehovah.
It is a quickening Word, which comforts in affliction, and is the reward of all who keep Jehovah's precepts.

MRS. BREWSTER MACPHERSON.

I AM beloved of the Prince of the garden of pleasure,
I am beloved;
I am his pearl, and his dove, and his heart's hidden treasure, I am approved;
To-day he has given his love, oh! his love without measure,
Which can never be moved.

He has called me 'Beloved of my soul', and my heart beats, repeating
'Beloved of my soul',
And my blood dances swift through my veins in a musical beating;
The twin currents roll,
Pouring forth their wild love, then again to their centre retreating
Under righteous control.

O king of my life's hidden spring! O lord of my being!
Beloved of my heart;
Our lips breathed one prayer, and our souls, in a sudden, agreeing,
Knit, joining each part
Of the long-severed Word that the prophets beheld in their seeing–
Belovèd thou art.

The long-severed name of the Lord we are loving and fearing;
Our Sabbaths of rest
Do welcome the Son; the Redeemed hail the Bride-groom's appearing–
His Name ever blest;
The Word in our hearts spoken now, in soft accents endearing,
With joy is confest.

Yea! Imrah–the Word, the Redeemed, the Bride of the Morning,
The joy of the earth;
O Imrah, beloved, whom the world had outcast in its scorning,
Rejoice in thy birth;
Ten thousands shall bless thee and bring thee thy gems of adorning,
And comfort thy dearth.

HAROLD MONRO

b. 1879

God

ONCE, long before the birth of time, a storm
Of white desire, by its own ardour hurled,
Flashed out of infinite Desire, took form,
Strove, won, survived: and God became the world.

Next, some internal force began to move
Within the bosom of that latest earth:
The spirit of an elemental love
Stirred outward from itself, and God was birth.

Then outward, upward, with heroic thew,
Savage from young and bursting blood of life,
Desire took form, and conquered, and anew
Strove, conquered, and took form: and God was strife

Thus, like a comet, fiery flight on flight;
Flash upon flash, and purple morn on morn:
But always out of agony–delight;
And out of death–God evermore reborn,

Till, waxing fair and subtle and supreme,
Desiring his own spirit to possess,
Man of the bright eyes and the ardent dream
Saw paradise, and God was consciousness.

He is that one Desire, that life, that breath,
That Soul which, with infinity of pain,
Passes through revelation and through death
Onward and upward to itself again.

Out of the lives of heroes and their deeds,
Out of the miracle of human thought,
Out of the songs of singers, God proceeds;
And of the soul of them his Soul is wrought.

Nothing is lost: all that is dreamed or done
Passes unaltered the eternal way,
Immerging in the everlasting One,
Who was the dayspring and who is the day.

ALFRED NOYES

b. 1880

The Loom of Years

IN the light of the silent stars that shine on the struggling sea,
In the weary cry of the wind and the whisper of flower and tree,
Under the breath of laughter, deep in the tide of tears,
I hear the Loom of the Weaver that weaves the Web of Years.

The leaves of the winter wither and sink in the forest mould
To colour the flowers of April with purple and white and gold:
Light and scent and music die and are born again
In the heart of a grey-haired woman who wakes in a world of pain.

The hound, the fawn, and the hawk, and the doves that croon and coo,
We are all one woof of the weaving and the one warp threads us through,
One flying cloud on the shuttle that carries our hopes and fears
As it goes thro' the Loom of the Weaver that weaves the Web of Years.

The green uncrumpling fern and the rustling dew-drenched rose
Pass with our hearts to the Silence where the wings of music close,
Pass and pass to the Timeless that never a moment mars,
Pass and pass to the Darkness that made the suns and stars.

Has the soul gone out in the Darkness? Is the dust sealed
from sight?
Ah, hush, for the woof of the ages returns thro' the warp
of the night!
Never that shuttle loses one thread of our hopes and fears,
As it comes thro' the Loom of the Weaver that weaves
the Web of Years.

O, woven in one wide Loom thro' the throbbing weft of
the whole,
One in spirit and flesh, one in body and soul,
Tho' the leaf were alone in its falling, the bird in its hour
to die,
The heart in its muffled anguish, the sea in its mournful
cry,

One with the flower of a day, one with the withered moon,
One with the granite mountains that melt into the noon,
One with the dream that triumphs beyond the light of
the spheres,
We come from the Loom of the Weaver that weaves the
Web of Years.

Art, the Herald

'The voice of one crying in the wilderness'

BEYOND; beyond; and yet again beyond!
What went ye out to seek, oh foolish-fond?
Is not the heart of all things here and now?
Is not the circle infinite, and the centre
Everywhere, if ye would but hear and enter?
Come; the porch bends and the great pillars bow

Come; come and see the secret of the sun;
The sorrow that holds the warring worlds in one;
  The pain that holds Eternity in an hour;
One God in every seed self-sacrificed,
One star-eyed, star-crowned universal Christ,
  Re-crucified in every wayside flower.

The Paradox

'I Am that I Am'

I

ALL that is broken shall be mended;
All that is lost shall be found;
  I will bind up every wound
When that which is begun shall be ended.
Not peace I brought among you but a sword
  To divide the night from the day,
When I sent My worlds forth in their battle-array
  To die and to live,
  To give and to receive,
  Saith the Lord.

II

Of old time they said none is good save our God;
But ye that have seen how the ages have shrunk from my rod,
And how red is the wine-press wherein at my bidding they trod,
Have answered and said that with Eden I fashioned the snake,
That I mould you of clay for a moment, then mar you and break,
And there is none evil but I, the supreme Evil, God.
  Lo, I say unto both, I am neither;
  But greater than either;

For meeting and mingling in Me they become neither evil nor good;
Their cycle is rounded, they know neither hunger nor food,
They need neither sickle nor seed-time, nor root nor fruit,
They are ultimate, infinite, absolute.
Therefore I say unto all that have sinned,
East and West and South and North
The wings of my measureless love go forth
To cover you all: they are free as the wings of the wind.

III

Consider the troubled waters of the sea
Which never rest;
As the wandering waves are ye;
Yet assuaged and appeased and forgiven,
As the seas are gathered together under the infinite glory of heaven,
I gather you all to my breast.
But the sins and the creeds and the sorrows that trouble the sea
Relapse and subside,
Chiming like chords in a world-wide symphony
As they cease to chide;
For they break and they are broken of sound and hue,
And they meet and they murmur and they mingle anew,
Interweaving, intervolving, like waves: they have no stay:
They are all made as one with the deep, when they sink and are vanished away;
Yea, all is toned at a turn of the tide
To a calm and golden harmony;
But I–shall I wonder or greatly care,
For their depth or their height?
Shall it be more than a song in my sight
How many wandering waves there were

Or how many colours and changes of light?
It is your eyes that see
And take heed of these things: they were fashioned for you, not for Me.

IV

With the stars and the clouds I have clothed Myself here for your eyes
To behold That which Is. I have set forth the strength of the skies
As one draweth a picture before you to make your hearts wise;
That the infinite souls I have fashioned may know as I know,
Visibly revealed
In the flowers of the field,
Yea, declared by the stars in their courses, the tides in their flow,
And the clash of the world's wide battle as it sways to and fro,
Flashing forth as a flame
The unnameable Name,
The ineffable Word,
I am the Lord.

V

I am the End to which the whole world strives:
Therefore are ye girdled with a wild desire and shod
With sorrow; for among you all no soul
Shall ever cease or sleep or reach its goal
Of union and communion with the Whole,
Or rest content with less than being God.
Still, as unending asymptotes, your lives
In all their myriad wandering ways
Approach Me with the progress of the golden days;
Approach Me; for my love contrives

That ye should have the glory of this
For ever; yea, that life should blend
With life and only vanish away
From day to wider wealthier day,
Like still increasing spheres of light that melt and merge in wider spheres
Even as the infinite years of the past melt in the infinite future years.
Each new delight of sense,
Each hope, each love, each fear,
Widens, relumes and recreates each sphere,
From a new ring and nimbus of pre-eminence.
I am the Sphere without circumference:
I only and for ever comprehend
All others that within me meet and blend.
Death is but the blinding kiss
Of two finite infinities;
Two finite infinite orbs
The splendour of the greater of which absorbs
The less, though both like Love have no beginning and no end.

VI

Therefore is Love's own breath
Like Knowledge, a continual death;
And all his laughter and kisses and tears,
And woven wiles of peace and strife,
That ever widen thus your temporal spheres,
Are making of the memory of your former years
A very death in life.

VII

I am that I am;
Ye are evil and good;
With colour and glory and story and song ye are fed as with food:

The cold and the heat,
The bitter and the sweet,
The calm and the tempest fulfil my Word;
Yet will ye complain of my two-edged sword
That has fashioned the finite and mortal and given you the sweetness of strife,
The blackness and whiteness,
The darkness and brightness,
Which sever your souls from the formless and void and hold you fast-fettered to life?

VIII

Behold now, is Life not good?
Yea, is it not also much more than the food,
More than the raiment, more than the breath?
Yet Strife is its name!
Say, which will ye cast out first from the furnace, the fuel or the flame?
Would ye all be as I am; and know neither evil nor good; neither life; neither death;
Or mix with the void and the formless till all were as one and the same?

IX

I am that I am; the Container of all things: kneel, lift up your hands
To the high Consummation of good and of evil which none understands;
The divine Paradox, the ineffable Word, in whose light the poor souls that ye trod
Underfoot as too vile for their fellows are at terrible union with God!
Am I not over both evil and good,
The righteous man and the shedder of blood?
Shall I save or slay?

I am neither the night nor the day,
Saith the Lord.
Judge not, oh ye that are round my footstool, judge not, ere the hour be born
That shall laugh you also to scorn.

X

Ah, yet I say unto all that have sinned,
East and West and South and North
The wings of my measureless love go forth
To cover you all: they are free as the wings of the wind.

XI

But one thing is needful; and ye shall be true
To yourselves and the goal and the God that ye seek;
Yea, the day and the night shall requite it to you
If ye love one another, if your love be not weak.

XII

Since I sent out my worlds in their battle-array
To die and to live,
To give and to receive,
Not peace, not peace, I have brought among you but a sword,
To divide the night from the day,
Saith the Lord;
Yet all that is broken shall be mended,
And all that is lost shall be found,
I will bind up every wound,
When that which is begun shall be ended.

Song

From 'The Forest of Wild Thyme'

WHAT is there hid in the heart of a rose,
Mother-mine?
Ah, who knows, who knows, who knows?
A man that died on a lonely hill
May tell you, perhaps, but none other will,
Little child.

What does it take to make a rose,
Mother-mine?
The God that died to make it knows
It takes the world's eternal wars,
It takes the moon and all the stars,
It takes the might of heaven and hell
And the everlasting Love as well,
Little child.

The Two Worlds

THIS outer world is but the pictured scroll
Of worlds within the soul,
A coloured chart, a blazoned missal-book
Whereon who rightly look
May spell the splendours with their mortal eyes
And steer to Paradise.

O, well for him that knows and early knows
In his own soul the rose
Secretly burgeons, of this earthly flower
The heavenly paramour:

And all these fairy dreams of green-wood fern,
    These waves that break and yearn,
Shadows and hieroglyphs, hills, clouds and seas,
    Faces and flowers and trees,
Terrestrial picture-parables, relate
    Each to its heavenly mate.

O, well for him that finds in sky and sea
    This two-fold mystery,
And loses not (as painfully he spells
    The fine-spun syllables)
The cadences, the burning inner gleam,
    The poet's heavenly dream.

Well for the poet if this earthly chart
    Be printed in his heart,
When to his world of spirit woods and seas
    With eager face he flees
And treads the untrodden fields of unknown flowers
    And threads the angelic bowers,
And hears that unheard nightingale whose moan
    Trembles within his own,
And lovers murmuring in the leafy lanes
    Of his own joys and pains.

For though he voyages further than the flight
    Of earthly day and night,
Traversing to the sky's remotest ends
    A world that he transcends,
Safe, he shall hear the hidden breakers roar
    Against the mystic shore;
Shall roam the yellow sands where sirens bare
    Their breasts and wind their hair;
Shall with their perfumed tresses blind his eyes,
    And still possess the skies.

He, where the deep unearthly jungles are,
    Beneath his Eastern star
Shall pass the tawny lion in his den
    And cross the quaking fen.
He learnt his path (and treads it undefiled)
    When, as a little child,
He bent his head with long and loving looks
    O'er earthly picture-books.
His earthly love nestles against his side,
    His young celestial guide.

RACHEL ANNAND TAYLOR

The Immortal Hour

STILL as great waters lying in the West,
    So is my spirit still.
I lay my folded hands within Thy breast,
    My will within Thy will.
O Fortune, idle pedlar, pass me by.
O Death, keep far from me who cannot die.
The passion-flowers are lacing o'er the sill
Of my low door.–As dews their sweetness fill,
    So do I rest in Thee.
It is mine hour. Let none set foot therein.
It is mine hour unflawed of pain or sin.
'Tis laid and steeped in silence, till it be
A solemn dazzling crystal, to outlast
And storm the eyes of poets when long-past
Is all the changing dream of Thee and Me.

The Night Obscure of the Soul

WHEN the Soul travails in her Night Obscure,
 The nadir of her desperate defeat,
What heavenly dream shall help her to endure,
 What flaming Wisdom be her Paraclete?
No curious Metaphysic can withhold
 The heart from that mandragora she craves:–
Unreasonable, old as Earth is old,
 The blind ecstatic miracle that saves.
Far off the pagan trumpeters of pride
 Call to the blood.–Love moans.–Some fiery fashion
Of rapture like the anguish of the bride
 Leaps from the dark perfection of the Passion,
Crying: 'O beautiful God, still torture me,
For if thou slay me, I will trust in Thee.'

The Question

I SAW the Son of God go by
 Crowned with the crown of Thorn.
'Was It not finished, Lord?' I said,
 'And all the anguish borne?'

He turned on me His awful eyes:
 'Hast thou not understood?
Lo! Every soul is Calvary,
 And every sin a Rood.'

ANONYMOUS

At the Feet of Isis

HER feet are set in darkness–at Her feet
We kneel, for She is Mother of us all–
A mighty Mother, with all love replete;
We, groping 'midst the shadow's dusky pall,
Ask not to see the upper vision bright,
Enough for us Her feet shine clear–all virgin white.

Her wings are tipped with golden light, but we
Ken but the shadow at Her pinions' base–
We kneel before Her feet, we cannot see
The glory that illuminates Her face,
For he who t'wards the vision gazeth up
Finds first the stricken breast–the sacrificial cup!

Her feet gleam in the darkness–at Her feet
We lay the price of those twin pearls of Heav'n–
All that man hath–an offering incomplete
Is his who yet his best would leave ungiv'n;
And as She stoops Her guerdon to bestow,
His life's blood in Her cup, outstretched there, needs
must flow!

Her wings are in the shadow–Lo! they cast
That shadow e'en o'er Heav'n's own light, we cry,
For in the darkness, terrible and vast,
She spreads the wing to which the soul must hie;
But, to that shelter led, our upward gaze
Beholds Her pinions formed of Light's celestial rays!

Her feet are in the darkness, but Her face
Is in high Heav'n–all Truth inhabits there;
All Knowledge and all Peace, and perfect grace,
And in the wonder of Her joy they share
Who, blindly clinging to Her feet erstwhile,
Obtained the priceless gift–the vision of Her smile.

A Ballade of the Centre

WHEN all the shores of knowledge fade
Beyond the realms of night and day,
When the quick stir of thought is stayed
And, as a dream of yesterday,
The bonds of striving fall away:
There dawns sometimes a point of fire
Burning the utter dark, that may
Fulfil our desperate desire.

Into the darkness, unafraid,
Wherein soft hands of silence lay
Their veil of peace upon the blade
Of too bright thought, we take our way.
In changing of desire we pay
Whatever price the gods require,
Knowing the end is theirs–and they
Fulfil our desperate desire.

Upon the stillness we have made
Between our working and our play
A deeper stillness yet is laid.
Like some white bird above the sway

Of summer waves within the bay
Peace lights upon us ere we tire,
And does (yet how, we cannot say)
Fulfil our desperate desire.

Envoi

God of the world, to Whom we pray,
Thou Inmost God to Whom aspire
All hopes that Thou wilt not betray–
Fulfil our desperate desire!

JOHN MASEFIELD

The Ballad of Sir Bors

WOULD I could win some quiet and rest, and a little ease,
In the cool grey hush of the dusk, in the dim green place of the trees,
Where the birds are singing, singing, singing, crying aloud
The song of the red, red rose that blossoms beyond the seas.

Would I could see it, the rose, when the light begins to fail,
And a lone white star in the West is glimmering on the mail;
The red, red passionate rose of the sacred blood of the Christ,
In the shining chalice of God, the cup of the Holy Grail.

The dusk comes gathering grey, and the darkness dims
the West,
The oxen low to the byre, and all bells ring to rest;
But I ride over the moors, for the dusk still bides and waits,
That brims my soul with the glow of the rose that ends
the Quest.

My horse is spavined and ribbed, and his bones come
through his hide,
My sword is rotten with rust, but I shake the reins and
ride,
For the bright white birds of God that nest in the rose
have called,
And never a township now is a town where I can bide.

It will happen at last, at dusk, as my horse limps down the
fell,
A star will glow like a note God strikes on a silver bell,
And the bright white birds of God will carry my soul
to Christ,
And the sight of the Rose, the Rose, will pay for the
years of hell.

The Seekers

FRIENDS and loves we have none, nor wealth nor
blessed abode,
But the hope of the City of God at the other end of the
road.

Not for us are content, and quiet, and peace of mind,
For we go seeking a city that we shall never find.

There is no solace on earth for us–for such as we–
Who search for a hidden city that we shall never see.

Only the road and the dawn, the sun, the wind, and the rain,
And the watch-fire under stars, and sleep, and the road again.

We seek the City of God, and the haunt where beauty dwells,
And we find the noisy mart and the sound of burial bells.

Never the golden city, where radiant people meet,
But the dolorous town where mourners are going about the street.

We travel the dusty road till the light of the day is dim,
And sunset shows us spires away on the world's rim.

We travel from dawn to dusk, till the day is past and by,
Seeking the Holy City beyond the rim of the sky.

Friends and loves we have none, nor wealth nor blest abode,
But the hope of the City of God at the other end of the road.

From 'The Everlasting Mercy'

I DID not think, I did not strive,
The deep peace burnt my me alive;
The bolted door had broken in,
I knew that I had done with sin.
I knew that Christ had given me birth
To brother all the souls on earth,
And every bird and every beast
Should share the crumbs broke at the feast.

O glory of the lighted mind.
How dead I'd been, how dumb, how blind.
The station brook, to my new eyes,
Was babbling out of Paradise,
The waters rushing from the rain
Were singing Christ has risen again.
I thought all earthly creatures knelt
From rapture of the joy I felt.
The narrow station-wall's brick ledge,
The wild hop withering in the hedge,
The lights in huntsman's upper story
Were parts of an eternal glory,
Were God's eternal garden flowers.
I stood in bliss at this for hours.

O glory of the lighted soul.
The dawn came up on Bradlow Knoll,
The dawn with glittering on the grasses,
The dawn which pass and never passes.

'It's dawn,' I said, 'And chimney's smoking,
And all the blessed fields are soaking.
It's dawn, and there's an engine shunting;
And hounds, for huntsman's going hunting.
It's dawn, and I must wander north
Along the road Christ led me forth.' . . .

O wet red swathe of earth laid bare,
O truth, O strength, O gleaming share,
O patient eyes that watch the goal,
O ploughman of the sinner's soul.
O Jesus, drive the coulter deep
To plough my living man from sleep.

Slow up the hill the plough team plod,
Old Callow at the task of God,
Helped by man's wit, helped by the brute
Turning a stubborn clay to fruit,
Hid eyes for ever on some sign
To help him plough a perfect line.
At top of rise the plough team stopped,
The fore-horse bent his head and cropped;
Then the chains chack, the brasses jingle,
The lean reins gather through the cringle,
The figures move against the sky,
The clay wave breaks as they go by.
I kneeled there in the muddy fallow,
I knew that Christ was there with Callow,
That Christ was standing there with me,
That Christ had taught me what to be,
That I should plough, and as I ploughed
My Saviour Christ would sing aloud,
And as I drove the clods apart
Christ would be ploughing in my heart,
Through rest-harrow and bitter roots,
Through all my bad life's rotten fruits.

O Christ who holds the open gate,
O Christ who drives the furrow straight,
O Christ, the plough, O Christ, the laughter
Of holy white birds flying after,
Lo, all my heart's field red and torn,
And Thou wilt bring the young green corn,
The young green corn divinely springing,
The young green corn forever singing;
And when the field is fresh and fair
Thy blessèd feet shall glitter there,
And we will walk the weeded field,
And tell the golden harvest's yield,

The corn that makes the holy bread
By which the soul of man is fed,
The holy bread, the food unpriced,
Thy everlasting mercy, Christ.

MICHAEL FIELD

Midsummer Night's Dream

BUT so deep the wild-bee hummeth,
And so still the glow-worm glows,
That we know a Saviour cometh,
And we lay our hearts with those–
All the mysteries earth strives with through the June
nights and the rose.

Strange the joy that sets us weeping–
Holy John, thy Feast is come!
Yea, we feel a Babe is leaping
In the womb where he is dumb
To the song that God's own Mother sings so loud to
Christendom.

High that singing, high and humble!
Lo, our Queen is taking rule:
Faint midsummer thunders rumble,
And gold lilies light the pool,
While the generations whisper that a Queen is taking rule.

'Where the Blessed Feet Have Trod'

NOT alone in Palestine those blessed Feet have trod,
For I catch their print,
I have seen their dint
On a plot of chalky ground,
Little villas dotted round;

On a sea-worn waste,
Where a priest, in haste,
Passeth with the Blessèd Sacrament to one dying, frail,
Through the yarrow, past the tamarisk, and the plaited
    snail:
Bright upon the grass I see
    Bleeding Feet of Calvary–
And I worship, and I clasp them round!
On this bit of chalky, English ground,
Jesu, Thou art found: my God I hail,
    My Lord, my God!

LASCELLES ABERCROMBIE

b. 1881

Emblems of Love

She

ONLY to be twin elements of joy
In this extravagance of Being, Love,
Were our divided natures shaped in twain;
And to this hour the whole world must consent.
Is it not very marvellous, our lives
Can only come to this out of a long
Strange sundering, with the years of the world between us?

He

Shall life do more than God? for hath not God
Striven with himself, when into known delight
His unaccomplisht joy he would put forth,–
This mystery of a world sign of his striving?
Else wherefore this, a thing to break the mind
With labouring in the wonder of it, that here
Being–the world and we–is suffered to be!–

But, lying on thy breast one notable day,
Sudden exceeding agony of love
Made my mind a trance of infinite knowledge.
I was not: yet I saw the will of God
As light unfashion'd, unendurable flame,
Interminable, not to be supposed;
And there was no more creature except light,–
The dreadful burning of the lonely God's
Unutter'd joy. And then, past telling, came
Shuddering and division in the light:
Therein, like trembling, was desire to know
Its own perfect beauty; and it became
A cloven fire, a double flaming, each
Adorable to each; against itself
Waging a burning love, which was the world;–
A moment satisfied in that love-strife
I knew the world!–And when I fell from there,
Then knew I also what this life would do
In being twain,–in being man and woman!
For it would do even as its endless Master,
Making the world, had done; yea, with itself
Would strive, and for the strife would into sex
Be cloven, double burning, made thereby
Desirable to itself. Contrivèd joy
Is sex in life; and by no other thing
Than by a perfect sundering, could life
Change the dark stream of unappointed joy
To perfect praise of itself, the glee that loves
And worships its own Being. This is ours!
Yet only for that we have been so long
Sundered desire: thence is our life all praise.–
But we, well knowing by our strength of joy
There is no sundering more, how far we love
From those sad lives that know a half-love only,

Alone thereby knowing themselves for ever
Sealed in division of love, and therefore made
To pour their strength always into their love's
Fierceness, as green wood bleeds its hissing sap
Into red heat of a fire! Not so do we:
The cloven anger, life, hath left to wage
Its flame against itself, here turned to one
Self-adoration.–Ah, what comes of this?
The joy falters a moment, with closed wings
Wearying in its upward journey, ere
Again it goes on high, bearing its song,
Its delight breathing and its vigour beating
The highest height of the air above the world.

She

What hast thou done to me!–I would have soul,
Before I knew thee, Love, a captive held
By flesh. Now, inly delighted with desire,
My body knows itself to be nought else
But thy heart's worship of me; and my soul
Therein is sunlight held by warm gold air.
Nay, all my body is become a song
Upon the breath of spirit, a love-song.

He

And mine is all like one rapt faculty,
As it were listening to the love in thee,
My whole mortality trembling to take
Thy body like heard singing of thy spirit.

She

Surely by this, Beloved, we must know
Our love is perfect here,–that not as holds
The common dullard thought, we are things lost

In an amazement that is all unware;
But wonderfully knowing what we are!
Lo, now that body is the song whereof
Spirit is mood, knoweth not our delight?
Knoweth not beautifully now our love,
That Life, here to this festival bid come
Clad in his splendour of worldly day and night,
Filled and empower'd by heavenly lust, is all
The glad imagination of the Spirit?

He

Were it not so, Love could not be at all:
Nought could be, but a yearning to fulfil
Desire of beauty, by vain reaching forth
Of sense to hold and understand the vision
Made by impassion'd body,–vision of thee!
But music mixt with music are, in love,
Bodily senses; and as flame hath light,
Spirit this nature hath imagined round it,
No way concealed therein, when love comes near,
Nor in the perfect wedding of desires
Suffering any hindrance.

She

Ah, but now,
Now am I given love's eternal secret!
Yea, thou and I who speak, are but the joy
Of our for ever mated spirits; but now
The wisdom of my gladness even through Spirit
Looks, divinely elate. Who hath for joy
Our Spirits? Who hath imagined them
Round him in fashion'd radiance of desire,
As into light of these exulting bodies
Flaming Spirit is uttered?

He

Yea, here the end
Of love's astonishment! Now know we Spirit,
And Who, for ease of joy, contriveth Spirit.
Now all life's loveliness and power we have
Dissolved in this one moment, and our burning
Carries all shining upward, till in us
Life is not life, but the desire of God,
Himself desiring and himself accepting.
Now what was prophecy in us is made
Fulfilment: we are the hour and we are the joy,
We in our marvellousness of single knowledge,
Of Spirit breaking down the room of fate
And drawing into his light the greeting fire
Of God,–God known in ecstasy of love
Wedding himself to utterance of himself.

JOSEPH MARY PLUNKETT

1887-1916

I saw the Sun at Midnight, rising red

I SAW the Sun at midnight, rising red,
Deep-hued yet glowing, heavy with the stain
Of blood-compassion, and I saw It gain
Swiftly in size and growing till It spread
Over the stars; the heavens bowed their head
As from Its heart slow dripped a crimson rain,
Then a great tremor shook It, as of pain–
The night fell, moaning, as It hung there dead.

O Sun, O Christ, O bleeding Heart of flame!
Thou giv'st Thine agony as our life's worth,
And mak'st it infinite, lest we have dearth
Of rights wherewith to call upon thy Name;
Thou pawnest Heaven as a pledge for Earth,
And for our glory sufferest all shame.

I see His Blood upon the Rose

I SEE his blood upon the rose
And in the stars the glory of his eyes,
His body gleams amid eternal snows,
His tears fall from the skies.

I see his face in every flower;
The thunder and the singing of the birds
Are but his voice–and carven by his power
Rocks are his written words.

All pathways by his feet are worn,
His strong heart stirs the ever-beating sea,
His crown of thorns is twined with every thorn,
His cross is every tree.

DAVID ATWOOD WASSON

1823-1887

The Mystic

i. Knowledge

THE Secret of the World is lowly,
  Self-sung nigh my pleading ear;
It presses close, enchanting, holy,
  Murmuring,–what, I cannot hear:
A dream embosoming all my waking,
  Solace shaming all my fear.

In hours serenest and profoundest,
  List I 'yond the breadth of time:
Over the sea of calm *Thou* soundest;
  Now I catch the tune, the rhyme,
And now shall know!–Alas! the silence
  Ripples, broken; dies the chime.

Partial, the universal Mother
    Tells her secret to the stars:
And they intone it each to other,
    Trooping in their silver cars.
Winging and witching comes the echo,
    But mine ear the meaning bars.

When the sunlight, aether flooding,
    Rains its richness down the sky,
The Face on every beam is brooding,
    And on every leaf an eye
Implanteth, where the dauntless, dimless,
    Godlike vision I espy.

The psalmist pine-tree, sounding, sweeping
    One great chord forevermore;
Deep-chested Ocean's chant, as, keeping
    Time upon the throbbing shore,
His billowy palm still falls and rises,–
    Both recount that wondrous lore.

The World is rich, it hath possession;
    Joy of wealth fills land and sea;
The fields in bloom, the stars in session,
    Birds and blades on bough and lea,
All know the truth, the joy, the wonder,
    Not revealed to man, to me.

Nature, be just in thy bestowing!
    Best to best shouldst thou confide.
Oh! why from him, whose bliss is knowing,
    Knowledge, cruel, dost thou hide?
Since, that withholden, naught is given;
    Given, naught withheld beside.

ii. Life

A goblet drained is all my knowing,–
Cup whence I have quaffed the wine:
From out the Unknown comes the flowing
And exhaustless juice divine,
That lends the blood its priceless crimson,
And the eye its living shine.

Embrace me, Mystery of Being;
Fill my arteries, flood my brain,
And through me pour thy heart, till seeing,
Thought, are drowned, like dew in rain,
In powerful, pure participation:
Separate life is separate pain.

Temple unseen of Truth immortal,
Thought hath brought me to thy door;
Never passes he the portal,
I am drawn the threshold o'er;
And lo! I am a leaf that quivers
In God's joy-wind evermore!

Now are the light-waves round me rolling,
Now the love-tides through me run,
Body and soul anew ensouling:
Seeing and being melt in one.
The ear is self-same with the music,
Beam with vision, eye with sun.

CLARENCE A. WALWORTH

Musa Extatica

THE altar tiles are under her feet,
Buff and blue;
The tiles lie smooth beneath her feet,
But touch not her sandal shoe.
Her eyes entranced might seem to gaze
Where arches concentrate and meet
In a maze;
But the arches are not in view.
Where does the vision lie?
What fixes the maiden's eye?
What makes her smile?
Is it far, or is it near?
What makes her garments float so clear
Above the bed of tile?
They are not lifted by the air.
Why hold her hands behind her head,
Dipped in that foam of golden hair,
As if she heard some distant tread,
And stood prepared to call?
Why does her bosom rise and fall?
Its even swell of deep emotion
Is like the roll on a placid ocean
Of billows from afar.
Who can tell what these billows are?
Is it joy coming, or desire outgoing?
Does she command, or is she wooing?
Why does she smile? why bend her brow?
Why nod? why beckon now,
Whiles censuring, and whiles approving,
Is she conveying her desire
To some viewless choir,
Or a crowd of spirits moving?

Wait! wait! Now she is still.
If thou hast a poet's ear
For sacred song, come near!
The beating of her heart will tell.

'Lo! me on holy ground,
With burning bushes all around.
Oh! whither shall I turn?
I burn! I burn!
Electric currents come and go.
They thread my spirit through and through:
And a crowding tide of thought
Holds my spirit overwrought,
And urges love to fond despair.
Oh! give me air!
I die! I die!
Blow on me from the upper sky,
Or joy that has no breath,
Unsung must end in death.
Oh! give me air divine!
Brace me with the breath of wine!
Give me such milk as flows from the breast
Of the all-hallowing Eucharist,
That I may troll
Sweet carols to the Oversoul.
Either fill me
With blood of song, or kill me.

'Oh! I am drunk, but not with drink;
Wild, but not all beyond command.
How could imagination think
To gauge, by law of plumb and line,
A vision reared by heavenly wand,
A beauty all entrancing and divine,
Which makes thought reel as if with wine?

It steals my reason, yet I own it;
It steals my thought to crown it.
My heart in sweet delirium
Lies safe at home.
It gives me more than it can take,
Though I leave all for its dear sake;
A mighty vision haunts me,
Enchants and disenchants me,
Heals my wounds, yet makes me bleed.
Not for the world would I dispel it.
Oh! could I, as I see it, tell it,
I were a bard indeed.

'Oh! I am mad, but not with folly,
Sad am I without melancholy,
Glad, but with sober merriment;
Fond am I, without detriment
To reason. Bonded to higher will
That may not be denied,
My own I seek to kill,
All fearless of the suicide.
Oh! I am calm,
I know where I am.
Yea, when most overwrought
I still am mistress of my thought;
Though oft to others I may seem
A vessel driving to the coast
On the foam of a dream,
And utterly lost,
There's method in my madness,
There's measure in my gladness;
And into rhythmic rule I bring
True anthems to my Lord and King.
Of love, all ruling love, I sing.

By love inspired, by love oppressed,
Within my breast
Electric forces gathering
Leap into buds;
Thoughts crystallize into thick geodes
The grasses wave their myriad flags;
Hills helmeted with lofty crags
Rein up like warriors;
The hemlocks bending low,
Like water carriers,
Beneath their yokes of snow,
Keep measure with their feet
To the time I beat;
Pines, crowding to look o'er
The common score,
Bend eagerly down till their bonnets meet;
Clouds march in groups;
Waves march in columns over the sea;
Stars gallop in troops;
Nights and days keep time;
The fuguing seasons chime
With nature and with me;–
All praise the Lord together.
To the last cliffs of space I shout,
My choristers to gather.
Sing out! sing out!
Keep tune, keep time,
To the pitch and motion of my rhyme!
Faster! faster! faster!
Look at me!
One! two! three!
'Tis the measure of the mighty Master.
So beats revolving life in Trinity.
'Tis the secret of infinity–

Who keeps true time shall time outlast;
Who loses, stubbornly slow,
From heaven shall be outcast,
And its music shall never know.
Sing all! sing out!
Prolong the chant with joyous shout.
Faith praises with untiring tongue.
The hearts that weary die unblest,
Harps must not be unstrung,
Love may repose but never rest.'

ALFRED GURNEY

The New World

'That new world which is the old.'–TENNYSON.

A NEW world did Columbus find?
  Ah! 'tis not so *that* world is found;
God's golden harvest-sheaves who bind
  Are tillers of another ground.

No new world like the old we need;
  One thing suffices–one alone,
A garnered world-harvest from seed
  The wounded Hands of Christ have sown.

No earthly Paradise avails,
  No Eldorado in the West;
The Spirit's Breath must fill their sails
  Who seek the Highlands of the Blest.

By stripes is healing wrought, and stars
  Point ever to a central Sun;
He flies the conquering flag, whose scars,
  Transfigured, speak of Victory won.

O Royal Heart, Thy Kingdom come!
  All else may change; all else may go:
Not eastward, westward, is our Home,
  But *onward, upward:*–even so!

One Sign alone is love-designed,
  God's Evergreen, the Eternal Rood;
Happy the home-seekers who find
  Its meaning plain–*a world renewed!*

EDWIN J. ELLIS

Preface to 'Fate in Arcadia'

HERE kneels my word, that may not say
  Even to the inward ear of night
More than the laughter of the day
  Or the soft weeping of twilight.

No waking hours, no sleep shall find
  The world's continual dream revealed.
The Living Word is silent mind,
  And every book is closed and sealed.

Our Mother Earth for daily things
  Has given the daily mother-tongue;
But the mute wonder that she brings,
  All lips have kissed; no voice has sung.

And even now the usual word
  Spread like an empty couch and cold
Measures the sound our fathers heard,
  But holds no more the hint untold.

For He is risen whom we seek:
    The linen clothes without the form
Are folded, lest too clear they speak
    The Divine Body, buried warm.

Then every song is free from blame,
    Though silence veil her inmost part
Like the dark centre of the flame,
    Or the hot patience of the heart.

The Wanderer

AH, Christ, it were enough to know
    That brooding on the unborn things
Thou gatherest up the years that go
    Like a hen's brood beneath her wings.

It were enough to know that those,
    More evil than the years that fall,
Who heard Thee mocked Thy safe repose
    And would not trust Thee at Thy call.

It were enough that Thou hast died,
    Because Thyself Thou couldst not save,
Unless by losing from Thy side
    Thy sons that drove Thee to Thy grave.

Yet more and more we know and see,
    For Golgotha the shade retains
Of Him who died, the Form of Thee,
    Of Him who bore Thy fleshly pains.

Nor there alone this Form shall be
    Still seen within us, Thou dost say
Until there shine on earth and sea
    Light of the unforeboded Day.

O Christ the Wanderer, marked as Cain,
We know the sign upon Thy brow;
We know the trailing cross, the stain;
The passing footstep whispers now.

It was Thy hand, we learn at last,
That nailed Thee in that far-off year;
Thy hand as now Thou wanderest past,
Drives deep within Thy side the spear.

While evil holds the world in grip
And men revile the eternal powers,
This vision holds Thee lip to lip
Close to our love and makes Thee ours.

JOHN GRAY

The Tree of Knowledge

FROM what meek jewel seed
Did this tree spring?
How first beat its new life in bleak abode
Of virgin rock, strange metals for its food,
Towards its last hewn mould, the bitter rood?
First did it sprout, indeed,
A double wing.

Earth hung with its gross weight
Its loins unto:
The tender wings, with hope in every vein,
Beat feebly upward, saying: 'Is this the pain
The Sooth spake of; to lift to God again
This blackness' dark estate
Reformed anew?

'Mine 'tis, of fruit mine own,
To work this deed:
Earnest of promise absolute, these green
Sweet wings; a million engines pulse therein.
Yet can I leave not for a space, to lean
Upon a fulcrum known,
To know my need.'

With which, the seed upthrust
To God a scale;
Wondering at its fibre and tough growth;
Saying, the while it purposed: 'For He knoweth
My sore extremity, how I am loth
To cleave unto the dust
Which makes me hale.'

Long while the scale increased
In height and girth;
Cast many branches forth and many wings;
Wherein and under, formed and fashioned things
Had great content and speech and twitterings:
Insect and fowl and beast
And sons of earth.

Stern, netherward did grope
Each resolute root
Of the tree, making question in the deep
Of spirits, where the mighty metals sleep,
How long ere from its base the rock should leap;
Saying: 'Yet have I hope
Of that my fruit.'

Sprang from its topmost bough
The hope at length
Fearsome and fierce and passionate. The sire
Warmed his son's vitals with celestial fire,
Feeding him with sweet gum of strong desire,
Lest be not stanch enow
His godly strength.

Until the gardener came
With his white spouse,
Wounding the tree, and ravishing the son,
(Whence curses fallen and a world undone.)
For that rape, wrathfully a shining one
Drave them with fearful flame
Without their house.

Race upon savage race,
Rough brood on brood,
Defiled before it, whiles the tree scanned each;
Leaned leaf and branch to grapple and beseech;
Till, on a certain day, requiring speech
Of the tree, at its base
The whole world stood:

'What hast thou given us,
Thou barren tree?
"Knowledge," thou answerest? Thou hast set agape
The door of Knowledge only. Thy limbs ape
Some truth. We love thee not, nor love thy shape.
Imposture, thus and thus
We fashion thee.'

Sorely then handled it
The gardener's sons.
Strangely they built it newly, having cleft
Its being all asunder; stem bereft
Of quivering limbs, save one to right and left,
Urging the self-same wit
It gave them once.

'Lo! all my glories fall.
Of these my woes,
What know those wrathful men, save, in yon place,
Perhaps, yon athlete, stripped for my embrace?
If longing cheat me not, writ in his face,
He knows about it all,
He knows, he knows.

'Sorrow! What sin they now,
Those wrathful men?
Passion! thou'rt come to me again too soon:
Too hot thou givst me back the fiery boon
I gave thee; love consumes me, that I swoon;
Thou on my topmost bough,
My fruit again.'

On the Holy Trinity

ERE aught began,
Beyond the span
Of sense, the Word
(O priceless hoard!)
Was, which God fashioned in his youth.

O Fatherbreast,
Wherefrom, with zest,
The Word did bloom!
Yet did the womb
Retain the Word in very truth.
Of twain a fount,
Love paramount,
The double troth,
Known unto both,
The ever gentle Spirit flows.
Equal, and none
Can make but one;
One are the three;
Yet what it be
That triple spirit only knows.
The triple crown
Hath deep renown;
Ring without clasp
No sense can grasp,
It is a depth without a floor.
Is rest, is grace,
Shape, form and space;
The source, the ring
Of everything;
A point which never moveth more.
To its abode
There is no road;
Curiously
It beareth thee
Into a desert strangely strange.
Is wide, is broad,
Unmeasured road;
The desert has
Nor time nor space,
Its way is wonderfully strange.

That desert plot
No foot hath trod;
Created wit
Ne'er came to it;
It is, and no man knoweth what.
Is there, is here,
Is far, is near,
Is deep, is high,
And none reply
Whether this thing be this or that.
Is light, is pure,
Is most obscure,
Nameless, alone,
It is unknown,
Free both of end and origin.
It standeth dark,
Is bare and stark;
Reveal his face
Who knows its place,
And say what fashion it is in.
Become a child,
Deaf, blind and mild;
Be eye and thought
Reduced to naught,
Self and negation driven back,
Space, time resign,
And every sign,
No leader hath
The narrow path,
So com'st thou to the desert track.
O soul, abroad,
Go in to God;
Sink as a yes
In nothingness,
Sink in unfathomable flood.

I fly from thee,
Thou greetest me;
Self left behind,
If I but find
Thee, O thou good of every good!

EUGENE MASON

b. 1862

Apparition

HOW shall I find Him, who can be my guide?
Wears He a human form, a tear-marred face,
By blood-red raiment may He be descried,
Or broods He far withdrawn through stellar space?
Perchance, informing all, His coils entwine
And bind the monstrous fabric cell to cell,
Or, veiled in service, 'neath this Bread and Wine
A homely God, He deigns with men to dwell.
Lo! just beyond the skyline He may stand,
Speak just without the waftage of mine ear,
I all but touch Him with my outstretched hand,
Clear to my senses He may straight appear.

I hush my drumming heart, I stay my breath
To catch His step, to hearken what He saith.

FRED. G. BOWLES

Resurrection

AS the slow Evening gather'd in her grey,
And one clear star its ancient pathway trod–
With long, low cadences of dear delay
The lark, descending, left his song with God!

And Peace came, like a reverential soul,
With far-off tremors of a further world,
And thro' the silver mist of twilight stole
Unto the heart of all. And upward curl'd
The April moon, resurgent of the sun,
To the blue dusk of the exalted dome
Of heav'n; and the white wind-flowers, one by one,
Shook in light slumber on their hilly home.
It was so sweet to stoop and feel around!
Each blade of grass a breathing lyre of life
Whereon the wind, in arias of sound,
Told subtle music; how the great World, rife
With scent of violet, and primrose-strewn,
Strain'd tender fingers from each dewy sod
To the dear Christ of chrysalis and moon–
And, dusk descending, left her soul with God!

An Insurgent of Art

LIKE a tired lover I rest on her bosom,
I, the Insurgent of Art . . . Thou, the Glory,
Worshipped of Cherubim, leaning toward me;
Now through the yellowing clouds of the rushes,
Now o'er the music of waters melodic,
Now from the wavering blue fields of heaven,
Or from the daffodil's soundless pale trumpet,
Drawing my soul with miraculous ardours!
What is thy purpose? Ah! What is thy doing?
White stars are water-blooms set in the ocean,
Young lives are petals from one burning Blossom,
Fallen from altitudes starry and primal–
Welcome the wind that shall blow them to shelter,
Breathe on their circumstance, shape the Soul's eddy,

Separately fire and transform all this wonder.
I, thy lost lover, long-waiting, have found Thee,
I, who had seen Thy sheathed colours, descending,
Melt into violets, flow into pansies,
Know that the Master hath need of the artist!
Out of the force of His Being, atomic,
Came I, and go I, ripe seed of His sowing;
Reticent, mutinous, still have I found Thee,
Steadfast I worship, for Thou art so near me–
Set in a Soul, my one Holy of Holies!

NORA CHESSON

Hertha

I AM the spirit of all that lives,
Labours and loses and forgives.
My breath's the wind among the reeds;
I'm wounded when a birch-tree bleeds.
I am the clay nest 'neath the eaves
And the young life wherewith it brims.
The silver minnow where it swims
Under a roof of lily-leaves
Beats with my pulses; from my eyes
The violet gathered amethyst.
I am the rose of winter skies,
The moonlight conquering the mist.

I am the bird the falcon strikes;
My strength is in the kestrel's wing,
My cruelty is in the shrikes.
My pity bids the dock-leaves grow
Large, that a little child may know

Where he shall heal the nettle's sting.
I am the snowdrop and the snow,
Dead amber, and the living fir–
The corn-sheaf and the harvester.

My craft is breathed into the fox
When, a red cub, he snarls and plays
With his red vixen. Yea, I am
The wolf, the hunter, and the lamb;
I am the slayer and the slain,
The thought new-shapen in the brain.
I am the ageless strength of rocks,
The weakness that is all a grace,
Being the weakness of a flower.

The secret on the dead man's face
Written in his last living hour,
The endless trouble of the seas
That fret and struggle with the shore,
Strive and are striven with evermore–
The changeless beauty that they wear
Through all their changes–all of these
Are mine. The brazen streets of hell
I know, and heaven's gold ways as well.
Mortality, eternity,
Change, death, and life are mine–are me.

EVA GORE-BOOTH

The Quest

FOR years I sought the Many in the One,
I thought to find lost waves and broken rays,
The rainbow's faded colours in the sun–
The dawns and twilights of forgotten days.

But now I seek the One in every form,
Scorning no vision that a dewdrop holds,
The gentle Light that shines behind the storm,
The Dream that many a twilight hour enfolds.

Harvest

THOUGH the long seasons seem to separate
Sower and reaper or deeds dreamed and done,
Yet when a man reaches the Ivory Gate
Labour and life and seed and corn are one.

Because thou art the doer and the deed,
Because thou art the thinker and the thought,
Because thou art the helper and the need,
And the cold doubt that brings all things to nought.

Therefore in every gracious form and shape
The world's dear open secret shalt thou find,
From the One Beauty there is no escape
Nor from the sunshine of the Eternal mind.

The patient labourer, with guesses dim,
Follows this wisdom to its secret goal.
He knows all deeds and dreams exist in him,
And all men's God in every human soul.

Form

THE buried statue through the marble gleams,
Praying for freedom, an unwilling guest,
Yet flooding with the light of her strange dreams
The hard stone folded round her uncarved breast.

Founded in granite, wrapped in serpentine,
Light of all life and heart of every storm,
Doth the uncarven image, the Divine,
Deep in the heart of each man, wait for form.

SUSAN MITCHELL

The Living Chalice

THE Mother sent me on the holy quest,
Timid and proud and curiously dressed
In vestures by her hand wrought wondrously;
An eager burning heart she gave to me.
The Bridegroom's Feast was set and I drew nigh–
Master of Life, Thy Cup has passed me by.

Before new-dressed I from the Mother came,
In dreams I saw the wondrous Cup of Flame.
Ah, Divine Chalice, how my heart drank deep,
Waking I sought the Love I knew asleep.
The Feast of Life was set and I drew nigh–
Master of Life, Thy Cup has passed me by.

Eye of the Soul, awake, awake and see
Growing within the Ruby Radiant Tree,
Sharp pain hath wrung the Clusters of my Vine;
My heart is rose-red with its brimmèd wine.
Thou hast new-set the Feast and I draw nigh–
Master of Life, take me, Thy Cup am I.

Immortality

AGE cannot reach me where the veils of God
Have shut me in,
For me the myriad births of stars and suns
Do but begin,
And here how fragrantly there blows to me
The holy breath,
Sweet from the flowers and stars and hearts of men,
From life and death.

We are not old, O heart, we are not old,
The breath that blows
The soul aflame is still a wandering wind
That comes and goes;
And the stirred heart with sudden raptured life
A moment glows.

A moment here–a bulrush's brown head
In the grey rain,
A moment there–a child drowned and a heart
Quickened with pain;
The name of Death, the blue deep heaven, the scent
Of the salt sea,
The spicy grass, the honey robbed
From the wild bee.

Awhile we walk the world on its wide roads
And narrow ways,
And they pass by, the countless shadowy troops
Of nights and days;
We know them not, O happy heart,
For you and I
Watch where within a slow dawn lightens up
Another sky.

Love's Mendicant

WHAT do I want of thee?
No gift of smile or tear
Nor casual company,
But in still speech to me
Only thy heart to hear.

Others contentedly
Go lonely here and there;
I cannot pass thee by,
Love's Mendicant am I
Who meet thee everywhere.

No merchandise I make;
Thou mayst not give to me
The counterfeits they take.
I claim Him for Love's sake,
The Hidden One in thee.

JAMES H. COUSINS

The Quest

THEY said: 'She dwelleth in some place apart,
Immortal Truth, within whose eyes
Who looks may find the secret of the skies
And healing for life's smart!'

I sought Her in loud caverns underground,–
On heights where lightnings flashed and fell;
I scaled high Heaven; I stormed the gates of Hell,
But Her I never found

Till thro' the tumults of my Quest I caught
A whisper: 'Here, within thy heart,
I dwell; for I am thou: behold, thou art
The Seeker–and the Sought.'

Vision

WHEN I from life's unrest had earned the grace
Of utter ease beside a quiet stream;
When all that was had mingled in a dream
To eyes awakened out of time and place;
Then in the cup of one great moment's space
Was crushed the living wine from things that seem;
I drank the joy of very Beauty's gleam,
And saw God's glory face to shining face.

Almost my brow was chastened to the ground,
But for an inner Voice that said: 'Arise!
Wisdom is wisdom only to the wise:
Thou art thyself the Royal thou hast crowned:
In Beauty thine own beauty thou hast found,
And thou hast looked on God with God's own eyes.'

ALICE MARY BUCKTON

The Great Response

LET me come nearer Thee,
O Perfect Soul!
Down-looking on me, whereso'er I tread,
With earnest gaze from cliff, and sky o'erhead,
From clustered leaves and buds and bowers of green–
Let me come nearer Thee!

Seeking Thine intercourse
I wander wide
O'er hills and valleys, under moon and stars,
Rapt in a secret tumult of delight
At every passing cloud, and changing light
On stream and mountain side.

I kiss thy cheek, fair rose!
Its pearly hue
Reflects the darker passion blood of mine:
Thy tender breath, responding to the lips,
Is sweeter to the soul than new-mixt wine.

Young veinèd leaf uncurled,
And tendril green,
Clinging about my finger slenderly,
Thou seëst not: what wouldst thou have of me?
What happy sense hast thou, to know the touch
Of the unseen?

Blue dome of heaven that guards
The living world
Like a green gem within a casket rare,
Fretted with brooks, and set in silver seas,
What Breast contains ye both, the moving Earth
And the free Air?

And lo! within my soul
Some happy Thing
Betrayed the secret sigh of heart's content:
And, from the hollows of the breathless hills
There came a quiet Voice: Look round on Me,
The Presence, the Desire that moves and fills,
The whole–the part!

I rise upon the winds:
I draw the stars
Thro' realms of night, on paths of trackless dawn!
Mine Eye contains the light of Day: mine Arm
Unfurls the cloud, and flings the grateful shade
On hill and lawn!

In glimmering regions, yet unfound,
I penetrate
The Abyss of Being, and the Springs of Thought:
I order things that be: and blamelessly
Divide the heavens and earth, reproved of nought,
Of Joy and Power, insatiate!

I linger in the twilight land of grief:
With health divine
Breathing on frozen hearts that know me not;
They lift their marred and chilly lips to me,
Swooning into my bosom dreamlessly,
For Grief and Death are mine!

I gather up the fleeting Souls that seem
All day to die:
Their beauty, melting, passeth not away!
Woven into the golden mist of Life
They 'merge again upon the teeming Strife
That worketh endlessly!

And Man, the fairest of my children! Thou
That battlest darkly with thy Destiny,
Whom I have made for god-like liberty,
And fain had lifted up to be with Me–
My son and fellow-worker! know

I only Am: unhasting, uncontrolled,
My Perfect Will
Fulfils its perfect Self, around, above!
My HIDDEN NAME is Joy! O mortal, yield
Unto the Breath that would thy being fill,
The Breath of Love!

Before the Dawn

THOU, for whom words have exhausted their sweet-
ness–
Thou, the All-End of all human desire–
Thou, in whose Presence the ages are hourless,
Gather me nigher!

Husht in the chambers where Reason lies sleeping,
Ere the Day claim us, to which we are told,–
Wrapped in the veil of Thy slumbering Beauty,
Fold me, oh fold!

Fill me afresh with the wonder of wakening–
Draw me again with Thy splendour and might–
Open my lids but a moment, and grant me
Sight of Thy sight!

Out of the furthest high Throne of Thy Dwelling,
A motionless Flame on the Bosom of Thought,
Deign to uncover Thyself, O Eternal
Seeker and Sought!

Pure in the Body that offers Thee homage,
Blest in the Thought that embraces Thee far,
Next to Thy secret and innermost Breathing
Thy worshippers are!

Forth to the Day that I know not awaiting,
Out to the highway Thy glory hath trod,
Glad as a child, and as passionless, fearless,
Lead me, O God!

ANNA BUNSTON (MRS. DE BARY)

A Basque Peasant returning from Church

O LITTLE lark, you need not fly
To seek your Master in the sky,
He treads our native sod;
Why should you sing aloft, apart?
Sing to the heaven of my heart;
In me, in me, in me is God!

O strangers passing in your car,
You pity me who come so far
On dusty feet, ill shod;
You cannot guess, you cannot know
Upon what wings of joy I go
Who travel home with God.

From far-off lands they bring your fare,
Earth's choicest morsels are your share,
And prize of gun and rod;
At richer boards I take my seat,
Have dainties angels may not eat:
In me, in me, in me is God!

O little lark, sing loud and long
To Him who gave you flight and song,
And me a heart aflame.
He loveth them of low degree,
And He hath magnified me,
And holy, holy, holy is His Name!

A Great Mystery

Shall I, the gnat which dances in Thy ray,
Dare to be Reverent?–Coventry Patmore

STRANGELY, strangely, Lord, this morning
    Camest Thou beneath my roof,
Shorn of all Thy royal adorning,
    Stripp'd of judgement and reproof,
The King of kings yet gladly scorning,
    Every plea but love's behoof.
'Can this be God?' I said, 'who enters,
    This be God who climbs my stair?
God sits high in heavenly centres,
    And though He hath us in His care,
'Tis as His adopted children,
    Slaves redeemed from Satan's snare.
God is mightier than the mountains,
    Far more majesty would wear,
This One comes like summer fountains,
    Hath no snow upon His hair.
With eagle pinions God will cover
    Those who seek for refuge there,
But these are dove-like wings that hover,
    God was never half so fair.'
Then with voice like falling water
    Viewless angels sang to me,
Fear not thou, O virgin daughter,
    Thy King desires thy poverty.

At that 'Ave Maria'
    I arose and I obeyed;
O my King Cophetua,
    I, Thy blessed beggar-maid,

Who once lay among the potsherds
    Stand in silver plumes arrayed;
I, who lonely in the vineyards
    Morn and noon and evening strayed,
Now am wrapt in Thine embraces,
    'Neath Thy banner 'Love' am laid,
Made partaker of Thy graces,
    I, the outcast beggar-maid.

No excuse and no invention
    Makes me less unworthy Thee,
No prostration, no pretension
    Of unique humility,
But Thy glorious condescension
    Blazes through my misery,
And Thy love finds full extension
    In the nothingness of me.
Dark my soul, yet Thou hast sought her,
    My night allows Thy day to shine,
Thou the grape art, I the water–
    Both together make the wine.
I the clay and Thou the craftsman,
    I the boat and Thou the strand,
I the pencil, Thou the draughtsman,
    I the harp and Thou the hand.

But the world with envy raging
    Fain would snatch me, Lord, from Thee,
And Death and Hell their war are waging,
    Therefore go not far from me.
By the mystery of this housel,
    By this momentary truth,
By the love of this espousal,
    By this kindness of my youth,

By Thy promise of remembrance,
By that sweet perversity
That makes my dark uncomely semblance
Seem desirable to Thee–
Leave me not lest faith should falter,
O! secure my fealty,
I the victim on Thine altar,
Thou the fire consuming me.

'O Sovereign Lord, Thou Lover of Men's Souls!'

THOU hope of all Humanity,
What of all this that meets the sight,
The blood, the tears, the misery?
Raiment of needlework outspread
Wrought curiously with golden thread,
That my bride may be fitly adorned to-night.

But, oh thou Bridegroom of the Soul,
What of the sounds, the sounds of fear,
The groans of men, the bells that toll?
Thou hearest the minstrels tune their lutes,
Thou hearest the young men try their flutes
For the feast of the marriage that draweth near.

Yet, oh thou Bridegroom of the Soul,
What of the mind's captivity?
What of the spirit's doubt and dole?
Out of the ebony halls of night,
Aloes, cassia, myrrh, delight,
The bride in her palace of ivory.

Then, oh thou Bridegroom of the Soul,
What of the songs from woods new-clothed,
The laughing flowers, the sunlit knoll?
    My footsteps that follow along the shore,
    My fingers about the latch and door,
My face at the window of my betrothed.

Under a Wiltshire Apple Tree

SOME folk as can afford,
So I've heard say,
Set up a sort of cross
Right in the garden way
To mind 'em of the Lord.

But I, when I do see
Thik apple tree
An' stoopin' limb
All spread wi' moss,
I think of Him
And how He talks wi' me.

I think of God
And how He trod
That garden long ago;
He walked, I reckon, to and fro
And then sat down
Upon the groun'
Or some low limb
What suited Him
Such as you see

On many a tree,
And on thik very one
Where I at set o' sun
Do sit and talk wi' He.

And, mornings too, I rise and come
An' sit down where the branch be low;
A bird do sing, a bee do hum,
The flowers in the border blow,
And all my heart's so glad and clear
As pools when mists do disappear:
As pools a-laughing in the light
When mornin' air is swep' an' bright,
As pools what got all Heaven in sight
So's my heart's cheer
When He be near.

He never pushed the garden door,
He left no footmark on the floor;
I never heard 'Un stir nor tread
And yet His Hand do bless my head,
And when 'tis time for work to start
I takes Him with me in my heart.

And when I die, pray God I see
At very last thik apple tree
An' stoopin' limb,
And think of Him
And all He been to me.

DARRELL FIGGIS

Slaibh Mor

I STOOD among the ancient hills,
While all the dusk eve's blue array
Swept round with softly rustling wings
To still the glamour of the day.
The murmur of persistent rills,
A lone thrush with his communings
Of music, folded in some trees,
A piping robin ere he flew,
And the soft touch of a calm breeze
Sighing across the heavenly view,
Were the sole voices whispering round
The slope hills with reflective sound,
So still the whole earth was:
So very still it was.
The solemn conclave of the hills,
In an erect fraternity,
Expectant of the hour to be,
Were trembling in the calm that fills
The house of Being with its peace.
A measured rhythm flowed abroad
From old Earth of the heart so strong,
That was itself a manner of song,
Bidding the day's tame tumults cease
Before the coming of her lord.
The throstle, as he communed low,
Enchanted seemed, and tranced, and spelled,
To catch the measure of that flow
That from the mighty heart upwelled,
That his own song thereby should be
Lost in the inner immensity.

The trickling music of the rills
Along the bosom of the hills
Was to that larger rhythm bent,
And in that larger silence played.
The very winds that came and went
Were in their courses stayed,
Hushed in a mute expectancy.
The silent Earth was bent in prayer.
And I, as I stood there,
Scarce witting what my body knew,
Was hushed to adoration too.

Like a charmed cadence throbbing low
Along her scarred, mute visage so,
Flowed the Earth's spirit thro' the air
Emerging from its ancient lair,–
Flowed round the dusk and glooming hills
That stood in solemn peacefulness,
Flowed thro' the shimmer of air that fills
The valleys with a shadowy tress,
Flowed up where stars began to peep,
Flowed where the hushed winds lay asleep,
And sank again while peace profound
Wrapped all the ancient hills around.
Not a breath stirred;
No voice or song was heard.
It was a silence vaster than the dead;
It was a silence where in all its power
Being raised up its mighty head an hour.
And I, tho' I scarce knew what chanced,
Caught in the measured rhythm, and tranced,
Was yet raised to a terrible dread
Of the great hush that wrapped the hills:
That spell upon the standing hills.

I could have fled, but that the awe
Of an unfurling and strange might
Had me transfigured in its law.
And yet the fear that stirred in me
Was mingled with a wild delight
That thrilled with very ecstasy
Thro' every nerve and vein and mesh
Building my quivering house of flesh.

Then a strange shudder shook the hills.
Some movement swayed them in eclipse,
As tho' a dread apocalypse
Were waiting till they were unfurled
With all the travail of the world.
They were transformed, and shadowy-high
They stood there, and yet floated by;
While from some inner place of flame
A boom of distant music came
Suddenly thro' the air,
And huge and silent chords of sound
Soared o'er the quivering hills around,
As I hung trembling there.
My house of flesh could scarce contain
The rolling chords that swept abroad
And undissolved remain,
My joy stirred in me with such pain.
Loosed on the silence that had been,
Obeying its symphonic lord,
The music rolled thro' time and space,
Booming in changing chord on chord
Amidst a silence that seemed still
Upon the old Earth's brooding face.
It rolled round each reverberate hill;
It crashed its high symphonic will

And floated all the vales between,
In clouds of colour mounting high,
In waves of music sweeping by,
Booming above the ancient peace
Betwixt the ancient silences.

What chanced I do not know.
How is it I should know?
Like rolling clouds before the day
The booming music rolled away;
And, like a storm of splendour past,
The silence seemed yet to outlast
The music it had ushered so.–
Then slowly the wise thrush arose
And mused away the evening's close.

CLIFFORD BAX

The Meaning of Man

Take courage; for the race of man is divine.
The Golden Verses.

DEAR and fair as Earth may be
Not from out her womb are we,–
Like an elder sister only, like a foster-mother, she,
For we come of heavenly lineage, of a pure undying race,
We who took the poppied potion of our life, and quaffing deep
Move enchanted now forever in the shadow world of sleep,
In the vast and lovely vision that is wrought of time and space.

Overhead the sun and moon
  Shining at the gates of birth
Give to each a common boon,–
  All the joy of earth;
Mountains lit with moving light,
  Forest, cavern, cloud and river,
Ebb and flow of day and night
  Around the world forever.
These and all the works of man may he who will behold,
Mighty shapes of bygone beauty, songs of beaten gold,
Starlike thoughts that once, in ages gone, were found by
    seër-sages,
All the throng'd and murmuring Past, the life men loved
    of old.
Yet sometimes at the birth of night when hours of heat
    and splendour
  Melt away in darkness, and the flaming sun has set
Across the brooding soul will sweep, like music sad and
    tender,
  Sudden waves of almost passionate regret,
For then the hills and meadowlands, the trees and flowerful
    grasses,
  All the world of wonder that our eyes have gazed upon,
Seems remote and mournful, as a rainbow when it
    passes
  Leaves the heart lamenting for the beauty come and
    gone,
And in the deep that is the soul there surges up a cry
'Whence are all the starry legions traversing the sky?
  Whence the olden planets and the sun and moon and
    earth?
Out of what came all of these and out of what came I?'
And far away within the same unfathomable deep
  Comes an answer rolling 'Earth and moon and sun,

All that is, that has been, or that ever time shall reap,
Is but moving home again, with mighty labours done,
The Many to the Everlasting One.'

And this is the meaning of man,
The task of the soul,
The labour of worlds, and the plan
That is set for the whole,
For the spark of the spirit imprisoned within it,
In all things one and the same,
Aeon by aeon and minute by minute,
Is longing to leap into flame,
To shatter the limits of life and be lost in a glory intense and profound
As the soul with a cry goes out into music and seeks to be one with the sound.

For as those that are sunken deep
In the green dim ocean of sleep,
In a thousand shapes for a thousand ages the one great Spirit is bound.
The air we inhale and the sea,
The warm brown earth and the sun,
Came forth at the Word of the One
From the same First Mother as we,
And now, as of old when the world began
The stars of the night are the kindred of man,
For all things move to a single goal,
The giant sun or the thinking soul.
Ah what though the Tree whose rise and fall
Of sap is fed from the Spirit of All,
With suns for blossoms and planets for leaves,
Be vaster yet than the mind conceives?
Earth is a leaf on the boundless Tree,
And the unborn soul of the earth are we.

O man is a hungering exiled people, a host in an unknown land,
A wandering mass in the vast with only a black horizon to face,
Yet still, though we toil for a time in the heat over measureless deserts of sand
The longing for beauty that shines in the soul is the guiding-star of the race.
It is this that alone may redeem
A world ignoble with strife,
This only bring all that we dream
From the shattered chaos of life.
And this that forever shall spur us and lead us from peak unto peak on the way
Till body and spirit be welded in one and the long Night fall on the Day,
And all the sonorous music of time, the hills and the woods and the wind and the sea,
The one great song of the whole creation, of all that is and that yet shall be,
Chanted aloud as a paean of joy by the Being whose home is the vast
Shall tremble away in silence, and all be gone at the last,
Save only afar in the Heart of the Singer of whom it was chanted and heard
Remembrance left of the music as a sunset-fire in the west,
Remembrance left of the mighty Enchanted Palace that rose at His Word,
This, and a joy everlasting, an immense inviolate rest.

ELSA BARKER

He who knows Love

HE who knows Love–becomes Love, and his eyes
Behold Love in the heart of everyone,
Even the loveless: as the light of the sun
Is one with all it touches. He is wise
With undivided wisdom, for he lies
In Wisdom's arms. His wanderings are done,
For he has found the Source whence all things run–
The guerdon of the quest, that satisfies.

He who knows Love becomes Love, and he knows
All beings are himself, twin-born of Love.
Melted in Love's own fire, his spirit flows
Into all earthly forms, below, above;
He is the breath and glamour of the rose,
He is the benediction of the dove.

The Slumberer

O THOU mysterious One, lying asleep
Within the lonely chamber of my soul!
Thou art my life's true goal,
Thine is the only altar that I keep.
Rapt in the contemplation of thy repose,
I see in thy still face that Mystic Rose
Whose perfume is my soul's imaginings,
And Beauty at whose awesomeness I weep
With over-plenitude of ecstasy.
Thy slumber is the great world-mystery–

The paradigm of all the latent things
That in their destined hour Time magnifies:
Its emblems are the intimate hush that lies
Over the moonlit lake;
The wonder and the ache
Of unborn love that trembles in its sleep;
The hope that thrills the heavy earth
With presage of becoming, and vast birth;
The secret of the caverns of the deep.

The Mystic Rose

I, WOMAN, am that wonder-breathing rose
    That blossoms in the garden of the King.
    In all the world there is no lovelier thing,
And the learned stars no secret can disclose
Deeper than mine–that almost no one knows.
    The perfume of my petals in the spring
    Is inspiration to all bards that sing
Of love, the spirit's lyric unrepose.

Under my veil is hid the mystery
    Of unaccomplished aeons, and my breath
    The Master-Lover's life replenisheth.
The mortal garment that is worn by me
The loom of Time renews continually;
    And when I die–the universe knows death.

Microprosopos

BEHIND the orient darkness of thine eyes,
The eyes of God interrogate my soul
With whelming love. The luminous waves that roll
Over thy body are His dream. It lies
On thee as the moon-glamour on the skies;
And all around–the yearning aureole
Of His effulgent being–broods the whole
Rapt universe, that our love magnifies.

O thou, through whom for me Infinity
Is manifest! Bitter and salt, thy tears
Are the heart-water of the passionate spheres,
With all their pain. I drink them thirstily!
While in thy smile is realized for me
The flaming joys of archangelic years.

PAUL HOOKHAM

A Meditation

'THE Self is Peace; that Self am I.
The Self is Strength; that Self am I.'
What needs this trembling strife
With phantom threats of Form and Time and Space?
Could once my Life
Be shorn of their illusion, and efface
From its clear heaven that stormful imagery,
My Self were seen
An Essence free, unchanging, strong, serene.

The Self is Peace. How placid dawns
The Summer's parent hour
Over the dewy maze that drapes the fields,
Each drooped wild flower,
Or where the lordship of the garden shields
Select Court beauties and exclusive lawns!
'Tis but the show
And fitful dream of Peace the Self can know.

The Self is Strength. Let Nature rave,
And tear her maddened breast,
Now doom the drifting ship, with blackest frown,
Or now, possessed
With rarer frenzy, wreck the quaking town,
And bury quick beneath her earthy wave–
She cannot break
One fibre of that Strength, one atom shake.

The Self is one with the Supreme
Father in fashioning,
Though clothed in perishable weeds that feel
Pain's mortal sting,
The unlifting care, the wound that will not heal;
Yet these are not the Self–they only seem.
From faintest jar
Of whirring worlds the true Self broods afar.

Afar he whispers to the mind
To rest on the Good Law,
To know that naught can fall without its range,
Nor any flaw
Of Chance disturb its reign, or shadow of Change;
That what can bind the life the Law must bind–
Whatever hand
Dispose the lot, it is by that Command;

To know no suffering can beset
Our lives, that is not due,
That is not forged by our own act and will;
Calmly to view
Whate'er betide of seeming good or ill.
The worst we can conceive but pays some debt,
Or breaks some seal,
To free us from the bondage of the Wheel.

WILFRED ROWLAND CHILDE

Foreword

A Song of the Little City

AT intervals of tunes
And under lonely towers,
Where silences of noons
Cover their secret flowers,
In places no one knows,
Where winding ways go down,
In the dim heart of a rose,
I find the Little Town.

When my soul wearieth
Of cities proud and great,
Whose skies are dark as death,
But gold is in their gate:
When my soul sorry is
For ships of great renown,
And rich men's palaces,
I seek the Little Town.

Upon a hill it stands,
Built up with quiet walls,
Guarding inviolate lands,
A place of festivals,
A place of happy bells,
Where comes no earthly one,
Beyond the heavens and hells,
Between the moon and sun.

Between the moon and sun,
Far, far beyond the stars,
Where comes not any one,
Nor roll the great world's cars,
With an angel all day through,
That wears a golden crown,
And is robed in red and blue,
I find the Little Town.

Fountains are playing there,
And children dance all day,
Who are far lovelier
Than any fabled fay,
And in their festivals
Far, far away behold,
From the high carven walls,
Dim mountains made of gold.

And high above it all,
With arches rich and fine,
A minster towering tall
Proclaims the place divine:
Where none to veil Him be,
And the birds of Eden sing,
I find the lord of me,
The Little City's King.

Turris Eburnea

A Song of God's Fool the Mystic

MY soul is like a fencèd tower,
And holds a secret room:
I hide me in it many an hour
Amid its dim perfume:
I have my holy bloom,
The Rose of Heaven in flower:
I hold my inner bower
In strait and dreaming gloom,
My soul my fencèd tower.

The Rose of soil angelical,
That shines not over earth,
I have its buds and petals all,
Inestimable of worth,
Its blood-red calyces
Dyed with the wine of God,
Roots earthy from that sod,
Which dews in Syon bless,
And leaves of loveliness.

Its radiant heart unfolds to me,
Its starry soul is plain
In glimmering felicity,
Dyed deep with love and pain:
And while my glad eyes gaze
Upon its petalled crown,
I hear a song come down
With thanksgiving and praise
Of the celestial town.

The moon, that torch Dianian,
Dreams ever paganly:
But I am only a simple man
In a white tower by the sea:
There comes a liturgy,
Even for a little span,
Great voices Christian,
Songs of my Lord to me,
To me, a simple man.

A tower of ivory it is
Beside a shoreless sea:
I look out of my lattices
And the saints appear to me,
A singing company
From heaven's high palaces,
Chaunting their litanies:
White luting Cecily
Their first choir-maiden is.

The sea-wave crashes in my ears;
Again their viols cease:
I have been here for endless years,
And the room is full of peace.
Dim-sliding harmonies
And dreaming voice of seers
Come past all barriers:
With God I have no fears,
And round me roll His seas.

610

SAROJINI NAYADU

The Soul's Prayer

IN childhood's pride I said to Thee:
'O Thou, who mad'st me of Thy breath,
Speak, Master, and reveal to me
Thine inmost laws of life and death.

'Give me to drink each joy and pain
Which Thine eternal hand can mete,
For my insatiate soul would drain
Earth's utmost bitter, utmost sweet.

'Spare me no bliss, no pang of strife,
Withhold no gift or grief I crave,
The intricate lore of love and life
And mystic knowledge of the grave.'

Lord, Thou didst answer stern and low:
'Child, I will hearken to thy prayer,
And thy unconquered soul shall know
All passionate rapture and despair.

'Thou shalt drink deep of joy and fame,
And love shall burn thee like a fire,
And pain shall cleanse thee like a flame,
To purge the dross from thy desire.

'So shall thy chastened spirit yearn
To seek from its blind prayer release,
And spent and pardoned, sue to learn
The simple secret of My peace.

'I, bending from my sevenfold height,
Will teach thee of My quickening grace,
Life is a prism of My light,
And Death the shadow of My face.'

In Salutation to the Eternal Peace

MEN say the world is full of fear and hate,
And all life's ripening harvest-fields await
The restless sickle of relentless fate.

But I, sweet Soul, rejoice that I was born,
When from the climbing terraces of corn
I watch the golden orioles of Thy morn.

What care I for the world's desire and pride,
Who know the silver wings that gleam and glide,
The homing pigeons of Thine eventide?

What care I for the world's loud weariness,
Who dream in twilight granaries Thou dost bless
With delicate sheaves of mellow silences?

Say, shall I heed dull presages of doom,
Or dread the rumoured loneliness and gloom,
The mute and mythic terror of the tomb?

For my glad heart is drunk and drenched with Thee,
O inmost wine of living ecstasy!
O intimate essence of eternity!

To a Buddha seated on a Lotus

LORD BUDDHA, on thy lotus-throne,
With praying eyes and hands elate,
What mystic rapture dost thou own,
Immutable and ultimate?
What peace, unravished of our ken,
Annihilate from the world of men?

The wind of change for ever blows
Across the tumult of our way,
To-morrow's unborn griefs depose
The sorrows of our yesterday.
Dream yields to dream, strife follows strife,
And Death unweaves the webs of Life.

For us the travail and the heat,
The broken secrets of our pride,
The strenuous lessons of defeat,
The flower deferred, the fruit denied;
But not the peace, supremely won,
Lord Buddha, of thy Lotus-throne.

With futile hands we seek to gain
Our inaccessible desire,
Diviner summits to attain,
With faith that sinks and feet that tire
But nought shall conquer or control
The heavenward hunger of our soul.

The end, elusive and afar,
Still lures us with its beckoning flight,
And all our mortal moments are
A session of the Infinite.
How shall we reach the great, unknown
Nirvana of thy Lotus-throne?

R.A. ERIC SHEPHERD

Intimations

I THINK that in the savour of some flowers
God hides the loveliness we fain would know;
And that He makes it poignant with His showers
To lure us on toward what He longs to show.
I know He seeks in tiny wistful airs
To give my soul bright gleams of what shall be,
And that in plainsong endings quick despairs
Glitter like angels o'er a shadowed sea.
There is no thing God may not make His own
That smelleth sweet and is of good report. . . .
The leastest thing that we have longest known
May truth reveal beyond the range of thought.
And so each tiniest act and merest ploy
May grow instinct with sacramental joy!

C.M. VERSCHOYLE

Crucifixion on the Mountain

The soul would endure splendid martyrdoms, but her Lord lays upon her the ultimate reward of failure and of death.

I FOUND full many a hindrance on the road
That led up to the summit of desire,
Sharp rocks and wounding thorns; and in the mire
I fell, and soiled the garment I had care
To keep so fair
For the great rites awaiting me in Love's abode.
Yet on I pressed,
Dreaming of rest
That should be sweeter for toil undergone,
When on my Saviour's breast
Divine and human should be one.

Deep ran the chasms across the way,
Chasms my wilfulness had made,
But Love had cast a bridge above the spray
Flung by the roaring waters far below;
And with the cross my strength, the cross my guide,
My worser self for ever crucified,
I climbed toward the line of snow
That Love had laid
Far up, to mark the final stage
Of chill forlorn desertion, that should close
My pilgrimage.

High on the summit shone the mystic cross
Beside which life is death, and riches dross;
Not such the cross that companies my way,
A harsh rude copy meet for every day,
Beauty it lacks, untrimmed and harsh the wood,
And bitter as Christ's rood;
Heavy as death, no staff to life is this,
But such a weight
As leaves the soul unsoothed, disconsolate,
And drags the body down to the abyss.

Upward I crawl, the dream of joy is past,
I, that would share the sorrow of my Lord
And feel the piercing sword
Divide my flesh and spirit, now at last,
Discern the failure I am forced to share,
And see the garment I would keep so fair,
Foul from the dirt of many a foolish fall
The world might mock at. When I set my feet
Upon the path I said–
A martyrdom were sweet;
Come sword, come fire,

All tortures are less sharp than my desire.
  Let me have flints for bed,
And thorns, such as once wove my Master's crown,
Spurring me on to share in His renown.
  And lo! I faint
Beneath a common cross I cannot raise.
Mankind might jeer, but on celestial praise
  Free from all envious taint
I counted; wherefore then this loneliness
  Weighted with death?
Give me the nails, the spear, oppress
  My soul with every pang till my last breath,
  And then, the victor's wreath.

Yet I climbed still, the bitter words I spoke
Fell into silence and no echoes woke;
  But in my heart a small voice murmuring
  Whispered,–thy King
Humbly exchanged celestial gain for loss,
  Requiring no place to lay Him down,
  No victor's crown,
But only wood enough to make a cross.

I bowed my head in shame, and upward went
Slowly, beneath my burden bent;
  Deep in the snow my bleeding feet
  Sank at each step, and on the sheet
Of dazzling white left scarlet stains.
My eyes grew blind, my trembling knees gave way,
My body was a mass of fiery pains:
    And still I rose and fell,
  And struggled on a space,
Half dreaming broken words from far away,

The heavenward way,–
The pains of hell,–
And murmuring, weeping, falling,
Upon my Master calling,
Unconscious now of all save agony,
I still endured, until I lay
On the appointed place
Upon the summit, faint and like to die.

So, I thought, heaven is won,
Gone is the burden that so long I carried;
Yet still the summoning angels tarried.
I lay alone,
Almost desiring back the fardel gone,
That was my bliss and bale;
And so methought a thousand years
Of silence passed.
At last
I raised my eyes to see
Some angel that should bind my wounds and wipe my tears,
But there was Calvary,
And black and gaunt three crosses rose
Untenanted, among the snows.

Then, deep within, the silence spoke,–
Now thou hast left Gethsemane,
Stretch thy rebellious limbs upon the tree,
Giving thy body up for Me.
And I obeyed,
And laid
My feet and hands to bear the stroke
Of piercing nails.
And so I hung another thousand years.

The wind arose, and far below me tossed
    A sea of sombre-crested pines; the cloudy skies
Burst with the gale, and showed an orange rent,
And heavy clouds, like boats with tattered sails,
    Flapped low, and dipped and raced about the height
    Until they sank in mist that swathed my sight.
Then I closed my eyes,
    And tore my way from the poor earthly tent,
    And free, I knew my labours all well spent,
And no pang lost.

Abandoned hung the earthly form
While round it swayed and shrieked the storm;
    But my soul, being free,
    Rejoiced most thankfully,
Until a voice cried,–nay,
Still must thou lay
    Thy soul upon the rood.
So my stripped soul was fastened there,
        And that cross stood
Beside the centre, towering gaunt and bare
        While other thousand years went by;
Till my purged spirit burst its sheath,
And free of soul and body knelt beneath
The triple emblem of a conquered death.

Now let my spirit rise to God who gave–
Not through the grave,
    But upward into light.
Aye, chanted seraphs with their dulcimers,
The ladder it prefers
    Is the great midmost cross.
My spirit trembled, but I clomb–
    Ah, then fell night;
This, this is not my home.

And in a horror far too deep to tell
I knew the pains of hell,
And for a thousand years I drank this bitter cup,
Until my spirit yielded itself up,
And hands of love
Stretched from above
Upraised me in a most delicious rest,
Upon that cross and ladder of delight,
Which now I knew was but my Master's breast.

The Deliverer

(THE city quakes, the earth is filled with blood–
I, I that love Thee raised Thee on this Rood!)

Lord, I am least of all Thy followers,
Yet greatest in my love: devotion spurs
Me on to strange deep thoughts and stranger deeds
My roughness planned not erst,
For all unversed
In ways of love I would content Thy needs,
Delight Thee with a flower, a word, a song,
Striving to make Thy toilsome way less long,
Its stones less bitter, its rebuffs less rude,
To guard Thee 'gainst the sharp ingratitude
Of those who beg Time and Eternity,
Both worlds at once, abusing clemency.

Dazzle them, Master, with a word
Such as the universe has never heard;
Whisper it till the earth's foundations quake,
And fiery worlds awake
And shake

Their burning pinions, and ring out the cry
    That shrilly echoes
Where between whirling planets flows
The ardent stream of palpitating light.
    Destroy the worlds, Oh Lord,
    With the one whispered word,
And with consuming flame illume the sight
    Of all those muddy souls who love Thee not:
Or bid the flying circles cease
And a great peace
    Thunder across immensity,
Enwrapping heaven and earth and sky.
    Bid the air cease to hum
    And all the murmuring orbs be dumb,
Suddenly, utterly,
    And shatter them with silence–

Yea, Master, I have borne to see Thee weep,
More deep
    The iron scarce could pierce my suffering soul;
Have seen Thee fast and pray,
    Struggle and sweat.
While the eleven slept the night away
    My brow was wet,
My heart beat high,
    For, lo, I read
    The scroll of Heaven emblazonèd,
And knew Thy triumph nigh–

(The city quakes, the air is full of blood–
I, I that love Thee raised Thee on this Rood!)

Scourged, spit upon, denied,
    I suffered all with Thee ;
Raising Thee high that all should bend the knee.

That very royal crown of thorns
    That crimsoneth Thy brow–
So might gleam rubies set on snow,–
    I offered it; dear Master, look on me,
    Say, have I not done well?
    How my poor heart would swell
At praise from Thee–
    For see, without my deed,
Thy deed had not been done;
This be my meed
    Thy battle won–
And that down future ages, lighted by the torch
    That Thou dost kindle, men shall say–

(The city quaked, the air was full of blood,
Judas that loved Him raised Him on the Rood!)

Peter in the porch
    Warmed his chilled hands as he denied,
While Judas' teeth did chatter before Caiaphas;
My darkness seemed a heavy monstrous mass
    With but one quivering light–Thy tortured death–
    Ay, for it pierced beneath
My heart into my spirit–yet I knew
Before the worlds that task I had to do;
    God set it me, let me fulfil
    His very bitter will–

Master, my voice is harsh, mine eyes are dim,
I should rejoice and hymn
    Thy great uplifting, high above all towers–
    Follow the circle round, there Judas cowers,
Lonely, forsaken, outcast, anguish-swayed;
Yet we are one, betrayer and Betrayed;

Thou drinkest of my cup, I drink of Thine,
Thou art immortal, I shall be divine;
Dreaming, Thou risest from Thy painful Throne,
Waking, Thou drawest to Thee me, Thine own.
I kissed Thee gently–Thou hast understood?
Out on the silly cowards who deserted Thee,
Whom men call good.
Thou and I are free,
We see not as the others see,
We dream–
And that is times away.
Far down the stream
Of heavenly ways we see our paths unite
Where the veils fall, and day
For me replaces night–

(The city quakes, the earth is full of blood–
I, I that love Thee raised Thee on this Rood!)

Farewell, my Love, my Master, I have dared
For Thee that lesser men had left undone,
Be my love hereby proved, I have not spared
To give my God where God but gave His Son.
I bear such pains, my body was not formed
To see the struggles of a dying God,
Or hold the terror of a prisoned soul
Striving for freedom: I am fain
Of silence, and the peace of night again.
Night brooding over Galilee,
And our small company
Each with his portioned dole
Quietly laid about Thee on the sod,
Beneath which, now, there is no peace for me,
For Thou and I have work to do–Oh God!

Forsaken, helpless, therefore doubly to be loved–
See how I yearn o'er Thee!

Yet are Thy throes soon past,
  And mine, aeonial, scarce begun,
For where Thy name is honoured, I am cursed;
  Outcast, reviled, I down the ages go,
Death but delivers me to greater woe.
  But where Thy passion is rehearsed
Our names are linkèd still,
And Thine shall such a heavenly dew distil
  That mine shall be washed pure and sweet some day,
And children's lips sing 'Judas', like a kiss,
  But in no softer way
  Than fell that kiss with which I did betray
Thy sad humanity,
Freeing the Godhead for eternity–

(The city quakes, the air is full of blood,–
Judas that loves Thee raised Thee on this Rood!)

These triumphs are too keen, we die,
So sharp the sacrifice, the agony.
  Keep Thou the hapless Judas in Thy heart,
Nor fail me on that far-off day
When all that erred in my sad deed is purged away.
  My lowly part
Was just to make the sacrifice complete,
Adding to heavenly stature earthly feet:
  Thou art uplifted, I shall be cast down,
  Master, farewell, until my destined crown
Is won, and all Thou strivest for fulfilled.
I am not worthy that my blood be spilled
  Like Thine: in grosser pangs be spirit torn
  From my gross body, let the wide world scorn

So I but join Thee aeons after
Where the soft laughter
    Of the redeemed echoes about the heavenly space;
    And find, crouched at Thy feet, a little quiet place.
Then, when my courage grows, after awhile,
Murmur to me, with Thy celestial smile–

Judas! for the great love I bear to Thee
I grant thee to be crucified with Me!

AMY K. CLARKE

'Vision of Him'

THROUGH the Uncreated,
    Uncleft, Untrod,
Breathed for a moment
    Sorrow of God.

And lo! it fell starlike–
    Trembling to cease
In His Infinite gladness
    Infinite peace.

Out of that tremor
    Time was made,
Worlds crept into being
    Young and afraid.

Slowly, by beauty,
    His creatures grew wise,
Slow dawned its wonder
    On opening eyes.

Men watched adoring
His waters roll,
Deep flowed His colours
Through sense and soul.

Moan of creation–
Rapture that stirs–
Blindly they learned it,
Years upon years.

Till clearly one spirit
Cried on His Name
From all her lovely
And earthly frame.

Light could not veil it,
Nor darkness dim,
Flesh but receive it–
Vision of Him.

Deep sunk His answer,
The Word that sufficed–
Out of her Body
Cometh His Christ.

RUTH TEMPLE LINDSAY

The Hunters

'The Devil, as a roaring lion, goeth about seeking whom he may devour.'

THE Lion, he prowleth far and near,
Nor swerves for pain or rue;
He heedeth nought of sloth nor fear,
He prowleth–prowleth through

The silent glade and the weary street,
In the empty dark and the full noon heat;
And a little Lamb with aching Feet–
He prowleth too.

The Lion croucheth alert, apart–
With patience doth he woo;
He waiteth long by the shuttered heart,
And the Lamb–He waiteth too.
Up the lurid passes of dreams that kill,
Through the twisting maze of the great Untrue,
The Lion followeth the fainting will–
And the Lamb–He followeth too.

From the thickets dim of the hidden way
Where the debts of Hell accrue,
The Lion leapeth upon his prey:
But the Lamb–He leapeth too.
Ah! loose the leash of the sins that damn,
Mark Devil and God as goals,
In the panting love of a famished Lamb,
Gone mad with the need of souls.

The Lion, he strayeth near and far;
What heights hath he left untrod?
He crawleth nigh to the purest star,
On the trail of the saints of God.
And throughout the darkness of things unclean,
In the depths where the sin-ghouls brood,
There prowleth ever with yearning mien–
A Lamb as white as Blood!

HORACE HOLLEY

The Stricken King

O WHAT am I that the cold wind affrays,
O What am I the ocean could confound
A fort so open to the rebel days
And nature's mutiny and human wound?
O What am I so weak against the world,
Yea, weaker in my heart that should be strong,
On whom this double warfare is unfurled,
Of outer violence first, then inward wrong?
I am a fair, a fleeting glimpse of God
One moment visible in mortal state,
A bit of heaven caught i' the prison-clod,
That I nor nature's self may violate;
    Ev'n as a jewel lost from kingly crown
    That's royal still, though fingered by a clown. . . .

We of the world who shuffle to our doom,
Who dull with common lead the gold of time,
Despoiling where we may the tender bloom
Of all unworldly souls that rise sublime;
Still scourging wisdom nobler than our use
And scorning pity bent on our despair,
Fouling earth's seldom beauty by abuse
In rage at strength too strong, at fair too fair;
Nathless we suffer pain with them we slay,
And more than they, as we their death survive.
Weep not for them so glorious in decay,–
Weep thou for us, inglorious and alive:
    Stricken ourselves in their destruction, till
    That inward Saviour come we cannot kill. . . .

Yet, longer dwelling in that ruined court
Where man, the stricken king, so ill does reign
I find his folly wiser than report
And his defilement daughter of his pain.
He's like a king who never knew repose
But lives in constant dread to be o'erthrown,
Buying a half-obedience from his foes
And half-a-king to them who would have none.
And so his robe is stained, his front dismayed,
His court a mock, himself but half a king;
And so his magnanimity's arrayed,
So foully gowned, a self-impeaching thing.
'Tis so his royalty would be a scorn
If it were not too piteous and forlorn.

Himself his foe and bitter regicide,
Himself the faction risen in his state,
Himself his spy and minister, to chide
Himself to wrath, and nourish his own hate;
Himself his fool that can himself beguile,
Himself his scullion, foul to that degree,
Himself his beggar, skilled in cunning wile
Himself to plead in his necessity;
Yet king withal, and proved by future act
When all that baser self he may resign,
Leagued with himself and firm in his own pact
To live a monarch, noble in his line!
A king withal, and nowise made more clear:
His knavish self his lordly self does fear.

JOHN OXENHAM

Everymaid

KING'S Daughter!
Would'st thou be all fair,
Without–within–
Peerless and beautiful,
A very Queen?

Know then:–
Not as men build unto the Silent One,–
With clang and clamour,
Traffic of rude voices,
Clink of steel on stone,
And din of hammer;–
Not so the temple of thy grace is reared.
But,–in the inmost shrine
Must thou begin,
And build with care
A Holy Place,
A place unseen,
Each stone a prayer.
Then, having built,
Thy shrine sweep bare
Of self and sin,
And all that might demean;
And, with endeavour,
Watching ever, praying ever,
Keep it fragrant-sweet, and clean:
So, by God's grace, it be fit place,–
His Christ shall enter and shall dwell therein.
Not as in earthly fane–where chase
Of steel on stone may strive to win
Some outward grace,–
Thy temple face is chiselled from within.

JOHN SPENCER MUIRHEAD

Quiet

THERE is a flame within me that has stood
Unmoved, untroubled through a mist of years,
Knowing nor love nor laughter, hope nor fears,
Nor foolish throb of ill, nor wine of good.
I feel no shadow of the winds that brood,
I hear no whisper of a tide that veers,
I weave no thought of passion, nor of tears,
Unfettered I of time, of habitude.
I know no birth, I know no death that chills;
I fear no fate nor fashion, cause nor creed,
I shall outdream the slumber of the hills,
I am the bud, the flower, I the seed:
For I do know that in whate'er I see
I am the part and it the soul of me.

GERTRUDE M. HORT

The Paradox

I

WHEN I have gained the Hill
Where beats the clear and rigid light of God
Full on the path by fearless comrades trod;
When I have tuned to theirs my will and word,
And by my prompting voice their ranks are stirred
To hail each height with 'Higher! Higher still!'
That luring glow which from the Valley streams
Warns me *I* am not what my spirit seems.

II

But when my life descends
Into the Hollow, where no wild thoughts reach,
And all that lawful yearning can beseech
Sits at my hearth, or in my garden grows;
When I need match no more with noble foes,
Nor share the yoke with unrelenting friends,
That strange veiled star which o'er the Hill-top beams,
Shows me *I* am not what my body dreams!

Thanksgiving

I

SOME thank Thee that they ne'er were so forsaken
In dust of death, in whirling gulfs of shame,
But by one kindred soul their part was taken,
One far-off prayer vibrated with their name!
I thank Thee too–for times no man can number,
When I went down the rayless stairs of Hell,
And to my comrades, at their feast or slumber,
The echoes cried: 'All's well!'

II

Some thank Thee for the stern and splendid vision,
Of truth, that never let them shrink or swerve!
Till on their dearest dream they poured derision,
And broke the idols they had sworn to serve!
I thank Thee that, for me, some mystic terror
Still haunts the accustomed shrine, the accustomed way,–
So, though Truth calls me with the mouth of error,
I need not disobey!

III

Some thank Thee for the Voice that sounds unbidden,
Above the altar of their sacrifice;
For that great Light wherein they stood unchidden,
And watched, reflected, in each other's eyes.
I too–for whom came never word or token,
Whose prayer into a seeming Void descends,
I praise Thee for the trustful hush unbroken,
The right of perfect friends!

HAROLD E. GOAD

Spring's Sacrament

'LIFT up your hearts!' The holy dews
Asperge the woodland throng;
Dawn after dawn the lark renews
His miracle of song;
While taper-like the crocus pricks
Athwart the yearning sod;
The primrose lifts his golden pyx,
And God looks forth to God.

The symbols blind, the visions fail,
Our souls strain out to Thee;
Within the leaf, the light, the veil,
Is Thy Felicity.
O Heart of all the world's desire,
Breathe from around, above,
The mystic kiss of Fire to fire
That Love will yield to love!

Index Of Authors

Index Of Authors

Index of First Lines

Index of First Lines

Index of First Lines

Index of First Lines

Index of First Lines